You never ask questions
When God's on your side

BOB DYLAN

"Christians, Jews and Muslims and those without religious affiliation will welcome Aftab Malik's brave efforts to create a dialogue about terrorism. Pulpits and parliaments have provided platforms for illegitimate and simple hate messages that cannot be justified by the core values of the Abrahamic faiths or the founding principles of democratic states. This book helps to create a rational and informed counterweight to those who pour oil on the flames."
— **PROFESSOR ROBIN COHEN**
University of Warwick, England

"...an admirable and significant *tour de force* which probes the back room architects of the invasion of Iraq, the theological underpinnings of the Christian Zionists; how they have sanctified Empire, Islamicized evil and wrapped the shroud of Jesus around Israel."
— **DR. S. J. NOUMOFF**
McGill University, Canada

"Speaking the truth about Israel and Zionism must include an honest discussion of the Bush administration's war on Iraq. It must also acknowledge the role of Israel-first ideologues who strive to 'redraw the map of the Middle East' and to forge the relationship between the US and the rest of the world analogous to the relationship of the hammer to the nail. This book goes a long way in speaking these truths."
— **PROFESSOR DANIEL A. MCGOWAN**
Director, Deir Yassin Remembered, www.DeirYassin.org

"...incisively and mercilessly exposes and analyzes government lies most of us live by, many of us kill by, and many more of us get killed by. This book is a must for anyone who is interested in awakening a human mind that has been duped by false propaganda."
— **PROFESSOR RACHEL GIORA**
Tel Aviv University, Israel

"This book departs from the prevalent Western tendency to portray Islamic extremism as an isolated religious aberration rather than as a response to historical and political developments in the Islamic world. Not only does it point out that continuing American, Israeli and Russian aggression against Islamic peoples has fomented religious-based militancy among Muslims, but it draws needed attention to the fact that religious extremists within Christianity and Judaism have routinely supported such aggression. What a refreshing contrast to the endless propaganda of American and Israeli 'terrorism experts' who systematically obfuscate any serious inquiry into the causes of political violence in the Middle East."

— **PROFESSOR TOMIS KAPITAN**
Northern Illinois University, Illinois, US

"Scholarly, incisive, and a must read for individuals committed to confronting misinformation, illusions, and spin from the Bush administration and the media about Iraq, Palestine and the Middle East. Aftab Malik has done a masterful job of pulling together some of the best scholars in the field and this book will almost certainly become required reading for students and scholars alike. This is a breath of fresh air in the midst of a very toxic moment in our history."

— **PROFESSOR JESS GHANNAM**
University of California, San Francisco, US

"This timely and richly sourced book spans the roots of the 'War on Terrorism' from Halliburton to the neo-cons to the Apocalypse... it unmasks a vast web of deceit consisting of media pundits, greedy executives and religious fanatics...."

— **ISRAEL ADAM SHAMIR**
Author of The Galilee Flowers

"A well-documented contribution to a critical understanding of the forces of current US policies in the Middle East."

— **PROFESSOR GÖRAN THERBORN**
Uppsala University, Sweden

"At Nuremberg in 1946, the Allied Tribunal rejected the German argument for pre-emptive war (the Bush doctrine) with the statement: 'To initiate a war of aggression is not only an international crime; it is the supreme international crime differing only from other war crimes in that it contains within itself the accumulated evil of the whole.' Since the Anglo-American-Zionist 'axis of good' has opted for the wanton disregard for human life and criminal unconcern for human misery while calling immoral actions 'moral,' and illegal actions 'legal,' the cauterized collective conscience of members of the US government and their supporters can only be matched by the moralized drivel produced by ever-aggrieved Israel. This collection of articles serves as an illuminating and pointed examination of conscience for persons interested in scrutinizing their attitudes toward what has been happening in the Middle East."

— **PROFESSOR BRUCE J. MALINA**
Creighton University, Nebraska, US

"... extremely timely and informative....an excellent book to read!"

— **PROFESSOR FATMA WAHDAN ANTAR**
Manchester, Connecticut, US

"The architects of the 'war on terrorism' and the war in Iraq have made a shameful art out of ignoring mountains of facts, creating others, and distorting the rest. In the face of such madness and the disdain for human life that it represents, this powerful book asserts what appears to be a radical idea: that the facts matter, and that they must be pursued, proclaimed and contextualized regardless of how uncomfortable this may be for those in power. In the finest public intellectual tradition, the contributors have produced work that is bold, engaging, humane, and deeply relevant to the troubling times in which we live."

— **DR. JOHN COLLINS**
St. Lawrence University, Canton, New York, US

"This book asks the tough questions: What is terrorism and how does it differ from state terrorism? Who are the neo-conservatives and what accounts for their focus on Iraq? What is Israel's role in the War on Terror? How do conservative Christians and Biblical prophecy fit into this volatile mix? What is the relation between Islamic theology and political violence? *With God on Our Side* is a must read for those not satisfied with explanations offered by mainstream media."

— **STEPHEN A. HARMON *PH.D***
Pittsburg State University, Kansas, US

WITH GOD ON OUR SIDE

Do not cause people to loathe the worship of God
SAYING OF THE PROPHET MUHAMMAD

WITH GOD
ON OUR SIDE
Politics & Theology of the War on Terrorism

Foreword by
JOHN L. ESPOSITO

Introduction by
KHALED ABOU EL FADL

Edited by
AFTAB AHMAD MALIK

 AMAL PRESS
BRISTOL • ENGLAND

Amal Press, PO Box 688, Bristol BS99 3ZR. England

http://www.amalpress.com
info@amalpress.com

A catalogue record for this book is available from the British Library

ISBN 0-9540544-6-6 paperback

Printed in United States of America
Cover Concept: Aftab Malik; Design: Mukhtar Sanders
Typesetting: Zain ul-Abedin, Partners in Print UK.

CONTENTS

PART IV: SHATTERING ILLUSIONS

AFTAB AHMAD MALIK is the editor of *The Empire and the Crescent: Global Implications for a New American Century* (2003) and *Shattered Illusions: Analyzing the War on Terrorism* (2002). Both books are published by Amal Press. He also serves as an editorial advisor for *Islamica Magazine.*

AS´AD ABUKHALIL is Associate Professor of political science at California State University, Stanislaus and Research Fellow at the Center for Middle Eastern Studies at the University of California, Berkeley. He is the author of *Bin Laden, Islam, and America's New "War on Terrorism"* (NY: Seven Stories Press, 2002).

BILL CHRISTISON joined the CIA in 1950, and served on the analysis side of the Agency for 28 years. From the early 1970s, he served as National Intelligence Officer (principal advisor to the Director of Central Intelligence on certain areas) at various times for Southeast Asia, South Asia and Africa. Before he retired in 1979 he was Director of the CIA's Office of Regional and Political Analysis, a 250-person unit.

CORINNE WHITLATCH is the Executive Director of Churches for Middle East Peace, a coalition of 19 national church bodies – Protestant, Catholic, and Orthodox – which are working to bring a just and peaceful solution to the Arab-Israeli conflict and other disputes in the Middle East.

DONALD E. WAGNER is Professor of Religion and Director of the Center for Middle Eastern Studies North Park University, Chicago, Illinois. His publications include: *Dying in the Land of Promise: Palestine and Palestinian Christianity from Pentecost-2000* (Melisende, 2003); *Anxious for Armageddon* (Herald Press, 1995), *Peace or Armageddon* (Harper & Row-Zondervan, 1993), and *All in the Name of the Bible* (Amana Press, 1986).

FRANCIS A. BOYLE is Professor of International Law. He obtained his Doctor of Law (1976) from Harvard Law School. His Master's Degree (1978) and Ph.D. (1983) were also obtained from Harvard University, in political science, specializing in international relations and international politics. He is the author of a number of books, including: *Palestine, Palestinians and International Law* (Clarity Press Inc., 2003); *The Criminality of Nuclear Deterrence: Could the US War on Terrorism Go Nuclear?* (Clarity Press Inc., 2002); *The Future of International Law* (Transnational Publishers Inc., 1989) and *Defending Civil Resistance Under International Law* (Juris Publishers Inc., 1987). He has also written a number of major articles on a range of related international law and human rights issues.

GARY LEUPP is Professor of History at Tufts University, and Adjunct Professor of Comparative Religion. He is the author of several books including: *Servants, Shophands and Laborers in the Cities of Tokugawa Japan* (Princeton University Press, 1994) and *Interracial Intimacy in Japan: Western Men and Japanese Women, 1543-1900* (Continuum International Publishing Group, 2003)

GLEN RANGWALA is a lecturer at the Department of Politics, University of Cambridge, UK, and a fellow of Trinity College. Trained as a political theorist at Cambridge, Glen switched to the study of international law, and then returned to Cambridge to complete a doctorate in political and legal rhetoric in the Arab Middle East. His specific interest is in Palestinian politics from 1967 to 1977, and the rhetorical relations between the West Bank resident population and the leadership of the Palestinian resistance movement in exile. He is also published on a number of other themes, including international humanitarian law, comparative human rights law, Iraq and nuclear weapons. His book on the American occupation of Iraq will be published by Hurst publishers in 2005.

JASON VEST is a Washington reporter whose work has appeared in the *Washington Post, US News & World Report,* the *American Prospect,* and the *Village Voice.*

JIM WALLIS is a Christian leader for social change. He is a speaker, author, activist, and international commentator on ethics and public life. Jim was a founder of *Sojourners*—Christians for justice and peace—more than 30 years ago and continues to serve as the editor of *Sojourners* magazine, covering faith, politics and culture. In 1995, Wallis was instrumental in forming "Call to Renewal," a national federation of churches, denominations, and faith-based organizations from across the theological and political spectrum working to overcome poverty. In 1979, *Time* magazine named Wallis one of the "50 Faces for America's Future." His books include *Faith Works* (2000), *The Soul of Politics: A Practical and Prophetic Vision for Change* (1994), *Who Speaks for God? A New Politics of Compassion, Community, and Civility* (1996) and *Call to Conversion* (1981).

JOHN CHUCKMAN is a columnist for YellowTimes.org. He is former chief economist for a large Canadian oil company. John writes with a passionate desire for honesty, the rule of reason, and concern for human decency. He is a member of no political party and takes exception to what has been called America's "culture of complaint" with its habit of reducing every important issue to an unproductive argument between two simplistically-defined groups. He lives in Canada, which he is fond of calling "the peaceable kingdom."

JOHN L. ESPOSITO is University Professor and Professor of Religion and International Affairs at Georgetown University's Walsh School of Foreign Service. Founding Director of the Center for Muslim-Christian Understanding, Esposito is Editor-in-Chief of *The Oxford Encyclopedia of the Modern Islamic World* and *The Oxford History of Islam*. His other publications include: *Unholy War: Terror in the Name of Islam*; *What Everyone Needs to Know about Islam*; *The Islamic Threat: Myth or Reality?*; *Islam: The Straight Path; Islam and Politics; Islam and Democracy and Makers of Contemporary Islam* (with John O. Voll); *Political Islam: Revolution, Radicalism, or Reform?* He was recently conferred Pakistan's highest civil award *Hilal-I-Ilal-I-Qaid-I-Azam* for his contributions to Literature and Islamic Studies.

KATHLEEN CHRISTISON worked for 16 years as a political analyst with the CIA, dealing first with Vietnam and then with the Middle East for her last seven years with the Agency before resigning in 1979. Since leaving the CIA, she has been a free-lance writer, dealing primarily with the Israeli-Palestinian conflict. Her book, *Perceptions of Palestine: Their Influence on US Middle East Policy*, was published by the University of California Press and reissued in paperback with an update in October 2001. Her second book, *The Wound of Dispossession: Telling the Palestinian Story*, was published in March 2002 by Sunlit Hills Press.

KEVIN B. MACDONALD is Professor of Psychology at California State University–Long Beach. He completed his Ph.D. in Bio-behavioural Sciences at the University of Connecticut in 1981 and writes in the areas of evolutionary personality psychology, evolutionary developmental psychology, and strategizing human groups. His publications include: *Social and Personality Development: An Evolutionary Synthesis* (New York: Plenum, 1988); *A People that Shall Dwell Alone: Judaism as a Group Evolutionary Strategy, with Diaspora Peoples* (Westport, CT: Praeger, 1998); *Separation and Its Discontents: Toward an Evolutionary Theory of Anti-Semitim* (Westport, CT: Praeger, 1998); *The Culture of Critique: An Evolutionary Analysis of Jewish Involvement in Twentieth-Century Intellectual and Political Movements* (Westport, CT: Praeger, 1998; Bloomington, IN: Authorhouse, 2002); Burgess, R. L., & MacDonald, K. B. (Eds.) *Evolutionary Perspectives on Human Development*, 2nd edition (Thousand Oaks, CA: Sage, 2004)

KHALED ABOU EL FADL is Professor of Law at the UCLA School of Law where he teaches National Security law, Islamic law and Immigration law. Dr. Abou El Fadl holds a B.A. in Political Science from Yale University, a J.D. from the University of Pennsylvania Law School, and an M.A. and Ph.D. in Islamic law from Princeton University. Dr. Abou El Fadl was recently appointed by President George W. Bush to serve as a commissioner on the US Commission on International Religious Freedom. He is also a member of the Board of Directors of Human Rights Watch, and on the Advisory Board of Middle East Watch. He regularly serves as an expert in a wide variety of cases involving human rights, terrorism, political asylum, and international and commercial law. He is the author of eight books including: *Islam and the Challenge of Democracy* (Princeton University Press, 2004); *The Place of Tolerance in Islam* (Beacon Press, 2002); *And God Knows the Soldiers: The Authoritative and Authoritarian in Islamic Discourses* (University Press of America/Rowman and Littlefield, 2001) and *Rebellion and Violence in Islamic Law* (Cambridge University Press, 2001). He has written more than 50 articles on various topics in Islam and Islamic law, and his works have been translated in many countries including Malaysia, Singapore, Indonesia, Egypt, Turkey, Iran and France, among others.

LARRY EVEREST is a correspondent for the *Revolutionary Worker* newspaper and author of *Behind the Poison Cloud: Union Carbide's Bhopal Massacre.* He has reported from the Iran, the West Bank, Gaza, India, and Iraq, and his articles have appeared in publications across the US. In 1991, he traveled to Iraq and shot the video "Iraq: War Against the People." His recent book *Oil, Power and Empire: Iraq and the US Global Agenda,* is published by Common Courage Press. (2003) His website is www.larryeverest.com

NEIL LOWRIE is a Ph.D. student studying metallurgy at Loughborough University. His interest in the Middle East is as a result of having a Palestinian mother and being raised in Lebanon. He is an executive member of the Arab Media Watch.

PAUL S. BOYER is a Professor emeritus of history at the University of Wisconsin at Madison and currently a visiting professor of history at the College of William and Mary. He is the author of *When Time Shall Be No More: Prophecy Belief in Modern American Culture* (Harvard University Press, 1992).

PHILLIP CRYAN works for "Witness for Peace" in Colombia, bringing delegations from the US to see the effects of US military aid firsthand. He recently completed a Fellowship with Pesticide Action Network North America. Phillip received a BA in English, Summa Cum Laude, from UC-Berkeley in May 2001.

ROBERT DREYFUSS is a longtime Washington journalist and a contributing writer for *Mother Jones.* He has been rated by *The Columbia*

Journalism Review, as one of the "best unsung investigative journalists working in print."

SEYYED HOSSEIN NASR is one of the world's leading experts on Islamic science and spirituality. He is Professor of Islamic Studies at George Washington University and author of over fifty books (including *Man and Nature: the Spiritual Crisis of Modern Man* (Kazi Publications, 1998), *Religion and the Order of Nature* (Oxford, 1996) and *Knowledge and the Sacred* (SUNY, 1989) and five hundred articles which have been translated into several major Islamic, European and Asian languages.

SOUMAYYA GHANOUSHI is currently preparing her Ph.D. thesis at the University of Durham on the intellectual roots of the West's vision of Islam. She obtained her Bachelors and Masters Degrees in philosophy from the University of London. Previously she held the post of president of the University of London's Society for Islamic Philosophy & Thought and currently chairs the society of Students for Justice in Palestine (SJP). Soumayya is also a free- lance writer.

TANYA C. HSU is a senior analyst of Middle East political economy at the Institute for Research: Middle Eastern Policy. For almost two decades she has created and facilitated strong connections between Middle Eastern leaders, diplomats and business men and women. She continues an active role to promote progress, both economic and political, between the region and the United States. Ms. Hsu holds an Economics degree from the University of London. Ms. Hsu's analysis has been published in the US, Europe and the Middle East, including *Al Ahram*, and the Media Monitors Network. She appears on Palestinian, Jordanian and British television and radio as well as within the United States. Ms Hsu was an organizer of the 2003 Harvard Symposium "Promoting Understanding between the Arab World and the US," and serves on the Board of the Atlanta Chapter of the American-Arab Anti Discrimination Committee. Ms Hsu worked for ten years as a financial advisor serving clients in the United Kingdom and United States.

WILLIAM BLUM left the State Department in 1967, abandoning his aspiration of becoming a Foreign Service Officer because of his opposition to what the United States was doing in Vietnam. He then became one of the founders and editors of the *Washington Free Press,* the first "alternative" newspaper in the capital. In 1999, he was one of the recipients of Project Censored's awards for "exemplary journalism" for writing one of the top ten censored stories of 1998, an article on how, in the 1980s, the United States gave Iraq the material to develop a chemical and biological warfare capability. His books include: *Killing Hope: US Military and CIA Interventions Since World War II* (Zed Books, 2003) and the recently published *Freeing the World to Death: Essays on American Empire* (Common Courage Press, 2004)

WILLIAM D. HARTUNG is a Senior Fellow at the World Policy Institute and Director of the Arms Trade Resource Center. He is the author of *How Much Are You Making on the War, Daddy? A Quick and Dirty Guide to War Profiteering in the Bush Administration* (Nation Books/Avalon Group, 2004).

ZAID SHAKIR accepted Islam in 1977, while serving in the United States Air Force. Upon completion of his military service, in 1981, he enrolled in The American University in Washington, DC, where he earned a BA Degree in International Relations, with honors. He subsequently obtained an MA in Political Science from Rutgers University in 1986. After spending seven years in Syria studying Arabic and Islamic Sciences, he returned to the United States in November 2001, resuming the leadership of *Masjid al-Islam.* He later taught both Arabic and Political Science at Southern Connecticut State University. Zaid Shakir has lectured extensively on issues related to both Islam and African American life. He has also written numerous articles, which have been published in leading Islamic and academic periodicals. He has translated three books from Arabic into English, and is considered a leading authority on Islam in the American context.

AFTAB AHMAD MALIK

> O people, your creator is one.
> You are all from the same ancestor.
> All of you are from Adam
> — *Saying of the Prophet Muhammad*

> Has not one God created us?
> — *Malachi 2:10*

I NNOCENTS ARE BEING slaughtered. Whether it be done as a consequence of "collateral damage," resulting from secular violence or by the delusion of serving God's will through "religious" violence. This book was in page-proof when the taking of over 1,000 hostages consisting of school children, their parents and teachers occurred in Beslan, Russia. The end result was carnage. Under horrific circumstances, children were forced to drink their own urine[1] as the "rebels" refused anything more than a bucket of water to be shared amongst the children and adults under the sweltering heat. The sickness that pervades the minds of those individuals who use religion to justify the most grotesque and horrific acts should not and cannot be defended by anyone. Islam is suffering continuously at their hands and Muslims can no longer remain silent; our silence is our acquiescence to the crimes that are being carried out.

Innocent people have become targets of fanatical individuals who represent no-one but their own twisted minds and darkened hearts. Islam is free of these *muharibs*, rebels, vigilantes, these terrorists. Muslims are innocent of such crimes against humanity.

The world continues to grow in confusion as people are told that "Islam is a religion of peace" and they then witness the carnage which results from the hands of extremists being beamed across television channels world-wide. Despite the suffering of Muslims through state sponsored violence and the uneven application of international law, whether it is in Chechnya, the occupied Palestinian territories, or in Algeria, nothing can justify heinous actions that result in the spilling of innocent blood.

The books of Islam, the Qur'an and the sayings of the Prophet (*hadiths*) have both fallen victim and hostage to the "armies of ignorant people clashing in the darkness of ignorance."[2] Devoid of the necessary skills and tools to decipher the religious texts, these students of chaos have side stepped over one thousand years of scholasticism and Qur'anic exegesis to create their own deluded *Sharia*[3]—a new law couched in Islamic terminology established solely to be the antithesis of the West. Under this law, there is only hatred and rejection. Under this law, Muslims and non-Muslims alike are its victims.

Theology cannot be ignored when trying to understand this aberrant attitude that has spread like a virus within the Muslim world and has infected some of the minds of the unwary in the West.[4] This "war theology" has been derived from a literal understanding of the Qur'an, which has a disregard for the basic principles of jurisprudence and rejects the established consensus by the scholastic community. This reading of Islam has long been rejected and discarded by the scholars of Islam. The Chechens know first hand of how this brutal theology has devastated its traditional society, pitting father against son, family against family. The official Chechen rebel leader, Aslan Maskhadov, condemned the seizure of the school, describing the Beslan attackers as "madmen." He said that the acts of terror were "carried out by people whose desire for revenge against acts of brutality by Russian troops had driven them out of their senses."[5] Most commentators are aware how Chechnya's battle for independence has been to a large degree hijacked by a violent and radicalized reading of Islam that nutures itself on powerful emotions. This version of Islam has been quick to introduce the use of indiscriminate violence and terror,[6] which is justified as a response to the horrific deaths of thousands of Muslims at the hands of the Russian army. This blood-thirsty ideology has only served to impede the Chechen cause for independence.[7]

Muslims have to reject this exchange of indiscriminate violence which is a modern phenomenon; a *bid'a* (reprehensible innovation) that must be called by what it truly is. Human life, its sanctity and the human soul is precious and to be honored in Islam. Out of the hundreds of thousands of *hadiths*, only five hundred have the transmitted status of the Qur'an, (*mutawatir*) and among them is the saying that the Prophet continually forbade the killing of women and children. Muslims do not share the secular conception of "collateral damage." In Islam, the unjust killing of just one soul is akin to "taking the lives of all humanity."[8] Islam bestows dignity and honor for each and every soul, irrespective of being a believer or not.[9] It is related once that a funeral procession passed in front of the Prophet, and he stood up. Then he was told it was a bier of a Jew. The Prophet said, "Is he not a human soul?"[10]

It is a well known fact that in Islam, fighting has always been prescribed as a last resort and Muslims should never initiate hostilities. In addition, there are higher forms of *jihad* other than fighting.[11] The striking difference between a *jihad* conducted according to the principles of Islam to the current corrupted conception of *jihad* waged by Muslim vigilantes, can be epitomized in the example of Emir 'Abd al-Qadir al-Jaza'iri. Resisting French colonial efforts, as leader of the Muslim Algerian resistance between 1830 and 1847, the Emir fought for justice with justice. At a time when the French army was massacring entire tribes, collecting severed Arab heads as trophies and being paid for collecting Arab ears, the Emir insisted that captives should be treated well and he forbade any ill treatment.[12] When the Emir was questioned about the reward for a live French soldier, the Emir replied "eight douros." When he was further asked about the reward for a severed French head, he responded "twenty-five blows of the baton on the soles of the feet."[13] The Emir did not fight like with like. His mission was determined and shaped by the moral imperative as set in the Qur'an which forbids excess and aggression being carried out against people.[14] Even after being sent into exile in Damascus, the Emir did not allow his experiences fighting the (Christian) French army to distort his moral responsibilities. In 1860, during the civil war, he tried to avert an ensuing massacre of Christians. Unable to prevent it, no less, he and his followers were able to protect 15,000 Christians, among who were dignitaries and European ambassadors. It was Winston Churchill who said:

All the representatives of the Christian powers then residing in Damascus, without one single exception, had owed their lives to him [...] An Arab had thrown his guardian aegis over the outraged majesty of Europe. A descendent of the Prophet had sheltered and protected the Spouse of Christ.[15]

Collective responsibility was not an understanding that the Emir had. It isn't Qur'anic nor Prophetic. He understood that the Qur'an did not forbid Muslims from dealing justly nor from keeping friendship with those people who had neither persecuted Muslims because of their religion nor had driven them from there homes.[16] It was this action of the Emir, protecting the Christians, that was brought to the attention of another Muslim warrior, Imam Shamil al-Daghestani. Like the Emir, Imam Shamil was also leading a resistance, but against Russian Imperialism. Like the Emir, he too was regarded in awe by followers and enemies alike. In his letter to the Emir, he wrote:

> I was astonished at the blindness of the functionaries who have plunged into such excesses, forgetful of the words of the Prophet, peace be upon him, "Whoever shall be unjust towards a tributary,[17] who shall do him wrong, who shall lay on him any charge beyond his means, and finally who shall deprive him of anything without his own consent, it is I who will be his accuser in the day of Judgment."[18]

These two men knew that hatred and revenge had no role to play in their resistance against the brutalities of the French and Russian armies. They did not use collective guilt as a weapon to inflict massacres upon the innocent in retaliation for what their people had endured. They did not see a world divided between "good and evil," but rather, they distinguished between those people who fought them and those people who shared the same ethnicity and religion but did not fight them. They fought with a heart cleansed of hatred, revenge or anger. They adhered scrupulously to the moral and ethical imperatives of the Qur'an. They understood that aggression and excess were forbidden and that mercy, compassion and forbearance were the benchmarks of human dignity. There really can be no greater contrast between them and the so called *jihadists* that are the scourge the earth today. In words written over 140 years ago, that ring ever so true today, the Emir 'Abd al-Qadir contemplated:

When we think how few men of real religion there are, how small the number of defenders and champions of the truth—when one sees ignorant persons imagining that the principle of Islam is hardness, severity, extravagance and barbarity—it is time to repeat these words: *'Patience is beautiful and God is the source of all succour.'*[19] [Qur'an 12:18]

Muslims need to reassert their Abrahamic heritage that calls to the highest morality. Jews and Christians who are called by the honorific title *Ahl al-Kitab* (People of the Book) have been targeted and killed unjustly in the name of Islam. The Qur'an speaks in clear terms about these religious traditions saying, [...] *We believe in God, and in what has been revealed to us [Muhammad], and what was revealed to Abraham, Ishmael, Isaac, Jacob and the Tribes, and in what was given to Moses, Jesus and the prophets from their Lord. We make no distinction between any of them.*[20] The Qur'an further teaches mutual respect between these traditions asserting; *from the people of Moses, there is a community that leads with truth and establishes justice,*[21] and referring to the Christians, we are told that *among them in affection to the believers will you find those who say 'We are Christians.'*[22] Tolerance in Islam is a directive of the Qur'an that has been implemented and lived by traditional Muslims across the world and throughout history, which has been ignored by the *jihadists* and extremist elements of Muslims.

With the growth of what has been described by the American scholar, Shaykh Hamza Yusuf, as a "tribal mentality," Muslims today shun other Muslims or look on in horror at those who seek to blame Muslims for acts of carnage. In the minds of the deluded, Islam has been reduced to a tribe; "bani-Islam." Like in the days of ignorance (*jahiliyya*) that preceded Islam, anyone who was slighted in any way had to reckon with the full force of the tribe in retaliation. The honor and integrity of the tribe was to be upheld zealously, even if its people were in the wrong. At the advent of Islam, the Prophet Muhammad did away with blood-feuds and tribal wars, replacing it with an understanding of brotherhood; one united on common ancestry. By uniting all of humankind to Adam and Eve, Islam had assured that no-one would be prejudiced against, regardless of creed, color or status. Today, this ethical gift of Islam has been discarded as love of co-religionists has superseded the love of God and of humanity.

It seems that post 9/11 Muslims are ever more obsessed with conspiracy theories, paranoia and self-deceit. The result has been a denial that Muslims could be capable of evil acts—and even the suggestion of this is seen as blasphemy. Instead, the tribal Muslims place the blame at the conspiracy of Jews or the shadowy secret American government, despite the fact that in the last fifty years, more Muslims have been killed by Muslims themselves.

It is hoped that Jews and Christians will also become aware of the crimes that are being carried out in their name and reject and distance themselves from what they see. When Zionists are understood to be speaking for all Jews, Jews around the world are seen to be complicit with the crimes that are carried out in Israel. We have seen the results in the unprovoked bombings by fanatics that have targeted and killed Jews in Turkey and North Africa. Christians need to be vocal in their rejection of the Christian Right and its apocalyptic reading of the Bible, which serves only to confirm to Muslims, that the West in general and the US in particular, is waging a new crusade against the Muslim world.

Muslims today must be strong and frank. We need to be supporters of justice, even be it against fellow Muslims and indeed, even if it is against our very own selves.[23] Islam teaches that with infliction comes the strengthening of belief, not its corruption. When faced by threat and persecution, Muslims turn to the prayer of Prophets; *God is enough for us—and what an excellent guardian!*[24] This is how faith is articulated when we have trust in God at all times. When faith is replaced by tribalism, the response is different; Muslims experience the states of hopelessness, blame, resentment and helplessness. Prayer is substituted for rhetoric and rhetoric leads to hate. In this state, Islam has been enmeshed by the emotions of anger, hate and revenge; emotions which Islam views as detrimental to the human heart and soul.[25] Rather than following the example of the Prophet, it seems that a parallel prophet has been construed through the skewed reading of the traditional texts. This prophet is a "shadow" prophet; one that moves in the shadows, characterized by rage, the zeal for war, showing no mercy towards his enemies, be they women, children or non-combatants. In contradistinction to this, authentic accounts of the Prophet show him to be a man "brilliantly spiritual, stern in matters of right yet compassionate and clement, rich in dignity yet extremely modest and humble [...] a manly and valorous warrior who was most kind and gentle with women and children."[26]

T HE PURPOSE OF this anthology, along with the two that have preceded it,[27] has been best explained by Professor Khaled Abou El Fadl in his introduction to *Shattered Illusions.* In attempting to understand a crime, lawyers try to understand the causes that lead to it. While doing so, they don't seek to justify the crime rather they try to fathom why it occurred and who benefits. The articles in all three anthologies are an attempt to explain to the reader not only why people in general and Muslims in particular have grievances with the unethical foreign policy of the US, but of the disastrous consequences that result.

If Western powers need to rethink and reassess their policies, mainstream Muslims also face critical choices and challenges. In the West, and especially in places like the US and Britain, Muslims have not fully convinced the public of their aversion and rejection of extremism, when we have extremists in our midst, celebrating the atrocities of September 11. The existence of extremists in Islam should hardly be surprising. All religious traditions have suffered at one time or another at their hands, and despite the Prophet's clear warning concerning extremism, Islam sadly, is no exception. From the grotesque beheading of innocents in Riyadh and Iraq to the mass wave of suicide bombings across Europe and North Africa, these Muslims have broken from a tradition that promotes mercy and justice[28] and have turned it into an ideology of blood and brutality, and for this, Muslims cannot blame the West.

For the integrity of Islam, these individuals and their organizations need to be seen as they are: marginal and heretical. Muslims need to be brave enough to hold them to account to their destruction that they have created on the earth. Islam is a religion of order and governance and it rejects vigilantes and renegades. In his famous statement, the first century scholar, Imam Malik remarked that sixty years of oppression is better than one moment of anarchy where tribulation (*fitna*) reigns. It is evident however, that there are growing numbers of Muslims in the West who seek the revivification of an authentic, traditional wisdom; one that discredits the angry rhetoric and the blind fury of the orphans of modernity,[29] and replaces it with the Prophetic notions of trust, courtesy and wisdom.

Ignorance and suspicion only serve to breed hatred. We all need to study the problems and possibilities confronting us, and begin debating what to do about them. If we all fail to understand the causes of this hate, our failure will only exacerbate and replicate the threatening conditions that afflict us.

In this scenario, there can only be losers.

W
HILE IT IS clear that this book is highly critical of American foreign policy, this should not be interpreted as an endorsement for anti-Americanism. America and Americans should *not* be defined by foreign policy—that would be a great injustice. I feel passionately that most Americans would be appalled if they truly knew what was being carried out thousands of miles away in their name. This is, in fact, part of the problem: Americans need to make themselves more aware of what is going on in the world and of America's role in it. Americans need to better understand who these 'other' people are: their customs and history, their views of America and their justifications for viewing her as they do. What Americans would soon discover is that the world is full of people who aspire to travel to America, and if possible, live there. There will be people who view America as arrogant and there will be those who view America as benevolent. Americans would also find people who object to what they see as America's domineering foreign policy. They see how America is able to side-step international law while being insistent that everyone else should abide by its letter.[30] It is this sad reality that alienates America's allies and infuriates its enemies.[31] The danger here is blindingly obvious: when the lines between Americans, America and its foreign policy begin to blur, American foreign policy becomes the criterion by which to judge Americans and America by, just as terrorists are often used to judge Muslims and Islam.

For those who cannot differentiate between Americans and American foreign policy, I would remind them of the hundreds of thousands of

Americans who have protested, and who continue to protest, at the way that their country has been dragged into an unrelenting war. In fact, on February 15, 2003 in more than 100 nations around the world (including America, Britain, France, Germany and Israel) over 30 million people marched in protest against the impending war against Iraq. Certainly, these people did not want to see a "clash" with the Muslim world nor wanted a war with Islam for that matter. Muslims need to recognize the need to cease talking about "hating the West" when they themselves have benefited in many ways from the West. From enjoying Western food, clothing and movies to having life-saving surgery and medicines developed in the West, flying to make Pilgrimage (*Hajj*) on planes built and engineered by the West and earning their livelihood based on cars produced by the West—Muslims need to be fair and just. Speaking as though the West were a monolith is the precise fault that most Muslims accuse Westerners of when they speak of Islam. While many people in the West have a certain degree of fear of Islam and many Muslims hold onto resentment, by allowing a small group of people to manipulate these emotions, this global political elite intends that people across the world should speak in absolutisms: "hating Islam" and "hating the West." For those Muslims who speak in such a way, they need to reflect again upon their religious principles and understand that Islam teaches that no individual can carry the blame of another and so, anti-Americanism and being anti-West cannot be Islamic concepts. Tribal religion and tribal nationalism should be rejected in favor of seeing the human race as an extension of the family of Adam and Eve, with every member of the family having an inherent and inalienable right to dignity and honor.

NOTES

1. See Paul Quinn-Judge, "They are Killing us all," *Time,* September 13, 2004, pp.43-45

2. Faraz Rabbani, "Where ignorant armies clash by night", Web-blog, http://blog.masud.co.uk/faraz.htm posted 7th September 2004.

3. Meaning "a path to something," the *sharia* has come to be seen as a primitive form of law that is concerned with oppression and characterized by its anti-intellectualism. Very much a legal tradition that sees no dichotomy between

reason and faith, the *sharia* is at once flexible and dynamic; something that was unique and advanced in its methodology and understanding, in the pre-modern world. Rather than being reduced to a set of political paradigms and Muslims assumed as actors of a political movement, the *sharia* is concerned with human nature, and is a means of achieving equilibrium.

4. In this regard, see T.J. Winter, *British Muslim Identity: Past, problems, prospects* (Cambridge: Muslim Academic Trust, 2003) pp.12-17. Also see Bill Powell, "Struggle for the soul of Islam" *Time* op cit., p.56 for an example at how protest against American foreign policy is articulated by a member of *Al-Muhajirun*. On the first anniversary of 9/11, many Muslims and non-Muslims looked at horror and in disgust as posters and flyers depicting the 19 suicide hijackers as the "Magnificent 19" appeared around areas of London and Birmingham. *Al-Muhajirun's* spokesman, Abu Omar told the BBC that Muslims who condemned the September 11 attacks were "apostates" and whose opinions carry no weight. He continued to exclaim that "many of the activities that have taken place since 9/11 are completely justified in the light of *sharia.*"

5. See Stephen Mulvey, "Analysis: The hostage-takers," BBC News UK edition, 6th September 2004, http://news.bbc.co.uk/1/hi/world/europe/3627586.stm

6. Introduced first to Chechenya in 1991, the militant-Wahhabi brand of Islam began to use tactics of terror that included kidnapping, torturing and executing of hostages. Maskhadov has always remained strongly anti-Wahhabi. In 1998, he announced that "the Chechen leadership has enough force to stop the spread in Chechnya of the anti-Islamic pernicious Wahhabi doctrine." His promise that Wahhabis would "stand before a *sharia* court and be punished for their bid to fuel a civil war in Chechnya," seems to have been unsuccessful. See Abd el-Wahid Miranda, "Why Extremism Always Fails: Spanish Muslim Perspectives," http://www.masud.co.uk/ISLAM/misc/extremism.htm, also see "How *Jihadis* entrenched themselves in Dagestan" in *The Times of India*, http://209.157.64.200/focus/f-news/900847/posts as to how Wahhabis were able to take advantage of the economic climate to propagate their doctrine. The Chechen Mufti, Akhmed Kadyrov has also been relentless in his criticism of Wahhabism which, he claims is "diametrically opposed to the Chechen way of life." His outspoken criticism has prompted a series of failed assassination attempts. Erik Batuev, "Trouble at the Top" Institute for War and Peace Reporting, http://www.iwpr.net/index.pl?archive/cau/cau_200001_15_02_eng.txt

For centuries, Chechen society has been based around Sufi brotherhoods (*tariqas*) of the *Naqshbandiyya* and *Qadariyya* branches. As Sufism is in direct conflict with the Wahhabi reading of Islam, most ordinary Chechens despise the Wahhabi groups. For greater understanding of the Wahhabi doctrine and its rejection by Sunni scholars throughout the centuries, see 'Abdal Hakim Murad, *Understanding the Four Madhabs* (Cambridge: Muslim Academic Press, 2001) and Hamid Algar, *Wahhabism: A Critical Essay* (New York: Islamic Publications International, 2002). Also see Abdal Hakim Murad, "Recapturing Islam from the Terrorists" http://www.masud.co.uk/ISLAM/ahm/recapturing.htm which explains why Muslims need to engage in an internal debate concerning the "cultural and doctrinal foundations of extremism," and the consequences of not doing so. More than often, Wahhabis are described as "extreme" or as "conservative" Sunnis. However, most of the early Sunni scholars who were writing at the time the Wahhabis appeared, did not include them amongst the Sunnis, because of their condemnation and rejection of almost all the practices, traditions and beliefs integral to Sunni Islam.

7. In his incisive article, Svante Cornell makes clear that by employing Wahhabi tactics of guerrilla warfare, the Chechen struggle for independence "is being increasingly depicted as an Islamic terrorist assault against Russia and Europe" which "fuel's Moscow's insistence on crushing the Chechen rebellion by force." See Svante E. Cornell, "The War Against Terrorism and the Conflict in Chechnya: A Case for Distinction," *The Fletcher Forum of World Affairs*, vol. 27:2 Summer/Fall 2003 p. 179, particularly see from page 174 onwards. In addition to explaining the growing influence of the Wahhabi form of Islam in this conflict, the article sets the historical circumstances of the conflict in Chechnya and points to the horrific circumstances that the Chechen's have had to endure which "defies description." *Human Rights Watch* documents "torture," "disappearances," "indiscriminate shootings," the killing of "numerous civilians," as well as the indiscriminate selection of males between the ages of 14 and 60 who are beaten, tortured, raped and killed. See pp.172-173. Svante concludes that the Russian war against Chechnya is actually a "brutal assault against an entire people," which is "genocidal" in nature. See p.182. For detailed insights to the connection between violent acts and the Wahhabi perpetrators, see Patrick Armstrong, "Conflict in Chechnya: A Background Perspective," *The Journal of Conflict Studies*, November 1999; Mark Galeotti, "Chechen Militants Bring Their War to Moscow," *Jane's Intelligence Review*, volume 14, Number 12, December 2002; David Holley and Alexei V. Kuznetsov, "Chechen Rebel's Rise and Fall,"

Los Angeles Times, October 26, 2002; Julius Strauss, "The Leader: The Unknown Soldier," *The Telegraph*, October 26, 2002; Anne Penketh, "Rebel Leader From a Family of Notorious Chechen Killers," *The Independent*, October 26, 2002; Johanna McGeary and Paul Quinn-Judge, "Theater of War: The Chechens Who Dared Seize a Theater in Russia's Capital Are Put Down, But Their Cause is on Center Stage," *Time* Europe, vol. 160 No. 19, Nov. 4, 2002

8. The verse in the Qur'an is *He who kills anyone, unless it be a person guilty of manslaughter or spreading corruption in the lands, will be as though he had killed all humanity; and whoever saves a life will be as though he saved the entire human race.* 5:32

9. In this regard, see Mohammed Hashim Kamali, *The Dignity of Man: An Islamic Perspective* (Cambridge: Islamic Texts Society, 2002) which provides an insightful analysis on this topic.

10. Related by Bukhari in his *sahih*.

11. The Prophet once asked his companions: "Shall I tell you about the best of all deeds, the best act of piety in the eyes of your Lord, which will elevate your status in the Hereafter, and carries more virtue than the spending of gold and silver in the service of God or taking part in *jihad* in the path of God? [It is] the remembrance (*dhikr*) of God." Related in Malik's *Muwatta'*, the *Musnad* of Ahmad, the *Sunan* of Tirmidhi, *Ibn Majah*, and the *Mustadrak* of Hakim. Al-Bayhaqi, Hakim and others declared it *sahih*. In another saying of the Prophet, he said that "the most excellent *jihad* is the uttering of truth in the presence of an unjust ruler." Related by al-Tirmidhi.

12. Reza Shah Kazemi, "Recollecting the Spirit of *Jihad*" in Joseph E. B. Lumbard (ed), *Islam, Fundamentalism, and the Betrayal of Tradition* (Bloomington, Indiana: World Wisdom Inc., 2004) p.132

13. Ibid.

14. The verse of the Qur'an states *O you who believe! Be upright for God, witnesses in justice; and let not hatred of a people cause you to be unjust. Be just— that is closer to piety.* 5:8

15. Reza Shah Kazemi, op. cit., p.133

16. *God has not forbidden you to be charitable and just to those who have not fought you over religion or driven you from your homes, for God loves the just.* Qur'an 60:8

17. That is a non-Muslim who enjoys the protection of the Muslim state

18. Reza Shah Kazemi, op. cit., p.133

19. Ibid., p.121

20. Qur'an 3:84

21. Qur'an 7:159

22. Qur'an 5:82-83

23. Qur'an 4:135

24. Qur'an 3:173

25. For a book that examines and seeks to remedy various diseases of the heart, see Hamza Yusuf (trans.), *Purification of the Heart: Signs, Symptoms and Cures of the Spiritual Diseases of the Heart* (Chicago: Starlatch Press, 2004). In Islam, the heart is seen as the source from which actions manifest. The state of the heart will dictate the nature of one's action. The Prophet said: "There is in the body a lump of flesh—if it becomes good, the whole body becomes good and if it becomes bad, the whole body becomes bad. And indeed it is the heart." Bukhari's *sahih.* In another saying, the Prophet describes how "In the last times, men will come forth who will fraudulently use religion for worldly ends" and will show outward signs of piety, but "their hearts will be the hearts of wolves." Related by al-Tirmidhi. With respect to this, *Jihad* has always been understood that it could not be carried out with "a murderous heart." Indeed, the Qur'an speaks in many places of the necessity of also purifying the soul and ego, for without its restraint, the soul remains one that enjoins evil. It has been authenticated by many *hadith* masters that the *mujahid* (one who partakes in a *jihad*) is one who "makes *jihad* against his *naffs*" (ego). See Ibn Hibban (#1624, 2519): Authentic; Shu`ayb al-Arna'ut (Commentary on *Ibn Hibban*): authentic; al-Hakim: *sahih*; al-'Iraqi confirms him; it is also in Tirmidhi, Ahmad, and Tabarani.

26. Thomas Cleary (trans.), *The Wisdom of the Prophet: Sayings of Muhammad* (Boston, Massachusetts: Shambhala, 2001) p. ix

27. This anthology contains seven of the original essays that appeared in *Shattered Illusions*. The remaining sixteen essays are new.

28. The Qur'an brings back its message to the overriding imperative of mercy and compassion. There are various commandments that urge Muslims to show these qualities at all times; *On those who show compassion, God is the most compassionate.* Qur'an 12:64; *Your God is one God. There is no God but He, the Compassionate, the Merciful.* Qur'an 2:163; *Wrong not, and you will not be wronged.* Qur'an 2:279; *If you pardon and overlook and forgive, then surely God is Forgiving, Merciful.* Qur'an 64:14. Likewise, the *hadith* literature are replete with words of Prophet Muhammad urging the believers to be just, compassionate and

merciful; The Prophet related that God said "O My servants, I have forbidden Myself injustice, and have made it forbidden to you; so do not be unjust." The Prophet said "Whoever is guilty of injustice against a fellow human being, whether in regard to his honor or anything else, let him seek his pardon for the Day of Resurrection [...]." In another saying, he said "God has rendered Mercy into a hundred parts, keeping ninety-nine parts and sending one part down to earth. By virtue of that one portion, creatures are merciful to one another, such that even the mare lifts her hooves away from her foal, fearing she may step on it." Related by Bukhari in his *sahih*. In a saying collected by the *Hanbalite* scholar, Ibn al-Jawziyya, the Prophet is said to have said, "He [God] is Compassionate and loves those who are compassionate. He is gentle and loves those who are gentle to others. Whoever is merciful to creatures, to him is God Merciful. Whoever does good for people, to him will God do good. Whoever is generous to them, to him will God be generous. Whoever benefits the people, God will benefit him." Michael Abdurrahman Fitzgerald and Moulay Youssef Slitine (trans.), *The Invocation of God; al Wabil al-Sayyib min al-Kalim al-Tayyib* (Cambridge: Islamic Texts Society, 2000) p.41. The Prophet Muhammad said "Have mercy on people so you may receive mercy; forgive people so [that] you may be forgiven." In short, Muslims believe that divine *compassion encompasses all things* (Qur'an 7:156) and that the divine Mercy takes precedence over the divine Wrath (Bukhari). As the contemporary scholar, Dr 'Umar Faruq 'Abd-Allah makes clear, although Islam is often described as a religion of "peace," "theologically, it is more accurate to refer to it as the 'religion of mercy.'" Dr. Umar Faruq 'Abd-Allah, "Mercy: The Stamp of Creation," Nawawi Foundation paper, http://www.nawawi.org/downloads/article1.pdf

29. See Khaled Abou El Fadl, "The Orphans of Modernity and the Clash of Civilizations," *Global Dialogue*, vol. 4 (2) pp.1-16

30. See Graham E. Fuller, "Muslims Abhor The Double Standard" *Los Angeles Times*, 5 October 2001; William Blum, *Rogue State: A Guide to the World's Only Superpower* (London: Zed Books, 2002) and Noam Chomsky, *Rogue States: The Rule of Force in World Affairs* (London: Pluto Press, 2000)

31. In this regard, see Mark Hertsgaard, *The Eagle's Shadow: Why America Fascinates and Infuriates the World* (London: Bloomsbury, 2003) and Ziauddin Sardar and Merryl Wyn Davies, *Why Do People Hate America?* (Cambridge: Icon Books Ltd, 2002)

JOHN L. ESPOSITO

MORE THAN THREE years after 9/11, the US-led war on global terrorism continues, as do terrorist attacks which have occurred from Morocco and Spain to Saudi Arabia and Indonesia. America remains a significant presence and force in Iraq and Afghanistan, anti-Americanism has increased exponentially and terrorism experts warn that despite the war on terrorism, religious extremism is growing rather than diminishing.

This new and substantially revised edition of *Shattered Illusions*, recast and re-titled *With God on Our Side: Politics and Theology of the War on Terrorism*, rises to the challenge of addressing the critical issues and questions that continue to affect relations between the Muslim world and the West post 9/11, from examining the causes and costs of the war in Iraq; the realities and myths of international terrorism; the multiple and interrelated roles and influence of neo-conservatives and the militant Christian Zionist Right to the theological sources of Muslim violence and extremism, and the influences and realities of US policy in the Middle East.

The question asked about Islam and Muslims in the days after 9/11—*what went wrong?*—is now relevant when assessing the Bush administration and American foreign policy in the Middle East. The American-led war on global terrorism has not destroyed al-Qa'ida, limited the growth of extremist groups or lessened the threat of global terrorism. Studies and polls show that both extremism and anti-Americanism have in fact increased. The war in Iraq, a war that did not enjoy the support of a broad-based coalition, did remove a bloody dictator. But Saddam was not, as maintained by the Bush administration, a regional or global threat who possessed WMDs, or a major supporter of Osama bin Laden and al-Qa'ida.

In many parts of the Muslim world, the war against global terrorism has continued to be viewed as a war against Islam and Muslims, as well as an attempt to redraw the map of the Middle East and the Muslim world. US policies have alienated many friends and long time allies in Europe and the Arab world. It has fueled anti-Americanism within and outside the Muslim world. Many in the Muslim world and elsewhere worry about the influence of an unholy alliance of neo-conservatives and the militant Christian Right, in a common attempt to implement a New American Century, to expand America's global influence and power.

Almost three years after 9/11, the Bush administration's track record and legacy have been challenged by those who charge that basic American democratic principles and values (the rule of law, civil liberties and human rights) have been sacrificed to a militant neo-conservative ideology. The administration circumvented international law: it embraced the doctrine of preemptive strikes, side-stepped the Geneva Accords, sought to exempt the US from accountability before international tribunals and, through domestic legislation and government policies and actions, compromised civil liberties. It undertook a war condemned by the heads of many mainstream religious faiths, including President Bush's own denomination, as unjust but supported by a neo-conservative and militant Christian Right minority.

The most serious risk to the future is the continued failure to adequately address the root causes of global terrorism and of anti-Americanism. Although the Bush administration quite correctly talked about a three-pronged strategy (military, economic and public diplomacy), the tendency has been to reduce public diplomacy to a public relations campaign rather than a serious re-examination of American foreign policy. In the search for legitimacy in the lead up to the invasion of Iraq, the Bush administration announced its new commitment to promote democracy and dedication to implement a Roadmap to resolve the Palestinian-Israeli conflict. However, the appeal to democracy and to the Roadmap proved to be a two-edged sword, a yardstick by which the administration would be judged. Failure to find Saddam's WMDs and to prove a substantive al-Qa'ida connection and the faltering and failed policies of the provisional authority increasingly brought the charge that the liberation of Iraq had become an occupation and that democratization meant a "guided democracy" under American trusteeship. The images from Abu Ghuraib, accompanied by attempts to deny or minimize the significance of its egregious violation of human rights, outraged not only Iraqis but many across the world. Bush's continued failure to match his tough stand with Arafat on terrorism with an equally tough stand against Ariel Sharon's use of violence and terror to destroy the political, economic and institutional infrastructure in Palestine, discredited the American Roadmap and fed extremism. The end result has been the further erosion of America's moral leadership and credibility, increased anti-Americanism among many of its allies and hatred of America among extremists.

9/11 and the threat of global terrorism has become a further excuse for many governments in the Middle East, Central, South and South East Asia to become more autocratic, to tighten their grip on power and limit dissent. Many countries remain authoritarian/security states where civil society and freedom of association are severely limited. Freedom of thought and expression in the press, media, schools and universities are subordinated to the state. Independent-minded intellectuals, secular and Islamic, continue to be silenced or intimidated, caught often between state security forces or radical Islamists. At the same time, religious extremism grows, violence and terror continue in the name of Islam.

9/11 highlighted the struggle for the heart and soul of Islam that has been going on in recent decades. Terrorist attacks from the World Trade Center and the Pentagon to Madrid to Bali led many to ask, "What is the relationship of Islam to global terrorism?" Moreover, the fact that Osama bin Laden and many of the 9/11 hijackers were from Saudi Arabia as well as Saudi support for some Islamic groups and *madrasas* (seminaries) in countries like Afghanistan and Pakistan raised questions about the role and influence of Wahhabism in global terrorism. Across the Muslim world there has been a growing recognition of the need to address issues of the relationship of Islam to violence and terror, pluralism and tolerance, to counter and contain advocates of theologies of hate.

Formidable challenges and obstacles must be overcome: the ultra conservatism of many (though not all) *ulama*; reform in the curriculum and training of religious scholars, leaders, and students; the discrediting of militant *jihadist* ideas and ideologies; and reform of those *madrasas* and universities that perpetuate a "theology of hate" and train *jihadis*. Like the Reformation in the West, it is a process not only of intellectual ferment and religious debate but also of religious and political unrest and violence. The struggle of Islam today is between the competing voices and visions of mainstream Muslims and a dangerous and deadly minority of terrorists like Osama bin Laden and al-Qa'ida. The lessons of the Protestant Reformation and the Catholic Counter-Reformation demonstrate that widespread religious reform takes time and is often accompanied not only by discussion and debate but also by conflict and violence.

The "war on global terrorism" continues to witness the mixing of politics and religion, the significant use of religious symbols, theology and discourse by the Bush administration and by Muslim extremists, both of whom believe "God is on our side." Policymakers, religious leaders, academics and public intellectuals face a daunting challenge to more critically identify and address the political and theological issues that are root causes for the perpetuation and growth of global terrorism.

INTRODUCTION TO SECOND EDITION
KHALED ABOU EL FADL

N OT MUCH TIME has passed between the first edition of *Shattered Illusions* and this substantially revised second edition, and yet in this relatively short time, so much that is de-stabilizing, deconstructive, demoralizing, and in fact down-right shattering, has taken place. At the most fundamental and basic level, so many lives have been destroyed and so many others have been denied liberty, physically assaulted and tortured, that one struggles with the feeling that it is the very concept of humanity that has been shattered.

The sheer magnitude of the hypocrisy that has been acted out before the world in the past couple of years has made a mockery of the idea of the universal applicability of human rights standards and democracy. After the claim that Iraq possessed weapons of mass destruction had become completely discredited, the Bush administration has persistently relied on the idea that it is building a democratic society in Iraq. Moreover, the Bush administration has made broader and more grandiose claims about inducing reform in the Arab world, and in fact building a new Middle East that is constructed on the principles of free markets, political liberalism, human rights, and democratic governance.

Meanwhile, however, it has become irrefutable that not only has the Bush administration engaged in proxy torture but it has directly and without mediators engaged in torturing detainees in Iraq and in Guantanamo Bay. Furthermore, although the US admitted that is it an occupying power in Iraq, the Bush administration has consistently violated the Geneva Conventions, which among other things, clearly define the duties and obligations of an occupying power. The US government installed a puppet administration in Iraq and adopted the illegal practice of bombardments in order to subdue Iraqi national liberation groups. The attitude of the Bush administration towards the ever mounting list of civilian casualties has been simply one of denial or in some cases, the payment of inadequate reparations. The sheer amount of violence committed in Iraq after the end of the official war demonstrated unequivocally that we have returned to the paradigms of colonialism and the White Man's Burden according to which a Western power assumes that it knows what is in the best interests of a racially non-white people, and continues pounding them with blow after blow until they submit—submit to the higher wisdom, sagacity, and civility of the white man.

Most troublesome is that the reaction of the non-Muslim and Muslim worlds to the slaughter and torture taking place in Iraq has been mild at best. Few, if any countries seem to be taking seriously the ideas of human rights and democracy—most countries have been far more interested in the possible business opportunities that Iraq offered than in enforcing the Geneva Conventions or the so-called Universal Bill of Human Rights. In fact, the irony is that for all the talk about building a new civil Middle East, a most troubling process has started unfolding. Countries friendly to the US in the Middle East, under the guise of fighting terrorism, unapologetically increased repressive measures against their own citizenry to silence any dissent regarding the reactions of their governments towards US policies in Iraq. There were new arrests of Islamists in Jordan and Egypt, and the passage of a new draconian anti-speech law in Kuwait and Saudi Arabia. The US administration and the rest of the Western world were not interested in the marked deterioration in human rights practices in countries friendly to the US. Instead the US and Europe remained obsessed with Syria and Iran. In the same way that we were consistently told that Iraq poses a frightening threat to world peace, so we are told that Syria and Iran pose the same threat. The world somehow managed to calm down about the threat posed by North Korea, but not Syria and Iran.

Of course, during all of this, there is one country that can own as many nuclear weapons as it wants, engage in as many extrajudicial killings as it wishes, indulge in as many preventive detentions as its heart desires, bomb civilian populations, blow up homes, and destroy farmlands. In other words, it is free to violate the Geneva Conventions in whichever way it desires, and pretty much invent its own version of international law without a single word of protest from the US and with mild abashed murmurings of slight displeasure from the Europeans. Of course, this country is Israel, which unlike Syria or Iran can never pose a danger to world peace, democracy, or human rights.

With all of this, so many humanistic and ethical convictions have more and more started to look like illusions that are being shattered by the realities of a strange world that seems oblivious to any standards of substantive justice.

But as illusions are being shattered, others are becoming constructed. At one point in history, after having invaded and dominated Khurasan, the Mongols were threatening to invade Iraq and destroy the weak Caliphate sitting in Baghdad. The Muslim Emir in Syria was forming an alliance with the Crusader state in Jerusalem against the Muslim state in Egypt. The King of France, meanwhile, threatened to start a new crusade by attacking Egypt or Syria. In short, the Muslim world looked like it was in terrible shape, threatened from all sides. But the Muslims, after suffering severe blows, managed to get their affairs together and repel both the Crusaders and Mongols.

Today, to the average Muslim, it seems that the Western world acts as if the only sources of danger or concern that need to be addressed are exclusively in the Muslim world. Afghanistan is occupied with a puppet government installed, and so is Iraq. Syria and Iran are constantly and consistently threatened. Sudan has become a new target for the Security Council and its possible sanctions. Kashmir and Chechnya? Forget these two—they have become terrorist causes.

This Western obsessive engagement with Muslim countries as the only possible sources of danger and the trouble makers of our age is convincing many Muslims that there is a one-sided war going on in the world today. Instead of fighting terrorism and going after terrorists, the US and Europe are fighting the dreams, hopes, aspirations, historical causes, and sense of self-determination of Muslims. Muslims suffer an increasing sense of siege that is only augmented by the remarkably Islamophobic acts and speech that is jovially perpetuated and tolerated in Western societies.

After World War II and in the post-colonial era, there was a virtual edifice of humanistic principles constructed with the distinct purpose of maintaining the integrity of nation-states, communities, and individuals. During this period, ethical and legal principles such as the prohibition against the use of force except in self-defense, non-aggression, self-determination, the right of people to national liberation, and the right to resist foreign domination and occupation were constructed to insure that colonialism and interference in the affairs of other nations were things of the past. Remarkably, in the past few years, for Muslims, this whole international edifice has started looking like an illusion that is being relentlessly shattered. It appears that international law is no longer available for the benefit of Muslims—the only law applied to Muslims by their own governments and by the West is that of the law of anti-terrorism. The law of anti-terrorism is no law at all.

One belief that, far from being shattered, became painfully confirmed is the utter impotence of Muslim governments to control their destinies or offer their people any security whatsoever. Muslim governments could not protect the Bosnians as they were being slaughtered, did not have a single say in the invasions of Iraq and Afghanistan, and sat around solely on the receiving end of all Western policies.

This is a material difference between the threat felt by Muslims during the Mongol and Crusader invasions and the threat felt today. In the past, Muslims could do something to control their own destinies, but today they are entirely defenseless.

This is why these recent years have raised the fearful specter of colonialism—perhaps it is not an illusion to think that the days of colonial domination are back again, or maybe that they never left in the first place but only pretended to lay dormant until it took an aggressively proselytizing administration to wake it from its dormancy. After all, we cannot forget that colonialism claimed that it shouldered the burden of civilizing the savages, and of teaching Muslims the virtues of democracy, free markets, and rationality. These turned out to be excuses for destroying the institutions of Islamic learning, especially *Sharia*, and for uprooting the Islamic tradition as a whole. In other words, these lofty excuses of civilization and so on acted like the sword that severed Muslims from their past and made them into orphans in the modern age. Muslims did not become entirely Westernized, but they also no longer held an authentic identity rooted in an Islamic historical continuity.

This state of uprootedness, more than anything else, is what created the terrorists of today. The true horror is that there is more than a fair chance that the Western policies of today are doing it all over again. If so, it is an illusion that the plague of terrorism will be extinguished. Tomorrow, the world can only look forward to and await a new breed of terrorists who were spawned by the disillusionments suffered by the new forms of colonialism practiced today.

JOHN L. ESPOSITO

EPTEMBER 11 SHATTERED many illusions. The attacks against the World Trade Center and the Pentagon, the symbols of American political, economic and military power, shattered the lives of many families and with it the illusion that somehow America was invincible—able to wage its wars overseas while mainland and mainstream America remained secure at home. It also signaled the vulnerability of European countries to the presence and threat of religious extremists in their midst. The fallout from September 11 surfaced the extent of a broad-based anti-Americanism and anti-Westernism, challenging the illusion of many in America and Europe who were oblivious to the depth of discontent, disillusionment and, among a deadly minority, hatred that exists. At the same time, while Muslims have increasingly become a visible presence in the West and Islam has become better known, September 11 resurfaced old (ancient and more recent) fears, animosities and stereotypes. Although many political and religious leaders took the lead of President George Walker Bush in distinguishing Islam from the acts of extremists and the war against global terrorism from a war against Islam, others did not. The vilification of Islam, its beliefs and heritage, has been widespread, raising persistent questions about the nature of Islam and its relationship to violence, terror, modernization, democratization, the abuse of women and human rights. For many who had thought that significant progress had been made in better understanding Islam and in Christian-Muslim relations, their beliefs now seemed illusory.

Many policymakers, commentators, the media and the general public succumb to the pitfall of seeing Islam through explosive headline events and slogans like a "clash of civilizations." They judge the many by the acts of a minority, the mainstream by an extremist fringe. The distinction between the religion of Islam and the actions of extremists, who hijack Islamic discourse and belief to justify their acts of terrorism, is obscured, leading to the tendency to equate Islamic fundamentalism and terrorism with all Islamic movements, political and social, non-violent and violent. Osama bin Laden and al-Qa'ida are no more representative of Islam, than Christians who blow up abortion clinics or Dr. Baruch Goldstein who slaughtered Muslims in the Hebron mosque is representative of mainstream Judaism.

Absence of a context, one that exists for Judaism and Christianity, in which the acts of extremists are quickly and easily disassociated from mainstream Islam, has made Muslim responses and outreach even more critical. Post-September 11 generated many books and a great deal of media coverage, some seeking to clarify and many to exploit and incite. In the midst of this crisis the visibility and voices of Muslims in particular alongside those of non-Muslims have become critical. This awareness is reflected in this publication by Amal Press, a publication house whose primary purpose is to publish Islamic classical texts on law, jurisprudence, theology and human psychology. Realizing the critical need to move beyond ignorance, stereotypes, media images, sound-bites, and pundits, this volume addresses many of the major issues that September 11 and the subsequent war against global terror have raised.

Making sense of Islam, Muslim politics and relations between the Muslim world and the West requires not only an awareness of the faith and its diverse interpretations but also the multiple roles that Islam plays in Muslim politics today. It is this awareness that will take us beyond monolithic, essentialist notions of Islam and Muslims to the vast, complex and multifaceted realities of the global Muslim experience. The 1.2 billion Muslims of the world live in some fifty-six Muslim countries, from Africa to Asia, as well as in Europe and America where Islam is the second and third largest religion, respectively. Governments range from monarchies to republics, the religious to the more secular, from America's and Europe's allies to their enemies.

A CLASH OF CIVILIZATIONS?

The September 11 terrorist attacks have led some to signal a new clash in the 21st century between Islam and Western civilization, portraying it as a clash of civilizations, between Islam and the West, or between the civilized world and global terrorism. Astonishingly, this approach has been initiated by prominent historians and social scientists, like Bernard Lewis and Samuel Huntington, who ought to know better. It has taken many guises: from talk of an age old clash between Islamic civilization and the West to a clash between "our" way of life and values and "theirs." Rulers in Tunisia, Algeria, Egypt, Turkey, Indonesia, and the Central Asian Republics as well as Israel, India and the Philippines have used the danger of Islamic radicalism to attract American and European foreign aid and to deflect from the failures of their governments or the indiscriminate suppression of opposition movements, mainstream as well as extremists.

Charges of a clash of civilizations are based upon outdated monolithic notions of civilizations. Civilizations like countries are complex, encompassing multiple and diverse identities, beliefs, values, interests and forces. Great diversity and differences (political and cultural) exist not only among but also within Muslim and Western countries and societies. Moreover, while some common beliefs or characteristics (language, religion, or customs) may exist in the West or in the Muslim world, history reveals the extent to which national identities and interests, political and economic forces, often belie that unity. The Iran-Iraq war and the conflicts between Muslim countries, in particular self-styled "Islamic" states and republics such as Saudi Arabia, Iran, the Taliban's Afghanistan, and Pakistan stand alongside twentieth century conflicts between Germany and France or Britain etc.

A clash of civilizations can become the clarion call that justifies aggression and warfare. However, today's and future global threats are and will be due less to a clash of "civilizations" than a clash of interests, political, economic and otherwise. While there are distinctive differences of doctrine, law, institutions, and values between Judaism, Christianity, and Islam, there are also a host of similarities. They all see themselves as Children of Abraham, are monotheists, believe in prophet-hood and divine revelation, have a concept of moral responsibility and accountability. This shared perspective has been recognized in recent years by the notion of a Judeo/Christian tradition, a concept that is slowly being extended by some who speak of a Judeo/Christian/Islamic tradition.

Historic clashes and violent confrontations have occurred, but they do not represent the total picture. Positive interaction and influence have also taken place. Islamic civilization was indebted to the West for many of the sources that enabled it to borrow, translate and then to develop a high civilization that made its own remarkable contributions in philosophy, the sciences and technology while the West went into eclipse in the Dark Ages. The West in turn reclaimed a renovated philosophical and scientific heritage from Islamic civilization, retranslating and re-appropriating that knowledge, which then became the foundation for its Renaissance.

In the modern period, Muslims have freely appropriated the accomplishments of science and technology. In many ways, they face a period of re-examination, reformation, and revitalization.

ISLAM IN THE WEST

Although great care was taken by American officials to distinguish between Islam and terrorism, a lack of awareness regarding Muslim perceptions of history was illustrated by George W. Bush's use of "crusade" to characterize America's war against global terrorism and the Pentagon's use of "Infinite Justice" to herald our exclusive God-given mandate to achieve justice. Is it not ironic that we decry the mixing of religion and politics as dangerous and antithetical to a modern (secular) state but, when useful, we ourselves rush to appeal to religion to justify our actions? More importantly, the administration has often proved incapable or unwilling to balance attention on stopping terrorists, in particular Osama bin Laden, with an equally important focus on the core political issues that help to explain a growing anti-Americanism in the Middle East and broader Muslim world.

Initially, President Bush and many Western political and religious leaders emphasized that extremists should not be equated with mainstream Islam, and that Arab and Muslim Americans should be respected and afforded the same freedoms and tolerance enjoyed by all other citizens. However, these special admonitions on behalf of Arabs and Muslims also reflect awareness that Islam is not judged by the same standards as Judaism and Christianity. Indeed, in seeking to understand Islam, many still struggle within a vacuum, relying on stereotypes born of negative and violent headlines and commentators whose own political agenda is less about America's national interest and more about discrediting Arabs and Muslims from Palestine to South Asia. Understanding of this Abrahamic faith (Islam belongs within a broader Judeo-Christian-Islamic tradition) as well as the everyday, normal lives of the mainstream Muslim majority is obscured by a radical minority, leading headlong into reporters, members of Congress, students, and colleagues with questions along the lines of: "Why do the majority of Muslims hate us?" and "What is it in the Qur'an that justifies terrorism and hijackings?" If the terrorists were members of Christian or Jewish groups that had legitimated their militancy and violence with a twisted interpretation of the Bible or Christianity, media coverage and government responses would reflexively treat these acts, as they have done in the past, as those of extremists or fanatics.

THE CAUSES OF ANTI-AMERICANISM

Many who have puzzled about anti-Western attitudes, in particular Americanism, in the Middle East and Muslim world, have often failed to realize that they see more than we see. Unlike the past, today an international Arab and Muslim media, no longer solely dependent on Western reporters and channels, provides daily coverage of the violence, the disproportionate firepower and number of Palestinian deaths and casualties, as well as the use of American weapons including F16s and Apache helicopters provided to Israel for use against Palestinians. Yasser Arafat's Palestinian Authority, Hamas, and Israel must all be held accountable for unacceptable acts of violence. However, the administration's soft-glove treatment of Israeli Prime Minister Ariel Sharon's heavy-handed policies in the West Bank and Gaza and relatively uncritical US support of Israel—witnessed in its levels of aid to Israel, the US voting record in the United Nations, and official statements by the administration and State Department—have proved a lightning rod.

Anti-Americanism is a broad-based phenomenon that cuts across Arab and Muslim societies. It is driven not by a blind hatred of America or religious zealotry, but by frustration and anger with US policy in the Muslim world. America's espousal of self-determination, democratization, and human rights are often seen in the Muslim world as a hypocritical double standard when compared to political and economic issues such as the impact of sanctions on more than a half million Iraqi children and sanctions against Pakistan but a failure to press Israel and

India on their nuclear developments. Similarly, the moral will, so evident in Kosovo is seen as totally absent in an American policy of permissive neglect in the Chechnyan and Kashmiri conflicts. Critics believe that the significant continued presence of US military and arms in the Gulf risks a new-colonialist military influence leading to uncritical support for authoritarian regimes as well as pressures on Arab governments to comply with US foreign policy objectives, especially with respect to Israel and Palestine. Such a litany sparks the anger of many mainstream Arabs and Muslims, both overseas and in America and Europe.

The temptation is to seek easy justifications to explain away anti-Americanism as simply irrationality, ingratitude, jealousy of our success or hatred for "our way of life." As a native born American convert to Islam and former government consultant has observed: "America's bizarre complicity in the genocidal destruction of Chechnya, its tacit support of India's incredibly brutal occupation of Kashmir, its passivity in the ethnic cleansing of Bosnia, and even America's insistence on zero casualties in stopping the ethnic cleansing of Kosovo all contribute to the terrorist mentality that is growing all over the world."

At the same time, the American media's coverage and editorials often reveal glaring contrasts with those of Europe and the Arab and Muslim world. The differences between programming on the BBC or al-Jazeera versus CNN and Fox News, the sharp contrast between headlines and coverage of Jenin, Nablus, and Bethlehem as well as assessments of the Bush administration in *The New York Times, Wall Street Journal, The Washington Post* and their counterparts in Europe is glaring. Moreover, the depth and breadth of media bias is reflected in editorials, op-eds and articles of commentators such as Bernard Lewis, Daniel Pipes, Charles Krauthammer, William Safire, Steven Emerson, Judith Miller, Martin Kramer, AM Rosenethal, William Kristol, George Will, Martin Peretz, Morton Zuckerman, Norman Podhoretz and others in publications like the *Wall Street Journal, The New York Times, The Washington Post, The New York Post, The New Republic, The Weekly Standard,* and *National Review.* However different, they all tie the war on terrorism and an anti-Islam rhetoric to an uncritical, pro-Israel position. As a result, the Palestinians are painted consistently as the brutal aggressors and the Israelis as innocent victims despite Israel's disproportionate firepower and the far greater Palestinian deaths and injuries. Articles underscore the growth of anti-Semitism but are silent about a comparable growth of anti-Arabism and anti-Islamic sentiment. Arafat is portrayed as responsible for acts of terrorism but Sharon's current and past (Shatila and Sabra) record is ignored. There is no balance in underscoring the failures of both Arafat and Sharon; no balance in depicting both Palestinians and Israelis as warriors as well as victims. At the same time, the alliance between the Christian Right and Republican neo-conservatives who espouse a theological/ideological pro-Israel, Zionist agenda exacerbates the situation. Their calls for the targeting of "terrorist" states from Libya and Sudan to Iran, Iraq and Syria seemingly confirm the charge of a widespread "conspiracy" against Islam.

The resultant image of America and American foreign policy is increasingly that of an "imperial" America whose overwhelming military and political power is used unilaterally, disproportionately and indiscriminately in a war not just against global terrorism and religious extremists but also against Islam and the Muslim world. The failure of the American administration to practice a parity of rhetoric and politics in Palestine-Israel, India-Pakistan, Russia-Chechnya feeds anti-American sentiment among the mainstream as well as the hatred of America among militant extremists. Across the political spectrum there is a growing tendency to believe that a clash of civilizations is on the horizon, provoked by America as well as al-Qa'ida and other extremists.

A WAR AGAINST GLOBAL TERRORISM OR AGAINST ISLAM?

The unfolding trajectory of the war against terrorism has convinced many in the Muslim world that this is a war against Islam and Muslims. Several factors have reinforced this perception and belief, contributing significantly to a widespread anger and anti-Americanism that cuts across Muslim societies: the broadening of the American-led military campaign's scope beyond Afghanistan, the use of the term "axis of evil," and the continued "pro-Israel" policy during the current crisis and carnage on the part of the Bush administration and Congress.

The lack of balance in rhetoric and policy, in words and deeds, of the Bush administration has reinforced the perception among many

Muslims of a Bush-Sharon, American-Israeli alliance. The President and his officials have criticized and held Yasser Arafat fully accountable for suicide bombings but praised Sharon as "a man of peace" and, though initially calling upon Sharon to halt his incursions and destruction of Palestinian cities and villages, quietly acquiesced to Sharon's rebuff and continued reliance on a massive and widespread use of force. The failure to acknowledge and condemn Ariel Sharon's provocation of the second *Intifada* through his visit to the Temple Mount and subsequently, Israel's invasion and devastation of Palestinian Muslim and Christian cities and villages, the siege of the Church of the Manger in Bethlehem in its war against "Palestinian terrorism" has fed a rage among Palestinian and Arab Muslims and Christians that has been witnessed across the Muslim world.

If President Bush was initially sensitive to distinguishing the religion of Islam from the actions of terrorists, that sensitivity soon seemed to fade. The aggressive policies of the Attorney General and a number of government agencies in raids and arrests of Arabs, Muslims, and Muslim organizations have often looked more indiscriminate than focused. The number of cases of imprisonment and detention without trial and the closure of Islamic organizations, without much public evidence or timely trials and convictions, has raised significant questions about the erosion of civil liberties. At the same time, anti-Islam/Muslim statements by several prominent Christian Right ministers like Franklin Graham, Pat Robertson, Jerry Falwell and Jerry Vines, a number of whom are long-time Republicans with political influence, have raised serious concerns about the extent of their influence on a Bush administration that includes members of the Christian Right in senior government positions, including Attorney General John Ashcroft and President Bush himself.

While many of the Bush administration's criticisms of Arafat are merited, its wholesale condemnation of Arafat however, contradicts American principles of self-determination and democracy. Statements by President Bush and Secretary of State Colin Powell, that Arafat is the problem with no comparable recognition that Israel's Ariel Sharon has proven equally incapable of anything other than a warrior strategy, undermines Bush's ability to play a constructive role and instead unwittingly contribute to the spiral of violence and the life "under siege" experienced by most

Palestinians and Israelis. The administration continues to fail to combine a condemnation of suicide bombings and criticism of Arafat's serious shortcomings in political leadership, economic development, control of acts of terrorism with a forceful critique of Sharon's flawed policies: from the replacement of a land for peace policy with peace through the military cleansing of the West Bank and Gaza to the Israeli government's failure to provide a clear political program or alternative. If America is to use its power and leverage as a superpower, the Bush administration will have to work more multilaterally and constructively with its European and Arab and Muslim allies and adopt a more balanced use of rhetoric and policy.

WESTERN DEMOCRATIC PRINCIPLES AND VALUES

Prosecution of the war against global terrorism has been accompanied by a gradual erosion of important principles and values at home or become a green light to authoritarian regimes in the Muslim world to further limit the rule of law and civil society, or repress non-violent opposition. American and European responses must be proportionate; from military strikes and foreign policy to domestic security measures and anti-terrorism legislation. It must be balanced by evidence that establishes a direct connection of guilt and by strikes that are focused rather than wide-ranging and indiscriminate. A disproportionate response runs the risk of a backlash in the Middle East and the broader Muslim world—as well as among fellow American and European Muslim citizens—that will erode the good will and support of many and reinforce an image of a new imperial superpower placing itself above international law.

Ultimately, the fight against global terrorism will not be won by the military. The temptation will be to seek easy justifications to explain away anti-Americanism and anti-Westernism as irrationality, ingratitude, a clash of civilizations, and hatred for "our way of life." Yet, the extremists aside, the bulk of criticism comes from those who judge the West by its admirable democratic principles and values, science, technology and educational systems. Many (in government, business, academia, and the media) admire and/or have visited, lived, or studied in America and Europe. Continued failure to address the above foreign policy issues effectively will continue to contribute to the growth of anti-Americanism witnessed throughout much of the Muslim world and elsewhere as well as provide a breeding ground for hatred and radicalism, the rise of extremist movements, and recruits for the bin Ladens of the world. It is critical that the Bush administration and its European allies adopt a long- as well as a short-term strategy, based upon a re-examination of foreign policy and an openness to press Israel (as well as the PNA), India, Pakistan, Russia and China as well as to reconsider their policies, strategies, and tactics.

S INCE THE TERRORIST attacks of 9/11, President Bush and his
administration have consistently claimed that they are engaged in
battle between good and evil. The good is civilized and, naturally,
the evil is not. President Bush invited the world to choose sides: either
one had to join the good guys, the upholders of civilization and civility, or
conversely, be counted among the evildoers, the dwellers in the darkness
of barbarity. Having adopted this dichotomous worldview, the logical
next step was to sort through the people of the world, and figure out
which slot they ought to fit in. Thus, on the one side, will be the believers
in civilization, but on the other, will be the infidels—those heathens
who ungratefully turned away from the truth. One wishes that Bush was
simply indulging in irresponsible semantics, but unfortunately he was
not. Bush was perpetuating a fairly old colonial habit. Not just the habit
of seeing the world through a binary vision, but also assuming that the
world sees us through the same dichotomous view. It is not just that we
gaze onto the world as either civilized or uncivilized, but we also presume
the world to either be for us or against us—either the world sees us as
friends or enemies. In fact, the orientalists of old and new, attributed to
Islam the belief that the world is divided into two abodes—the abode
of Islam and the abode of infidels. But this was nothing more than the
colonial worldview projected onto Muslims. Colonialism divided the
world into the civilized and the uncivilized, and declared that the white
man's burden is to civilize the world by force if necessary.[1] Similarly,
colonialism projected the same exact paradigm upon Islam. Accordingly,
orientalists, who were often in the service of colonial powers, claimed
that Islam divided the world into two abodes, and they presumed that
Muslims wish to convert the whole world, by force if necessary, to Islam.
Following the age-old honored tradition of colonialists and orientalists,
Bush has convinced himself of an unfailingly confrontational and
destructive paradigm. We put ourselves in a closed circle by convincing

ourselves that we don't like the infidel (uncivilized) and the infidel does not like us. Nurtured by the theorists of the *Clash of Civilizations*, this closed circle has become like a noose around our neck, strangling us, denying us oxygen, blurring our vision, and, ultimately and fundamentally, obscuring the way that we see and understand the world.

The colonialists of old, like Bush, promised and swore that they bear Muslims no ill will. A historian cannot count the number of times he or she will find proclamations issued by colonial powers declaring to Muslims that they have come as friends to help them build and flourish. Even more, every orientalist who worked in the service of colonialism repeatedly assured Muslims that they have nothing whatsoever against their religion. Some, like Goldzhier, initially concealed his Jewish convictions, converted to Islam for a period, and then converted back to Judaism. Montgomery Watt's writings are replete with condescending passages in which he praises Islam as a good and decent religion, which is essentially good enough for the Arabs, but goes on to proclaim Christianity as the one and only universal religion.[2]

So now, Bush assures Muslims that his war against terrorism is not a war against Islam. In the same way that during the age of colonialism Muslims were told not to take offense at the occupation of their countries and the dismantling of their institutions, in the age of post-colonialism, Muslims were told not to be offended as Afghanistan was bombed, and as Iraq was invaded and then occupied, as we continue to support the slaughter of Palestinians, and as we continue to turn a blind eye to India's human rights violations in Kashmir. We, in the United States, do not seem at all concerned with the Hindu fundamentalist government in power in India or the apocalyptic visions of Christian fundamentalists and how these visions contribute to death and destruction. Our consecutive political administrations have consistently categorized Jewish and Christian fundamentalist movements and White supremacist terrorist groups as a low law enforcement and surveillance priority as compared to Islamic fundamentalist or pro-Palestinian groups functioning in the United States. Importantly, even after the terrorist attacks of 9/11, Muslim and Arab terrorism was responsible for no more than two percent of the sum total of terrorist incidents taking place in the United States. Nevertheless, our enforcement policies remain focused nearly exclusively on Muslim and Arab terrorism.[3] A powerful point in case is the anthrax attacks that took place in the United States. After it became clear that neither Muslims nor Arabs were responsible for these attacks, the media interest practically all but vanished, and the resources dedicated to apprehending the culprits were cut in half. To date, the anthrax attacks cases remain unsolved, there is no public outcry demanding the apprehension and prosecution of those responsible for terrorizing the United States, and it has ended up costing us billions of dollars in added security measures.[4]

The irony is that after the Bush administration counseled Muslims not to take offense, a string of events followed that could not be considered anything but offensive. As a harbinger of what was to come, a pro-Palestinian tenured professor at the University of South Florida was fired purportedly for "disrupting University operations." Incredibly, the professor's crime was that extremist pro-Israeli groups threatened him, and the University claimed it could no longer guarantee his safety. Not only did Florida Governor Jeb Bush support the firing, but even the Justice Department and Equal Employment Opportunity Commission refused to investigate the incident as a possible civil rights violation.[5] The Bush administration then proceeded to pass into law the Patriot Act, which targeted Arabs and Muslims in particular; instituted mass detentions without charges against them; froze the assets of many civil Muslim organizations simply on the basis of speculation that they aid terrorist attacks against Israel or because they provide humanitarian supplies to orphaned children in Palestine; and even searched and confiscated the properties of some well known moderate, but politically active, Muslims in the United States. Meanwhile, Bush has surrounded himself with extremist pro-Israeli advisors, and appointed Tom Ridge, a well-known Islamophobe and Arab hater, as the head of Homeland Security in the United States. Even when a Christian fundamentalist, Pastor Jerry Vines, accused the Prophet of being "a demon possessed pedophile," and Islam of being a terroristic religion, Bush reacted by merely noting his disagreement, instead of expressing outrage or condemning this type of religious bigotry.[6] In fact, earlier, the very day after the comments were made, Bush spoke via satellite to the same Southern Baptist convention, in which Vines spoke, and praised the group as "among the earliest champions of religious tolerance and freedom."[7] Instead of strongly

Khaled Abou El Fadl

condemning these remarks or expressing clear outrage, Ari Fleischer, the White House spokesman, merely noted that this is "something that the president definitely disagrees with."[8] In general, unfortunately, President Bush has not distanced himself from religious leaders who have promoted intolerance against Islam.[9] Compounding the problem, Ashcroft, Bush's Attorney General, and the one responsible for implementing the anti-terrorism laws against Muslims, made the remarkably ignorant assertion that the difference between Christianity and Islam is that in Christianity God sent His son to die for humankind, but in Islam God demands that humans send their sons to die for Him. To date, when asked to explain the basis for this claim, Ashcroft has refused to apologize or even acknowledge his woeful ignorance of Islamic theology or law.[10] Bush did speak strongly, however, in opposition to physical attacks and hate crimes directed at Muslims, but the end result was that he has refused to put his money where his mouth is. He has not attempted to bolster anti-hate legislation in America, which are woefully vague and ineffective, and has refused to allocate increased funding to police enforcement agencies investigating and prosecuting hate crimes directed at Muslims and Arabs. Adding insult to injury, instead of focusing on the means that our school curriculums could be modified to combat racism, religious bigotry, and the culture of hate that has become an endemic American ailment, or on dealing with the prejudiced and entirely inaccurate way that Islam is taught in our public schools, he had a distinctly different set of priorities. Acting upon the counsel of his rabidly pro-Israeli Middle East advisors, Bush arrogantly demanded that Muslim countries revise their educational curriculums, and especially the way Islamic theology and law is taught so as to combat bigotry and hate. Bush seemed to be worried about the type of hate that Muslims and Arabs purportedly learn in their schools, but not with any other form of hate, directed at anyone else, that for instance, might be found in America or Israel. As the ex-governor of Texas, Bush must have been well aware of the type of racism and bigotry that plagues our own educational systems. Considering our own history with racism, perhaps we should be tempering our recommendations to other cultures with a bit of humility. Interestingly, as part of his international initiative for the eradication of hate and bigotry, Bush did not dare ask Israel to modify any of its educational materials, which are filled with degrading and dehumanizing images of Muslims and Arabs. This prejudice perpetuating educational material can only contribute to violence in the Middle East, and yet, the Bush administration has not shown any interest in resisting negative stereotypes of Arabs and Muslims.[11] But crowning his dedicated efforts in the service of education he, for all practical purposes, called for the abolition of the *madrasa* system in the Muslim world. Considering everything that the Bush administration has said about the *madrasas* and their role, the ignorance of the American politicians about the anthropological and sociological function of the *madrasas* is embarrassing. As someone who has spent a good part of his life receiving instruction in the *madrasas* of Egypt, I can attest that Bush's proclamations are overbroad generalizations that are factually incorrect. But Bush's statements in this regard are awfully reminiscent of the systematic effort by colonial powers to dismantle traditional Islamic educational institutions in the 18th and 19th centuries as a part of their "civilizing mission" in the Muslim world.[12] In short, it is as if Bush, like so many Western leaders and orientalists from the past and present, are saying to Muslims: "Do not take any of this personally—we have absolutely nothing against your wonderful tourist attractions, authentic looking flowing robes, and exotic prayer rugs and beads, but, for your own good, we are just going to have to emasculate you."

All of this is hardly surprising when one considers that the current American administration, on all matters relating to Arabs and Muslims, attentively listens only to a few sages, which it considers authoritative and dispositive. Those so-called sages are fanatically pro-Israeli, and fanatically hateful of everything Muslim or Arab. Their writings are plagued by conspiratorial delusions, as if the authors salivate over the prospect of any harm that might befall Muslims. After 9/11, these so-called experts have suddenly been propelled into prominence, where they consistently speak to Senate hearings, attend White House meetings, and appear on virtually every major television or radio program. Their hate-tracts fill the chambers of senators and representatives, and the offices of the intelligence community in the United States. This has reached the point that a State Department official, who is very skeptical about the legitimacy and veracity of these writers, expressed to me that he is forced not to openly voice his opinions to his colleagues about these so-called experts because he is made to feel as if voicing skepticism on this point has become politically incorrect in the culture of the Bush administration.[13] Frequently, again, acting upon misguided advice, the Bush administration has stumbled into remarkably odd, and logic defying, political positions. One can only presume that Bush is well-aware of the fact that most regimes in the Middle East are systematic human rights abusers and authoritarian. The long list includes Egypt, Saudi Arabia, Jordan, and Israel. Israel is one of the few countries in the Middle East in which torture is legally sanctioned, the other country being Iraq, and like most other Middle Eastern countries, its human rights record is abysmal.[14] In addition, Israel's democracy does not extend to its administration of the occupied territories, and it is not inclusive of Palestinians who do not carry Israeli citizenship.[15] Nevertheless, in what appeared to many Arabs are a remarkably hypocritical stance, Bush condemned Yasser Arafat's autocratic administration, and declared that a proper Palestinian democracy is a pre-requisite for peace with Israel. In doing so, Bush, of course, ignored the dictatorial and corrupt governments of so many other countries such as Egypt and Saudi Arabia, and held the Palestinian administration to a standard that none of the American allies in the Middle East could meet.[16] In addition, Bush and his predecessors have never voiced any level of concern over the human rights violations that take place in Israel, and consistently understate the human rights record of countries such as Kuwait and Saudi Arabia. Both countries would receive failing marks on the human rights front. Adding tragedy upon tragedy, Bush even went as far as calling Ariel Sharon "a man of peace." But as Professor Francis Boyle has pointed, Sharon, as well as Major General Amos Yaron, Director-General of the Israeli Defense Ministry, is a war criminal.[17]

To an extent, there is nothing entirely new about all of this. At least since the Kissenger years, we have cared little for Palestinian suffering under occupation, and we have systematically supported autocratic governments in Middle East. Our support of the Shah of Iran and Saddam Hussein of Iraq, until he got too greedy and invaded Kuwait, is still fresh in memory. But the material difference this time is that our administration has bought into a dangerous paradigm, espoused by certain Islamophobes, known as the *Clash of Civilizations*. The so-called experts of this paradigm, such as Samuel Huntington, Daniel Pipes, and Steven Emerson are specialists in what might be called the science of crisis development—they are particularly adept in exasperating an already complicated and highly tense situation. There is already a rather large body of literature on the myth of the clash of civilizations,[18] and this is not the place to provide an exhaustive exposition on the subject, but it is useful to note some basic criticisms of this paradigm.

Proponents of the notion of clash of civilizations seem to rely on an unfounded claim about the specificity and purity of particular values. Accordingly, they are willing to classify particular values as squarely Judeo-Christian while others are Islamic. It is as if values have a genealogy that can be clearly and precisely ascertained, which then can be utilized in classifying what properly belongs to the West and what belongs to the Islamic "other." But the origin and lineage of values are as much of a socio-historical construct as are claims about racial genealogical purity. Considering the numerous cultural interactions and cross-intellectual transmissions between the Muslim world and Europe, it is highly likely that every significant Western value has a measure of Muslim blood in it.[19] But this is not merely a matter of acknowledging the Muslim contribution to Western thought. Rather, by recognizing the mixed lineage of ideas, a simple and straightforward taxonomy of civilizations and what they are supposed to stand for becomes much more problematic. Like racial categories, one ought to recognize that civilizational categories are artificial political constructs that cannot be made consistent with socio-historical realities.

Often the attempt to identify one's own civilization and distinguish it from the "other," has much more to do with one's own aspirations than the reality of the "other." Put differently, descriptions of the "other," whoever the other may be, often tell us much more about the author of the description than the subject of the description.[20] For instance, when Westerners attempt to describe the Islamic civilization and what it represents, there is a real risk that the constructed image of the Islamic civilization will only reflect the aspirations and anxieties of those Westerners. Therefore, for example, if those Westerners aspire to achieve a greater degree of democracy, or are anxious about their own shortcomings vis-à-vis women's rights, it is likely that they will invent an image of the Muslim "other" as the exact antithesis of their own aspirations. By constructing the other as the exact antithesis, one is then able to be more satisfied and secure about one's own cultural achievements. The colonial images of the orient—its exoticness, mystique, and harems—had much more to do with the anxieties and fantasies of Western colonizer than it did with the sociological reality of the orient.

The problem is that claims about civilizational clashes must necessarily reduce complex social and historical dynamics into essentialized and artificially coherent categories. From a pedagogical point of view, such claims are likely to degenerate into powerful vehicles for the expression of prejudice.[21] As such, they tend to further misunderstandings and promote conflict. It is no wonder that when one examines the arguments of the Western proponents of the clash of civilizations, one finds that these proponents invariably ascribe most of what they perceive to be good and desirable to the West, and most of what they find distasteful or objectionable to Islam. Then quite often the proponents of a clash of civilizations condescendingly contend that the values of the "other," as terrible as they might be for Westerners, are good enough for the exotic other. Despotism, oppression, and degradation, for example, might be terrible for Westerners, but they are acceptable for Muslims because, after all, Muslims, themselves, are naturally accustomed to despotism, oppression, and degradation.[22] Muslims protests of being aggrieved and offended cannot be taken too seriously because they have a distinctly different set of social and cultural expectations than the Judeo-Christian West.

The supporters of Bush, however, will surely protest by asserting that this war is not about culture or religion; it is about terrorism. We are at war with terrorists, and fundamentalists, and can any one in good faith defend those people? But this simply begs a whole set of questions: Why have so many supporters of Bush's war against terrorism, become convinced that this is a war against Islam? What explains the fact that there have been a shocking number of books and articles cheering Bush's war, and in the same breath declaring a war on Islam, and celebrating notion of the clash of civilizations? Why has the war against terrorism been transformed, in the imagination of so many writers and commentators, into a war against the Muslim barbarians and the Islamic threat? Although bigots exist in every time and age, if the social dynamics that prevail within a society are marked by tolerance and basic decency, such bigots will often be shamed into silence. It is fairly clear that the way that the public discourse has been phrased in the United States has encouraged many Islamophobes to express their bigotry openly and defiantly. Post-9/11, there has been a virtual avalanche of publications that express unrestrained animosity to Islam, as a religion, and Muslims, as a people.[23] So the question is: In what ways has, what might be called, the barrier of civil-shame been breached in American society as in regards to the Islamic religion?

First, it is important to note the fact that terrorism and fundamentalism are not objective categories that can be studied and documented with scientific precision. The Russians called the Afghanis who resisted their occupation terrorists, and they continue to use the same label against the Chechnyans. The Serbs called the Bosnians and Kosovans fundamentalists and terrorists as well, and even the Nazis called the rebels of the Warsaw ghetto, terrorists. During the age of colonialism, every Muslim who protested at the dismantling of the institutions of his society and the spread of foreign power was called a Muslim zealot. Interestingly, even the Romans called the Jews who rebelled and ended up dying at the Masada, religious zealots. In fact, we ought not forget that it was not that long ago when the Irgun and Stern Jewish organizations were considered terrorist organizations by the British and local Palestinian governments.

The point is not that the word terrorism is so negotiated and abused that it has become meaningless. In fact, Islamic law, itself, adopted a clear definition of the concept: It defined it as the act of attacking non-combatants by stealth and without warning under such circumstances that the victims are unable to defend themselves or escape.[24] Many other national legal systems and international conventions have attempted to produce technical definitions of terrorism, but there has not been much success in reaching a universal consensus on the elements of such a crime.[25] Importantly, however, terrorism is not so much a legal category as it is a symbolic social and political construct. The word terrorism in the modern age, which historically did not always carry a negative connotation, signifies a level of ugliness that ought to be considered unacceptable and indecent. Whether societies used the expressions such as pirates, bandits, brigands, pillagers and looters, or terrorism, such expressions were always considered the antithesis of civilization—the undoing of civilized and ordered society. Roman law jurists expressed this concept in the phrase *hostis humani generis* (an enemy of human kind). Muslim jurists expressed the same idea in the notion of *muharib*—someone who wages war against all of society. Such an individual was seen as so threatening to human society that he was deemed an enemy of all societies, and therefore, was refused quarter or sanctuary anywhere on the earth.[26]

There ought to be little doubt that what took place on 9/11 is the undoing of all that is civilized or decent. By any legal or moral definition, it is not just terrorism, but also a suicidal and destructive psychosis. There ought not be any real question that those responsible are both *muharibs* and *hostis humani generis,* and should be dealt with accordingly. Importantly, however, when one is confronted with socially psychotic behavior, it is both unwise, and immoral, not to carefully reflect upon both the cause and response for this type of psychosis. Addressing the response first, it is important to keep in mind that both concepts of *muharibs* and *hostis humani generis* deal with particular and specific criminal elements, and not with collective guilt. Specific individuals or groups, not whole nations, commit the crime of terror. Responses to any crime in a fashion that are not discriminating and disproportionate are akin to responding to the commission of a crime by committing a crime.

The Qur'an teaches the sagacious lesson that: *No one should be made to suffer for the faults of another.*[27] This is a basic principle of justice that ought to guide any legal or moral response to any crime, including terrorism. As noted above, terrorism is a term that is often exploited by political forces that want to point to the illegitimacy of "the other", and label the "other" as barbaric. There are several aspects of our anti-terrorism policies that contribute to a symbolic leap from a "declared war against terrorism" to a "war against Islam." The moment that we intimate that we, in the West, are civilized and Islam is barbaric, we effectively equate Islam with terrorism. This is a frame of mind that is inherent in the very idea of the clash of civilizations because no one, not even Huntington and his supporters, truly believes the claim that the purportedly "clashing civilizations" are equal in moral merit or ethical value. Logically, it is possible for the good to clash with the good, but psychologically, emotively, and metaphysically this is a theoretical possibility that is difficult to accept. If two civilizations are clashing, the natural assumption will be that one is good and the other is bad. After all, why else would they clash? This is especially so because the American administration has solidified already a dichotomous view of the world. According to this view, the world can be divided into good or evil—there are no nuances or in betweens. Since the American administration has asserted our goodness, then, by definition, whomever we clash with must necessarily be evil.[28] This is all the more so when we adopt paradigms such as the axis of evil or rhetorical concepts such as rogue states. The language of axis of evil and rogue states runs counter to the idea of specific and individual liability and fault, and significantly contributes to the idea of collective and generalizable fault. Effectively, what this type of language connotes is that there are bad nations of people, and not just guilty individuals. Again, at the symbolic and emotive level, this type of language contributes to an environment in which bigotry and prejudice thrives. At the essence of bigotry and prejudice is the willingness to generalize about a people, and to consider these generalizations incontrovertible and unassailable. When our leadership presumes itself capable of generalizing about whole nations, branding them as evil, we set a terrible moral example.[29]

Beyond the quality of our political discourse, its symbolism, and the way it contributes toward fomenting an atmosphere in which bigotry is legitimated and even encouraged, there is also the issue of our actual concrete responses to psychotic behavior. Put simply, if our response to criminal behavior is criminal as well, all we accomplish is to contribute to the diluting of the standards of justice and morality. Here, I refer to our dismissive, and nearly callous, attitude towards the suffering of the innocent "other." Our campaign in Afghanistan has been shrouded in secrecy, including secrecy about civilian casualties that we might have inflicted upon innocent Afghanis. However, secrecy means that we are not taking responsibility for our mistakes, even if such mistakes were justifiable, and the refusal to take responsibility, in turn, de-legitimates the very moral standards that we avowedly are trying to uphold. By effectively sending out the message to the world that we refuse to be held accountable for our mistakes, and refuse to adhere to any standards other than the ones we deem appropriate for ourselves, we adopt the very logic of barbarism. Particularly in the historical setting in which we are conducting our campaign, we are also perpetuating the historical practices of colonialism, which were premised on policies of privilege and exceptionalism. It is imperative that we understand that colonialism cast the colonized in the frame of the immature and dependent. Colonialism treated the colonized as too backward to be capable of being treated with transparency or honesty. Put bluntly, the colonized had to be kept in the dark because the colonizer distrusted the colonized with information. Our attitude towards the transmission of information invokes this painful historical memory for many people in the Islamic world. In the conflict in Afghanistan, we have resisted, and continue to resist, applying the Geneva Conventions of 1949, which by all measures are an earmark of human civilization, and we have refused to disclose or discuss any information about reported massacres, and civilian casualties.[30]

It is important to recall that this same attitude has marked our reaction to charges of civilian casualties and excessive killing in the Gulf War. Despite considerable amount of evidence suggesting that violations of humanitarian law had taken place, our attitude can only be described as dismissive, and even bordering on the callous.[31] Furthermore, to date, we have been completely oblivious to our role in supporting the continuing human rights violations committed against Palestinians living under a military occupation in the West Bank and Gaza, and we even resisted an international investigation on the reported massacres that took place in Jenin and elsewhere. In essence, we took a firm stand against one form of barbarism, namely suicide bombings that killed and maimed Israeli civilians, but we took an entirely deferential and unprincipled stand on another form of barbarism, namely reported massacres and other human rights violations by Israeli forces. Without investigation, or a demand for transparency of information, we simply reaffirmed Israel's right to defend itself, which is a self-evident right, but which is also not the point. Palestinians have the right to defend themselves as well, but both Israelis and Palestinians do not have the right to defend themselves through immoral means, or by violating the rules of war. We, however, did not seem keen about investigating or ascertaining facts, despite the existence of reasonable grounds to believe that violations of humanitarian laws had, in fact, taken place. Without transparency of information and accountability, we simply confirm the barbarism of the colonial legacy and practice.

When confronted by the type of suicidal psychosis that was inflicted upon the United States on 9/11, we cannot afford to ignore the social and political dynamics that can produce this level of criminality and destructiveness. The magnitude of 9/11 is such that everyone who was affected, directly or indirectly, by this tragedy is under a moral duty to engage in a conscientious pause, and critically evaluate any direct or indirect responsibility that they might bear for this act of mass murder. I have taken a very critical stance towards certain theological and moral orientations that, in my opinion, contributed to these terrorist attacks.[32] This critical stance did not emanate from a belief in the collective guilt of Muslims for this criminal act. Rather, it was motivated by a desire to force a critical self-evaluation of the state of moral thought in the Muslim world, and the ways that each individual Muslim might have contributed directly or indirectly to a massacre of innocent lives of this magnitude. Naturally, some Muslims did not appreciate this critical stance, and accused me of creating divisiveness among Muslims or of betraying Islam. Nevertheless, the Qur'an advises human beings to hold steadfast to the truth of justice, and to bear witness on its behalf even if such testimony is against one's loved ones or even against oneself.[33] This basic moral principle ought to guide all attempts at critical self-appraisal.

Critically examining the underlying causes for criminal acts does not mean supporting or otherwise justifying the crime or even sympathizing with the criminal. For instance, a person who takes a gun into a school and commits mass murder should be punished. Investigating the social, economic, or political conditions that might have contributed to the making of such a monster does not mean that we condone the crime or the criminal. Rather, critically evaluating the root causes is a moral obligation owed to the victims of the crime, and also owed to any individuals who could potentially become the victims of a similar criminal act. Although this seems to be an obvious point, it is necessary to state it because of the tendency among many to equate critical self-evaluations with apologetics on behalf of crime, or, in this case, terrorism. Punishment and prevention might be related questions, but they are not identical. This is all the more so when one is dealing with an ideologically motivated crime such as terrorism. In my view, it is morally erroneous and socially irresponsible not to try to understand and prevent such psychotic behavior.

As a part of the process of critical self-evaluation, we must ask: In what ways does our own behavior towards the world in general, and the Muslim world, in particular, provide ideological fodder for terrorists? Adopting the attitude, which has become prevalent recently, that "those people are just crazy by their very nature!" or "it doesn't matter what we do because they're just irrational!" is a form of barbarism not materially different from the type of stereotypes adopted by those who support terrorists. Furthermore, the image of the irrational, non-reasoning, and illogical Muslim, who has no concept of reality, is a mental set that has been persistent throughout the history of colonialism in the Muslim world. The colonizer had to invent the image of the colonized as infantile, being incapable of reasoning in order to justify, morally and politically, the colonial project. Embarrassingly, the image of the Muslim as someone who has no concept of concrete reality, time, history, or place still persists in what is supposed to be serious modern scholarship.[34] But we ought to recognize that these types of stereotypes about Muslims are a part of our own barbarism, which only serves to contribute to mutual hostility and distrust.

Among the elements that we should think about are our own policies, as the main superpower in world, towards Muslims at large and the Arab world specifically. I have already alluded to the problem of supporting autocratic and corrupt regimes in the Arab world. We shamefully ignored the human rights violations of our former ally, Saddam Hussein, as long as he served our political interests in the same way that we continue to ignore the human rights violations of our current allies in the Middle East. Graham Fuller, the former vice-chairman of the National Intelligence Council at the CIA noted in an article that, in his experience, he has found that most Muslims actually respect most American values—such as liberty, freedom, and democracy. But Fuller questioned whether the US is constant to its own values abroad, which he noted the US "rarely" promotes in the Muslim world.[35] In a recent article in the *Guardian* and *Washington Post*, for instance, it was reported that the United States has been illegally transporting dozens of individuals suspected of having connections to al-Qaʿida to countries such as Egypt and Jordan for the explicit purpose of torturing the suspects in order to extract information. This practice, which is known as "rendition," is a violation of all civilized international treaties and conventions such as the Geneva Conventions of 1949, the convention on political and civil rights, the convention on the protection and non-refoulement of refugees, and the convention on the prohibition of torture,[36] all of which the United States has signed and ratified, not to mention all norms of morality and decency.[37] Quoting American diplomats, these reports allege that the Bush administration does not wish to conduct the torture itself, so it sends these suspects to places with the understanding that they will be tortured and the information extracted will then be conveyed to American intelligence.[38] It is not possible to overstate the impact that reports such as this, or the reports regarding the conditions under which prisoners were being held in Guantanamo Bay, has on the credibility of the United States in the Middle East. Such practices re-confirm the historical experience of Muslims in the colonial period. Colonial powers maintained two standards of human rights, one that was implemented in their own countries, and an entirely different standard—or perhaps the lack of a standard—that was implemented as to the colonized.[39] With policies such as these, it is difficult for the United States to avoid the appearance of reproducing the same destructive legacy.

A pivotal part of the American response to terrorism is our policies regarding Israel. I have already touched upon this subject, but it is important to re-emphasize that the dispossession and systematic suffering of the Palestinian people for over fifty years will continue to be a major source for radicalism until this problem is solved. Understandably, often supporters of Israel are uncomfortable about pointing the finger at the US-Israel special relationship as a major impetus for radicalization and terrorism. There is a reasonable component to this discomfort and that is the fact that consecutive Arab governments have used the conflict with Israel as a scapegoat for their own autocracy and incompetence. These governments have projected the blame for their failure to achieve any reasonable degree of success at development or effective governance on Israel, and, in fact, used the threat of Israel in order to justify suppression of free expression or civil rights. Nevertheless, there is also no doubt that the persistent brutalization of the Palestinians, living under occupation, and our tacit support of this brutalization is a major contributor to our questionable credibility in the Muslim world. It is not only that we are Israel's primary military, political, and economic supporters, but we also play this role regardless of the particular policies that Israel chooses to pursue. Importantly, even the language that we utilize vis-à-vis Israel reflects a regrettable duality in our standards. Every time there is a terrorist attack against Israeli civilians we, rightly, condemn such attacks in the strongest language possible. Meanwhile, our responses to the killing of Palestinian civilians are quite subdued, to say the least.

One of the main problems that we must honestly and bravely confront is that there is an entrenched belief in the Muslim world that we, Americans, do not place much value on a Muslim life. Understandably, this belief emerged slowly but surely during the colonial era, and became ingrained as a result of our policies during the post-colonial age. But Arabs or Muslims do not hold this belief alone. For instance, George Galloway, the (former) Labor MP from England, stated:

> "I have walked in the ashes of cities under attack. People being crushed by falling masonry and steel or incinerated by fire from an aerial attack, look, sound, and smell exactly the same whether they are in Beirut, the West Bank, Baghdad, or Manhattan. Arabs and Muslims believe, and they are right to believe, that we do not consider their blood as valuable as our own—as our policy in decades of our history makes abundantly clear."[40]

In order to understand this sentiment we do not have to go far back into history. The humanitarian tragedy caused by the US led sanctions against Iraq is staggering. The results of the sanctions, which include the death of one million Iraqi children, has been described as genocidal, and yet, various British and American administrations have not shown much concern.[41]

The inescapable conclusion that we, not as Americans or Arabs, or Muslims or non-Muslims, but as human beings, must confront and overcome the legacy of double-standards, colonialism, dominance, and oppression. As human beings, we must move beyond essentialisms, stereotypes, mutual distrust, and hate. We must avoid acting barbarically in the name of fighting barbarity, and the first step towards that goal is to shatter our comfortable illusions, and to confront the barbarity within ourselves. The person who confesses his or her own barbarity has started down the path of humility and the vanquishing of hate. The articles in this volume are by brave authors who strive to give a different perspective on what we think we know. The purpose of this collection is to challenge us to question our assumptions, and see or engage a perspective that we rarely find represented in the mainstream media. As such, this collection is in the best tradition of the West and East, and the best traditions of Judaism, Christianity, and Islam: the tradition of freedom of conscience and honest testimonials. The point of this collection is not to blame one party or another and the point is not to perpetuate hate. The point is to understand. The Persian poet Hafiz is reported to have said:

What would you say if you were invited to a banquet by God, and when you got there you saw everybody else who shared the earth with you at the same banquet. The Muslim, the Jew, the Christian, and the Hindu—all of them had been invited to the same banquet. How would you treat those people?

Then he said:

Hafiz knows that everyone here is a guest of God.

May we come to know this truth as well.

NOTES

1. On the so-called civilizing mission of colonialism and its destructive impact, see the classic work: Aime Cesaire, *Discourse on Colonialism*, Joan Pinkham, trans. (New York: New York University Press, 2000).

2. The classic studies on orientalism and its effects remain those of Edward Said, *Orientalism* (New York: Random House, 1979), and *Culture and Imperialism* (New York: Vintage Books, 1994).

3. For the terrorist threat posed by white supremacist groups, see Howard L. Bushart, John R. Craig, and Myra Barnes, *Soldiers of God: White Supremacists and Their Holy War for America* (New Jersey: Kensington Publishers Corp. 2000); Betty A. Dobartz and Stephanie L. Shanks-Meile, *The White Supremacist Movement in the United States: White Power, White Pride* (Richmond: John Hopkins University Press, 2000).

4. For detailed studies on the prejudice that seems to plague our anti-terrorist policies in the United States, see Susan M. Akram, "Schehrezade Meets Kafka: Two Dozen Sordid Tales of Ideological Exclusion," *14 Georgetown Immigration Law Journal 51* (1999); James X Dempsey and David Cole, *Terrorism and the Constitution: Sacrificing Civil Liberties in the Name of National Security* (Los Angeles: First Amendment Foundation, 1999); Natsu Taylor Saito, "Symbolism Under Siege: Japanese American Redress and the Racing of Arab Americans as Terrorists," *8 Asian Law Journal 1* (2001); Michael J. Whidden, "Unequal Justice: Arabs in America and United States Antiterrorism Legislation," *69 Fordham Law Review 2825* (2001).

5. The 12 members of the Board of Trustees of the University of South Florida gave notice to the professor of the meeting that decided his fate 24 hours before it took place. Professor Al-Arian was not allowed to attend the meeting, and his lawyer, who was permitted to attend, was not allowed to speak. Incidentally, the FBI had previously investigated the professor for possible ties with terrorist groups, and cleared him of all wrongdoing. See Bill Berkowitz, "Witch Hunt in South Florida: Pro-Palestinian Professor is First Casualty of Post 9/11 Conservative Correctness," at www.workingforchange.com, 12/21/01.

6. The accusation of pedophilia is not new; Jewish and Christian bigots have exploited it for many years. For example the United Soul Winners, a Christian group, states: "Khoemeni claimed Rushdie insulted Islam and its pedophile prophet, Muhammad. There is no insult when you are telling the truth. Many

elements within Islam are barbaric, violent and authoritarian. The only insult Rushdie committed was exposing those facts to the international community." www.fishbowlministries.org. November 2001. For an example from extremist Jewish quarters, we can find the following: "The conclusion is that the Jews have much greater right to Medina—the second most holy city of Islam than Arabs/ Muslims have to Jerusalem which they never built and which they invaded only after the death of the pedophile pervert prophet Mohammad." http://pub43. ezboard.com. The evangelical Robert A. Morey, the author of notorious *The Islamic Invasion: Confronting the World's Fastest Growing Religion* (New York: Harvest House Publishers, 1992), a hate-filled tract that is of the same genre as Hitler's *Mein Kemp*, accused the Prophet Muhammad of being a racist, a murderer, an irrational zealot, and a pedophile. In fact, after September 11, Morey announced a crusade against Islam, and invited Christians to sign the following pledge:

> In response to the Muslim Holy War now being waged against us, We, the undersigned, following the example of the Christian Church since the 7th century, do commit ourselves, our wealth, and our families to join in a Holy Crusade to fight against Islam and its false god, false prophet, and false book. We, the undersigned, believe that Islam is the root of all Muslim terrorism, which is the fruit of Islam.

See James A. Bevereley, "Is Islam a Religion of Peace?" at www.christianitytoday. com. We do not know how many people signed his pledge. On his website, www. faithdefenders.com, Morey calls upon Christians to sign on to what he calls a "certificate of valor," which reads: "The religion of Islam stands to be the greatest threat against humanity that the world has ever known. I therefore agree with this statement and will pledge my support. I also understand that my donation will further the efforts of Faith Defenders to reach these lost souls for the sake of Christ. I stand firm with Faith Defenders and further understand that at this time in history, we are in a crisis of epic proportions." Apparently, an earlier statement read: "I wish to join in the Crusade of Christ against Islam. To that end, and to demonstrate in the crusade against Islam, I hereby donate toward emergency wartime funds."

7. Susan Sachs, "Baptist Pastor Attacks Islam, Inciting Cries of Intolerance," *New York Times* 6/15/2002; Guest Column: Anti-Muslim Words Adds to Danger

for Christians," at www.gomemphis.com, 6/28/2002.

8. This was reported by Associated Press 6/20/02. The reality is that religious bigots have leveled the same accusation of pedophilia against Christianity and Jews as well. For the view that Jesus was a pedophile, see "Jesus was a Pedophile" at http://www.Theta.btinternet.co.uk 7/1/02. For the view that Judaism condones pedophilia, see "Girls Married at the Age of 3 According to the Jews' Holiest book, the Talmud." www.answering-christianity.com. The point is that every religious tradition is open to attack by bigots who are not interested in history or social context, but are simply interested in maligning the "other's" religious tradition, and so the challenge is not, as President Bush seems to think, to merely note disagreement, but to recognize that these claims are motivated by hate, not misinformation, and thus, ought to be treated as hate-speech and condemned in the strongest terms possible. While President Bush reacted strongly to physical attacks against Muslims and Arabs in the United States, at least in the sense of expressing outrage, he has been largely oblivious to the frenzy of hate speech directed at Muslims and Arabs after 9/11.

9. See Bessy Reyna, "Intolerance is Un-American," *The Hartford Courant*, 6/21/2002 at www.ctnow.com.

10. Dan Eggen, "Ashcroft Invokes Religion in US War on Terrorism," *Washington Post* 2/20/2002. Speaking about Islam in an interview with syndicated columnist and radio commentator Cal Thomas, Aschroft said: "Islam is a religion in which God requires you to send your son to die for Him. Christianity is a faith in which God sends His son to die for you." Ashcroft's remarks were first reported on Thomas' radio segment "Men of Faith in Washington D.C." on November 9.

11. On this, see Ilan Gur-Ze'Ev, *Destroying the Other's Collective Memory* (New York: Peter Lang Publishing, 2002); Sami Khalil Mar'i, *Arab Education in Israel* (Syracuse: Syracuse University Press, 1978). Also, see Israel Shahak, *Jewish History, Jewish Religion: The Weight of Three Thousand Years* (London: Pluto Press, 1994), parts of this book deals with the inaccurate and hate-filled material taught to Israeli school children about Arabs.

12. As Amilcar Cabral put it: "The colonialists usually say that it was they who brought us into history: today we show that this is not so. They made us leave history, our history, to follow them, right at the back, to follow the progress of their history." Amilcar Cabral, *Revolution in Guinea: An African People's Struggle* (London: Stage 1 Publications, 1969) p.63. On colonialism and the displacement of the cultures of the colonized, see Bernard S. Cohn, *Colonialism and Its Forms*

of Knowledge (Princeton: Princeton University Press, 1996); Patrick Colm Hogan, *Colonialism and Cultural Identity: Crises of Tradition in the Anglophone Literatures of India, Africa, and the Caribbean* (New York: New York University Press, 2000); Edward Said, "Secular Interpretation, the Geographical Element, and the Methodology of Imperialism," in Gyan Prakash (ed.) *After Colonialism: Imperial Histories and Postcolonial Displacements* (Princeton: Princeton University Press, 1995)pp. 21-39; Robert J. C. Young, *Postcolonialism: An Historical Introduction* (Oxford: Blackwell Publishers, 2001) pp. 200-3, 288-92.

13. Of course, here I am referring to the like of Steven Emerson, Daniel Pipes, and Samuel Huntington. The three-some are the ones most cited by politicians in private conversations, but they are the quintessential example of Islamophobes. For Daniel Pipes' endless spew of articles on the dangers and threats of Islam and the blessings and virtues of Israel, see www.amisraelhai.org For an analysis of Steven Emerson's endless campaign to malign Islam and unconditionally support Israel, see "Who Is Steven Emerson?" at www.cair-net.org.

14. In 1999, the Israeli Supreme Court issued a decision that outlawed certain forms of physical coercions under a particular set of conditions. Commendably, the Israeli Supreme Court recognized that torture is an affront to human dignity, but refused to endorse an unequivocal prohibition against the use of torture, see Alexandre Cockburn, "Israel's Torture Ban," *The Nation*, 9/27/1999; David Kretzmer, *The Occupation of Justice: The Supreme Court of Israel and the Occupied Territories* (Albany, New York: SUNY Press, 2002) pp.140-141. For a contra, but dated view, see Haim J. Zadok, "The High Court of Justice Did Not Sanction Torture," *Yediot Ahronot*, 3/12/96. Human rights NGOs have documented the systematic use of torture against Palestinian detainees. The Israeli human rights NGO B'Tselem has reported cases of torture against Palestinian minors occurring between October 2000 and January 2001. Yael Stein, "Torture of Palestinian Minors in the Gush Etzion Police Station," B'Tselem Information Sheet, July 2001. For further accounts of torture, see Amnesty International's report "Israel and the Occupied Territories: Mass detention in cruel, inhuman, and degrading conditions," May 2002, pp. 13-15 (available on-line at: http://web.amnesty.org/ai.nsf/index/mde150742002?opendocument&of=countries\ israel/occupied+territories).

In addition, see Amnesty International Report, "Israel and the Occupied Territories in 1988 (June, 1989). Also, see Al-Haq Staff: *Law in the Service of Man, Punishing a Nation: Human Rights Violations During the Palestinian Uprising*

December 1987 to December 1988 (South End Press, 1990); Human Rights Watch Report, "Torture and Ill-Treatment: Israel's Interrogation of Palestinians from the Occupied Territories," (June, 1994); Human Rights Watch Report, "A License to Kill: Israeli Operations Against Wanted and Masked Palestinians," (August, 1993).

15. Norman G. Finkelstein, *Image and Reality of the Israel-Palestine Conflict* (London: Verso Books, 2001); Amira Hass, *Drinking the Sea at Gaza: Days and Nights in a Land Under Siege*, Elana Wesley (trans.) (New York: Owl Books, 2000).

16. See Howard Schneider, "Arabs Under Autocratic Rule Question Bush Speech: Calls for Democracy Seen as Selective," *Washington Post* 6/28/2002; Susan Sachs, "How to Rig a Democracy," *New York Times* 6/30/2002.

17. See Francis A. Boyle, "Barak Appoints War Criminal Yaron." http://www.derechos.org/human-rights/mena/doc/boyle2.html

18. On this issue, see Samuel P. Huntington, *The Clash of Civilizations: Remaking of World Order* (New York: Touchstone Press, 1996); John Esposito, *The Islamic Threat: Myth or Reality?* (Oxford: Oxford University Press, rev ed. 1995); Fred Halliday, *Islam and the Myth of Confrontation* (London: I.B. Tauris, 1995); Colin Chapman, *Islam and the West: Conflict, Co-Existence or Conversion?* (Carlisle, U.K.: Paternoster Press, 1998); Karim H. Karim, *The Islamic Peril: Media and Global Violence* (Montreal: Black Rose Books, 2000); Dieter Senghaas, *The Clash Within Civilizations: Coming to Terms with Cultural Conflicts* (London: Rout-ledge, 1998). For excellent studies on the historical misconceptions about Islam prevalent in Europe, see Franco Cardini, *Europe and Islam* (Oxford: Blackwell Press, 2001); Albert Hourani, *Islam in European Thought* (Cambridge: Cambridge University Press, 1991). The best work on the subject remains: Norman Daniel, *Islam and the West: The Making of an Image* (Oxford: Oneworld Press, 1960, reprinted 2000). A particularly useful and sophisticated collection of studies, see: John Victor Tolan, *Medieval Christian Perceptions of Islam* (London: Routledge, 2000). For the impact of the Huntington thesis and misconceptions about Islam on American foreign policy, see Maria do Ceu Pinto, *Political Islam and the United States: A Study of U.S. Policy Towards Islamist Movements in the Middle East* (Reading, U.K.: Ithaca Press, 1999)

19. There are many works that document the influence of Islamic culture and thought on Europe. Two impressive works are: George Makdisi, *The Rise of Humanism in Classical Islam and the Christian West* (Edinburgh: Edinburgh

University Press, 1990); Mourad Wahba and Mona Abousenna (eds.) *Averroes and the Enlightenment* (New York: Prometheus Books, 1996). Even when preserving the Greek philosophical tradition, Muslim scholars did not act as mere transmitters, but substantially developed and built upon Greek philosophy. In a fascinating text which demonstrates the level of penetration that Islamic thought achieved in Europe, Thomas Aquinas, in an attempt to refute Ibn Rushd (aka Averroes), whom he labels as a "perverter of Peripatetic philosophy" and Ibn Sina (Avicenna), ends up quoting Hamid al-Ghazali in support of his arguments against Ibn Rushd's. Both al-Ghazali and Ibn Rushd were medieval Muslim philosophers and jurists. *Thomas Aquinas, On the Unity of the Intellect Against the Averroists*, Beatrice Zedler, trans. (Milwaukee: Marquette University Press, 1968) pp. 46-7. For a collection of articles that demonstrate cross-intellectual influences, see John Inglis, *Medieval Philosophy and the Classical Tradition: In Islam, Judaism, and Christianity* (Richmond, U.K.: Curzon Press, 2002). For an awe inspiring example of the contributions of medieval Muslim scholars to Greek philosophy, see Kwame Gyekye, *Arabic Logic: Ibn al-Tayyib's Commentary on Porphyry's Eisagoge* (Albany: State University of New York Press, 1979).

20. For an analysis of this process of projection and construction of an image of Islamic law, see Abou El Fadl, "Islamic Law and Ambivalent Scholarship," *Michigan Law Review* (2002).

21. Not surprisingly, writers who clearly do not like Muslims very much have exploited Huntington's thesis. For an example of paranoid Islamophobia, a work that was unfortunately highly praised by various American politicians, see Anthony J. Dennis, *The Rise of the Islamic Empire and the Threat to the West* (Bristol, IN: Wyndham Hall Press, 1996). For another example of a work, written from the perspective of a Christian fundamentalist, that exploits Huntington's argument and that is hostile to Islam, see George Grant, *The Blood of the Moon: Understanding the Historic Struggle Between Islam and Western Civilization* (New York: Thomas Nelson Press, rev. ed. 2001). Typically, in this genre of literature, Christianity, Judaism, and Western culture is, rather jovially, all bundled up in a single unitary mass, placed in one corner, and then it is pitted against the enemy in the other corner: the fantasized concept of The Islam.

22. This is the gist of Huntington's argument about the wrongfulness of believing in universal Western values, Huntington, *The Clash*, pp. 308-312. This is also Lawrence Rosen's argument is his *The Justice of Islam: Comparative Perspectives on Islamic Law and Society* (Oxford: Oxford University Press, 2000)

pp. 153-175. Also, see Ann Mayer, *Islam and Human Rights: Tradition and Politics* (Boulder, Colorado: Westview Press, 3rd, 1999) pp. 6-9.

23. There has been an alarming amount of anti-Islamic propaganda published after 9/11. Two particularly sinister works that attempt to demonize all politically active Muslim individuals or organizations are: Steven Emerson, *American Jihad: The Terrorists Among Us* (New York: Simon & Schuster, 2002), & Daniel Pipes, *Militant Islam Reaches America* (New York: W.W. Norton Co., 2002). Both of these works brand all American Muslims who are critical of Israeli policies as potential terrorist threats, and they incite suspicion against American Muslims by claiming that many of those Muslims are taking part in a secret conspiracy to promote terrorism in America. For a partial list of Islamophobic works that were published or reissued after 9/11, see: Dan Benjamin, *The Age of Sacred Terror: Radical Islam's War Against America* (New York: Random House Publishers, 2002); Anthony J. Dennis, *The Rise of the Islamic Empire and the Threat to the West* (New York: Wyndham Hall Press, 2001); Mark A. Gabriel, *Islam and Terrorism: What the Quran Really Teaches About Christianity, Violence, and the Goals of the Islamic Jihad* (New York: Charisma House, 2002); George Grant, *The Blood of the Moon: Understanding the Historic Struggle Between Islam and Western Civilization* (New York: Thomas Nelson Press, rev. ed. 2001); David Earle Johnson, *Conspiracy in Mecca: What You Need to Know About the Islamic Threat* (New York: David Johnson Books, 2002); Sumrall Lester, *Jihad—The Holy War: Time Bomb in the Middle East* (New York: Sumrall Publishing, 2002); John F. MacArthur, *Terrorism, Jihad, and the Bible* (New York: W Publishing Co., 2001); John F. Murphy Jr., *The Sword of Islam: Muslim Extremism from the Arab Conquests to the Attack on America* (New York: Prometheus Books, 2002); Adam Parfrey (ed.), *Extreme Islam: Anti-American Propaganda of Muslim Fundamentalism* (New York: Feral House, 2002); Robert Spencer, *Islam Unveiled: Disturbing Questions About the World's Fastest Growing Faith* (New York: Encounter Books, 2002); Larry Spargimino, *Religion of Peace or Refuge for Terror?* (New York: Hearthstone: 2002); Marvin Yakos, *Jesus vs. Jihad* (New York: Creation House, 2001). For a scholarly study on the subject of holy war in Islam, see John Esposito, *Unholy War: Terror in the Name of Islam* (Oxford: Oxford University Press, 2002).

24. On the subject, see Khaled Abou El Fadl, *Rebellion and Violence in Islamic Law* (Cambridge: Cambridge University Press, 2001).

25. See John F. Murphy, "International Terrorism: The Definitional Quagmire," in *State Support of International Terrorism: Legal, Political, and Economic*

Dimensions (Boulder, CO.: Westview Press, 1989). Barton L. Ingraham, "Problems of Definition: Is Political Crime 'Criminal'?" in *Political Crime in Europe: A Comparative Study of France, Germany, and England* (Los Angeles: University Press of California, 1979) pp. 3-36. For a useful collection of articles on the subject, see Conor Gearty (ed.), *Terrorism* (London: Dartmouth Publishing Co., 1996).

26. On the subject, see Khaled Abou El Fadl, "Political Crime in Islamic Jurisprudence and Western Legal History," 4:1 University of California at Davis *Journal of International Law and Policy* 1-28 (1998).

27. Qur'an 6:164, 17:15, 35:18, 39:7, 53:38.

28. This means that Huntington's claim that his clash of civilizations paradigm is a value-neutral and objective fact of history is disingenuous. Of course, it is not value-neutral, and it has a powerful emotional impact that results in the de-legitimating of the other.

29. On the myth of rogue nations and evil axis, see Noam Chomsky, *Rogue States: The Rule of Force in World Affairs* (London: South End Press, 2000); Noam Chomsky and Edward Said, *Acts of Aggression: Policing Rogue States* (New York: Seven Stories Press, 2002).

30. For a very critical view of the violations of the laws of war by the United States in Afghanistan and elsewhere post-9/11, see John K. Cooley, *Unholy Wars: Afghanistan, America, and International Terrorism* (London: Pluto Press, 3rd ed. rev'd, 2002); Phyllis Bennis, *Before and After: U.S. Foreign Policy and the September 11th Crisis* (London: Olive Branch Press, 2002); Noam Chomsky, *American Power and the New Mandarins: Historical and Political Essays* (New York: New Press, 2002).

31. Reportedly, more than a hundred thousand Iraqis were killed by American forces in this war. On the subject of war crimes committed during the Gulf War, see Human Rights Watch Report, *Needless Deaths in the Gulf War: Civilian Casualties During the Air Campaign and Violations of the Laws of War* (New York: Human Rights Watch, 1991); Ramsey Clark, *War Crimes: A Report on United States Crimes Against Iraq* (Wash. D.C.: Maisonneuve Press, 1992); Ramsey Clark, *The Fire This Time: U.S. War Crimes in the Gulf* (New York: Thunder's Mouth Press, 1992); Hassan A. El-Najjar, *The Gulf War: Overreaction and Excessiveness* (New York: Amazone Press, 2001); Thomas C. Fox, *Iraq Military Victory, Moral Defeat* (London: Sheed and Ward Publishers, 1991). There is also a considerable amount of data documenting war crimes collected in Arthur Henson, *The War*

Against Iraq: Handbook for the Anti-Imperialist (New York: Unity and Struggle Publications, 1992).

32. See Khaled Abou El Fadl, "Islam and the Theology of Power," in this collection.

33. Qur'an 4:135, 5:8.

34. For instance, see Lawrence Rosen's argument is his *The Justice of Islam: Comparative Perspectives on Islamic Law and Society* (Oxford: Oxford University Press, 2000). Rosen argues that Arabs and Muslims have no sense of set reality, and their only realities are highly negotiated and contingent. Rosen advises that in attempting to resolve the Arab-Israeli conflict, and making peace, Westerners must understand the Arab particular sense of justice. Arabs can only seek to make peace "against [a] tangled, ambivalent, refractory, and transcendent feeling of justice ...which shapes their expectations and hopes." p. 175.

35. Graham E. Fuller, "Muslims Abhor the Double Standard," *Los Angeles Times*, 10/5/2001.

36. The "Convention Against Torture and Other Cruel, Inhuman or Degrading Treatment or Punishment" was ratified by the USA in 1994.

37. What is has been called "torture by proxy" is a crime in United States, see 18 United States Code sections 241 & 242. However, in at least one case, a Federal court held that a confession obtained through torture in Egypt is admissible in a criminal prosecution in the United States. From a human rights and moral perspective, this is a very unfortunate decision, see U.S. v. Salameh, 54 F.Supp.2d 236, S.D.N.Y.,1999 (June 21, 1999)

38. Duncan Campbell, "U.S. Sends Suspects to Face Torture," *The Guardian*, 4/12/2002; Karen L. Snell, "Torture By Proxy," *The Recorder* 11/9/2001. One of those suspects, Muhammad Sa'ad Iqbal Madni was grabbed in Indonesia, and flown to Egypt on a US-registered GulfStream jet to be "interrogated" by Egyptian intelligence agents, and then to be handed over again to the US agents. According to Snell, Attorney General Ashcroft, appearing on the television show "Nightline", defended this policy of torture by proxy. Also, see Noam Chomsky, *The Umbrella of U.S. Power: The Universal Declaration of Human Rights and the Contradictions of U.S. Policy* (New York: Steven Stories Press, 1999); Richard Falk, *Winning (and Losing) the War Against Global Terror* (London: Olive Branch Publications, 2002).

39. For a disturbing memoir about the use of torture by the French in Algeria, see General Paul Aussaresses, *The Battle of the Casbah: Terrorism and Counter*

Terrorism in Algeria 1955-1957, Robert L. Miller (trans.) (New York: Enigma Books, 2002). Interestingly, in the introduction to this book, the publisher invokes the events of 9/11, and cites the shameful view of Alan Dershowitz, Harvard law professor, that torture is justified under certain circumstances. It is no coincidence that Dershowitz, who is a staunch supporter of Israel, has also justified the use of collective punishments against the villages of Palestinian terrorists. For a critique of Dershowitz's position, see Steve Randall, "Pro-Pain Pundits: Torture Advocates Defy U.S. and International law" at www.fair.org January/February 2002.

40. *The News International*, London Edition, 9/15/2001.

41. See Anthony Arnove (ed) *Iraq Under Siege: The Deadly Impact of Sanctions and War* (London: South End Press, 2000); Ramsey Clark, *The Impact of Sanctions on Iraq: The Children are Dying* (New York: World View Forum, 1996); Ramsey Clark, *A Challenge to Genocide: Let Iraq Live* (New York: International Action Center, 1998); Tim Niblock, *Pariah States and Sanctions in the Middle East: Iraq, Libya, and Sudan* (New York: Lynne Rienner Publishers, 2002).

Chapter 1 WORDS OF MASS DECEPTION

[Saddam Hussein] has not developed any significant capability with
respect to weapons of mass destruction. He is unable to project
conventional power against his neighbors.
—*Secretary of State, Colin Powel, February 24, 2001*

Simply stated, there is no doubt that Saddam Hussein now has
weapons of mass destruction.
—*Dick Cheney August 26, 2002*

Right now, Iraq is expanding and improving facilities that were used
for the production of biological weapons.
—*George W. Bush September 12, 2002*

It [the intelligence service] concludes that Iraq has chemical and
biological weapons; that Saddam has continued to produce them,
that he has existing and active military plans for the use of chemical
and biological weapons, which could be activated within 45
minutes, including against his own Shia population; and that he is
actively trying to acquire nuclear weapons capability [...]
—*Tony Blair, September 24, 2002*

If he declares he has none, then we will know that Saddam Hussein
is once again misleading the world.
—*Ari Fleischer December 2, 2002*

We know for a fact that there are weapons there.
—*Ari Fleischer January 9, 2003*

Our intelligence officials estimate that Saddam Hussein had the
materials to produce as much as 500 tons of sarin, mustard and VX
nerve agents.
—*George W. Bush January 28, 2003*

We have sources that tell us that Saddam Hussein recently
authorized Iraqi field commanders to use chemical weapons—the
very weapons the dictator tells us he does not have.
—*George W. Bush February 8, 2003*

So has the strategic decision been made to disarm Iraq of its
weapons of mass destruction by the leadership in Baghdad? I think
our judgment has to be clearly not.
—*Colin Powell March 8, 2003*

We are asked now seriously to accept that in the last few years-
contrary to all history, contrary to all intelligence—Saddam decided
unilaterally to destroy those weapons. I say that such a claim is
palpably absurd.
—*Tony Blair, 18 March, 2003*

Intelligence gathered by this and other governments leaves no doubt
that the Iraq regime continues to possess and conceal some of the
most lethal weapons ever devised.
—*George W. Bush March 18, 2003*

Well, there is no question that we have evidence and information
that Iraq has weapons of mass destruction, biological and chemical
particularly [...] all this will be made clear in the course of the

operation, for whatever duration it takes.
—*Ari Fleischer March 21, 2003*

One of our top objectives is to find and destroy the WMD. There are a number of sites.
—*Pentagon Spokeswoman, Victoria Clark March 22, 2003*

I have no doubt we're going to find big stores of weapons of mass destruction.
—*Kenneth Adelman, Defense Policy Board , March 23, 2003*

We know where they are. They are in the area around Tikrit and Baghdad.
—*Donald Rumsfeld March 30, 2003*

Saddam's removal is necessary to eradicate the threat from his weapons of mass destruction.
—*Jack Straw 2 April, 2003*

Obviously the administration intends to publicize all the weapons of mass destruction US forces find—and there will be plenty.
—*Robert Kagan April 9, 2003*

I think you have always heard, and you continue to hear from officials, a measure of high confidence that, indeed, the weapons of mass destruction will be found.
—*Ari Fleischer April 10, 2003*

There are people who in large measure have information that we need [...] so that we can track down the weapons of mass destruction in that country.
—*Donald Rumsfeld April 25, 2003*

Before people crow about the absence of weapons of mass destruction, I suggest they wait a bit.
—*Tony Blair 28 April, 2003*

I never believed that we'd just tumble over weapons of mass
destruction in that country.
—Donald Rumsfeld May 4, 2003

I just don't know whether it was all destroyed years ago [...] I mean,
there's no question that there were chemical weapons years ago
[...] whether they were destroyed right before the war, [or] whether
they're still hidden.
—*Major General David Petraeus.*
Commander 101st Airborne May 13. 2003

They may have had time to destroy them, and I don't know the
answer.
—*Donald Rumsfeld May 27, 2003*

For bureaucratic reasons, we settled on one issue, weapons of mass
destruction [as justification for invading Iraq] because it was the
one reason everyone could agree on.
—*Paul Wolfowitz May 28, 2003*

I have to accept we haven't found them and we may never find
them, We don't know what has happened to them.
—*Tony Blair, July 6, 2004*

[...] Saddam Hussein is a liar. He lies every single day [...] He is still
claiming that he won the war. His people are being told every day
that they won. It was a great victory in 1991 when he was thrown
out of Kuwait and chased back to Baghdad. Now, it seems to me
that almost every time you quote something from him, you should
preface it by saying 'here's a man who has lied all the time and
consistently.'
— *Secretary of Defense Donald Rumsfeld, 2003*

1 | The Lie Factory

ROBERT DREYFUSS &
JASON WEST

S IX MONTHS AFTER the end of major combat in Iraq, the United States had spent $300 million trying to find banned weapons in Iraq, and President Bush was seeking $600 million more to extend the search. Not found were Iraq's Scuds and other long-range missiles, thousands of barrels and tons of anthrax and botulism stock, sarin and VX nerve agents, mustard gas, biological and chemical munitions, mobile labs for producing biological weapons, and any and all evidence of a reconstituted nuclear-arms program, all of which had been repeatedly cited as justification for the war. Also missing was evidence of Iraqi collaboration with al-Qaʻida.

The reports, virtually all false, of Iraqi weapons and terrorism ties emanated from an apparatus that began to gestate almost as soon as the Bush administration took power. In the very first meeting of the Bush national-security team, one day after President Bush took the oath of office in January 2001, the issue of invading Iraq was raised, according to one of the participants in the meeting—and officials all the way down the line started to get the message, long before 9/11. Indeed, the Bush team at the Pentagon hadn't even been formally installed before Paul Wolfowitz, the deputy secretary of Defense, and Douglas J. Feith, undersecretary of Defense for policy, began putting together what would become the vanguard for regime change in Iraq.

Both Wolfowitz and Feith have deep roots in the neo-conservative movement. One of the most influential Washington neo-conservatives in the foreign-policy establishment during the Republicans' wilderness years of the 1990s, Wolfowitz has long held that not taking Baghdad in 1991 was a grievous mistake. He and others now prominent in the administration said so repeatedly over the past decade in a slew of letters and policy papers from neo-conservative groups like the Project for the New American Century and the Committee for the Liberation of Iraq. Feith, a former aide to Richard Perle at the Pentagon in the 1980s and an activist in far-right Zionist circles, held the view that there was no difference between US and Israeli security policy and that the best way to secure both countries' future was to solve the Israeli-Palestinian problem not by serving as a broker, but with the United States as a force for "regime change" in the region.

Called in to help organize the Iraq war-planning team was a longtime Pentagon official, Harold Rhode, a specialist on Islam who speaks Hebrew, Arabic, Turkish, and Farsi. Though Feith would not be officially confirmed until July 2001, career military and civilian officials in NESA began to watch his office with concern after Rhode set up shop in Feith's office in early January. Rhode, seen by many veteran staffers as an ideological gadfly, was officially assigned to the Pentagon's Office of Net Assessment, an in-house Pentagon think tank headed by fellow neo-con Andrew Marshall. Rhode helped Feith lay down the law about the department's new anti-Iraq, and broadly anti-Arab, orientation. In one telling incident, Rhode accosted and harangued a visiting senior Arab diplomat, telling him that there would be no "bartering in the bazaar anymore [...] You're going to have to sit up and pay attention when we say so."

Rhode refused to be interviewed for this story, saying cryptically, "Those who speak, pay."

According to insiders, Rhode worked with Feith to purge career Defense officials who weren't sufficiently enthusiastic about the muscular anti-Iraq crusade that Wolfowitz and Feith wanted. Rhode appeared to be "pulling people out of nooks and crannies of the Defense Intelligence Agency and other places to replace us with," says a former analyst. "They wanted nothing to do with the professional staff. And they wanted us the f*** out of there."

The unofficial, off-site recruitment office for Feith and Rhode was the American Enterprise Institute, a right-wing think tank whose 12th floor conference room in Washington is named for the dean of neo-conservative defense strategists, the late Albert Wohlstetter, an influential RAND analyst and University of Chicago mathematician. Headquartered at AEI is Richard Perle, Wohlstetter's prize protege, the godfather of the AEI-Defense Department nexus of neo-conservatives who was chairman of the Pentagon's influential Defense Policy Board. Rhode, along with Michael Rubin, a former AEI staffer who is also now at the Pentagon, was a ubiquitous presence at AEI conferences on Iraq over the past two years, and the two Pentagon officials seemed almost to be serving as stage managers for the AEI events, often sitting in the front row and speaking in stage whispers to panelists and AEI officials. Just after September 11, 2001, Feith and Rhode recruited David Wurmser, the director of Middle East studies for AEI, to serve as a Pentagon consultant.

Wurmser would be the founding participant of the unnamed, secret intelligence unit at the Pentagon, set up in Feith's office, which would be the nucleus of the Defense Department's Iraq disinformation campaign that was established within weeks of the attacks in New York and Washington. While the CIA and other intelligence agencies concentrated on Osama bin Laden's al-Qa'ida as the culprit in the 9/11 attacks, Wolfowitz and Feith obsessively focused on Iraq. It was a theory that was discredited, even ridiculed, among intelligence professionals. Daniel Benjamin, co-author of *The Age of Sacred Terror*, was director of counterterrorism at the National Security Council in the late 1990s. "In 1998, we went through every piece of intelligence we could find to see if there was a link between al-Qa'ida and Iraq," he says. "We came to the conclusion that our intelligence agencies had it right: There was no noteworthy relationship between al-Qa'ida and Iraq. I know that for a fact." Indeed, that was the consensus among virtually all anti-terrorism specialists.

In short, Wurmser, backed by Feith and Rhode, set out to prove what didn't exist.

IN AN ADMINISTRATION devoted to the notion of "Feith-based intelligence," Wurmser was ideal. For years, he'd been a shrill ideologue, part of the minority crusade during the 1990s that was beating the drums for war against Iraq. Along with Perle and Feith, in 1996 Wurmser and his wife, Meyrav, wrote a provocative strategy paper for Israeli prime minister Benjamin Netanyahu called *A Clean Break: A New Strategy for Securing the Realm*. It called on Israel to work with Jordan and Turkey to "contain, destabilize and roll back" various states in the region, overthrow Saddam Hussein in Iraq, press Jordan to restore a scion of the Hashemite dynasty to the Iraqi throne, and, above all, launch military assaults against Lebanon and Syria as a "prelude to a redrawing of the map of the Middle East which would threaten Syria's territorial integrity."

In 1997, Wurmser wrote a column in the *Wall Street Journal* called "Iraq Needs a Revolution" and the next year co-signed a letter with Perle calling for all-out US support of the Iraqi National Congress (INC), an exile group led by Ahmad Chalabi, in promoting an insurgency in Iraq. At AEI, Wurmser wrote *Tyranny's Ally: America's Failure to Defeat Saddam Hussein*, essentially a book-length version of *A Clean Break* that proposed an alliance between Jordan and the INC to redraw the map of the Middle East. Among the mentors cited by Wurmser in the book: Chalabi, Perle, and Feith.

The purpose of the unnamed intelligence unit, often described as a Pentagon "cell," was to scour reports from the CIA, the Defense Intelligence Agency, the National Security Agency, and other agencies to find nuggets of information linking Iraq, al-Qa'ida, terrorism, and the existence of Iraqi weapons of mass destruction (WMD). In a controversial press briefing in October 2002, a year after Wurmser's unit was established, Secretary of Defense Donald Rumsfeld acknowledged that a primary purpose of the unit was to cull factoids, which were then used to disparage, undermine, and contradict the CIA's reporting, which was far more cautious and nuanced than Rumsfeld, Wolfowitz, and Feith wanted. Rumsfeld particularly enjoyed harassing the CIA staffer who briefed him every morning, using the type of data produced by the intelligence unit. "What I could do is say, 'Gee, what about this?'" Rumsfeld noted. "Or what about that? Has somebody thought of this?" Last June, when Feith was questioned on the same topic at a briefing, he acknowledged that the secret unit in fact looked at the connection between Iraq and terrorism, saying, "You can't rely on deterrence to deal with the problem of weapons of mass destruction in the hands of state sponsors of terrorism because [of] the possibility that those state sponsors might employ chemical weapons or biological weapons by means of a terrorist organization proxy [...]"

Though Feith, in that briefing, described Wurmser's unit as an innocent project, "a global exercise" that was not meant to put pressure on other intelligence agencies or create skewed intelligence to fit preconceived policy notions, many other sources assert that it did exactly that. That the White House and the Pentagon put enormous pressure on the CIA to go along with its version of events has been widely reported, highlighted by visits to CIA headquarters by Vice President Cheney and Lewis Libby, his chief of staff. Led by Perle, the neo-cons seethed with contempt for the CIA. The CIA's analysis, said Perle, "isn't worth the paper it's printed on." Standing in a crowded hallway during an AEI event, Perle added, "The CIA is status quo oriented. They don't want to take risks."

That became the mantra of the shadow agency within an agency.

Putting Wurmser in charge of the unit meant that it was being run by a pro-Iraq-war ideologue who'd spent years calling for a preemptive invasion of Baghdad and who was clearly predisposed to find what he wanted to see. Adding another layer of dubious quality to the endeavor was the man partnered with Wurmser, F. Michael Maloof. Maloof, a former aide to Perle in the 1980s Pentagon, was twice stripped of his high-level security clearances—once in late 2001 and again last spring, for various infractions. Maloof was also reportedly involved in a bizarre scheme to broker contacts between Iraqi officials and the Pentagon, channeled through Perle, in what one report called a "rogue [intelligence] operation" outside official CIA and Defense Intelligence Agency channels.

As the momentum for war began to build in early 2002, Wolfowitz and Feith beefed up the intelligence unit and created an Iraq war-planning unit in the Pentagon's Near East and South Asia Affairs section, run by Deputy Undersecretary of Defense William Luti, under the rubric "Office of Special Plans," or OSP; the new unit's director was Abram N. Shulsky. By then, Wurmser had moved on to a post as senior advisor to Undersecretary of State John Bolton, yet another neo-con, who was in charge of the State Department's disarmament, proliferation, and WMD office and was promoting the Iraq war strategy there. Shulsky's OSP, which incorporated the secret intelligence unit, took control, banishing veteran experts—including Joseph McMillan, James Russell, Larry Hanauer, and Marybeth McDevitt—who, despite years of service to NESA, either were shuffled off to other positions or retired. For the next year, Luti and

Shulsky not only would oversee war plans but would act aggressively to shape the intelligence product received by the White House.

Both Luti and Shulsky were neo-conservatives who were ideological soulmates of Wolfowitz and Feith. But Luti was more than that. He'd come to the Pentagon directly from the office of Vice President Cheney. That gave Luti, a recently retired, decorated Navy captain whose career ran from combat aviation to command of a helicopter assault ship, extra clout. Along with his colleague Colonel William Bruner, Luti had done a stint as an aide to Newt Gingrich in 1996 and, like Perle and Wolfowitz, was an acolyte of Wohlstetter's. "He makes Ollie North look like a moderate," says a NESA veteran.

Shulsky had been on the Washington scene since the mid-1970s. As a Senate intelligence committee staffer for Senator Daniel Patrick Moynihan, he began to work with early neo-conservatives like Perle, who was then an aide to Senator Henry Jackson. Later, in the Reagan years, Shulsky followed Perle to the Pentagon as Perle's arms-control advisor. In the '90s, Shulsky co-authored a book on intelligence called *Silent Warfare*, with Gary Schmitt. Shulsky had served with Schmitt on Moynihan's staff and they had remained friends. Asked about the Pentagon's Iraq intelligence "cell," Schmitt—who is currently the executive director of the Project for the New American Century—says that he can't say much about it "because one of my best friends is running it."

According to Lt. Colonel Kwiatkowski, Luti and Shulsky ran NESA and the Office of Special Plans with brutal efficiency, purging people they disagreed with and enforcing the party line. "It was organized like a machine," she says. "The people working on the neo-con agenda had a narrow, well-defined political agenda. They had a sense of mission." At NESA, Shulsky, she says, began "hot-desking," or taking an office wherever he could find one, working with Feith and Luti, before formally taking the reins of the newly created OSP. Together, she says, Luti and Shulsky turned cherry-picked pieces of uncorroborated, anti-Iraq intelligence into talking points, on issues like Iraq's WMD and its links to al-Qa'ida. Shulsky constantly updated these papers, drawing on the intelligence unit, and circulated them to Pentagon officials, including Rumsfeld, and to Vice President Cheney. "Of course, we never thought they'd go directly to the White House," she adds.

Kwiatkowski recalls one meeting in which Luti, pressed to finish a report, told the staff, "I've got to get this over to 'Scooter' right away." She later found out that "Scooter" was none other than Lewis "Scooter" Libby, Vice President Cheney's chief of staff. According to Kwiatkowski, Cheney had direct ties through Luti into NESA/OSP, a connection that was highly unorthodox.

"Never, ever, ever would a deputy undersecretary of Defense work directly on a project for the vice president," she says. "It was a little clue that we had an informal network into Vice President Cheney's office."

Although Feith insists that the OSP did not seek to gather its own intelligence, Kwiatkowski and others sharply disagree. Staff working for Luti and Shulsky in NESA/OSP churned out propaganda-style intelligence, she says. As an example, she cited the work of a US intelligence officer and Arabic specialist, Navy Lt. Commander Youssef Aboul-Enein, who was a special assistant to Luti. "His job was to peruse the Arabic-language media to find articles that would incriminate Saddam Hussein about terrorism, and he translated these." Such raw intelligence is usually subject to a thorough vetting process, tracked, verified, and checked by intelligence professionals. But not at OSP—the material that it produced found its way directly into speeches by Bush, Cheney, and other officials.

According to Melvin Goodman, a former CIA official and an intelligence specialist at the National War College, the OSP officials routinely pushed lower-ranking staff around on intelligence matters. "People were being pulled aside [and being told], 'We saw your last piece and it's not what we're looking for,'" he says. "It was pretty blatant." Two State Department intelligence officials, Greg Thielmann and Christian Westermann, have both charged that pressure was being put on them to shape intelligence to fit policy, in particular from Bolton's office. "The al-Qaʻida connection and nuclear weapons issue were the only two ways that you could link Iraq to an imminent security threat to the US," Thielmann told the *New York Times*. "And the administration was grossly distorting the intelligence on both things."

BESIDES CHENEY, KEY members of the Pentagon's Defense Policy Board, including Perle and ex-House Speaker Newt Gingrich, all Iraq hawks, had direct input into NESA/OSP. The offices Of NESA were located on the Pentagon's fourth floor, seventh corridor of D Ring, and the Policy Board's offices were directly below, on the third floor. During the run-up to the Iraq war, Gingrich often came up for closed-door meetings with Luti, who in 1996 had served as a congressional fellow in Speaker of the House Gingrich's office.

As OSP got rolling, Luti brought in Colonel Bruner, a former military aide to Gingrich, and, together, Luti and Bruner opened the door to a vast flow of bogus intelligence red to the Pentagon by Iraqi defectors associated with Chalabi's Iraqi National Congress group of exiles. Chalabi founded the Iraqi National Congress in 1992, with the help of a shadowy CIA-connected public-relations firm called the Rendon Group, one of whose former employees, Francis Brooke, has been a top aide to Chalabi ever since. A scion of an aristocratic Iraqi family, Chalabi fled Baghdad at the age of 13, in 1958, when the corrupt Iraqi Hashemite monarchy was overthrown by a coalition of communists and the Iraqi military. In the late 1960s, Chalabi studied mathematics at the University of Chicago with Wohlstetter, who introduced him to Richard Perle more than a decade later. Long associated with the heart of the neo-conservative movement, Chalabi founded Petra Bank in Jordan, which grew to be Jordan's third-largest bank by the 1980s. But Chalabi was accused of bank fraud, embezzlement, and currency manipulation, and he barely escaped before Jordanian authorities could arrest him; in 1992, he was convicted and sentenced in absentia to more than 20 years of hard labor. After founding the INC, Chalabi's bungling, unreliability, and penchant for mismanaging funds caused the CIA to sour on him, but he never lost the support of Perle, Feith, Gingrich, and their allies; once, soon after 9/11, Perle invited Chalabi to address the Defense Policy Board.

According to multiple sources, Chalabi's Iraqi National Congress sent a steady stream of misleading and often faked intelligence reports into US intelligence channels. That information would flow sometimes into NESA/OSP directly, sometimes through Defense Intelligence Agency debriefings of Iraqi defectors via the Defense Human Intelligence Service, and sometimes through the INC's own US-funded Intelligence Collection Program, which was overseen by the Pentagon. The INC's intelligence "isn't reliable at all," according to Vincent Cannistraro, a former CIA chief of counterterrorism. "Much of it is propaganda. Much of it is telling the Defense Department what they want to hear, using alleged informants and defectors who say what Chalabi wants them to say, [creating] cooked information that goes right into presidential and vice presidential speeches."

Bruner, the aide to Luti and Gingrich's former staffer, "was Chalabi's handler," says Kwiatkowski. "He would arrange meetings with Chalabi and Chalabi's folks," she says, adding that the INC leader often brought people into the NESA/OSP offices for debriefings. Chalabi claims to have introduced only three actual defectors to the Pentagon, a figure Thielmann considers "awfully low." However, according to an investigation by the *Los Angeles Times*, the three defectors provided by Chalabi turned up exactly zero useful intelligence. The first, an Iraqi engineer, claimed to have specific information about biological weapons, but his information didn't pan out; the second claimed to know about mobile labs, but that information, too, was worthless; and the third, who claimed to have data about Iraq's nuclear program, proved to be a fraud. Chalabi also claimed to have given the Pentagon information about Iraqi support for al-Qa'ida. "We gave the names of people who were doing the links," he told an interviewer from PBS's Frontline. Those links, of course, have not been discovered. Thielmann told the same Frontline interviewer that the Office of Special Plans didn't apply strict intelligence-verification standards to "some of the information coming out of Chalabi and the INC that OSP and the Pentagon ran with."

In the war's aftermath, the Defense Intelligence Agency—which is not beholden to the neo-conservative civilians at the Pentagon—leaked a report it prepared, concluding that few, if any, of the INC's informants provided worthwhile intelligence.

SO FAR, DESPITE all of the investigations under way, there is little sign that any of them are going to delve into the operations of the Luti-Shulsky Office of Special Plans and its secret intelligence unit. Because it operates in the Pentagon's policy shop, it is not officially part of the intelligence community, and so it is seemingly immune to congressional oversight.

With each passing day, it is becoming excruciatingly clearer just how wrong US intelligence was in regard to Iraqi weapons and support for terrorism. The American teams of inspectors in the Iraq Survey Group, which has employed up to 1,400 people to scour the country and analyze the findings, have not been able to find a shred of evidence of anything other than dusty old plans and records of weapons apparently destroyed more than a decade ago. Countless examples of fruitless searches have been reported in the media. To cite one example: US soldiers followed an intelligence report claiming that a complex built for Uday Hussein, Saddam's son, hid a weapons warehouse with poison-gas storage tanks. "Well," US Army Major Ronald Hann Jr. told the *Los Angeles Times*, "the warehouse was a carport. It still had two cars inside. And the tanks had propane for the kitchen."

Countless other errors and exaggerations have become evident. The thousands of aluminum tubes supposedly imported by Iraq for uranium enrichment were fairly conclusively found to be designed to build noncontroversial rockets. The long-range unmanned aerial vehicles, allegedly built to deliver bioweapons, were small, rickety, experimental planes with wood frames. The mobile bioweapon labs turned out to have had other, civilian purposes. And the granddaddy of all falsehoods, the charge that Iraq sought uranium in the West African country of Niger, was based on forged documents—documents that the CIA, the State Department, and other agencies knew were fake nearly a year before President Bush highlighted the issue in his State of the Union address in January 2003.

"Either the system broke down," said former Ambassador Joseph Wilson, who was sent by the CIA to visit Niger and whose findings helped show that the documents were forged, "or there was selective use of bits of information to justify a decision to go to war that had already been taken."

Edward Luttwak, a neo-conservative scholar and author, says flatly that the Bush administration lied about the Intelligence it had because it was afraid to go to the American people and say that the war was simply about getting rid of Saddam Hussein. Instead, says Luttwak, the White House was groping for a rationale to satisfy the United Nations' criteria for war. "Cheney was forced into this fake posture of worrying about weapons of mass destruction," he says. "The ties to al-Qa'ida? That's complete nonsense."

In the Senate, Senator Jay Rockefeller is pressing for the Intelligence Committee to extend its investigation to look into the specific role of the Pentagon's Office of Special Plans, but there is strong Republican resistance to the idea.

In the House, Rep. Henry Waxman has introduced legislation calling for a commission to investigate the intelligence mess and has collected more than a hundred Democrats—but no Republicans—in support of it. "I think they need to be looked at pretty carefully," Waxman replied when asked about the Office of Special Plans. "I'd like to know whether the political people pushed the intelligence people to slant their conclusions." Congressman Waxman, meet Lt. Colonel Kwiatkowski.

Bodyguard of Lies:
Dissecting US Pretexts for War

LARRY EVEREST

Of course, this conjures up Winston Churchill's famous phrase when he
said—don't quote me on this, okay? I don't want to be quoted on this, so
don't quote me. He said "sometimes the truth is so precious it must be
accompanied by a bodyguard of lies."

—*Donald Rumsfeld, US Department of Defense Briefing,*
September 25, 2001[1]

To build its case for war with Iraq, the Bush administration argued that
Saddam Hussein had weapons of mass destruction, but some officials now
privately acknowledge the White House had another reason for war—a
global show of American power and democracy.

Officials inside government and advisors outside told ABC News the
administration emphasized the danger of Saddam's weapons to gain the
legal justification for war from the United Nations and to stress the danger
at home to Americans.

"We were not lying," said one official. "But it was just a matter of
emphasis."

— *ABC News, April 25, 2003*[2]

IN FACT, THEY were lying. Following September 11, 2001 attacks,
the US government relentlessly created pretexts to wage war against
Iraq. Charges were featured daily on the front pages of newspapers
and as lead stories on TV. As the truth leaked out before the war, it was
buried, downplayed, or barely reported. No wonder a *USA Today* poll

reported that over fifty percent of Americans believed there was a direct link between the Sept. 11 attacks and Saddam Hussein,[3] even though there was no evidence of such a connection.

The main pretexts that the US used to argue for war on Iraq were that:

1. Iraq possessed weapons of mass destruction in violation of UN resolutions;
2. with such weapons, Iraq posed a significant threat to the US and neighboring countries; and
3. Iraq was linked to alleged terrorist organizations, such as al-Qa'ida.

Yet, as of this writing, no "weapons of mass destruction" have been found in Iraq, more than one year after the US invasion and it seems very unlikely that the US will ever find anything resembling the quantities alleged to justify the invasion. In addition, no credible link had been established between the Iraqi government and al-Qa'ida, the Ansar al Islam group, September 11, or any attack against the US in at least ten years. What emerges is a portrait of a big power willing to use any fig leaf, no matter how flimsy, to cover its naked imperialist motives for waging war on Iraq.

In fact, by the end of the summer 2003, in the face of the failure to find any weapons of mass destruction and some exposure of the "intelligence" relied upon by the White House, the Bush administration began to revise its reasons for invading Iraq, downplaying the WMD pretext. Rather than charge that Iraq actually had weapons of mass destruction, the administration began to claim only that Iraq had a WMD "program," that the invasion was intended to "liberate" the people of Iraq, and that it was part of an overall effort to transform the Middle East. *The Washington Post* noted,

> As the search for weapons in Iraq continues without success, the Bush administration has moved to emphasize a different rationale for the war against Saddam Hussein: using Iraq as the "linchpin" to transform the Middle East and thereby reduce the terrorist threat to the United States. President Bush, who has stopped talking about Iraq weapons, said [...] that

"the rise of a free and peaceful Iraq is critical to the stability of the Middle East, and a stable Middle East is critical" to the security of the American people.[4]

Deputy Defense Secretary Wolfowitz, after a trip to Iraq, said flat out, "I'm not concerned about weapons of mass destruction [....] I'm concerned about getting Iraq on its feet. I didn't come [to Iraq] on a search for weapons of mass destruction."[5]

The following discussion examines some of the charges that were raised to justify the attack on Iraq. It also examines government statements during and after the war related to weapons of mass destruction and Iraq's alleged links to terrorism.

ALLEGED IRAQI LINKS TO AL-QAʿIDA & TERRORISM

Assertion:

The New York Times, September 27, 2002:

Defense Secretary Donald H. Rumsfeld said today that American intelligence had "bulletproof" evidence of links between al-Qaʿida and the government of President Saddam Hussein of Iraq.

Mr. Rumsfeld said that recently declassified intelligence reports about suspected ties between al-Qaʿida and the Iraqi government, including the presence of senior members of al-Qaʿida in Baghdad in "recent periods," were "factual" and exactly accurate."[6]

The Facts:

• No evidence has emerged of Iraqi involvement in the September 11 attacks or of links between Iraq and al-Qaʿida.

• Shortly after the September 11 attacks, even the *Wall Street Journal* noted that "few US officials believe that any real alliance between Iraq and al-Qaʿida ever emerged[...] The two groups share few aims and have very different motivations[...]"[7]

• According to the *New York Times*, intelligence officials from Jordan, Israel and Saudi Arabia do not believe there is any serious Hussein bin Laden connection.[8]

• Former UNSCOM inspector Scott Ritter says with regard to the alleged Iraq/al-Qaʻida link: "This one is patently absurd. He has spent the last thirty years declaring war against Islamic fundamentalism, crushing it[....] Osama bin Laden has a history of hating Saddam Hussein."[9] In fact, Ritter thinks a more likely scenario is that if al-Qaʻida obtained a nuclear device the group would use it against Saddam Hussein.

• The State Department's own report on terrorism, released in April 2001, stated that Iraq had not attempted an anti Western attack since 1993.[10]

• At the Federal Bureau of Investigation, some investigators said they were baffled by the Bush administration's insistence on a solid link between Iraq and Osama bin Laden's network. "We've been looking at this hard for more than a year and you know what, we just don't think it's there," a government official said. Mr. Bush asserted in his State of the Union address that Iraq was protecting and aiding al-Qaʻida operatives, but American intelligence and law enforcement officials said the evidence was fragmentary and inconclusive. "It's more than just skepticism," said one official, describing the feelings of some analysts in the intelligence agencies. "I think there is also a sense of disappointment with the community's leadership that they are not standing up for them at a time when the intelligence is obviously being politicized."[11]

• British intelligence also said there was no Iraq-al-Qaʻida link. As reported by the BBC: "There are no current links between the Iraqi regime and the al-Qaʻida network, according to an official British intelligence report seen by BBC News. The classified document, written by defense intelligence staff three weeks ago, says there has been contact between the two in the past[...] The defense intelligence staff document, seen by BBC defense correspondent Andrew Gilligan, is classified Top Secret and was sent to UK Prime Minister Tony Blair and other senior members of the government. It says al-Qaʻida leader Osama bin Laden views Iraq's ruling Baʼath party as running contrary to his religion, calling it an 'apostate regime.'"[12]

• Greg Thielman, the director of the strategic, proliferation, and military affairs division at the State Department's Bureau of Intelligence and Research until September 2002, says "Based on the terrorism experts I met with during my period of government, I never heard anyone make the claim that there was a significant tie between al-Qaʿida and Saddam Hussein." He added, "The Bush administration [...] was 'misleading the public in implying there was a close connection.'"[13]

• On August 1, 2003, Deputy Defense Secretary Wolfowitz was asked on The Laura Ingraham Show when exactly he started to think that Iraq had something to do with the September 11, 2001 attacks. In what was believed to be the first such admission by the Bush administration by that date, Wolfowitz conceded that "I'm not sure even now that perhaps Iraq had something to do with it."[14]

• Former US intelligence officials also doubt the alleged connection between Iraq and al-Qaʿida. A Pentagon unit, the Office of Special Plans, had been formed to try to find links between Iraq and al-Qaʿida, but was disbanded late in 2002. "About a dozen former CIA intelligence officials have been quoted as saying that the Office of Special Plans cherrypicked intelligence, much of which was gathered by unreliable Iraqi defectors, to make a stronger case for war and delivered directly to Vice President Dick Cheney's office and National Security Advisor Condoleezza Rice without first being vetted by the CIA."[15]

IRAQ AND THE ANTHRAX LETTERS

Assertion:

On October 15, 2001 Senator Tom Daschle announced that his office had received a letter laced with "weapons grade" anthrax. On October 18, the *Wall Street Journal* featured three articles blaming Iraq: a front page article accused Iraq of being "at the top of [the] suspect list"; the lead editorial said that "by far the likeliest supplier [of the anthrax in the letter to Daschlel] is Saddam Hussein"; and an opinion piece by CIA chief James Woolsey, titled "The Iraq Connection," which claimed, "There are substantial and growing indications that a state may, behind the scene, be involved in the attacks."[16]

Washington Post columnist Richard Cohen screamed, "Saddam and his bloody bugs have to go."[17]

Two days later, two top senators, McCain and Lieberman, advocated attacking Iraq.

The Facts:

• The anthrax mailed to Senator Daschle was most likely "Made in the USA." When the anthrax spores in the Daschle letter and other samples were analyzed, they turned out to be the "Ames" strain; the strain of anthrax bacteria developed in the US which the US military tried to "weaponize" in the 1960s. It is not the vollum strain that Iraq had been working with (after buying it from American Type Culture Collection, a Maryland company which sells biological material such as anthrax worldwide).

• Researchers also discovered silica in the anthrax in the Daschle letter. Silica is the agent that US weapons makers mixed with anthrax so that it could more easily disperse through the air. Iraq reportedly used bentonite, which was not found.[18]

• A US government official admitted that the "evidence at hand involving not just the coatings, but also genetic analysis of the bacteria and other intelligence suggested that it was unlikely that the spores were originally produced in the former Soviet Union or Iraq."[19]

WEAPONS OF MASS DESTRUCTION

NUCLEAR WEAPONS:
IRAQ SIX MONTHS AWAY FROM DEVELOPING
A NUCLEAR WEAPON

Assertion:

I would remind you that when the inspectors first went into Iraq and were denied, finally denied access, a report came out of the IAEA [International Atomic Energy Agency] that they were six months away from developing a weapon. I don't know what more evidence we need.[20]

—*George W Bush, September 7, 2002*

The Facts:

• The IAEA denied ever issuing such a report.[21] The IAEA did issue a report in 1998, around the time weapons inspectors were denied access to Iraq for the final time, but the report made no such assertion. It declared: "[...] based on all credible information to date [...] the IAEA has found no indication of Iraq having achieved its program goal of producing nuclear weapons or of Iraq having retained a physical capability for the production of weapon useable nuclear material or having clandestinely obtained such material."[22]

• In his first major report to Congress on the status of the US effort to find weapons of mass destruction, in October 2003, David Kay, the Bush administration's chief inspector for the Iraq Survey Group (ISG), had to concede "that Iraq's nuclear program was in only 'the very most rudimentary state.'"[23] The report (Kay Report) also stated "[...]to date we have not uncovered evidence that Iraq undertook significant post-1998 steps to actually build nuclear weapons or produce fissile material."[24]

ALUMINUM TUBES TO BE USED TO ENRICH URANIUM
FOR A NUCLEAR WEAPON

Assertion:

Powell at the UN:

Saddam Hussein is determined to get his hands on a nuclear bomb. He is so determined that he has made repeated covert attempts to acquire high specification aluminum from 11 different countries, even after inspections resumed [...] These tubes are manufactured to a tolerance that far exceeds US requirements for comparable rockets.[25]

The Facts:

• "While the matter is still under investigation and further verification is foreseen, the IAEAs analysis to date indicates that the specifications of the aluminum tubes sought by Iraq in 2001 and 2002 appear to be consistent with reverse engineering of rockets. While it would be possible to modify such tubes for the manufacture of centrifuges, they are not directly suitable for it."[26]

—*Dr. Mohammed El Baradei in IAEA report,*
The New York Times, January 10, 2003

• "A source close to the inspectors said the US military uses similar tubes for a rocket known as the Hydra 70."[27]

—*Dan Stober, San Jose Mercury News, March 18, 2003*

• In February 2003, prior to the invasion, "UN sources have told CBS News that American tips have lead to one dead end after another." Example: "Interviews with scientists about the aluminum tubes the US says Iraq has imported for enriching uranium, but which the Iraqis say are for making rockets. Given the size and specifications of the tubes, the UN calls the 'Iraqi alibi air tight.'"[28]

IRAQI URANIUM PURCHASE FROM NIGER

Assertion:

As a result of the intelligence we judge that Iraq has [...] sought significant quantities of uranium from Africa, despite having no active civil nuclear program that could require it [...][29]

—*September 2002 "Blair Dossier"*

The British government has learned that Saddam Hussein recently sought significant quantities of uranium from Africa. [...] Saddam Hussein has not credibly explained these activities. He clearly has much to hide.[30]

—*George W. Bush, State of the Union Address, January 28, 2003*

The Facts:

• UN Weapons Inspector Hans Blix on the supposed purchase of uranium from Niger:

Consider the case of the production of contracts for a presumed Iraqi purchase of enriched uranium from Niger. This was a crude lie. All false. The information was provided to the International Atomic Energy Agency by the US intelligence services [...] When one sees the things that the United States tried to do to show that the Iraqis had nuclear arms, one does have many questions.[31]

Mohamed El Baradei, head of the International Atomic Energy Agency charged that:

• "Documents provided by unidentified states may have been faked to suggest that the African country of Niger sold uranium to Iraq between 1999 and 2001." He said inspectors concluded that the documents were "not authentic" after scrutinizing "the form, format, contents, and signatures [...] of the alleged procurement related documentation."[32]
• The CIA had expressed doubts about this claim to the White House months earlier than the State of the Union Address. "The CIA sent two memos to the White House in October [2002] voicing strong doubts about a claim President Bush made three months later in the State of the Union address that Iraq was trying to buy nuclear material in Africa, White House officials said yesterday." "The acknowledgment of the memos, which were sent on the eve of a major presidential speech in Cincinnati about Iraq, comes four days after the White House said the CIA objected only to technical specifics of the Africa charge, not its general accuracy."[33]
• Former diplomat Joseph Wilson had reported to the CIA nearly a year earlier, in February 2002, that the alleged Iraqi purchase was highly unlikely. After spending eight days in Niger investigating this claim at the request of the CIA, retired diplomat Joseph Wilson "made an oral report" back to the Agency that the Iraqi uranium purchase was 'highly unlikely."[34] The report was quietly forgotten until reported in the

Washington Post on June 12, 2003, setting off a firestorm of controversy about the validity of the claim.

• Wilson then became the object of a White House smear campaign, telling NBC News that "the White House deliberately leaked his wife's identity as a covert CIA operative, damaging her career and compromising past missions [...]"[35]

• Others had also warned the Administration that the claim didn't check out. "[...] Ambassador to Niger Barbro Owens Fitzpatrick reported it was false in February 2002. So did fourstar Marine Gen. Carlton Fulford two months later."[36]

• The US then warned Niger to stay out of the controversy. "America has warned the Niger government to keep out of the row over claims that Saddam Hussein sought to buy uranium for his nuclear weapons programme from the impoverished West African state." Mr. Hama Hamadou told the British newspaper *The Telegraph* that "[...] the Niger government had never had discussions with Iraq about uranium and called on Tony Blair to produce the 'evidence' he claims to have to confirm that Iraq sought uranium from Niger in the 1990s."[37]

• Officials repeated the same allegation both before and after the State of the Union speech. The allegation of the uranium purchase was made not just in the Bush State of the Union speech, but several times. "..[In] the days before and after the State of the Union address, the allegation was repeated by national security advisor Condoleezza Rice, Secretary of State Colin L. Powell, Defense Secretary Donald H. Rumsfeld, Deputy Secretary of Defense Paul D. Wolfowitz, and in at least two documents sent out by the White House."[38]

CHENEY ON THE PERIL OF A NUCLEAR IRAQ

Assertion:

The New York Times:

Vice President Dick Cheney today presented the administration's most forceful and comprehensive rationale yet for attacking Iraq, warning that Saddam Hussein would "fairly soon" have nuclear weapons. "[...] What he wants is time, and more time to husband his resources to invest in his ongoing chemical and biological weapons program, and to gain possession of nuclear weapons," Mr. Cheney said. "The risks of inaction," he said, "are far greater than the risk of action."[39]

The Facts:

• IAEA Director General Dr. Mohamed El Baradei on Iraq's Nuclear Program:

There is no indication of resumed nuclear activities in those buildings that were identified through the use of satellite imagery as being reconstructed or newly erected since 1998, nor any indication of nuclear related prohibited activities at any inspected sites.

There is no indication that Iraq has attempted to import uranium since 1990.

There is no indication that Iraq has attempted to import aluminum tubes for use in centrifuge enrichment. Moreover, even had Iraq pursued such a plan, it would have encountered practical difficulties in manufacturing centrifuges out of the aluminum tubes in question.

Although we are still reviewing issues related to magnets and magnet production, there is no indication to date that Iraq imported magnets for use in a centrifuge enrichment programme.

After three months of intrusive inspections, we have to date found no evidence or plausible indication of the revival of a nuclear weapons programme in Iraq. We intend to continue our inspection activities, making use of all the additional rights granted to us by resolution 1441 and all additional tools that might be available to us, including reconnaissance platforms and all relevant technologies. We also hope to continue to receive from states actionable information relevant to our mandate. I should note that, in the past three weeks, possibly as a result of ever increasing pressure by the international community, Iraq has been forthcoming in its co operation, particularly with regard to the conduct of private interviews and in making available evidence that could contribute to the resolution of matters of IAEA concern. I do hope that Iraq will continue to expand the scope and accelerate the pace of its cooperation. [40]

IRAQ'S CHEMICAL AND BIOLOGICAL
WEAPONS PROGRAM AND INVENTORY

Assertion:

George Bush, January 28, 2003:

Our intelligence officials estimate that Saddam Hussein had the materials
to produce as much as 500 tons of satin, mustard, and VX nerve agent
[...] upward of 30,000 munitions capable of delivering chemical agents
[...] materials sufficient to produce more than 38,000 liters of botulinum
toxin.[41]

At the Geneva biological weapons conference the US claimed, "Iraq
has taken advantage of three years of no UN inspections to improve all
phases of its offensive biological weapons program [...] The existence of
Iraq's program is beyond dispute."[42]

The Facts:

• The charges related to Iraq's WMD inventory were largely based on
Iraq's inability to definitively "verify" the destruction of certain stocks
to UN inspectors in the 1990s. As Scott Ritter has discussed in his book
with William Rivers Pitt, *War on Iraq,* simply because UNSCOM did not
verify that all the chemical weapons (CW) inventory had been destroyed
did not mean Iraq still maintained that inventory. In addition, CW agents
have a "shelf life" after which they are no longer useful. Ritter explained
that, by 2003, virtually all of the CW agents that may have existed even as
late as 1998 had likely degraded and were no longer useful.[43]
• Secretary of State Colin Powell in February 2001 told reporters during
a trip to Egypt that Saddam Hussein "has not developed any significant
capability with respect to weapons of mass destruction. He is unable to
project conventional power against his neighbors."[44]
• The Pentagon's own intelligence group said it had no reliable
information on Iraqi chemical weapons. It wasn't until June 2003,
after the US invasion, that the existence of a second intelligence report

was revealed, a report that contradicted the earlier, highly publicized CIA report on chemical weapons. In November 2002, the Pentagon's Defense Intelligence Agency (DIA) "issued a report stating that there was 'no reliable information' showing that Iraq was actually producing or stockpiling, chemical weapons [...]" In fact, the DIAs November assessment "mirrors a September [2002] analysis that the agency made on the same subject." The DIA report is titled "Iraq's Nuclear, Biological, and Chemical Weapon and Missile Program: Progress, Prospects, and Potential Vulnerabilities." Specifically, the DIA report says, "No reliable information indicates whether Iraq is producing or stockpiling chemical weapons or where the country has or will establish its chemical agent production facility."[45]

 • After the 2003 war had begun, no weapons were found at the top sites identified by US intelligence. After searching more than 80 of the top 100 sites that US intelligence had labeled as possible Iraqi hiding places for chemical and biological weapons, no stockpiles have been found and the search team said they were setting aside their "intelligence" reports for the time being.[46]

 • After the 2003 US invasion, reports of discoveries of chemical or biological weapons in each case turned out to be false. For example:

  • On April 7, 2003, at an Iraqi military camp near Karbala, US troops discovered two dozen drums that allegedly tested positive for sarin and mustard gas.[47] Later, the US military determined the chemicals were ordinary pesticides.

  • MSNBC/NBC News, reported on May 11, 2003 that "military teams searching for biological and chemical weapons in Iraq found three trailers believed to be mobile biological weapons laboratories capable of producing deadly germs for weapons."[48] Later, the Defense Intelligence Agency determined that hydrogen for weather balloons was made in the trailers, not biological weapons. "Engineering experts from the Defense Intelligence Agency have come to believe that the most likely use for two mysterious trailers found in Iraq was to produce hydrogen for weather balloons rather than to make biological weapons, government officials say. The classified findings by a majority of the engineering experts differ from the view put forward in a white paper made public on May

28, 2003 by the CIA and Defense Intelligence Agency, which said that the trailers were for making biological weapons."[49]

• On April 27, 2003, AP reported out of Baiji, Iraq: "US troops found about a dozen 55 gallon drums in an open field near this northern Iraqi town, and initial tests indicated one of them contained a mixture of a nerve agent and mustard gas, an American officer said Sunday." "A chemical team checked the drums, one of which tested positive for cyclosarin, a nerve agent, and a blister agent which could have been mustard gas," a US military officer said.[50] However, the material in the drums turned out to be rocket fuel.[51]

• As of October 2004, no chemical or biological weapons have been found in Iraq. In October 2003, the Kay Report admitted that the ISG had "not yet found stocks of weapons." The Kay Report also acknowledged that "information found to date suggests that Iraq's large scale capability to develop, produce and fill new CW munitions was reduced—if not entirely destroyed during Operations Desert Storm and Desert Fox, 13 years of UN sanctions and UN inspections.[52]

SOURCES OF INFORMATION FOR
WEAPONS OF MASS DESTRUCTION

.

Powell's Claims of Solid Evidence

Assertion:

My colleagues, every statement I make today is backed up by sources, solid sources. These are not assertions. What we're giving you are facts and conclusions based on solid intelligence. I will cite some examples, and these are from human sources.[53]

—*Colin Powell at UN, February 5, 2003*

The Facts:

• Analysts believe that much of the US's information on WMDs has come from Ahmed Chalabi's Iraqi National Congress (INC) which received Pentagon money for intelligence gathering. "The INC saw the demand and provided what was needed," an analyst told the *Independent* newspaper in the UK. "The implication is that they polluted the whole US intelligence effort."[54]

• Another human source that Powell cites are detainees being held in Guantanamo, who are being held in horrific conditions, denied access to attorneys or the media, and who are threatened with torture (if not actually being tortured).

IRAQ'S FAILURE TO ALLOW UN
UNRESTRICTED ACCESS TO SCIENTISTS

Assertion:

You know the basic facts. Iraq has not complied with its obligation to allow immediate, unimpeded, unrestricted and private access to all officials and other persons as required by Resolution 1441.

The regime only allows interviews with inspectors in the presence of an Iraqi official, a minder. The official Iraqi organization charged with facilitating inspections announced, announced publicly and announced ominously that, quote, "Nobody is ready to leave Iraq to be interviewed."

Iraqi Vice President Ramadan accused the inspectors of conducting espionage, a veiled threat that anyone cooperating with UN inspectors was committing treason.[55]

—Colin Powell at UN, February 5, 2003

The Facts:

• Once Saddam Hussein was removed, according to US logic, the scientists and others would feel free to reveal the secrets about Iraq's suspected hidden arsenal. But few have come forward. And US officials say that those in custody are sticking to their stories—that Iraq hadn't had a chemical, biological or nuclear weapons program in years.[56]

• In fact the scientists' denials come despite the pressure that the US is putting on them. Rumsfeld announced that the US will pay a reward to anyone providing evidence of Iraqi weapons of mass destruction and he has threatened Iraqi scientists that if they don't cooperate they would be taken to a detention facility for interrogation and ultimately could be charged with war crimes.[57]

BRITISH INTELLIGENCE DOCUMENTS

Assertion:

I would call my colleagues attention to the fine paper that the United Kingdom distributed yesterday, which describes in exquisite detail Iraqi deception activities.[58]

—*Colin Powell at UN, February 5, 2003*

The Facts:

• It turns out that the British report plagiarized from two earlier sources. Britain's intelligence document entitled "Iraq: It's Infrastructure of Concealment Deception and Intimidation" plagiarized from articles from the military magazine *Jane's Intelligence Review* and from a school thesis by a postgraduate student in California. The author of the articles from *Jane's* said, "I don't like to think that anything I wrote has been used as an argument for war. I am concerned because I am against the war." The student, Ibrahim al Marashi said, "this is wholesale deception. How can the British public trust the government if it is up to these sort of tricks? People will treat any other information they publish with a lot of skepticism from now on." Both of the authors said that their figures had been altered in the British document.[59]

• The BBC reported that the British government exaggerated claims of Iraqi weapons, and was then hounded by the government to reveal its source. In late May/early June 2003, the BBC quoted an unnamed government official alleging that the British government wanted the "Blair Dossier" 'sexed up' with a reference to Saddam Hussein's ability to launch a biological or chemical attack within 45 minutes. The British government sequently hounded the BBC about its source for the state and demanded that the BBC confirm or deny that Dr. David Kelly was the source. Ten days later, Kelly was found dead, an apparent suicide.[60]

IRAQ'S DISCLOSURE STATEMENT

Assertion:

My colleagues, operative paragraph four of UN Resolution 1441, which we lingered over so long last fall, clearly states that false statements and omissions in the declaration and a failure by Iraq at any time to comply with and cooperate fully in the implementation of this resolution shall constitute—the facts speak for themselves—shall constitute a further material breach of its obligation.

We wrote it this way to give Iraq an early test to give Iraq an early test. Would they give an honest declaration and would they early on indicate a willingness to cooperate with the inspectors? It was designed to be an early test. They failed that test. By this standard, the standard of this operative paragraph, I believe that Iraq is now in further material breach of its obligations. I believe this conclusion is irrefutable and undeniable.[61]

—*Colin Powell at UN, February 5, 2003*

The Facts:

• The United States edited out more than 8,000 crucial pages of Iraq's 11,800 page dossier on weapons before passing on a sanitized version to the 10 non permanent members of the United Nations Security Council.

• A UN source in New York said: "The question being asked is valid. What did the US take out? And if weapons inspectors are supposed to be checking against the dossier's content, how can any future claim be verified? In effect the US was saying trust us and there are many who will not."

• Current and former UN diplomats are said to be "livid" at what some have called the "theft" of the Iraqi documents by the US. Hans von Sponeck, the former assistant secretary general of the UN and the UN's humanitarian coordinator in Iraq until 2000 said: "This is an outrageous attempt by the US to mislead."[62]

WEAPONS INSPECTIONS

Assertion:

National Security Adviser Condoleezza Rice: "I don't understand how anyone can say the inspections are working."[63]

The Facts:

• IAEA Director General Dr. Mohamed El Baradei:

In the past three months they have conducted over 200 inspections at more than 140 locations, entering without prior notice into Iraqi industrial facilities, munitions factories, military establishments, private residences, and presidential palaces, following up on inspection leads provided by other states, confiscating nuclear related Iraqi documents for further scrutiny, interviewing scientists and engineers known to have played a key role in Iraq's past nuclear weapons programme, lowering themselves by rope into abandoned underground reactor chambers, and—taking advantage of the "signature" of radioactive materials—conducting radiation surveys over thousands of kilometres of Iraqi roads and collecting samples of soil, air, water, and vegetation and particulate matter from key locations in Iraq for laboratory analysis. In short, the nuclear inspectors in Iraq have been far from idle, and their efforts far from futile. The IAEA's inspectors have systematically examined the contents and operations of all Iraqi buildings and facilities that were identified, through satellite surveillance, as having been modified or newly constructed since December 1998, when inspections were brought to a halt. They have determined the whereabouts and functionality of Iraq's known "dual use" equipment— that is, equipment that has legitimate industrial uses, such as precision machining, but that could also be used for the high precision manufacture of components relevant to a nuclear weapons programme [...]

Nuclear weapons inspections in Iraq are making marked progress. To date, we have found no substantiated evidence of the revival in Iraq of a nuclear weapons programme the most lethal of the weapons of mass destruction [....] The IAEA should be able, in the near future, to provide the Security Council with credible assurance regarding the presence or absence of a nuclear weapons programme in Iraq.[64]

Hans Blix, February 14, 2003:

The eight helicopters are fully operational. With the resolution of the problems raised by Iraq for the transportation of minders into the no fly zones, our mobility in these zones has improved. We expect to increase utilization of the helicopters.

Since we arrived in Iraq, we have conducted more than 400 inspections covering more than 300 sites. All inspections were performed without notice, and access was almost always provided promptly. In no case have we seen convincing evidence that the Iraqi side knew in advance that the inspectors were coming.

The inspections have taken place throughout Iraq at industrial sites, ammunition depots, research centres, universities, presidential sites, mobile laboratories, private houses, missile production facilities, military camps and agricultural sites. At all sites which had been inspected before 1998, re-baselining activities were performed. This included the identification of the function and contents of each building, new or old, at a site. It also included verification of previously tagged equipment, application of seals and tags, taking samples and discussions with the site personnel regarding past and present activities. At certain sites, ground penetrating radar was used to look for underground structures or buried equipment.

Through the inspections conducted so far, we have obtained a good knowledge of the industrial and scientific landscape of Iraq, as well as of its missile capability but, as before, we do not know every cave and corner. Inspections are effectively helping to bridge the gap in knowledge that arose due to the absence of inspections between December 1998 and November 2002.

More than 200 chemical and more than 100 biological samples have been collected at different sites. Three quarters of these have been screened using our own analytical laboratory capabilities at the Baghdad Centre (BOMVIC). The results to date have been consistent with Iraq's declarations.

The total number of staff in Iraq now exceeds 250 from 60 countries.

This includes about 100 UNMOVIC inspectors, 15 IAEA inspectors, 50 aircrew, and 65 support staff.[65]

NOTES

1. US Department of Defense News Briefing, Presenter: Secretary of Defense Donald Rumsfeld, September 25, 2001

2. John Cochran, "Reason for War?: White House Officials Say Privately the Sept. 11 Attacks Changed Everything," ABC News, April 25, 2003

3. Romesh Ratnesar, *Iraq & al-Qa'ida: Is There a Link?*" CNN.com, August 26, 2002

4. Dana Milbank and Mike Alien, "US Shifts Rhetoric on Its Goals in Iraq: New Emphasis: Middle East Stability," *Washington Post*, August 1, 2003

5. Robert Bums, "Deputy Defense Secretary Says Weapons Issue is Now Secondary in Iraq," *Associated Press*, July 21, 2003

6. Eric Schmitt, "Rumsfeld Says US Has 'Bulletproof' Evidence of Iraq's Links to Al-Qa'ida," *New York Times*, September 27, 2002

7. Hugh Pope and Neil King, Jr., "US Officials Discount Any Role by Iraq in Terrorist Attacks," *Wall Street Journal*, September 19, 2001

8. Bonnet, *New York Times*, October 11, 2001

9. William Rivers Pitt with Scott Ritter, *War on Iraq: What the Team Bush Doesn't Want You to Know* (New York: Context Books, 2002), p 49

10. Alan Simpson and Dr. Glen Rangwala, "Labour Against the War's Counter Dossier," September 17, 2002

11. James Risen and David Johnston, "Split at CIA & FBI on Iraqi Ties to Al-Qa'ida," *New York Times*, February 2, 2003

12. "Leaked Report Rejects Iraqi al-Qa'ida Link," BBC, February 5, 2003

13. Peter S. Canellos and Bryan Bender, "Questions Grow Over Iraq Links to al-Qa'ida," *Boston Globe*, August 3, 2003

14. US Department of Defense, "News Transcript: Deputy Secretary Wolfowitz Interview with The Laura Ingraham Show," August 1, 2003

15. Leopold, Antiwar.com, August 7, 2003. See also Matt Kelley, "Ex Officials Dispute Iraq Tie to al-Qa'ida," *Newsday*, July 13, 2003

16. Carla Anne Robbins, Marilyn Chase and Hugh Pope, "Spreading Fear:

Sophistication of Anthrax Raises New Questions About Germs' Source"; R. James Woolsey, "The Iraq Connection"; "The Anthrax War" (editorial), all from *Wall Street Journal*, October 18, 2001

17. Michael Massin, "Seven Days in October," *The Nation*, November 12, 2001

18. For discussion of anthrax mailings, see: Sabin Russell, "Silica grains detected in anthrax letter are tiny clues," *San Francisco Chronicle*, October 30, 2001; Mark Schoofs, Gary Fields, and Jerry Markhon, "Killer's Trail: Linguistic, Other Analyses Hint at Unabomber Type, Implying Long Search," *Wall Street Journal*, November 12, 2001; "Anthrax Attacks Likely Came from US Government Laboratory Expert," *Dow Jones Newswires*, November 21, 200 1; William J. Broad, "The Spores: Terror Anthrax Linked to Type Made by US," *New York Times*, December 3, 2001; William J. Broad with David Johnston, "US Inquiry, Tried, but Failed, to Link Iraq to Anthrax Attack," *New York Times*, December 22, 2001

19. Rick Weiss and Dan Eggen, "Lethal formula in anthrax mail points to labs of three countries," *International Herald Tribune*, October 26, 2001

20. White House, "President Bush, Prime Minister Blair Discuss Keeping the Peace," September 7, 2002 (www.whitehouse.gov/news/releases/2002/09/200209 07 2.html)

21. Joseph Curl, "Agency disavows report on Iraq arms," *Washington Times*, September 27, 2002

22. IAEA Press Release, "IAEA Submits Six Monthly Progress Report on its Verification Activities in Iraq," October 7, 1998

23. Priest and Pincus, *Washington Post*, October 3, 2003

24. Kay Report, October 2, 2003

25. Full Text of Colin Powell's Speech, *Guardian* (UK), February 5, 2003

26. Michael R. Gordon, "Agency Challenges Evidence Against Iraq Cited by Bush," *New York Times*, January 10, 2003

27. Dan Stober, "Nuclear inspectors reportedly angry," *San Jose Mercury News*, March 18, 2003

28. Phillips, CBS News, February 20, 2003

29. "Iraq's Weapons of Mass Destruction: The Assessment of the British Government," September 2002

30. "Bush's State of the Union speech," CNN.com, January 29, 2003

31. "Hans Blix: War Planned 'Long in Advance,'" News24.com, April 9, 2003. It is unclear who concocted the documents. New Zealand's *Herald* cites the

New Yorker's Seymour Hersh, who speculates that British intelligence may have forged the documents to help Bush quell congressional opposition to the war: In September, late September, before the Senate voted on a resolution authorizing the war, [the documents were displayed] at a series of top secret briefings in a secure room over in the Congress." Roger Franklin, 'Layers of deceit that built a case for war," *New Zealand Herald*, April 29, 2003

32. Bob Drogin and Greg Miller, "Top Inspectors Criticize CIA Data on Iraqi Sites," *Los Angeles Times*, March 8, 2003

33. Dana Milbank and Walter Pincus, "Bush Aides Disclose Warnings from the CIA," *Washington Post*, July 23, 2003

34. Robert Novak, "Mission to Niger," Townhall.com, July 14, 2003

35. Andrea Mitchell, "White House Striking Back?" NBC News, July 21, 2003

36. Mitchell, NBC News, July 21, 2003

37. David Harrison, "America Silences Niger Leaders in Iraq Nuclear Row," *Telegraph* (UK), August 3, 2003

38. Walter Pincus, "Bush Team Kept Airing Iraqi Allegation," *Washington Post*, August 8, 2003

39. Elisabeth Bumiller and James Dao, "Cheney Says Peril of a Nuclear Iraq Justifies an Attack," *New York Times*, August 27, 2002

40. "Statement to the United Nations Security Council by IAEA Director General Dr. Mohamed ElBaradei," March 7, 2003

41. "Bush's State of the Union speech," CNN.com, January 29, 2003

42. Alexander Higgins, "US Accuses Rogue States of Developing Bio Weapons," *Associated Press*, November 19, 2001

43. Pitt and Ritter, 28-29, 33-37

44. Walter Pincus and Dana Priest, Interim US report on arms indefinite," *San Francisco Chronicle*, September 25, 2003

45. David E. Kaplan and Mark Mazetti. "Second Intelligence Report: 'No Reliable Information' Iraqis Stockpiling Chemical Weapons," *US. News and World Report*, June 13, 2003

46. Pauline Jelinelc, "More than half of Iraq's top 'weapons sites' searched with no result," *Associated Press*, April 23, 2003

47. For example, see Bernard Weintaub, "Chemical Agents; American Soldiers Find Drums Possibly Storing Chemical Agents," *New York Times*, April 8, 2003

48. "Suspected Bioweapons Lab Found," MSNBC, May 11, 2003

49. Douglas Jehl, "Iraqi Trailers Said to Make Hydrogen, Not Biological Arms,"

New York Times, August 9, 2003

50. Louis Meixler, "US troops said to have found evidence of sarin, blister agents north of Baghdad," *Associated Press*, April 27, 2003

51. Guy Taylor, "Final tests find no nerve agents in Iraqi chemical," *Washington Times*, May 2, 2003

52. Kay Report, October 2, 2003

53. Powell, *Guardian* (UK), February 5, 2003

54. Whitaker, *Independent*, April 27, 2003

55. Powell, *Guardian* (UK), February 5, 2003

56. Daftia Linzer, "Iraqis won't admit to banned weapons," *Associated Press*, May 3, 2003

57. Doyle McManus and Bob Drogan, "US to step up its search for banned arms," *Los Angeles Times*, April 20, 2003

58. Powell, *Guardian* (UK), February 5, 2003

59. Gary Jones and Alexandra Williams, "Real Authors of Iraq Dossier Blast Blair," *Daily Mirror* (UK), February 8, 2003

60. "Timeline: The Gilligan Affair," *Guardian* (UK), July 18, 2003

61. Powell, *Guardian* (UK), February 5, 2003

62. James Cusick and Felicity Arbuthnot, "America Tore Out 8000 Pages of Iraq Dossier," *Sunday Herald* (Scotland), December 22, 2002

63. Sgt. 1st Class Doug Sample, "Saddam Has 'Weeks, Not Months,' Says Security Adviser Rice," *American Forces Press Service*, February 16, 2003

64. Dr. Mohamed El Baradei, "Mission Possible: Nuclear Weapons Inspections in Iraq," *Wall Street Journal*, March 7, 2003

65. Blix, *Guardian* (UK), February 14, 2003

3 | The Issue with the Butler Report

GLEN RANGWALA

THERE ARE THREE major lines that the Butler[1] report brings out. Naturally, there are a number of subsidiary issues well worth raising, but the following is a review of these three lines.

1. DISCLOSURE

The Butler report reveals that the government and intelligence services had a great deal of material that would undermine the case that Mr. Blair was presenting to the public about Iraq's weapons, but which was held back from public scrutiny. As a result, the public and MPs were not able to make a properly informed judgment on the scale of the threat posed by Iraq. Naturally, much information cannot be released for security reasons, but it is difficult to see how keeping the following information secret could be justified in this way:

A. THE LOW NUMBER OF SOURCES INSIDE IRAQ

Over *four-fifths* of the intelligence about Iraqi deception and concealment activities came from only *two sources*; two-thirds came from just one individual (§355; both of these sources are now recognized as being of questionable reliability). On Iraqi weapons, two-thirds of all intelligence reports that were circulated came from just *two sources* (§401): one reported only indirectly, and the validity of the other is now open to "serious doubt" (§403).

Butler also remarks that the "vast majority of the intelligence" on purported Iraqi mobile biological capacity came from just one individual (presumably, "Curveball," the INC-linked individual, held by Germany's Federal Intelligence Service), with whom no British official had even met prior to the war.

In total, therefore, the considerable majority of British intelligence on Iraq beyond what was already in the public realm came from just five individuals. It is in this regard that Butler remarks: "we were struck by the relative thinness of the intelligence base supporting the greater firmness of the Joint Intelligence Committee's (JIC) judgments on Iraqi production and possession of chemical and biological weapons" (§304).

There has been no explanation of why this information was not released to the public. It would have enabled the public to have a much better ability to judge the plausibility of the Prime Minister's claim[2] that Iraq was "a current and serious threat to the UK national interest" (dossier of Sept 02, foreword).

It is difficult to see how releasing this information would have endangered these sources. After all, US Secretary of State Colin Powell gave a clear account[3] of the four individuals he claimed were reliable sources on mobile biological laboratories in his presentation to the UN Security Council on 5 February 2003. There seems to be little reason why the UK could not have done the same.

At the very least, the Prime Minister could not have misled the House of Commons on 24 September 2002 by claiming that the intelligence picture painted in the dossier "is extensive, detailed and authoritative." Many would have taken from this claim that the amount of intelligence the UK had on Iraq was much greater than it really was.

Similarly, the dossier's allegations about mobile biological laboratories are alleged to be based upon "evidence from defectors [which] has indicated the existence of such facilities." Given that the "vast majority" of the claims came from just one individual, the claim that "defectors" (in the plural) were responsible for the evidence was simply misleading.

B. DEFECTORS AND SOURCES WHO GAVE A DIFFERENT PICTURE

The single most prominent defector from Iraq was Hussein Kamil, Saddam Hussein's son-in-law and director of Iraq's Military

Industrialization Corporation, who had been in charge of Iraq's weapons program. After he defected to Jordan on 7 August 1995, he told[4] UN inspectors that "I ordered destruction of all chemical weapons. All weapons —biological, chemical, missile, nuclear were destroyed."

Butler confirms that this was known to the British intelligence services. JIC reported on 24 August 1995 that: "Hussein Kamil claims there are no remaining stockpiles of agent" (§177). This information was only released to the public seven and a half years later through a leak (to me) of the transcript[5] of Hussein Kamil's interview, on 26 February 2003.

There has been no explanation of why this information was held back by the Government. It clearly undermined the Government's case, particularly insofar as Hussein Kamil's name was invoked by many— including the Prime Minister himself (to the *Independent on Sunday*, 2 March 2003[6])—to justify the claim that Iraq was a current threat. There was no danger to anyone from releasing this information, as Kamil had already been killed in 1996.

Similarly, Butler records that two sources "regarded as reliable" by the intelligence services "tended to present a less worrying view of Iraqi chemical and biological weapons capability" (§404). The decision to favor those sources with alarmist perspectives over those who presented a "less worrying view" was therefore not based upon a question of their reliability; it was a political choice, one that starkly influenced the discussion of the scale of the threat Iraq posed.

C. CHANGING PERSPECTIVES ON THE THREAT FROM IRAQ

Butler mentions that reports on a source who "had a major effect on the certainty of statements in the Government's dossier of September 2002" (§401) were withdrawn by MI6 in July 2003 (§405). This was not made public until the Butler report was released in July 2004, even though it has allowed a more honest public assessment of the case that had been made for war.

Mr. Blair claims that he was not aware of the withdrawal of this report until the Butler process was complete. If it was the case that this source had the "major effect" that Butler describes, the Prime Minister needs to explain how it was that he was in such a serious position of ignorance for twelve months, during which he continued to profess his certainty about Iraq's weapons. Shouldn't someone pay the price for allowing Mr. Blair to look like a fool for so long?

2. FAILURE TO INVESTIGATE ALARMIST PERSPECTIVES

In a considerable number of cases, Butler demonstrates how sources or claims of dubious reliability but of a highly alarmingly nature were not evaluated thoroughly. Butler explains the lack of checks upon sources by pointing to how the relevant staff—"Requirements" officers, in the jargon - were "junior officers," who were in those positions "in order to make overall staff savings." (§414)

However, the failure to investigate properly the claims of alarming sources on such a crucial issue reflects a lack of political priority in evaluating these claims with appropriate skepticism. It is difficult to imagine that if Mr. Blair had seriously pressed MI6 or JIC about how reliable their information sources were, it would have been left to "junior officers" to make all the checks on reliability. Two key examples recounted by Butler are:

A. URANIUM FROM NIGER

The basis of the government's case, as reported by Butler, was that: "During 2002, the UK received further intelligence from additional sources which identified the purpose of [an Iraqi official's] visit to Niger as having been to negotiate the purchase of uranium ore." (§495)

Although these "additional sources" are not described by Butler, one of them was not the Iraqi official at the centre of the allegations— Ambassador Wissam al-Zahawi, referred to by Butler at §502. After he retired from Iraqi government service in 2001, Zahawi was resident in Amman, Jordan (where there is also a large MI6 station) and paid a number of visits to the UK in 2001 and 2002. At no point did British officials contact him to discuss his trip to Niger. The news media in 1999 had quoted him as being the official visiting Niger; when I wanted to contact Zahawi for an interview in 2003, I was able to obtain his telephone number and email address from a reputable academic database without any difficulty whatsoever.

The failure of the intelligence services to do this five minute task on an issue so crucial as to be key evidence for whether or not Iraq had an ongoing nuclear program reflects not just on the junior nature of the staff. It demonstrates the political inexpediency of making a serious attempt to investigate alarming allegations about Iraq for their actual plausibility.

Incidentally, the Butler report oddly does not include any reference to the claim from the CIA's director of Weapons Intelligence Non-Proliferation and Arms Control Centre (WINPAC), as recounted in the Senate intelligence committee[7] report of 7 July 2004 (pp.65, 66). He told the committee that the CIA had urged Britain to remove references to the uranium claim from the September dossier.

45 MINUTES

The Butler report demonstrates that the British intelligence services mentioned that the sub-source who provided the information that Iraq could use CBW of some sort within 45 minutes had "links to opposition groups and the possibility that his reports would be affected by that." (§403; this is the individual referred to as the sub-source for the 45 minutes claims at §512). This opposition group referred to seems to be the Iraqi National Accord (INA), led by interim Prime Minister Iyad Allawi, according to the INA's own statements. As a result, there was a clear incentive for the individual source to make alarming claims to British intelligence officials and their conduits. Butler mentions that "post-war validation by SIS has raised serious doubts about the reliability of reporting from this new sub-source." (§403) There seems to have been every possibility that further attempts to assess the reliability of the sub-source could have been made prior to incorporating his claim in such a categorical way into the September 2002 dossier. If it were the case that circumstances rendered it impossible to ascertain his reliability, then it would seem proper that the dubious provenance of the source—as well as the nature of the claim, relating to battlefield weapons—should have been made public.

B. FAILURE TO RE-EVALUATE CLAIMS AFTER THE INTRODUCTION OF INSPECTORS

Butler records how the British intelligence services were not asked for a re-evaluation of intelligence given the findings of the UN weapons inspectors during 2002-03. (§362)

This is remarkable, given that the inspectors were visiting many of the sites that the British government had previously named as sites of concern. Furthermore, UNMOVIC head, Hans Blix had told[8] the Security Council on 7 March 2003 that "the numerous initiatives, which are now taken by the Iraqi side with a view to resolving some long-standing open disarmament issues, can be seen as 'active', or even 'proactive.'"(Butler misstates Blix's position quite severely at his §362).

The British government's failure to re-evaluate its claims, despite this "proactive" cooperation from Iraq, demonstrates that there was no attempt to ascertain the likely state of Iraq's weapons prior to the invasion. Instead, the earlier alarming claims were allowed to stand, even though material had subsequently been found that would cast severe doubt upon their plausibility.

Equally, Butler mentions that there was not a full intelligence assessment of the *Iraqi declaration of 7 December 2002* (§363). Nevertheless, the Iraqi declaration was condemned by both Mr. Blair and Mr. Straw as being false. By contrast, Hans Blix had told[9] the Security Council on 27 January 2003: "In the field of missiles and biotechnology, the declaration contains a good deal of new material and information covering the period from 1998 and onward. This is welcome." It seems that the UK did not have intelligence material with which to disagree with Dr Blix's statement on the usefulness of the declaration. However, they continued to portray it as inadequate, and used this as part of the justification for war.

3. POLITICAL OVERSTATEMENT

Quite apart from the September dossier, the Butler report demonstrates that a considerable number of the claims that the Prime Minister was making on Iraq's weapons through 2002 and 2003 were not based upon intelligence assessments. Some were in direct contradiction with the intelligence assessments. There were two major forms of this misstatement:

A. CLAIMS ABOUT IRAQ S WEAPONS WHILST JIC ASSESSMENTS WERE STILL UNCERTAIN.

The Butler report (§296) shows that the Joint Intelligence Committee only gave a strong indication that Iraq had chemical and biological weapons in its assessment of 9 September 2002. Prior to the 21 August 2002 assessment (which was more ambiguous), JIC assessments emphasized how little was known about Iraqi chemical, biological and nuclear programs, and stopped short of any definitive claims either way. The JIC Assessment of 15 March 2002, for example states that:

> From the evidence available to us, we believe Iraq retains some production equipment, and some small stocks of CW agent precursors, and may have hidden small quantities of agents and weapons. [...] There is no intelligence on any BW agent production facilities... [10]

Despite the uncertainty expressed in the JIC assessments of this period, the Prime Minister continued to voice his certainty about Iraq weapons. For example, on 3 April 2002, Mr. Blair told[11] NBC news that "We know that he [Saddam Hussein] has stockpiles of major amounts of chemical and biological weapons, we know that he is trying to acquire nuclear capability, we know that he is trying to develop ballistic missile capability of a greater range."

This reference to "major amounts of chemical and biological weapons" is in direct contradiction with the latest JIC assessment, which stated only the *possibility* that Iraq had "small quantities of agents."

Similarly, Jack Straw had said in an interview[12] with David Frost on 24 March 2002 that "Iraq poses a threat to the world because of its manufacture and development of weapons of mass destruction." There was no indication in any of the intelligence material recounted in the Butler report that the hyperbolic claim about "a threat to the world" had the slightest basis in evidence.

Furthermore, it was in this context that the intelligence assessments had to be made. The Prime Minister and Foreign Secretary had already declared—without evidence—that Iraq had prohibited chemical and biological weapons. This left the intelligence services in a position where they knew that they would only be able to take on a significant role in policy-making if they were to provide material to justify these claims.

B. CLAIMS ABOUT UN WEAPONS INSPECTORS

The Butler report makes clear the extent to which the intelligence services recognized the UN weapons inspections during the 1991-98 period as having been successful in disarming Iraq. The JIC assessment of 4 February 1998 recorded that "UNSCOM and the IAEA have succeeded in destroying or controlling the vast majority of Saddam's 1991 weapons of mass destruction (WMD) capability." (§181)

This assessment, repeated in later JIC assessments, was directly contradicted by the Prime Minister. For example, he told the *Independent on Sunday*[13] on 2 March 2003 that "the UN has tried unsuccessfully for 12 years to get Saddam to disarm peacefully." At the House of Commons on 17 March 2003, in the debate that led to a vote for war, he presented[14] as still existing the "large quantities of WMD" left over from 1991 that were still "unaccounted for" when the US withdrew UN inspectors from Iraq in 1998. This was in direct contrast with JIC assessments, which had consistently claimed that little if any weapons were left over from the 1991 capability.

NOTES

1. The entire report is available from: http://www.butlerreview.org.uk/report/index.asp

2. For Tony Blair's foreword to the Iraq dossier see: http://www.number10.gov.uk/output/Page284.asp

3. Colin Powell's remarks can be found at: http://www.state.gov/secretary/rm/2003/17300.htm

4. See: http://middleeastreference.org.uk/kamel.html

5. Ibid

6. *The Independent on Sunday* "Blair: My Christian conscience is clear over the war" available at: http://news.independent.co.uk/uk/politics/story.jsp?story=383014

7. Available from: http://intelligence.senate.gov/

8. His transcript is available from: http://www.un.org/apps/news/infocusnewsiraq.asp?NewsID=414&sID=6

9. See: http://www.un.org/apps/news/infocusnewsiraq.asp?NewsID=354&sID=6

10. Annex B of the Butler report, pp.167-68

11. See: http://www.pm.gov.uk/output/Page1709.asp

12. See: http://www.iraqwatch.org/government/UK/FCO/uk-fco-straw-03-24-02.htm

13. "Blair: My Christian conscience is clear over the war" op.cit.

14. See http://www.pm.gov.uk/output/Page3294.asp

4 | The Price of Freedom in Iraq

CEARA DONNELLEY &

WILLIAM D. HARTUNG

Nᴜᴍʙᴇʀs ᴅᴏᴍɪɴᴀᴛᴇ ᴛʜᴇ recent headlines and sound bytes from Baghdad and the Pentagon:

• 147,000: the number of US ground troops on Iraqi soil.

• 237: the number of US service men and women killed since the beginning of ground operations.

• 99: the number of these deaths since May 1, the day that Bush declared combat victory for the coalition.

• 9: the number of months since members of the 3rd Infantry Division have seen their families.

• 3: the number of times their homecoming has been delayed.

• $3.9 billion: the number of US dollars, estimated by Donald Rumsfeld, it costs per month to support US efforts in Iraq.

• $400 billion: the projected military budget recently approved by Congress for FY 2004.

The list goes on.

What many reports lack, despite all of these statistics, are the real details. When it comes to who is doing what in Iraq, the facts are less clear. Your average CNN-watching American may be able to report the latest on soldiers killed or Iraqis successfully "found, killed or captured," but you'd be hard pressed to find an average American who could tell you how the scene is really unfolding. How many Americans know who supplied the war, who is in charge of reconstruction, how much they are being paid for it, and how they were hired?

The answer is not quite so simple as a predictable response—"the military." Few know the real details: how the projects and personnel planning post-war Iraq come from private American corporations making world-class lemonade out of the sour situation in the Persian Gulf.

From providing the weapons and tanks that took us to Baghdad, to the personnel rebuilding dams and bridges or operating ports, to the pencils and lesson plans revamping the education system for young Iraqis, private American corporations are spearheading US campaigns in Iraq and reaping the financial rewards of warfare.

Private corporations have played an unprecedented role in the Second Gulf War, and from the looks of just one more number—$680 million, the projected contract with Bechtel Group Inc. for its reconstructive work in Iraq—they will continue to do so.

Some of the jobs undertaken by the Bechtels and the Halliburtons, such as rebuilding water and electrical systems for instance, are necessary and important. Yet as a nation and as a democracy we must ponder seriously whether such private corporations, with such firm connections to our leadership, are necessarily the ones who should be handed these jobs. The privatization of the United States military is not a new controversy. P.W. Singer's new book *Corporate Warriors: The Rise of the Privatized Military Industry* (Ithaca, New York: Cornell University Press, 2003) offers insights into the questions that should be asked about the unprecedented levels of privatization of military planning, training, construction, and services that were pursued during the Clinton/Gore administration and have been accelerated under the Bush/Cheney administration. If the experience thus far in Iraq is any indication, we clearly have a long way to go before we establish the appropriate balance between profits and patriotism in the use of private corporations to implement our national security strategy.

From a taxpayer's perspective, the most important question is how many billions of dollars has our government paid private corporations to ensure a final victory in Operation Iraqi Freedom—whatever "victory" ultimately comes to mean?

What follows is a breakdown of the major corporations involved in Iraq from the incipient days of US military action to the forthcoming years of rebuilding.

RUN-UP TO WAR
WHO PUT THE SHOCK IN "SHOCK AND AWE?"

Long before the Bush administration could sufficiently sell its case to the United Nations, Congress, and the American people, it was planning for war against Saddam and his Republican Guard. For companies like Raytheon, Boeing, and Lockheed Martin this meant a big boom in business in exchange for the big booms their weapons and bombs showered on Iraq months later. Though the ties that bind these companies to the Bush administration are not quite as controversial as those linking rebuilding and private military companies, such as Halliburton and Bechtel, it is still clear, by tracing overlapping personnel, that far from being a relic of the Cold War, the military-industrial complex is alive and well and thriving in George W. Bush's Washington.

LOCKHEED MARTIN

The Pentagon's No. 1 contractor has certainly benefited from military action in Iraq. The company reports eighty percent of its business is with the US Department of Defense and the US federal government agencies. It is also the largest provider of information technology (IT) services, systems integration, and training to the US government. Such business has grown substantially during the Bush tenure, especially in the fiscal year 2002, as plans for war were formulated, and expenditures in weapons and dollars calculated.

• The company was awarded $17 billion in defense contracts in 2002, up from $14.7 billion in 2001.[1]

• First quarter sales for 2003 were $7.1 billion, an eighteen percent increase from the corresponding quarter in 2002.

• In March of 2003, as the first bombs rained on Baghdad, the US Air Force awarded Lockheed Martin a $106.6 million contract for Paveway II GBU-12 and—16 Laser Guided Bomb (LGB) kits, as part of a $281 million contract characterized by "indefinite delivery, indefinite quantity"—a fancy term for an open-ended, cost-plus contract. The majority of the kits, also known as "smart bombs" (when fitted on warheads) were ordered to restock diminishing US Navy inventories.

• Also in March, the company received a $4 billion multi-year contract with the US Air Force and the Marine Corps for the acquisition of C-130J Super Hercules Aircraft, to deliver the additional planes (the two departments combined already own forty-one) from 2003 to 2008.

• Former Lockheed Martin Vice-President Bruce Jackson was a finance chair for the Bush for President campaign; Vice-Presidential spouse Lynne Cheney is a former board member of Lockheed Martin, and used to receive $120,000 per year from the company for attending a handful of semi-annual board meetings.[2]

• Chris Williams, lobbyist for Johnston & Associates, is one of nine members of the Defense Policy Board to have ties to defense companies. His firms represent Lockheed Martin, Boeing, TRW and Northrop Grumman.[3]

BOEING

Boeing is the Pentagon's No. 2 contractor as a supplier of war materials ranging from information technology to planes and the bombs that drop from them. The B-52, the aircraft made famous during the Korean War, remained the "workhorse" in Operation Iraqi Freedom. It has been upgraded to modern technological heights by "smart bombs" and precision-guided weapons like those produced by Lockheed Martin, as well as those devised by Boeing itself. In fact, Boeing's Joint Direct Attack Munitions (JDAMs) are the majority of the military's smart bomb arsenal, because they are cheap and effective: a $22,000 kit makes almost any bomb a precision munition.

• In 2002, Boeing received $16.6 billion in Pentagon contracts—up from $13 billion in 2001, $12 billion in 2000.

• While the Air Force originally ordered 87,000 JDAM kits, it expanded that order to more than 230,000 sometime before the March invasion. The going price was $378 million.[4]

• The company recently won a $9.7 billion contract from the DoD to build sixty additional C-17 transport planes, praised as the only aircraft capable of lifting the Army's heavy tanks, in addition to Apache helicopters, Humvees, and Bradley fighting vehicles. In a deployment that began in January 2003, the C-17's were operating constantly, delivering equipment to staging spots in the Persian Gulf.

• Other recent contracts include $60.3 million for additional production of one hundred and twenty Standoff Land Attack Missiles Expanded Response (SLAM-ER), $3.3 billion for the sale of 40 F-15K aircraft and weapons support for the Republic of Korea.

• Richard Perle, former Chairman, and now a mere member of the Defense Policy Board is a managing partner at venture-capital company Trireme Partners, L.P., which invests in homeland security and defense companies. Half of the $45 million in capital thus far comes from Boeing.[5]

• 58% of the $1.5 million in Soft Money and PAC contributions Boeing made during the 2000 campaign went to the Republican candidates. When Bush was declared victor, Boeing gave $100,000 for the inauguration.

RAYTHEON

The fourth largest defense contractor in the United States, Raytheon boasts involvement in over four thousand weapons programs.

The defense electronics company is best known for the publicity garnered during the 1991 Gulf conflict by its Patriot Air Defense missile that intercepted Iraqi Scud missiles. Since 1991 the Pentagon has spent $3 billion improving the accuracy of the weapon, which studies subsequent to Desert Storm revealed to be far less than perfect.

Raytheon also manufactures the Tomahawk land attack missile, another familiar name in times of combat. Raytheon's website morbidly celebrates its popularity: "Over three hundred Tomahawks were used in Operation Desert Storm alone. Since Desert Storm in 1991, more than one thousand Tomahawks have been fired." Estimates of the weapon's use the second time around predicted that eight hundred would be fired in just the first hours of war. In addition to these two well-known weapons of war, Raytheon produces a wide range of popular missile systems, radar and surveillance systems, and bombs. As a major arms exporter to countries including Israel, Egypt, Saudi Arabia, Turkey, and South Korea, the company is likely to doubly benefit from the militarization of world politics as nations clamor to bolster defense systems.

• Each Tomahawk missile costs between $600,000 and $ 1 million.

• Raytheon's fourth quarter operating report of January 2003 reported a doubling in profits.

• CEO Daniel Burnham is content with the course set by Bush and company, applauding the fact that "the market is higher today than we thought a year ago," and boasting that "We are perfectly aligned with the defense department's priorities."

• The Navy recently contracted a $1.2 billion deal to develop future ships like the DDX destroyer, for which Raytheon integrates electronics.

• The Air Force raised its request from $12.2 million to $80 million worth of 901 Javelin anti-tank missiles, co-produced by Raytheon and Lockheed Martin.

• Since 1996, Raytheon has donated more than $3.3 million in soft money and PAC donations, which places it fourth in donations among major defense contractors in the 2002 midterm electoral campaigns.

• Despite a traditional relationship with Massachusetts Democrats, Raytheon's contributions have increasingly leaned towards the Republican party culminating in a 58%/42% split, R/D, in the 2002 midterm Congressional elections.[6]

ALLIANT TECHSYSTEMS

Lesser known than defense giants like Boeing, Lockheed Martin, and Raytheon, Alliant nonetheless may be the defense company that profits most consistently from the war in Iraq and the wars for "regime change" that may be yet to come under the Bush administration's first-strike military doctrine. Alliant Tech supplies all of the Army's small arms munitions, used in rifles and machine guns, and approximately half of the medium-caliber rounds fired by tanks and antitank chain guns in attack helicopters. War strategies may change, favoring tanks over aircraft or vice versa, but soldiers will always need ammo and they will always need more ammo in times of combat. Alliant's recent sixteen percent increase in sales reflects that bottom line.

• Alliant's sales rose from $1.8 to $2.1 billion in FY 2002, a sixteen percent increase.

• Last year the Army awarded Alliant a $92 million dollar contract for two hundred and sixty-five million rounds of small-caliber ammunition, notably including cartridges for M-16 rifles.

• In February, Alliant received another $113 million in contracts to make ammunition for the Abrams battle tank.[7]

CLEANING UP THE MESS:
CONTRACTING THE REBUILDING OF IRAQ

P.W. Singer calls it the "service side" of war. Private military companies are on the rise as the purported defenders of freedom. During "Operation Iraqi Freedom," the United States deployed one private military worker for every ten soldiers—a tenfold increase since the 1991 Gulf War.

Between 1994 and 2002 the Pentagon entered into more than three thousand contracts with private military companies of varying notoriety.[8] Worldwide, private military contractors are a $100 billion annual business, and with the war on terrorism being described as the "endless war," there will be more money to be made in the years ahead.

Many Americans now know the link between private military contractor Halliburton and Vice President Cheney, yet the morally ambiguous relationships between military-industrial giants and the Washington elite do not end there. Mainstream news reports have also focused on the role played by Bechtel, another corporation that enjoys close ties with the Republican administration and is reaping billions as it rebuilds Iraq.

Along with these familiar examples, we should add Dyncorp, MPRI, Vinnell, Logicon, AirScan: these names should become familiar because their employees are being paid to do the dirty work alongside US soldiers in Iraq. One wonders whose salaries are higher.

HALLIBURTON

Halliburton first made headlines in this war, when it won the very first rebuilding contract without bidding and before US tanks even made it to Baghdad. In the shadow of Enron and seemingly ubiquitous corporate scandal, the relationship between Halliburton and its former CEO, Vice President Dick Cheney, raised a red flag.

In March 2003, Halliburton subsidiary Kellogg, Brown, and Root (KBR) was awarded the main contract to control oil fires and stabilize oil fields under US command; no limit was placed on the duration or dollars involved in this venture.

Halliburton is not all about oil; its profit from the war on Iraq runs deeper than the oil wells. Cheney's former company provides a wide range of services and is correspondingly contracted to perform them in private bidding sessions that exclude most competitors.

• Since September 11, the Bush administration has doled out over $2.2 billion in defense-related contracts to Cheney's former company.[9]

• Halliburton's contract to secure and protect oil fields in Iraq, secretly awarded by the Army without any competitive bidding, could be worth up to $1 billion.[10]

• From September 2002 to April 2003, Halliburton received over $443 million in defense related contracts to provide services ranging from logistical support to building enemy prisoner of war camps and refueling military tanks.

• From 1999 to 2002, Halliburton donated $708,770 in soft money and PAC contributions, 95% of that total going to Republicans.

• A recent *Newsweek* article reports that "while Defense Secretary in the first Bush administration, Cheney awarded KBR the Army's first private contract to manage troop tent cities. During the Clinton years Halliburton lost that contract after KBR came under fire for allegedly overcharging the government. But after Cheney was elected, KBR was again awarded that Army contract and has rung up $1.15 billion so far on the ten year deal."[11]

• Due to a decision he made upon leaving Halliburton, Cheney still receives annual deferred compensation of roughly $180,000 from his former company.

BECHTEL

Though contracts for rebuilding Iraq were awarded as soon as war was underway, if not sooner, as late as mid-April the big question was: who would win the grand prize, the jackpot in the current round in bidding a wide-ranging $600 million reconstruction contract awarded by USAID to cover the cost of rebuilding critical infrastructure: airports, roads, water and power systems, schools and hospitals?

After a secretive bidding process, Bechtel Group of San Francisco was announced as the winner, sparking a flurry of attention from the media and those who know of Bechtel's intricate ties to the Bush administration. As one *New York Times* article aptly put it:

> Awarding the first major contract for reconstruction in Iraq to a politically connected American company under restricted business procedures sends a deplorable message to a skeptical world [...] the award of a contract worth up to $680 million to the Bechtel Group of San Francisco in a competition limited to a handful of American companies can only add to the impression that the United States seeks to profit from the war it waged.[12]

Bechtel was widely regarded as a highly capable contender for the $600 million plus contract, yet its ties to Washington are so intricately and firmly woven that it's nearly impossible not to imagine what kind of pressure was on the contracting decision.

• As Secretary of State for Reagan (and former president of Bechtel), in 1983, George Schultz sent Donald Rumsfeld on a Middle East peace envoy to the city of Baghdad to meet with Saddam Hussein. Rumsfeld was instructed to ask for the leader's support in Bechtel's bid on construction of an oil pipeline from Iraq to the port of Aqaba. Twenty years later, Rumsfeld and his cohorts were in the position to once again launch Bechtel into a position of power in the Middle East, and they did so.[13]

• Jack Sheehan, a senior Vice President at Bechtel, is a member of the Defense Policy Board.[14]

• USAID administrator Andrew Natsios, the overseer of bidding contracts in Iraq, also has close ties to Bechtel; he headed Boston's massive "Big Dig" construction process, a disastrous $14 billion boondoggle that accounted for some of the biggest cost overruns in the history of American municipal public works. Bechtel is one the main contractors on the "Big Dig" project.[15]

• Just two months before war, President Bush appointed multi-billionaire Riley Bechtel (the 104th richest man in the world thanks to his family's company) to his Export Council to advise the government on how to create markets for American companies overseas.[16]

• From 1999 to 2001, Bechtel contributed $1.3 million to political campaigns; fifty-eight percent went to Republican candidates.[17]

DYNCORP

The celebratory images from the fall of Baghdad—giant Saddam statues falling, spontaneous exultation—were quickly replaced with grim reality of the consequences of destroying order in hopes of implementing a better one. Looting ran rampant: much needed medical equipment and supplies disappeared, precious and invaluable artifacts were stolen from museums. The US military, already stretched thin and committed to the continuing task of stabilizing the region, stood by helplessly.

It was clear something had to be done. Enter Dyncorp: a multi-billion dollar military contractor providing personnel that fits the description offered by one Pentagon official to the *New York Times*: "something a little more corporate and more efficient with cleaner lines of authority and responsibility [than United Nations peace-keeping troops]."[18] Corpwatch. org reporter Prattap Chatterjee has accurately characterized this service as rent-a-cop; Dyncorp' s website is still advertising lucrative positions to fill the Iraqi police force it has promised to build under contract to the US government. Former servicemen, police officers, and prison guards line up.

• The State Department awarded DynCorp a multi-million dollar contract in April to advise the Iraqi government on setting up effective law enforcement, judicial, and correctional facilities. The company estimates it will send one thousand American law enforcement experts to Iraq to meet the task. DynCorp projects a return of up to $50 million for the first year of the contract.[19]

• DynCorp contributed 74% of a total $276, 975 to the Republican party from 1999 to 2002.[20]

MORE CONTRACTS:
PRIVATIZATION BEYOND DEFENSE

The US government has not only hired companies to dramatically supplant the duties of the occupying military. American taxpayers are also paying for the specialized rebuilding of other essentials in Iraq. To appreciate fully the cost of the war and its aftermath, these contracts are listed below with brief summaries of tasks for which they were awarded.[21]

• $4.8 million to Stevedoring Services of America was awarded by USAID for "assessment and management" of the Umm Qasr port on southeastern Iraq.

• $10 million to Abt Associates Inc. to reform the Iraqi Ministry of Health and to deliver health services and supplies in the interim.

• $2.5 million to Skylink Air and Logistic Support (USA) Inc. to help reopen and manage Iraq's airports.

• $7 million to International Resources Group was awarded for a ninety-day period for the management of relief and rebuilding efforts.

• $7.9 million to Research Triangle Institute (RTI) to promote Iraqi civic participation in the reconstruction process. RTI will provide technical assistance and training systems in the effort to improve internal administrative skills and understanding of municipal government and services.

• $2 million over one year to Creative Associates International Inc. to address "immediate educational needs" of Iraq's primary and secondary schools. Contract provides for school supplies, training teachers, and developing testing methods to track student performance.

IRAQI OIL: FUNDING RECONSTRUCTION

The US has just recently lined up long-term oil deals with twelve companies around the world in a hastened effort to gain revenue to pay for reconstruction. According to its senior American advisor, Philip Carroll, a former executive of oil giant Royal Dutch Shell, Iraq's State Oil Marketing Organization plans to supply an average of seven hundred and twenty-five thousand to seven hundred and fifty-thousand barrels of oil a day to US firms like ExxonMobil, ChevronTexaco, ConocoPhilipps, Marathon and Valero Energy; as well as European giants like Shell, BP, Total, Repsol YPF; the Chinese firm Sinochem; Switzerland-based oil dealer Vitol and Japan's Mitsubishi.[22] The choices of oil contractors seem to be entirely political, with Carroll's former company on the list, along with National Security Advisor Condoleezza Rice's former firm,

Chevron. The contract with BP is may be a partial payback for the United Kingdom's commitment of combat troops to the US-led war against Hussein's regime; and the Japanese deal has been discussed as "bait" to lure the Japanese government into supplying personnel for security and policing functions in occupied Iraq. And, of course, while Washington's man from Royal Dutch Shell exercises veto power over the decisions of the new Iraqi oil ministry, the money for rebuilding Iraq's devastated oil producing infrastructure goes to Dick Cheney's former company, Halliburton, on a cost-plus basis.

CONCLUSION:
TIME FOR ACCOUNTABILITY

As costs mount for the US-led rebuilding and occupation of Iraq, the profits of companies like Lockheed Martin, Boeing, Raytheon, Bechtel, Halliburton, and Dyncorp are likely to rise substantially as a result of contracts steered their way by the Bush administration. Recently, the *New York Times* reported yet another example of favoritism that benefited Halliburton.[23]

After responding to pressure from Rep. Henry Waxman (D-CA) and rival companies to re-bid the longer-term portion of Halliburton's multi-year, multi-billion dollar contract for rebuilding and operating Iraq's oil infrastructure, it now appears that the bidding process is a sham, like so much else about the Bush administration's privatized rebuilding effort in Iraq. After going through the process of recruiting bidders for the contract and holding an all day meeting in Dallas in mid-July with companies interested in competing with Halliburton for the Iraqi oil industry rebuilding contract, the Army Corps of Engineers quietly revised the specs for the new contract so that the vast majority of the $1 billion in work that was supposed to be up for competition was in essence handed back to Halliburton. The work schedules for the alleged $1 billion bid were fixed so that the majority of the work (or at least the majority of the contract dollars) would be issued during calendar year 2003. Given that the bidding process for the second phase of rebuilding Iraq's oil sector won't yield a winner until October 15, 2003, at the earliest, this essentially meant that Halliburton would get the majority of phase two work by default. This led Bechtel, a major potential competitor for the phase two work, to withdraw from the bidding, arguing that so much of the work had essentially been handed to Halliburton in a back-door deal with the Army Corps that was not revealed during the initial rounds of bidding, that the notion of a true "competition" for the Army Corps' second phase contract was basically a sham.

It is clear that there needs to be more accountability—both to the people of Iraq and the American taxpayers—about how the privatized rebuilding process in Iraq is going to proceed. Contracts should be opened to true competitive bidding, involving not only US firms but competent companies from allied nations. The decisions about which tasks are appropriate for private corporations, as opposed to US government entities or non-profit, non-governmental organizations, should be made openly and transparently, with appropriate Congressional oversight and public input. Rebuilding contracts should be short-term, limited profit arrangements that do not pre-empt the ability of a future democratic government in Iraq to choose its own contractors and structure its own industries as the Iraqi people—not Washington bureaucrats or politically-wired companies like Bechtel and Halliburton—see fit. Companies which are profiting from the rebuilding of Iraq should take a pledge not to make contributions towards the 2004 presidential and Congressional campaigns, to avoid the unseemly appearance of payback, as if firms that have been rewarded by the Bush administration with contracts in Iraq are funneling a percentage of their profits back to Republican candidates. Ideally, if President Bush wants to set an appropriate moral tone, he should agree not to accept contributions for his re-election campaign from any company involved in the rebuilding of Iraq.

At the height of World War II, Senator Harry Truman of Missouri made a name for himself by uncovering profiteering and fraud by companies involved in providing supplies for the war effort. Given the high political and economic stakes in Iraq, a comparable investigation is in order now. Rep. Henry Waxman (D-CA) has been asking all of the right questions in his role as the ranking Democrat on the House Committee on Government Reform, but he needs to be joined by prominent colleagues of both parties, and in the Senate as well as the House, in digging up answers about the cost, effectiveness, and propriety of rebuilding Iraq via the via the secretive, privatized process that the Bush administration and the Pentagon have been pushing thus far.[24]

NOTES

1. "War in Iraq: We foot the billing, Corporations make a killing," www.citizensworks.org

2. Ibid.

3. "Advisors of Influence: Nine Members of the Defense Policy Board Have Ties to Defense Contractors," report by the Center for Public Integrity, www.publici.org

4. Ibid.

5. For more details on Boeing's role in Iraq and its connections to Washington see ATRC's April 4, 2003 update.

6. For additional information on Raytheon see ATRC's March 24, 2003 update.

7. Amy Cortese, "Quiet, but Central, Role for Ammunition Maker," *New York Times*, March 23, 2003.

8. P.W. Singer, "Have Guns, Will Travel," *New York Times*, July 21, 2003.

9. Michael Scherer, "The World According to Halliburton," www.motherjones.org

10. Keith Naughton and Michael Hirsch, "Fanning the Flames: Cheney's Halliburton ties," *Newsweek*, April 7, 2003.

11. Ibid.

12. "And the Winner is Bechtel," *New York Times*, April 19, 2003.

13. Pratap Chatterjee, "Bechtel's Friends in High Places," special to Corpwatch, April 24, 2003, www.corpwatch.org.

14. "Advisors of Influence," www.publici.org.

15. Chatterjee, April 24, 2003.

16. Ibid.

17. "Rebuilding Iraq—The Contractors," www.opensecrets.org.

18. Pratap Chatterjee, "DynCorp Rent-a-Cops May Head to Post-Saddam Iraq," special to Corpwatch, April 9, 2003, www.corpwatch.org.

19. "Rebuilding Iraq—The Contractors," www.opensecrets.org.

20. Ibid.

21. All statistics provided by the USAID fact sheet on reconstruction contracts for Iraq: www.usaid.gov/press/factsheets/2003/fs030620.html.

22. Chip Cummins, "Iraq Lines Up Long-Term Oil Deals," *Wall Street Journal*, July 29, 2003, company identification provided by Agence France Presse, July 31, 2003.

23. Neela Bannerjee, "Bechtel Ends Move for Work in Iraq, Seeing a Done Deal," *New York Times*, August 8, 2003

24. To see Waxman's excellent series of letters to the Army Corp of Engineers and other key Bush administration policy makers, go to the web site of the House Committee on Government Reform, www.house.gov/reform, and find the site for minority caucus.

5 | Too Many Smoking Guns to Ignore

BILL & KATHLEEN CHRISTISON

OST OF THE vociferously pro-Israeli neo-conservative policymakers in the Bush administration made no effort to hide the fact that at least part of their intention in promoting war against Iraq (and later perhaps against Syria, Iran, Hezbollah, and the Palestinians) is to guarantee Israel's security by eliminating its greatest military threats, forging a regional balance of power overwhelmingly in Israel's favor, and in general creating a more friendly atmosphere for Israel in the Middle East. Yet, despite the neo-cons' own openness, a great many of those on the left who opposed going to war with Iraq and opposed the neo-conservative doctrines of the Bush administration nonetheless utterly rejected any suggestion that Israel was pushing the United States into war, or was cooperating with the US, or even hoped to benefit by the war. Anyone who had the temerity to suggest any Israeli instigation of, or even involvement in, the Bush administration war planning was inevitably labeled somewhere along the way as an anti-Semite. Just whisper the word "domination" anywhere in the vicinity of the word "Israel," as in "US-Israeli domination of the Middle East" or "the US drive to assure global domination and guarantee security for Israel," and some leftist who otherwise opposed going to war against Iraq will trot out charges of promoting the *Protocols of the Elders of Zion*, the old czarist forgery that asserted a Jewish plan for world domination.

This is tiresome, to put it mildly. So it's useful to put forth the evidence for the assertion of Israeli complicity in the Bush administration during the planning for war with Iraq, which is voluminous, as the following recitation will show. Much of what is presented below could be classified as circumstantial, but much is from the mouths of the horses themselves, either the neo-con planners or Israeli government officials, and much of it is evidence that, even if Israel was not actively pushing for war, many Israelis did expect to benefit from it, and this despite their fear that the war could bring down on Israel a shower of Iraqi missiles.

The evidence below is listed chronologically, except for two items grouped separately at the end. Although deletions have been made for the sake of brevity, and emphasis has been added to occasional phrases and sentences, no editorial narrative has been added. The evidence speaks for itself.

> Benjamin Netanyahu's government comes in with a new set of ideas. While there are those who will counsel continuity, Israel has the opportunity to make a clean break; it can forge a peace process and strategy based on an entirely new intellectual foundation, one that restores strategic initiative. To secure the nation's streets and borders in the immediate future, Israel can [among other steps] work closely with Turkey and Jordan to contain, destabilize, and roll-back some of its most dangerous threats. This implies a clean break from the slogan, 'comprehensive peace' to a traditional concept of strategy based on balance of power. Israel can shape its strategic environment, in cooperation with Turkey and Jordan, by weakening, containing, and even rolling back Syria. This effort can focus on removing Saddam Hussein from power in Iraq, an important Israeli strategic objective in its own right, as a means of foiling Syria's regional ambitions. Jordan has challenged Syria's regional ambitions recently by suggesting the restoration of the Hashemites in Iraq. *Since Iraq's future could affect the strategic balance in the Middle East profoundly, it would be understandable that Israel has an interest in supporting the Hashemites in their efforts to redefine Iraq. Israel's new agenda can signal a clean break* by abandoning a policy which allowed strategic retreat, by reestablishing the principle of preemption, rather than retaliation alone and by ceasing to absorb blows to the nation without response.

> Israel's new strategic agenda can shape the regional environment in ways that grant Israel the room to refocus its energies back to where they are most needed: to rejuvenate its national idea. Ultimately, Israel can do more than simply manage the Arab-Israeli conflict through war. No amount of

weapons or victories will grant Israel the peace it seeks. When Israel is on a sound economic footing, and is free, powerful, and healthy internally, it will no longer simply manage the Arab-Israeli conflict; it will transcend it. As a senior Iraqi opposition leader said recently: "Israel must rejuvenate and revitalize its moral and intellectual leadership. It is an important, if not the most important, element in the history of the Middle East." Israel—proud, wealthy, solid, and strong—would be the basis of a truly new and peaceful Middle East.

> — *"A Clean Break: A New Strategy for Securing the Realm,"*
> *policy paper written for Israeli Prime Minister Benjamin Netanyahu,*
> *mid-1996, under the auspices of an Israeli think tank, the Institute for*
> *Advanced Strategic and Political Studies. Authors included Richard Perle,*
> *Douglas Feith, and David Wurmser, now all policymakers in or policy*
> *advisors to the Bush administration.*

Iraq's future will profoundly affect the strategic balance in the Middle East. The battle to dominate and define Iraq is, by extension, *the battle to dominate the balance of power in the Levant* over the long run. Iraq tried to take over its neighbor, Kuwait, a catastrophic mistake that has accelerated Iraq's descent into internal chaos. This chaos has created a vacuum in an area geo-strategically central, and rich with human and natural resources. The vacuum tempts Iraq's neighbors to intervene, especially Syria, which is also driven to control the region. Iraq's chaos and Syria's efforts simultaneously provide opportunities for the Jordanian monarchy. Jordan is best suited to manage the tribal politics that will define the Levant in the wake of failed secular-Arab nationalism. If Jordan wins, then Syria would be isolated and surrounded by a new pro-western Jordanian-*Israeli*-Iraqi-Turkish bloc. It would be prudent for *the United States and Israel* to abandon the quest for "comprehensive peace," including its "land for peace" provision with Syria, since it locks the United States into futile attempts to prop-up local tyrants and the unnatural states underneath them. Instead, the United States and Israel can use this competition over Iraq to improve *the regional balance of power* in favor of regional friends like Jordan.

> — *"Coping with Crumbling States: A Western and Israeli Balance of Power*

Strategy for the Levant," policy paper written for an Israeli think tank, the Institute for Advanced Strategic and Political Studies, December 1996, by David Wurmser, now a State Department official in the Bush administration.

In the [occupied] territories, the Arab world, and *in Israel*, Bush's support for Sharon is being credited to the pro-Israel lobby, meaning Jewish money and the Christian Right. [In April 2002] state department professionals convinced Bush that it was important to quell the violence in the territories before assaulting Iraq. The US military supported that view, emphasizing the critical importance of the ground bases in Saudi Arabia and Egypt, for the success of the mission. But according to a well-placed American source, the weather vane turned. Vice President Dick Cheney, Defense Secretary Donald Rumsfeld, and Rumsfeld's deputy, Paul Wolfowitz, asked Bush what kind of coalition-shmoalition he needed to win the war in Afghanistan. They calmed his concerns by saying there's no chance the situation in the territories will shake the regimes of Mubarak in Egypt and the Abdullahs in Jordan and Saudi Arabia. Last Saturday [April 20], the president convened his advisors in Camp David, for another discussion of the crisis in the territories and Iraq. They decided to sit on the fence.

— Israeli commentator Akiva Eldar, Ha'aretz, April 26, 2002

It echoes the hawks in the Bush administration, but Israel has its own agenda in backing a US attack on Iraq. As Egypt and other Arab allies issue vehement warnings to dissuade Washington, Israel's fear is that the US will back off. "If the Americans do not do this now," said Israeli Deputy Defense Minister and Labor Party member Weizman Shiry on Wednesday, "it will be harder to do it in the future. In a year or two, Saddam Hussein will be further along in developing weapons of mass destruction. It is a world interest, but especially an American interest to attack Iraq. And as deputy defense minister, I can tell you that the United States will receive any assistance it needs from Israel," he added.

Viewed through the eyes of Israel's hawkish leaders, however, a US strike is not about Iraq only. Decision makers believe it will strengthen Israel's hand on the Palestinian front and throughout the region. Deputy Interior

Minister Gideon Ezra suggested this week that a US attack on Iraq will help Israel impose a new order, *sans Arafat*, in the Palestinian territories. "The more aggressive the attack is, the more it will help Israel against the Palestinians. The understanding would be that what is good to do in Iraq, is also good for here," said Ezra. He said a US strike would "undoubtedly deal a psychological blow" to the Palestinians. Yuval Steinitz, a Likud party member of the Knesset's Foreign Affairs and Defense Committee, says he sees another advantage for Israel. The installation of a pro-American government in Iraq would help Israel vis-à-vis another enemy: Syria. "After Iraq is taken by US troops and we see a new regime installed as in Afghanistan, and Iraqi bases become American bases, it will be very easy to pressure Syria to stop supporting terrorist organizations like Hezbollah and Islamic Jihad, to allow the Lebanese army to dismantle Hezbollah, and maybe to put an end to the Syrian occupation in Lebanon," he says. "If this happens we will really see a new Middle East. It might be enough not to invade Syria but just to have an American or UN blockade so that no one can ship weapons to it," Steinitz adds. Mr. Ezra predicts a US strike would "calm down the entire region" by eliminating "the extremism of Saddam."

— *Ben Lynfield, Christian Science Monitor, August 30, 2002*

As the Bush administration debates going to war against Iraq, its most hawkish members are pushing a sweeping vision for the Middle East that sees the overthrow of President Saddam Hussein of Iraq as merely a first step in the region's transformation. The argument for reshaping the political landscape in the Mideast has been pushed for years by some Washington think tanks and in hawkish circles. It is now being considered as a possible US policy with the ascent of key hard-liners in the administration, from Paul Wolfowitz and Douglas Feith in the Pentagon to John Hannah and Lewis Libby on the vice president's staff and John Bolton in the State Department, analysts and officials say. Iraq, the hawks argue, is just the first piece of the puzzle. After an ouster of Hussein, they say, the United States will have more leverage to act against Syria and Iran, will be in a better position to resolve the Israeli-Palestinian conflict, and will be able to rely less on Saudi oil.

The thinking does not represent official US policy. But increasingly the argument has served as a justification for a military attack against Iraq, and elements of the strategy have emerged in speeches by administration officials, most prominently Vice President Dick Cheney. *A powerful corollary of the strategy is that a pro-US Iraq would make the region safer for Israel* and, indeed, its staunchest proponents are ardent supporters of the Israeli right-wing. Administration officials, meanwhile, have increasingly argued that the onset of an Iraq allied to the US would give the administration more sway in bringing about a settlement to the Israeli-Palestinian conflict, though Cheney and others have offered few details on precisely how. In its broadest terms, the advocates argue that a democratic Iraq would unleash similar change elsewhere in the Arab world. "Everyone will flip out, starting with the Saudis," said Meyrav Wurmser, director of the Center for Middle East Policy at the Hudson Institute in Washington [and another author of the 1996 policy paper written for Israel, above]. "It will send shock waves throughout the Arab world. Look, we already are pushing for democracy in the Palestinian Authority, though not with a huge amount of success, and we need a little bit more of a heavy-handed approach," she said. "But if we can get a democracy in the Palestinian Authority, democracy in Iraq, get the Egyptians to improve their human rights and open up their system, it will be a spectacular change. After a war with Iraq, then you really shape the region."

— *John Donnelly and Anthony Shadid,*
Boston Globe, September 10, 2002

Slowly, President Bush's war plan against Iraq is emerging from the thick fog. At first it looked like a collection of hazy slogans, but gradually it is becoming clear that it has definite, if hidden, aims. The war plan of the Bushies makes sense only if the US leadership is ready (more than that, is actually longing) for the occupation of Iraq in order to remain there for many, many years. But in the eyes of Bush and his advisors, this is a very worthwhile investment that would yield immense benefits. Among others:

- The main objective of the American economy
  (and therefore of American policy) is the oil of the Caspian Sea.

- The existence of a secure American base in the heart of the Arab world will also enable Washington to bully all the Arab regimes, lest they stray from the straight and narrow.
- The new situation will destroy the last remnants of Arab independence. Even today, almost all the Arab countries are dependent on America.

A massive American physical presence in their midst will put an end to any pretense of Arab power and unity. A grandiose, world-embracing, yet simple and logical design. What does it remind me of? In the early 80's, I heard about several plans like this from Ariel Sharon (which I published at the time). His head was full of grand designs for restructuring the Middle East, the creation of an Israeli "security zone" from Pakistan to Central Africa, the overthrow of regimes and installing others in their stead, moving a whole people (the Palestinians) and so forth. I can't help it, but the winds blowing now in Washington remind me of Sharon. I have absolutely no proof that the Bushies got their ideas from him, even if all of them seem to have been mesmerized by him. But the style is the same, a mixture of megalomania, creativity, arrogance, ignorance and superficiality—an explosive mixture.

Sharon's grand design floundered, as we know. The bold flights of imagination and the superficial logic did not help;—Sharon simply did not understand the real currents of history. I fear that the band of Bush, Cheney, Rumsfield, Rice, Wolfowitz, Perle *and all the other little Sharons* are suffering from the same syndrome. Sharon may believe that he will be the big winner of such an American move, though history may show that he brought a historical disaster on us. He may succeed in exploiting the ensuing anarchy in order to drive the Palestinians out of the country. But within a few years Israel could find itself surrounded by a new Middle East. A region full of hatred, dreaming of revenge, driven by religious and nationalist fanaticism. And in the end, the Americans will go home. We will be left here alone. But people like Bush and Sharon do not march to the beat of history. They are listening to a different drummer.

— Israeli peace activist Uri Avnery,

CounterPunch.org, September 10, 2002

Ever since the Bush administration ordered the CIA to nurture the exiled Iraqis, nothing happens to them by accident. [Jordanian] Prince Hasan didn't just happen to drop in [on a meeting of Iraqi exiles in London] because he was in town. The Hashemite dynasty has never given up its dream to revive the Iraqi throne. It could be a great job for Hasan, whose older brother [the late King Hussein] denied him the Jordanian kingdom at the last minute. It's true that restoring a monarchy in Iraq does not exactly fit the Bush administration's vision of a democratic Middle East. But there are signs that it fits some old dreams of a few of the key strategists around the Bush-Cheney-Rumsfeld triangle running America's Iraq policy. A few weeks ago, Richard Perle invited the Pentagon chiefs to a meeting with researchers from a Washington think tank. According to information that reached a former top official in the Israeli security services, the researchers showed two slides to the Pentagon officials. The first was a depiction of the three goals in the war on terror and the democratization of the Middle East: Iraq, a tactical goal; Saudi Arabia, a strategic goal; and Egypt, the great prize. The triangle in the next slide was no less interesting: Palestine is Israel, Jordan is Palestine, and Iraq is the Hashemite Kingdom.

—*Israeli commentator Akiva Eldar, Ha'aretz, October 1, 2002*

The summer of 1993 saw the emergence of two contradictory paths concerning Israel and its place in the Middle East. The signing of the Oslo agreement raised hopes for Israel's integration into a web of political, security and economic cooperation with its Arab neighbors. At the same time, Harvard Prof. Samuel Huntington published his essay, "The Clash of Civilizations," in which he argued that the conflicts around the world would no longer be over ideology, but over culture instead. "Islam has bloody borders," Huntington wrote, counting Israel as a "Western creation" on the fault lines of the conflict, along with Kashmir and Bosnia. The idea was accepted enthusiastically by the Israeli right wing. It also had some supporters on the left, most noticeably Ehud Barak, who described Israel as a Western fortress in the region, "a villa in the jungle."

As of now, it appears that the argument was settled in favor of the clash of civilizations theory, which has taken over the political and security establishment in Israel. The appeal of the clash of civilizations theory is also expressed in the Israeli enthusiasm for the expected American assault on Iraq, in the hope of showing the Arabs who's the boss in the region. *Israel is the only country to absolutely support the American decision, and has urged it to act, and quickly.* The tangible result of the change in consciousness has been deepening Israel's dependence on American defense and economic support. Sharon led that policy. The same Sharon says there are no free lunches in policy and is now begging for aid from Washington, trying to point the American cannon in the direction of its next target after Iraq.

—*Israeli correspondent Aluf Benn, Ha'aretz, November 14, 2002*

The embrace of US President George W. Bush is Ariel Sharon's chief asset as he vies for another term of office as prime minister. Sharon is finding it hard to show any achievements during his 20 months in power. The only card left in his hand is the diplomatic card, as personified by Israel's good relations with the White House, and all of Sharon's campaign revolves around it. Sharon and his cronies are now asking the voters for an extended period of grace, and are promising that next year will be the year that counts. All of their hopes and expectations are pointed toward Washington: *an American attack on Iraq is seen as the lever which can extricate Israel from its economic, security and social quagmire.* It is hoped that the removal of Saddam Hussein from power will set in motion a "domino effect," will end the Palestinian Intifada, bring about the end of Yasser Arafat's regime and eradicate the threat to Israel from Iran, Syria and Hezbollah.

—*Israeli correspondent Aluf Benn, Ha'aretz, November 18, 2002*

To understand the genesis of this extraordinary [US global] ambition, it is also necessary to grasp the moral, cultural and intellectual world of American nationalism in which it has taken shape. This nationalism existed long before last September, but it has been inflamed by those attacks and, equally dangerously, it has become *even more entwined with the nationalism of the Israeli Right.* The banal propaganda portrayal of Saddam as a crazed and suicidal dictator plays well on the American street, but I don't believe that it is a view shared by the Administration. Rather, their intention is partly to retain an absolute certainty of being able to defend the Gulf against an Iraqi attack, but, more important, to retain for the US and Israel a free hand for intervention in the Middle East as a whole. From the point of view of Israel, the Israeli lobby and their representatives in the Administration, the apparent benefits of such a free hand are clear enough. For the group around Cheney, the single most important consideration is guaranteed and unrestricted access to cheap oil, controlled as far as possible at its source. [A]s alternative technologies develop, they could become a real threat to the oil lobby, which, like the Israeli lobby, is deeply intertwined with the Bush Administration. War with Iraq can therefore be seen as a satisfactory outcome for both lobbies.[W]hat the Administration hopes is that by crushing another middle-sized state at minimal military cost, all the other states in the Muslim world will be terrified into full co-operation in tracking down and handing over suspected terrorists, and into forsaking the Palestinian cause. The idea, in other words, is to scare these states not only into helping with the hunt for al-Qaʻida, but into *capitulating to the US and, more important, Israeli agendas in the Middle East.*

"The road to Middle East peace lies through Baghdad" is a line that's peddled by the Bush Administration and the Israeli lobby. It is just possible that some members of the Administration really believe that by destroying Israel's most powerful remaining enemy they will gain such credit with Israelis and the Israeli lobby that they will be able to press compromises on Israel. But this is certainly not what public statements by members of the Administration, let alone those of its Likud allies in Israel, suggest. It's far more probable, therefore, that most members of the Bush and Sharon Administrations hope that the crushing of Iraq will so demoralize the Palestinians, and so reduce wider Arab support for them, that it will be possible to force them to accept a Bantustan settlement bearing no resemblance to independent statehood. From the point of view of the Arab-Israeli conflict, war with Iraq also has some of the character of a *Flucht nach vorn*, an "escape forwards," on the part of the US Administration. On the one hand, it has become clear that the conflict is integrally linked to everything else that happens in the Middle East, and therefore cannot simply be ignored, as the Bush Administration tried to do during its first year in office. On the other hand, even those members of the American political elite who have some understanding of the situation and a concern for justice are terrified of confronting Israel and the Israeli lobby in the ways which would be necessary to bring any chance of peace. When the US demands "democracy" in the Palestinian territories before it will re-engage in the peace process it is in part, and fairly cynically, trying to get out of this trap.

—Anatol Lieven, Senior Associate at the Carnegie Endowment for International Peace, London Review of Books, December 2002

If you want to know what the administration has in mind for Iraq, here's a hint: It has less to do with weapons of mass destruction than with implementing an ambitious US vision to redraw the map of the Middle East. The new map would be drawn with an eye to two main objectives: controlling the flow of oil and *ensuring Israel's continued regional military superiority.* [Patrick] Clawson [a policy analyst with the Washington Institute for Near East Policy], whose institute enjoys close ties with the Bush administration, was candid during a Capitol Hill forum on a post-Hussein Iraq in 1999: "US oil companies would have an opportunity to make significant profits," he said. "We should not be embarrassed about the commercial advantages that would come from a re-integration of Iraq into the world economy." [...] But taking over Iraq and remaking the global oil market is not necessarily the endgame. The next steps, favored by *hard-liners determined to elevate Israeli security above all other US foreign policy goals*, would be to destroy any remaining perceived threat to the Jewish state: namely, the regimes in Syria and Iran. In 1998, [David] Wurmser, now in the State Department, told the Jewish newspaper *Forward* that if [Iraqi opposition leader] Ahmad Chalabi were in power and extended a no-fly, no-drive zone in northern Iraq, it would provide the crucial piece for an anti-Syria, anti-Iran bloc. "It puts Scuds out of the range of Israel and provides the geographic beachhead between Turkey, Jordan and Israel," he said. "This should anchor the Middle East pro-Western coalition." [Richard] Perle, in the same 1998 article, told *Forward* that *a coalition of pro-Israeli groups* was "at the forefront with the legislation with regard to

Iran. One can only speculate what it might accomplish if it decided to focus its attention on Saddam Hussein."

Now, Israeli Prime Minister Ariel Sharon has joined the call against Tehran, arguing in a November interview with the *Times* of London that the US should shift its focus to Iran "the day after" the Iraq war ends.[T]he hard-liners in and around the administration seem to know in their hearts that the battle to carve up the Middle East would not be won without the blood of Americans and their allies. "One can only hope that we turn the region into a caldron, and faster, please," [Michael] Ledeen preached to the choir at *National Review Online* last August. "That's our mission in the war against terror."

— *UC Berkeley journalism professor Sandy Tolan, Los Angeles Times,*
December 1, 2002

The immediate and laudatory purpose of a United States military campaign against Iraq is to stamp out the regime of Saddam Hussein, the world's most psychopathic ruler, and to strike a blow against terrorism and the proliferation of weapons of mass destruction. As such this is *a welcome move from Israel's standpoint, whatever the consequences.* [T]he American planners, who display considerable disdain for most of the Muslim and Arab world, seem to think that the forcible removal of Saddam's evil regime and the consequent implantation of an American military presence in the wild Middle East will project a civilizing or liberating influence. They are not alone; not a few progressive Arab thinkers (and many Israelis) appear to welcome this American *deus ex machina* into the region.

— *Israeli military/political analyst, Yossi Alpher, bitterlemons.org,*
December 23, 2002

I think that the conquest of Iraq will really create a New Middle East. Put differently: the Middle East will enter a new age. For the time being this will happen without us, as long as there's no Palestinian solution. Many peoples in the region are ruled by frightened dictators who have to decide whom to fear more, the terrorists or the war against terrorism.

Asad fears for his legitimacy due to the war against terrorism. Arafat can also lose his legitimacy. The Saudis gave money for terrorism due to fear. No terrorist-sponsoring country is democratic. In those countries [that support terrorism] there will be revolutions. Television will play a role like in the collapse of the Iron Curtain. This will happen with the Palestinians, too. The Arab world is ripe for internal revolution like the USSR and China in the past decade.

— Former Israeli Prime Minister Shimon Peres, bitterlemons.org,
December 23, 2002

Republican Sen. Chuck Hagel of Nebraska, having just returned from a week-long fact-finding trip to the Middle East, addressed the Chicago Council of Foreign Relations Dec. 16 and said out loud what is whispered on Capitol Hill: "The road to Arab-Israeli peace will not likely go through Baghdad, as some may claim." The "some" are led by Israeli Prime Minister Ariel Sharon. In private conversation with Hagel and many other members of Congress, *the former general leaves no doubt that the greatest US assistance to Israel would be to overthrow Saddam Hussein's Iraqi regime.* That view is widely shared inside the Bush administration, and is *a major reason why US forces today are assembling for war.*

As the US gets ready for war, its standing in Islam, even among longtime allies, stands low. Yet, the Bush administration has tied itself firmly to Gen. Sharon and his policies. In private conversation, National Security Advisor Condoleezza Rice has insisted that Hezbollah, not al-Qa'ida, is the world's most dangerous terrorist organization. How could that be, considering al-Qa'ida's global record of mass carnage? In truth, Hezbollah is the world's most dangerous terrorist organization from Israel's standpoint. While viciously anti-American in rhetoric, the Lebanon-based Hezbollah is focused on the destruction of Israel. Thus, Rice's comments suggest that the US war against terrorism, accused of being Iraq-centric, actually is Israel-centric. That ties George W. Bush to Ariel Sharon. What is widely perceived as an indissoluble Bush-Sharon bond creates tension throughout Islam. On balance, war with Iraq may not be inevitable but is highly probable. *That it looks like Sharon's war* disturbs Americans such as Chuck Hagel, who have no use for Saddam Hussein but worry about the background of an attack against him.

—Robert Novak, Washington Post, December 26, 2002

With a scandal chipping away at his government, Prime Minister Ariel Sharon changed the subject to Iraq this week and found his country eager to listen. Mr. Sharon's remarks seemed to strike a chord with Israeli voters, who are concerned about an Iraqi attack and still traumatized by the events of 1991, when 39 Iraqi missiles landed in the country. To some Israeli commentators, the week's events highlighted the lingering effects of the first war with Iraq, and how Mr. Sharon, an incumbent prime minister with an unmatched reputation for toughness, is the likely beneficiary of any debate over a second one. "What happened in 1991 is an unfinished chapter," said Asher Arian, a senior fellow at the Israel Democracy Institute in Jerusalem. "*The Israeli public feels it has a score to settle.* When Sharon talks about Iraq, it has enormous resonance." Part of the explanation for the positive reception of Mr. Sharon is the genuine fear that many Israelis harbor of an Iraqi attack. The other factor, commentators here say, is the looming memory of the Persian Gulf war of 1991. For Israelis, proud of their military successes over the years, that war was a different experience. At American insistence, they endured Iraqi missile attacks without fighting back. "The gulf war was the first time in Israel's history where people had to hide and run way," said Itzhak Galnoor, former commissioner of the Israeli civil service. 'For Israelis to be helpless, that was very traumatic.'

— Dexter Filkins, New York Times, December 29, 2002

Authors' note: Given the prevailing atmosphere in the United States for debate on Israel, the frequency with which critics of Israel are accused of malicious ethnic motives, and the widespread skittishness about associating Israel or American Jews with war planning against Iraq, the following items are of particular interest. The first of these items reports a clear Jewish effort to suppress any evidence of Jewish support for war. The second is evidence, from a non-Jewish perspective, of the effect of the silence imposed on critics of Israel.

A group of US political consultants has sent pro-Israel leaders a memo urging them to keep quiet while the Bush administration pursues a possible war with Iraq. The six-page memo was sent by the Israel Project, a group funded by American Jewish organizations and individual donors. Its authors said the main audience was American Jewish leaders, but much of the memo's language is directed toward Israelis. The memo reflects a concern that involvement by Israel in a US-Iraq confrontation could hurt Israel's standing in American public opinion and undermine international support for a hard line against Iraqi President Saddam Hussein. "Let American politicians fight it out on the floor of Congress and in the media," the memo said. "Let the nations of the world argue in front of the UN. Your silence allows everyone to focus on Iraq rather than Israel."

An Israeli diplomat in Washington said the Israeli government did not request or fund the efforts of the Israel Project and that Israeli leaders were unlikely to follow all the advice. "These are professional public relations people," the diplomat said. "There's also a political-diplomatic side." The Iraq memo was issued in the past few weeks and labeled "confidential property of the Israel Project," which is led by Democratic consultant Jennifer Laszlo Mizrahi with help from Democratic pollster Stan Greenberg and Republican pollsters Neil Newhouse and Frank Luntz. Several of the consultants have advised Israeli politicians, and the group aired a pro-Israel ad earlier this year. "If your goal is regime change, you must be much more careful with your language because of the potential backlash," said the memo, titled "Talking About Iraq." It added: "*You do not want Americans to believe that the war on Iraq is being waged to protect Israel rather than to protect America.*" In particular, the memo urged Israelis to pipe down about the possibility of Israel responding to an Iraqi attack. "Such certainty may be Israeli policy, but asserting it publicly and so overtly will not sit well with a majority of Americans because it suggests a pre-determined outcome rather than a measured approach," it said.

— *Dana Milbank, Washington Post, November 27, 2002*

[We need to] demystify the question of why we have become unable to discuss our relationship with the current government of Israel. Whether the actions taken by that government constitute self-defense or a particularly inclusive form of self-immolation remains an open question. The question of course has a history. This open question, and its history, are discussed rationally and with considerable intellectual subtlety in Jerusalem and Tel Aviv. Where the question is not discussed rationally, where in fact the question is rarely discussed at all, since so few of us are willing to see our evenings turn toxic, is in New York and Washington and in those academic venues where the attitudes and apprehensions of New York and Washington have taken hold. The president of Harvard recently warned that criticisms of the current government of Israel could be construed as "anti-Semitic in their effect if not their intent." The very question of the US relationship with Israel, in other words, has come to be seen as unraisable, potentially lethal, the conversational equivalent of an unclaimed bag on a bus. We take cover. We wait for the entire subject to be defused, safely insulated behind baffles of invective and counter invective. Many opinions are expressed. Few are allowed to develop. Even fewer change.

— *Joan Didion, New York Review of Books, January 16, 2003*

For a prince must have two kinds of fear; one internal as regards his
subjects, one external as regards foreign powers.

—*Niccolo Machiavelli, The Prince*

If you once forfeit the confidence of your fellow citizens, you can
never regain their respect and esteem. It is true that you may fool all
the people some of the time; you can even fool some of the people all
of the time; but you can't fool all of the people all of the time.

—*Abraham Lincoln*

If the great essential truth about terrorism is that some people just
hate the United States, the obvious next question is, Why? But to the
Bush administration, that is of no interest. But it should be of great
interest to any concerned citizen.

—*Michael Kinsley, Washington Post, September 2004*

6 | Why do They Hate Us?[1]

DISINFOPEDIA

F ROM US PRESIDENT George W. Bush:

"Americans are asking, *why do they hate us?* They hate what we see right here in this chamber—a democratically elected government. Their leaders are self-appointed. They hate our freedoms—our freedom of religion, our freedom of speech, our freedom to vote and assemble and disagree with each other. They want to overthrow existing governments in many Muslim countries, such as Egypt, Saudi Arabia, and Jordan. They want to drive Israel out of the Middle East. They want to drive Christians and Jews out of vast regions of Asia and Africa."[2]

From the White House Press Secretary, Ari Fleischer 12th October 2001:

Question: "A number of news organizations have done some very in-depth reporting on why they hate us—if you want to use that phrase. And it's not just they don't understand our goodness. I mean, you hear a lot of policy issues—troops in Saudi Arabia, our Israeli policy, Iraqi women and children—you know, you hear those things over and over again. The President in his response to his question did not mention any of the policy things that some Muslims have problems with. Is there any reexamination of our policy going on right now?"

Mr. Fleischer: "No, the policies of the government remain the same and it's important to communicate those policies to people around the world."[3]

From Charley Reese:

"It is absurd to suppose that a human being sitting around suddenly stands up and says: 'You know, I hate freedom. I think I'll go blow myself up.'"[4]

From Zbigniew Brzezinski, national security advisor during the Carter administration: *National Catholic Reporter*, 26th October 2001. In a CNN interview, Brzezinski said the United States should be going after the terrorists and added:

"But we have to ask ourselves, what fuels them? What sustains them? What produces the terrorists?"

His answer:

"Political rage over a number of issues."[5]

From Osama bin Laden, 24th November 2002:

• "Because you attacked us and continue to attack us."
• "Under your supervision, consent and orders, the governments of our countries which act as your agents, attack us on a daily basis."
• "You steal our wealth and oil at paltry prices because of your international influence and military threats."
• "Your forces occupy our countries; you spread your military bases throughout them; you corrupt our lands, and you besiege our sanctities, to protect the security of the Jews and to ensure the continuity of your pillage of our treasures."
• "You have starved the Muslims of Iraq, where children die every day. It is a wonder that more than 1.5 million Iraqi children have died as a result of your sanctions, and you did not show concern. Yet when three thousand of your people died, the entire world rises and has not yet sat down."[6]

7th November 2001:

• "The American people should remember that they pay taxes to their government, they elect their president, their government manufactures arms and gives them to Israel and Israel uses them to massacre Palestinians. The American Congress endorses all government measures and this proves that the entire America is responsible for the atrocities perpetrated against Muslims."[7]

3rd November 2001:

• "[...] when we move to Palestine and Iraq, there can be no bounds to what can be said. Over one million children were killed in Iraq. The killing is continuing. As for what is taking place in Palestine these days, I can only say we have no one but God to complain to. What is taking place cannot be tolerated by any nation. I do not say from the nations of the human race, but from other creatures, from the animals. They would not tolerate what is taking place. A confidant of mine told me that he saw a butcher slaughtering a camel in front of another camel. The other camel got agitated while seeing the blood coming out of the other camel. Thus, it burst out with rage and bit the hand of the man and broke it. How can the weak mothers in Palestine endure the killing of their children in front of their eyes by the unjust Jewish executioners with US support and with US aircraft and tanks? Israel and US 'are one': Those who distinguish between America and Israel are the real enemies of the nation."[8]

29th March 1997:

• "We declared *jihad* against the US government, because the US government is unjust, criminal and tyrannical. It has committed acts that are extremely unjust, hideous and criminal whether directly or through its support of the Israeli occupation of the Prophet's Night Travel Land (Palestine). And we believe the US is directly responsible for those who were killed in Palestine, Lebanon and Iraq. The mention of the US reminds us before everything else of those innocent children who were dismembered, their heads and arms cut off in the recent explosion that took place in Qana (in Lebanon)."[9]

From the Pentagon's Defense Science Board in 1998:

"A strong correlation exists between US involvement in international situations and an increase in terrorist attacks against the United States. President Bill Clinton has also acknowledged that link. The board, however, has provided no empirical data to support its conclusion. This paper fills that gap by citing many examples of terrorist attacks on the United States in retaliation for US intervention overseas. The numerous incidents cataloged suggest that the United States could reduce the chances of such devastating—and potentially catastrophic—terrorist attacks by adopting a policy of military restraint overseas."[10]

From the Pew Research Center for the People and the Press:

"In 2002, in a survey of thirty-eight thousand people in forty-four countries, the Pew Research Center found that the US global image had slipped. But when we went back this spring after the war in Iraq—conducting another sixteen-thousand interviews in twenty countries and the Palestinian Authority—it was clear that favorable opinions of the US had plummeted."

"What is most striking, however, is how anti-Americanism has spread. It is not just limited to Western Europe or the Muslim world. Moreover, there is considerable evidence that the opinion many Muslims have of the United States has gone beyond mere loathing. In this year's Pew survey, majorities in seven of eight predominantly Muslims nations believe the US may someday threaten their country.
    • American policies and power fuel resentment for the US throughout the world.
    • Global publics believe the United States does too little to solve world problems and backs policies that increase the yawning global gap between rich and poor.
    • For Muslims, it has become an article of faith that the US unfairly sides with Israel in its conflict with the Palestinians—99% of Jordanians, 96% of Palestinians and 94% of Moroccans agree. So too do most Europeans. The only dissent comes from Americans, where a 47% plurality sees US policy as fair. Even in Israel, more respondents view US policy as

unfair than say it is fair.

    • Resentment of American power, as much as its policies or leadership, also drives anti-American sentiments. People around the world—and particularly in Western Europe and the Middle East—are suspicious of America's unrivaled power."[11]

Later, in 2004:

"A year after the war in Iraq, discontent with America and its policies has intensified rather than diminished. Opinion of the United States in France and Germany is at least as negative now as at the war's conclusion, and British views are decidedly more critical. Perceptions of American unilateralism remain widespread in European and Muslim nations, and the war in Iraq has undermined America's credibility abroad. Doubts about the motives behind the US-led war on terrorism abound, and a growing percentage of Europeans want foreign policy and security arrangements independent from the United States. Across Europe, there is considerable support for the European Union to become as powerful as the United States."[12]

From a report by the *Christian Science Monitor* 27th September 2001:

• "Most Arabs and Muslims knew the answer, even before they considered who was responsible."
• "And voices across the Muslim world are warning that if America doesn't wage its war on terrorism in a way that the Muslim world considers just, America risks creating even greater animosity."
• "Arabs do not share Mr. Bush's view that the perpetrators did what they did because 'they hate our freedoms.' Rather, they say, a mood of resentment toward America and its behavior around the world has become so commonplace in their countries that it was bound to breed hostility, and even hatred. And the buttons that Mr. bin Laden pushes in his statements and interviews win a good deal of popular sympathy. :
    • the injustice done to the Palestinians,
    • the cruelty of continued sanctions against Iraq,
    • the presence of US troops in Saudi Arabia,

> • the repressive and corrupt nature of US-backed Gulf governments."[13]

In one view published by the *Council on Foreign Relations* January/February 2003:

"Two groups have come under examination in the 'why do they hate us?' debate that has unfolded since September 11, 2001. One comprises the perpetrators of violence and terrorism—the Osama bin Ladens, the Mohammad Attas, and some suicide bombers. They are fanatics in every sense of the word. Their interpretations of politics and Islam are so extreme that they disparage the great majority of Muslim Middle Easterners as 'unbelievers.' They are not going to be deterred by debate, compromise, sanctions, or even the threat of death. The challenge they pose to the United States is a security issue, a matter to be dealt with through careful police work and military action. America's resources are adequate for dealing with this threat."

"The vastly larger group of Muslim Middle Easterners who express anger toward the United States and evince some sympathy for bin Laden pose a far more serious challenge. This group's members are afflicted by middle-class frustrations, governed by political systems that give them no voice, and burdened by economies that offer them few opportunities. They are witnessing a conflict over land and sacred places in which they perceive the United States as applying two standards of equity and two standards of measuring violence, each in favor of Israel. That resulting frustration and anger leads to expressions of sympathy for those who resort to violence against the United States."[14]

What the US papers said 12th September 2001:

"American newspapers have reacted with a mixture of defiance and patriotism to yesterday's attack. But none are jingoistic. Although many declare the attack as an 'act of war,' none calls for revenge."[15]

What the Middle East papers said 12th September 2001[16] and additionally 13th September 2001[17] :

"For all their differences, the media in the Middle East—from Iraq to Israel— seem to be agreed on one thing: whoever was to blame for yesterday's carnage in the US, the attacks are the result of American policies."

From the *Jerusalem Post* 13th December 2001:

"The answer is that America has been attacked not for what it has done wrong, but for what it has done right, and for being the hope of the entire world."[18]

Allegedly from the *Wall Street Journal* 12th September 2001:

"The east coast carnage was the fruit of the Clinton administration's Munich-like appeasement of the Palestinians."[19]

From Adam Young:

"The US sends billions in financial and military aid to Egypt, Saudi Arabia, and Jordan each year to prop up these regimes against 'fundamentalist' popular Islamic movements (which are the only way dissent can be expressed in these regimes, since Islam is the only thing these rulers can't outlaw). The US also gives political support to corrupt and oppressive dictatorships, such as exist in Algeria and Tunisia. Everywhere, the US favors and aids the status quo of political repression and dictatorship. This hypocrisy is what fuels Arab and Muslim anger."[20]

From Harry Browne and millions of clear minds around the world:

"There was only one possible motive for the 9/11 attackers: they were protesting the way the American government has been using force for half a century to overrule the wishes of people in the Middle East and elsewhere."[21]

US Secretary of Defense, Donald Rumsfeld suggested in a memo dated October 2003 that "the *madrassas* and the radical clerics are recruiting, training and deploying" terrorists against us.[22]

Col. Dan Smith (Ret.) responds that:

"Focusing on the *madrassas* and other institutions that promote narrowly focused viewpoints, whether directed against the US, the West, their own government, or international organizations, misses the crux of the problem. (Were this a problem in auto mechanics, the solution to eliminating harmful emissions will not be found at the output end—the tailpipe—but at the input—the engine combustion chamber.) It misses because the real problem is the repression of human and civil rights and liberties, often in the name of 'security,' in countries whose regimes have been supported or condoned by the US and other western nations."[23]

The Guardian, 12th September 2001:

"Nearly two days after the horrific suicide attacks on civilian workers in New York and Washington, it has become painfully clear that most Americans simply don't get it. From the president to passersby on the streets, the message seems to be the same: this is an inexplicable assault on freedom and democracy, which must be answered with overwhelming force—just as soon as someone can construct a credible account of who was actually responsible. [...] any glimmer of recognition of why people might have been driven to carry out such atrocities, sacrificing their own lives in the process—or why the United States is hated with such bitterness, not only in Arab and Muslim countries, but across the developing world—seems almost entirely absent."[24]

NOTES

1. Abridged by editor from http://www.disinfopedia.org

2. http://www.whitehouse.gov/news/releases/2001/09/20010920-8.html

3. http://www.whitehouse.gov/news/releases/2001/10/20011012-15.html

4. http://reese.king-online.com/Reese_20031107/index.php

5. http://www.findarticles.com/cf_dls/m1141/1_38/79965766/p1/article.jhtml

6. http://observer.guardian.co.uk/worldview/story/0,11581,845725,00.html and http://www.the7thfire.com/Politics%20and%20History/why_do_they_hate_us.htm

7. http://www.the7thfire.com/Politics%20and%20History/why_do_they_hate_us.htm

8. http://www.the7thfire.com/Politics%20and%20History/why_do_they_hate_us.htm

9. http://www.the7thfire.com/Politics%20and%20History/why_do_they_hate_us.htm

10. http://www.cato.org/pubs/fpbriefs/fpb-050es.html

11. http://people-press.org/commentary/display.php3?AnalysisID=77

12. http://people-press.org/reports/display.php3?ReportID=206

13. http://www.csmonitor.com/2001/0927/p1s1-wogi.html

14. http://www.foreignaffairs.org/20030101faessay10222/john-waterbury/hate-your-policies-love-your-institutions.html

15. http://media.guardian.co.uk/attack/story/0,1301,550616,00.html

16. http://media.guardian.co.uk/presspublishing/story/0,7495,550558,00.html and http://www.guardian.co.uk/september11/story/0,11209,600886,00.html

17. http://www.guardian.co.uk/september11/story/0,11209,600970,00.html

18. http://www.guardian.co.uk/september11/story/0,11209,600970,00.html

19. http://www.guardian.co.uk/september11/story/0,11209,600944,00.html

20. http://www.mises.org/fullarticle.asp?control=818

21. http://www.harrybrowne.org/articles/TerrorismReason.htm

22. As reported October 22, 2003, by Dave Moniz and Tom Squitieri, Defense memo: "A grim outlook" and Rumsfeld's war-on-terror memo in *USA Today*.

October 16, 2003

TO: Gen. Dick Myers, Paul Dundes Wolfowitz, Gen. Pete Pace, Doug Feith.

FROM: Donald Rumsfeld
SUBJECT: Global War on Terrorism

The questions I posed to combatant commanders this week were: Are we winning or losing the Global War on Terror? Is DoD changing fast enough to deal with the new 21st century security environment? Can a big institution change fast enough? Is the USG changing fast enough?

DoD has been organized, trained and equipped to fight big armies, navies and air forces. It is not possible to change DoD fast enough to successfully fight the global war on terror; an alternative might be to try to fashion a new institution, either within DoD or elsewhere — one that seamlessly focuses the capabilities of several departments and agencies on this key problem.

With respect to global terrorism, the record since Septermber 11th seems to be:

• We are having mixed results with Al-Qaida, although we have put considerable pressure on them — nonetheless, a great many remain at large.

• USG has made reasonable progress in capturing or killing the top 55 Iraqis.

• USG has made somewhat slower progress tracking down the Taliban — Omar, Hekmatyar, etc.

• With respect to the Ansar Al-Islam, we are just getting started.

• Have we fashioned the right mix of rewards, amnesty, protection and confidence in the US?

• Does DoD need to think through new ways to organize, train, equip and focus to deal with the global war on terror?

• Are the changes we have and are making too modest and incremental? My impression is that we have not yet made truly bold moves, although we have have made many sensible, logical moves in the right direction, but are they enough?

• Today, we lack metrics to know if we are winning or losing the global war on terror. Are we capturing, killing or deterring and dissuading more terrorists every day than the *madrassas* and the radical clerics are recruiting, training and deploying against us?

• Does the US need to fashion a broad, integrated plan to stop the next generation of terrorists? The US is putting relatively little effort into a long-range plan, but we are putting a great deal of effort into trying to stop terrorists. The cost-benefit ratio is against us! Our cost is billions against the terrorists' costs of millions.

- Do we need a new organization?
- How do we stop those who are financing the radical *madrassa* schools?
- Is our current situation such that "the harder we work, the behinder we get"?

It is pretty clear that the coalition can win in Afghanistan and Iraq in one way or another, but it will be a long, hard slog.

- Does CIA need a new finding?
- Should we create a private foundation to entice radical *madradssas* to a more moderate course?
- What else should we be considering?

Please be prepared to discuss this at our meeting on Saturday or Monday.
Thanks

See: http://www.usatoday.com/news/washington/executive/rumsfeld-memo.htm

23. http://www.fpif.org/papers/rumsfeldqa2003.html
24. http://www.guardian.co.uk/september11/story/0,11209,600944,00.html

Defining Terrorism

PHILLIP CRYAN

TERRORISM MAY BE the most important, powerful word in the world right now. In the name of doing away with terrorism, the United States bombed Afghanistan and continues to occupy Iraq. Political leaders around the world were quick to declare their support for the new US war, each seeking to re-name their own enemies as "terrorists."

According to the polls, many people in the US believe that war on the al-Qa'ida network is justified in retaliation for the September 11 attacks. The defined enemy of the US military campaign has not, however, been just the people responsible for the September 11 attacks, but "terrorism" in general. The US has declared a "War on Terrorism"—a war which also includes as enemies, as President Bush has made clear, "all those who harbor terrorists." What exactly do these words, "terrorism" and "harboring," mean? What definitions are we using?

LEGAL DEFINITION:
SEEKING INTERNATIONAL CONSENSUS

The difficulty of answering this question was stated concisely in a *New York Times* article: "immediately beyond al-Qa'ida, the high moral condemnations of global terrorism rapidly become relative, and the definition blurred." The international community has been actively seeking consensus on the definition of "terrorism" for many years, to no avail.

Twelve separate international conventions have been signed, each covering a specific type of criminal activity—seizure of airplanes, political assassination, the use of explosives, hostage-taking, etc. Broad ratification of these treaties has been difficult to achieve; and the more fundamental issue of creating a comprehensive, binding international convention against terrorism has been set aside, after repeated efforts, as practically irresolvable. As the UN puts it, "the question of a definition of terrorism has haunted the debate among States for decades."

One of the points of heated contention in this debate has been whether the term "terrorism" should apply to the actions of States in the same way that it applies to the actions of non-State groups. It's easy to see why this question would be so contentious: whatever one's overall view of the Israeli/Palestinian conflict, for example, it's pretty easy to admit that unjustifiable acts of terror and murder have been committed by both sides. Should the two sides be held equally accountable, even though one is an already-recognized State and one is a national liberation movement? These kinds of questions have been repeatedly raised, not only in regard to the Middle East but also in regard to State-sponsored acts of terrorism throughout the world.

Since international consensus has been so difficult to reach, for the purposes of this brief discussion of terrorism and "harboring" I'll use the FBI's definition: "Terrorism is the unlawful use of force or violence against persons or property to intimidate or coerce a government, the civilian population, or any segment thereof, in furtherance of political or social objectives." How does such a definition line up with the goals and strategies of the "War on Terrorism"?

JUSTICE

How does a definition of terrorism such as the FBI's get applied? Who has the authority to judge what counts as "terrorism" and what doesn't? Is there a level playing field, internationally, for the persecution of terrorists?

A comment made by Syria's Information Minister, Adnan Omran, frames these problems in a provocative, yet also precise and urgent, way: "The Americans say either you are with us or you are with the terrorists. That is something God should say." The original title given to the US military campaign in Afghanistan—"Operation Infinite Justice"—seems to confirm Omran's concern. President Bush has indeed stated, in an address to Congress, that "Every nation, in every region, now has a decision to make: either you are with us, or you are with the terrorists." Is our government in fact equating its judgments, policies and military actions with the meting out of a God-like "infinite justice"? If so, what kind of moral clarity do we ground such authority in?

A brief review of some US political and military interventions over the last few decades reveals just how far we are (sadly, tragically) as a nation from having the kind of track-record and integrity required to wage such a war with a clear conscience and certainty of purpose. Following the FBI definition, our government has repeatedly, in country after country, used "force or violence" "unlawfully," "to intimidate or coerce a government, [a] civilian population, or [a] segment thereof," in order to achieve "political or social objectives." I will mention only a few examples.

TERRORISM AND "HARBORING" OF TERRORISTS BY THE US

US intervention in Nicaragua provides an astounding, but by no means extraordinary, example. First, some background: by 1934, when the authoritarian Somoza regime was established, the US had already occupied the country militarily on at least four different occasions, established training schools for right-wing militia, dismantled two liberal governments, and helped to orchestrate fake elections. In 1981, the CIA began to organize the "Contras"—many of whom had already received training from the US military as members of the Somozas' National Guardsmen—to overthrow the progressive Sandinista government. In other words: the CIA "harbored," recruited, armed and trained the Contras, in order to "coerce" and overthrow a government, and terrorize a people, through violent means ("in furtherance of political [and] social objectives"). US intervention went well beyond "harboring," however, in this case. In 1984, the CIA mined three Nicaraguan harbors. When Nicaragua took this action to the World Court, an $18 billion judgment was brought against the US. The US response was to simply refuse to acknowledge the Court's jurisdiction.

Another striking example of US terrorist activity was the bombing of a suburban Beirut neighborhood in March 1985. This attack—which killed eighty people and wounded two hundred others, making it the single largest bombing attack against a civilian target in the modern history of the Middle East—was ordered by the director of the CIA (William Casey) and authorized by President Reagan. Another US attack on civilians, the 1986 bombing of Libya, is listed by the UN's Committee on the Legal Definition of Terrorism as a "classic case" of terrorism—on a short list that includes the bombing of PAN AM 103, the first attempt made on the World Trade Center, and the bombing of the Oklahoma City Federal Building.

Other instances of US support for, or direct engagement in, terrorist acts include:

• overthrow of the democratically elected Allende government in Chile in 1973—leading to widespread torture, rape and murder by the military regime, and to the termination of civil liberties;

• extensive support for a right-wing junta in El Salvador that was responsible for 35,000 civilian deaths between 1978 and 198;

• assassination attempts, exploded boats, industrial sabotage and the burning of sugar fields in Cuba;

• the training of thousands of Latin American military personnel in torture methods at the School of the Americas (now called the Western Hemisphere Institute for Security Cooperation);

• providing huge quantities of arms—far more than any other nation—to various combatants in the Middle East and West Asia, and

• massive support, in funds and arms, for Israeli attacks on Palestinian civilians.

The rationale provided for many of these interventions—in those cases where a rationale was in fact provided—was the "war on Communism." This often served as an alibi, however, for the protection of economic interests: access to natural resources (oil in particular), consumer markets and cheap labor for "First World" corporations.

DOUBLE STANDARDS

US officials successfully pressured the UN to impose sanctions on Libya for its initial refusal to extradite Libyan agents implicated in the

PAN AM 103 bombing; but they (US officials) have consistently refused to extradite US citizens—all of whom have ties to the CIA—charged with acts of terrorism in Costa Rica and Venezuela (including blowing up a Cuban airliner in 1976). We have provided no support for attempts to bring Augusto Pinochet (the Chilean military dictator responsible for the atrocities described above) to justice—probably not only because our own government was so heavily involved in his rise to power, but also because the prosecution of such an obvious State-terrorist would open the door, legally, for the likes of Henry Kissinger and Otto Reich to be tried for having ordered terrorist acts. Establishment of the International Criminal Court—which should be in operation before the end of 2002, since it has now been ratified by the required number of countries— has likewise been resisted by the US

The double standards at play, the hypocrisy and bad faith involved, in calling for the world to decide whether it is "with us" or "with the terrorists" should by now be fairly evident. To use President Bush's terms, our nation has—tragically—in reality championed "Fear" and suppressed "Freedom" in a great many countries, for millions of people. We have been directly responsible for acts of terrorism, and for the "harboring" of terrorists, on an almost unimaginable scale in terms of human death and the creation of fear. When Green Berets trained the Guatemalan army in the 1960s—leading to a campaign of bombings, death squads and "scorched earth" assaults that killed or "disappeared" two-hundred thousand—US Army Colonel John Webber called it "a technique of counter-terror." This comment can serve as a reminder and warning for us now—not that there are not real terrorist threats to our national security, but that we have to be incredibly careful about how we define terrorism, who defines it, and what tactics are used to uproot it. There is something truly chilling, as the Syrian Information Minister pointed out, in the apparent consensus within the United States that we stand for "Freedom" and all that is "Good" in the world, and that we are somehow entitled and equipped to mete out "infinite justice."

BLOWBACK

As most of us have read at some point since September 2001, the attacks on the Taliban and al-Qa'ida are complicated, politically and morally, by our military and economic support for the *Mujahideen* war against the USSR in the 1980s. We provided over $7 billion in arms and funds, plus training supplied through the Pakistani intelligence agency, ISI. The lesson: lines of distinction between "Good" and "Evil" are dramatically more blurred and complex than President Bush, Secretary Rumsfeld, and most voices in the media seem to want us to think. US training and funding of the *Mujahideen*—literally, US harboring of terrorists—were a crucial part of what enabled the Taliban to come to power in Afghanistan. This is what military analysts call "blowback."

A less frequently discussed but equally important instance of blowback is the US role in Iraq. Throughout the 1980s, the US actively supported Iraq as an ally against Iran and as a potentially profitable future source for raw goods and market for exports. Though the US government was clearly aware of Saddam Hussein's extermination of Kurds and his development of military and chemical weapons capacity (there is ample documentation of the extent of US leaders' knowledge), the US continued to support Hussein's government with billions of dollars in export credit insurance. This situation only changed when US oil access was threatened (by the invasion of Kuwait). Up until then, no matter how extreme the fiscal duplicity, military build-up or outright genocide committed by Hussein's regime, US officials urged "hard-headedness" and a recognition of Iraq's strategic and economic importance as an ally. Again, this brief outline of a piece of recent history complicates the current situation enormously: how can Hussein be "Evil" and "a terrorist," and we "Good" and the world's defenders of "Freedom," if we funded him through many of the atrocities he's committed, fully conscious that he was committing them? As with Afghanistan, a short memory on our part, together with a preference for black-and-white thinking, are likely to prove responsible for yet more suffering and violence now and down the road.

The situation in Iraq is perhaps more complex and tragic than any other, in terms of the US role past and future. US-imposed sanctions (almost every country in the UN opposed them) against Iraq have led to the deaths of approximately one million people. Two Assistants to the Secretary-General of the UN responsible for humanitarian aid to Iraq resigned in protest, calling the sanctions "genocide." Our government waged a methodical, hugely violent, daily war against the people of Iraq—attacking civilians in numbers that grotesquely dwarf the horrific tragedies of September 11. When asked in 1996 what she felt about the deaths of five-hundred thousand children caused by the sanctions, then-Secretary of State Madeleine Albright replied that it was "a very hard choice," but, all things considered, "we think the price is worth it." (It is worth pausing here, for a moment, perhaps, to try to take in the reality of such a statement.)

LANGUAGE'S DANGERS

In a world of such extreme violence, hypocrisy and moral ambiguity, we need to be careful about whom we listen to, whom we believe, and whose wars we fight. The phrase "War on Terrorism" has been quickly picked up by political leaders seeking to advance a host of different agendas domestically and internationally.

The phrase is likely to be with us for some time (Secretary Rumsfeld has described the war as "sustained, comprehensive and unrelenting"), used as the justification for all sorts of military, political and economic interventions abroad— not to mention its domestic effects: the removal of civil liberties (through the USA-Patriot Act and other new legislation) and the slashing of social programs in order to fund military expansion.

Some examples of international uses:

• The US sent military advisors to the Philippines, to assist the government in what it describes as a campaign against Muslim "terrorists." The number of "advisors" was later increased.

• Ariel Sharon's government has attempted to justify its campaign against Palestinians entirely through the rhetoric of "exterminating terrorism." Hundreds, perhaps thousands, of Palestinian civilians have been killed, countless homes have been destroyed, and the Israeli/Palestinian peace process has been set back many years if not decades.

• Sharon, with some help from the US, is responsible for introducing a pivotal new phrase into the "War on Terrorism's" rhetorical/political arsenal: "You can't negotiate with terrorists." This phrase has since been used, to the great benefit of State violence, in Colombia, the US and elsewhere; it serves to discredit peaceful diplomatic strategies and to justify the military repression of opponents. The phrase has spread rapidly: a landlord in Boston, Massachusetts, whose tenants used a Gandhian non-violent demonstration to pressure him to offer affordable housing, recently refused to meet with the tenants, stating: "you can't negotiate with terrorists."

• A *Heritage Foundation* report named Iraq, Iran, Syria, Sudan, and Libya as States which need to be "put on notice [...] that they will not escape America's wrath if they continue to support international terrorism." President Bush famously singled out North Korea, Iran and Iraq as an "Axis of Evil" in his State of the Union address.

• Colombian army officials switched, within just a few days of September 11, from calling the FARC and ELN rebels "narco-guerrillas" to calling them "narco-terrorists." Francis X. Taylor, head of the US Department of State's Office of Counterterrorism, stated in October that these Colombian groups will "get the same treatment as other terrorist groups," including "where appropriate—as we are doing in Afghanistan—the use of military power." A Supplemental bill currently under consideration in the US Congress seeks to free up the military support (helicopters, advisors, intelligence, etc.) provided to Colombia in recent years under the "War on Drugs" for direct "counter-terrorist" (i.e., counterinsurgency) efforts. The Bush administration's budget for 2003 included $98 million to protect a Colombian pipeline operated by Los Angeles-based Occidental Petroleum from "infrastructure terrorism."

• The ongoing US "War on Drugs" policy for Colombia—called "Plan Colombia"—involves a brand of chemical warfare, just what was feared so greatly last fall in the US Crop-duster planes spray broad-spectrum herbicides onto the Colombian countryside and the people who live there, leading to widespread illness, displacement, poverty and hunger.

• Russia has been seeking, since September 11, to cast Chechen rebels as terrorists, and Georgia as a terrorist-harboring State, in order to legitimate its use of violence in those two arenas.

• China is expected to use the justifying rhetoric of the "War on Terrorism" to further crack down on Uighur Muslims, Tibetans and Taiwan.

FINAL REMARKS

On October 4, 2001, Amnesty International published a report on the tightening of security in the wake of September 11. In the report, Amnesty observed that "some of the definitions of terrorism under discussion are so broad that they could be used to criminalize anyone out of favor with those in power." We must be careful with definitions; we must know what we mean. When asked to define "terrorism," Sir Jeremy Greenstock, the British diplomat initially charged with leading UN efforts to combat terrorism, replied: "What looks, smells and kills like terrorism is terrorism." It is, simply, not that simple. Such oversimplifications and appeals to "obviousness" are not only inaccurate but profoundly dangerous, as the Amnesty International report suggests. And clear delineation of definitions will become increasingly complicated and difficult to achieve over time, as more governments and special interests seek to advance the policies they favor by calling them "attacks on terrorism."

Who are we, the United States, in the end, to tell the world what Good and Evil are, after our history of unlawful military interventions, double standards, and outright engagement in acts of terrorism? President Bush's explanation for anti-US sentiment—"These people can't stand freedom"—is ludicrous, deplorable: it grotesquely misrepresents the realities of current world politics and the history of 20th century US foreign policy. In light of that history, and of the fact that the definition of "terrorism" has been debated without resolution for decades, it is our responsibility as US citizens and as human beings to think carefully, long and hard and well, about this war; to notice and question each use of the word "terrorism" that we come across; and to educate ourselves, and one another, about the reality of suffering in the world in which we live—its causes, and ways to truly uproot them.

SOURCES

"Definitions of Terrorism," The United Nations Office for Drug Control and Crime Prevention, October 9, 2001

Arundhati Roy, "The Algebra of Infinite Justice," *The Guardian*, September 29 2001

"Democratic Gains Falter With Tighter Security in Central Europe," *New York Times*, October 4, 2001

Kim R. Holmes, "America Strikes Back: Looking Ahead," *The Heritage Foundation*, October 8, 2001

Stephen Zunes, "International Terrorism," October 15, 2001

"A Growing List of Foes Now Suddenly Friends" *New York Times*, October 5, 2001

Iraqgate: Saddam Hussein, US Policy and the Prelude to the Persian Gulf War, 1980-1994, Digital National Security Archive, October 15, 2001

Legal Definition of Terrorism, GA: Legal Committee, October 9, 2001

Conventions Against Terrorism, the United Nations Office for Drug Control and Crime Prevention, on October 9, 2001

"The Challenges of Alliance with Russia," *New York Times* October 5, 2001

"Terrorist Threats Against America," testimony by Francis X. Taylor to the Committee on International Relations, on October 11, 2001

Mark Rosenfelder, US Interventions in Latin America, on October 15, 2001

Reyko Huang, *Lessons from History: US Policy Toward Afghanistan, 1978-2001*, Center for Defense Information Terrorism Project, October 15, 2001

"US May Use Military in Hemisphere," *Associated Press*, October 16, 2001

Nick Cooper, "Defining 'Terrorism,'" *Indymedia*, October 15, 2001

8 | Myth & Denial in the War against Terrorism
Just Why do Terrorists Terrorize?
WILLIAM BLUM

IT DIES HARD. It dies very hard. The notion that terrorist acts against the United States can be explained by envy and irrational hatred and not by what the United States does to the world—i.e., US foreign policy—is alive and well.

The fires were still burning intensely at Ground Zero when Colin Powell declared: "Once again, we see terrorism, we see terrorists, people who don't believe in democracy [...]"[1]

George W. picked up on that theme and ran with it. He's been its leading proponent ever since September 11 with his repeated insistence, in one wording or another, that terrorists are people who hate America and all that it stands for, its democracy, its freedom, its wealth, its secular government." (Ironically, the President and Attorney General John Ashcroft probably hate our secular government as much as anyone.)

Here he is more than a year after September 11: "The threats we face are global terrorist attacks. That's the threat. And the more you love freedom, the more likely it is you'll be attacked."[2]

In September 2002, the White House released the "National Security Strategy," purported to be chiefly the handiwork of Condoleezza Rice, which speaks of the "rogue states" which "sponsor terrorism around the globe; and reject basic human values and hate the United States and everything for which it stands."

In July of the following year, we could hear the spokesman for Homeland Security, Brian Roehrkasse, declare: "Terrorists hate our freedoms. They want to change our ways."[3]

Thomas Friedman, the renowned foreign policy analyst of the *New York Times*, would say *amen*. Terrorists, he wrote in 1998 after two US embassies in Africa had been attacked, "have no specific ideological program or demands. Rather, they are driven by a generalized hatred of the US, Israel and other supposed enemies of Islam."[4]

This *idée fixe*—that the rise of anti American terrorism owes nothing to American policies—in effect postulates an America that is always the aggrieved innocent in a treacherous world, a benign United States government peacefully going about its business but being "provoked" into taking extreme measures to defend its people, its freedom and its democracy. There consequently is no good reason to modify US foreign policy, and many people who might otherwise know better are scared into supporting the empire's wars out of the belief that there's no choice but to crush without mercy—or even without evidence—this irrational international force out there that hates the United States with an abiding passion.

Thus it was that Afghanistan and Iraq were bombed and invaded with seemingly little concern in Washington that this could well create many new anti American terrorists. And indeed, since the first strike on Afghanistan in October 2001 there have been literally scores of terrorist attacks against American institutions in the Middle East, South Asia and the Pacific, more than a dozen in Pakistan alone: military, civilian, Christian, and other targets associated with the United States, including the October 2002 bombings in Bali, Indonesia, which destroyed two nightclubs and killed more than 200 people, almost all of them Americans and their Australian and British allies. The following year brought the heavy bombing of the US managed Marriott Hotel in Jakarta, Indonesia, the site of diplomatic receptions and 4th of July celebrations held by the American Embassy.

A US State Department report on worldwide terrorist attacks showed that the year 2003 had more "significant" terrorist incidents than at any time since the department began issuing statistics in 1982; the 2003 figures do not include attacks on US troops in Iraq.[5]

TERRORISTS IN THEIR OWN WORDS

The word "terrorism" has been so overused in recent years that it's now commonly used simply to stigmatize any individual or group one doesn't like, for almost any kind of behavior involving force. But the word's *raison d'être* has traditionally been to convey a political meaning, something along the lines of the deliberate use of violence against civilians and property to intimidate or coerce a government or the population in furtherance of a political objective.

Terrorism is fundamentally propaganda, a very bloody form of propaganda. It follows that if the perpetrators of a terrorist act declare what their objective was, their statement should carry credibility, no matter what one thinks of the objective or the method used to achieve it. Let us look at some of their actual declarations.

The terrorists responsible for the bombing of the World Trade Center in 1993 sent a letter to the *New York Times* which stated, in part: "We declare our responsibility for the explosion on the mentioned building. This action was done in response for the American political, economical, and military support to Israel the state of terrorism and to the rest of the dictator countries in the region."[6]

Richard Reid, who tried to ignite a bomb in his shoe while aboard an American Airline flight to Miami in December 2001, told police that his planned suicide attack was an attempt to strike a blow against the US campaign in Afghanistan and the Western economy. In an e-mail sent to his mother, which he intended her to read after his death, Reid wrote that it was his duty "to help remove the oppressive American forces from the Muslims land."[7]

After the bombings in Bali, one of the leading suspects—later convicted—told police that the bombings were "revenge" for "what Americans have done to Muslims." He said that he wanted to "kill as many Americans as possible" because "America oppresses the Muslims."[8]

In November 2002, a taped message from Osama bin Laden began: "The road to safety begins by ending the aggression. Reciprocal treatment is part of justice. The [terrorist] incidents that have taken place [...] are only reactions and reciprocal actions."[9]

That same month, when Mir Aimal Kasi, who killed several people outside of CIA headquarters in 1993, was on death row, he declared: "What 1 did was a retaliation against the US government" for American policy in the Middle East and its support of Israel.[10]

It should be noted that the State Department warned at the time that the execution of Kasi could result in attacks against Americans around the world.[11] It did not warn that the attacks would result from foreigners hating or envying American democracy, freedom, wealth, or secular government.

Similarly, in the days following the start of US bombing of Afghanistan there were numerous warnings from US government officials about being prepared for retaliatory acts, and during the war in Iraq, the State Department announced: "Tensions remaining from the recent events in Iraq may increase the potential threat to US citizens and interests abroad, including by terrorist groups."[12]

Another example of the difficulty the Bush administration has in consistently maintaining its simplistic *idée fixe*: In June 2002, after a car bomb exploded outside the US Consulate in Karachi killing or injuring more than 60 people, the *Washington Post* reported that "US officials said the attack was likely the work of extremists angry at both the United States and Pakistan's president, Gen. Pervez Musharraf, for siding with the United States after September 11 and abandoning support for Afghanistan's ruling Taliban."[13]

George W. and others of his administration may or may not believe what they tell the world about the motivations behind anti American terrorism, but, as in the examples just given, some officials have questioned the party line for years. A Department of Defense study in 1997 concluded: "Historical data show a strong correlation between US involvement in international situations and an increase in terrorist attacks against the United States."[14]

Former US president Jimmy Carter told the *New York Times* in a 1989 interview:

> We sent Marines into Lebanon and you only have to go to Lebanon, to Syria or to Jordan to witness first hand the intense hatred among many people for the United States because we bombed and shelled and unmercifully killed totally innocent villagers—women and children and farmers and housewives—in those villages around Beirut. [...] As a result of that [...] we became kind of a Satan in the minds of those who are deeply resentful. That is what precipitated the taking of our hostages and that is what has precipitated some of the terrorist attacks."[15]

Colin Powell has also revealed that he knows better. Writing of this same 1983 Lebanon debacle in his memoir, he forgoes clichés about terrorists hating democracy: "The USS New Jersey started hurling 16 inch shells into the mountains above Beirut, in World War II style, as if we were softening up the beaches on some Pacific atoll prior to an invasion. What we tend to overlook in such situations is that other people will react much as we would."[16]

The ensuing terrorist attack against US Marine barracks in Lebanon took the lives of two hundred and forty-one American military personnel.

The bombardment of Beirut in 1983 and 1984 is but one of many examples of American violence against the Middle East and/or Muslims since the 1980s. The record includes:
• the shooting down of two Libyan planes in 1981
• the bombing of Libya in 1986
• the bombing and sinking of an Iranian ship in 1987
• the shooting down of an Iranian passenger plane in 1988
• the shooting down of two more Libyan planes in 1989
• the massive bombing of the Iraqi people in 1991
• the continuing bombings and sanctions against Iraq for the next 12 years
• the bombing of Afghanistan and Sudan in 1998
• the habitual support of Israel despite the routine devastation and torture it inflicts upon the Palestinian people
• the habitual condemnation of Palestinian resistance to this
• the abduction of "suspected terrorists" from Muslim countries, such as Malaysia, Pakistan, Lebanon and Albania, who are then taken to places like Egypt and Saudi Arabia, where they are tortured
• the large military and hi-tech presence in Islam's holiest land, Saudi Arabia, and elsewhere in the Persian Gulf region
• the support of undemocratic, authoritarian Middle East governments from the Shah of Iran to the Saudis.

"How do I respond when I see that in some Islamic countries there is vitriolic hatred for America?" asked George W. "I'll tell you how I respond: I'm amazed. I'm amazed that there's such misunderstanding of what our country is about that people would hate us. I am—like most Americans, I just can't believe it because I know how good we are."[17]

It's not just people in the Middle East who have good reason for hating what the US government does. The United States has created huge numbers of potential terrorists all over Latin America during a half century of American actions far worse than what it's done in the Middle East. If Latin Americans shared the belief of radical Muslims, that they would go directly to paradise for martyring themselves in the act of killing the great Satan enemy, by now we might have had decades of repeated terrorist horror coming from south of the border. As it is, there have been many non suicidal terrorist attacks against Americans and their buildings in Latin America over the years.

To what extent do Americans really believe the official disconnection between what the US does in the world and anti American terrorism? One indication that the public is somewhat skeptical came in the days immediately following the commencement of the bombing of Iraq on March 20 of this year. The airlines later announced that there had been a sharp increase in cancellations of flights and a sharp decrease in future flight reservations in those few days.[18]

In June, the Pew Research Center released the results of polling in twenty Muslim countries and the Palestinian territories that brought into question another official thesis, that support for anti American terrorism goes hand in hand with hatred of American society. The polling revealed that people interviewed had much more "confidence" in Osama bin Laden than in George W. Bush. However, "the survey suggested little correlation between support for bin Laden and hostility to American ideas and cultural products. People who expressed a favorable opinion of bin Laden were just as likely to appreciate American technology and cultural products as people opposed to bin Laden. Pro—and anti bin Laden respondents also differed little in their views on the workability of Western style democracy in the Arab world."[19]

THE IRAQI RESISTANCE

The official Washington mentality about the motivations of individuals they call terrorists is also manifested in current US occupation policy in Iraq. Secretary of War, Donald Rumsfeld has declared that there are five groups opposing US forces—looters, criminals, remnants of Saddam

Hussein's government, foreign terrorists and those influenced by Iran.[20] An American official in Iraq maintains that many of the people shooting at US troops are "poor young Iraqis" who have been paid between $20 and $100 to stage hit and run attacks on US soldiers. "They're not dedicated fighters," he said. "They're people who wanted to take a few potshots."[21]

With such language do American officials avoid dealing with the idea that any part of the resistance is composed of Iraqi citizens who are simply demonstrating their resentment about being bombed, invaded, occupied, and subjected to daily humiliations.

Some officials convinced themselves that it was largely the most loyal followers of Saddam Hussein and his two sons who were behind the daily attacks on Americans, and that with the capture or killing of the evil family, resistance would die out; tens of millions of dollars were offered as reward for information leading to this joyful prospect. Thus it was that the killing of the sons elated military personnel. US Army trucks with loudspeakers drove through small towns and villages to broadcast a message about the death of Hussein's sons. "Coalition forces have won a great victory over the Baath Party and the Saddam Hussein regime by killing Uday and Qusay Hussein in Mosul," said the message broadcast in Arabic. "The Baath Party has no power in Iraq. Renounce the Baath Party or you are in great danger." It called on all officials of Hussein's government to turn themselves in.[22]

What followed was several days of some of the deadliest attacks against American personnel since the guerrilla war began. Unfazed, American officials in Washington and Iraq continue to suggest that the elimination of Saddam will write *finis* to anti-American actions.

Another way in which the political origins of terrorism are obscured is by the common practice of blaming poverty or repression by Middle Eastern governments (as opposed to US support for such governments) for the creation of terrorists. Defenders of US foreign policy cite this also as a way of showing how enlightened they are. Here's Condoleezza Rice:

> [The Middle East] is a region where hopelessness provides a fertile ground
> for ideologies that convince promising youths to aspire not to a university
> education, a career or family, but to blowing themselves up, taking as many
> innocent lives with them as possible. We need to address the source of the

problem.[23]

Many on the left speak in a similar fashion, apparently unconscious of what they're obfuscating. This analysis confuses terrorism with revolution.

In light of the several instances mentioned above, among others which could be cited, of US officials giving the game away, in effect admitting that terrorists and guerrillas may be, or in fact are, reacting to actual hurts and injustices, it may be that George W. is the only true believer among them, if in fact *he is one*. The thought may visit leaders of the American Empire, at least occasionally, that all their expressed justifications for invading Iraq and Afghanistan and for their "War on Terrorism" are no more than fairy tales for young children and grown up innocents. But officialdom doesn't make statements to represent reality. It constructs stories to legitimize the pursuit of interests. And the interests here are irresistibly compelling: creating the most powerful empire in all history, enriching their class comrades, remaking the world in their own ideological image.

Being the target of terrorism is just one of the prices you pay for such prizes, and terrorist attacks provide a great excuse for the next intervention, the next expansion of the empire, the next expansion of the military budget.

A while ago, I heard a union person on the radio proposing what he called "a radical solution to poverty—pay people enough to live on."

Well, I'd like to propose a radical solution to anti American terrorism—stop giving terrorists the motivation to attack America. As long as the imperial mafia insist that anti American terrorists have no good or rational reason for retaliation against the United States for anything the US has ever done to their countries, as long as US foreign policy continues with its bloody and oppressive interventions, the war on terrorism is as doomed to failure as the war on drugs has been.

If I were the president, I could stop terrorist attacks against the United States in a few days. Permanently. I would first apologize—very publicly and very sincerely—to all the widows and orphans, the impoverished and the tortured, and all the many millions of other victims of American imperialism. Then I would announce to every corner of the world that

America's global military interventions have come to an end. I would then inform Israel that it is no longer the 51st state of the union but—oddly enough—a foreign country. Then I would reduce the military budget by at least 90% and use the savings to pay reparations to the victims and repair the damage from the many American bombings, invasions and sanctions. There would be more than enough money. One year's military budget in the United States is equal to more than $20,000 per hour for every hour since Jesus Christ was born. That's one year.

That's what I'd do on my first three days in the White House. On the fourth day, I'd be assassinated.

SEPTEMBER 11 COMMISSION

On June 16, 2004, the National Commission on Terrorist Attacks Upon the United States (investigating the events of September 11, 2001), issued a report which stated that Khalid Sheik Mohammed, regarded as the mastermind of the attacks, wanted to personally commandeer one aircraft and use it as a platform to denounce US policies in the Middle East. Instead of crashing it in a suicide attack, the report says, Mohammed planned to kill every adult male passenger on the plane, contact the media while airborne, and land at a US airport. There he would deliver his speech before releasing all the women and children.[24]

The question once again arises: Why was Mohammed planning on denouncing US policies in the Middle East? Why wasn't he instead planning to denounce America's democracy, freedom, wealth and secular government?

Two days later, Islamic militants in Saudi Arabia beheaded an employee of the leading US defense contractor, Lockheed Martin, maker of the Apache helicopter, on which the victim, Paul Johnson, Jr., had long worked. His kidnappers said he was singled out for that reason. "The infidel got his fair treatment [...] Let him taste something of what Muslims have long tasted from Apache helicopter fire and missiles."[25]

ADDENDUM:

TERRORISTS AS MENTALLY RETARDED

The reluctance to ascribe rational human motivations to militant political opponents is not confined to American leaders. Documents disclosed in 2002 in Spain reveal that during the 1936-39 civil war, the Spanish fascists subjected their leftist prisoners to a battery of physical and psychological tests for the purpose of finding some inherent deformity that would explain their bizarre ideology. Unsurprisingly, they concluded that amongst the captured members of the pro republican International Brigades, almost a third of the British nationals were "mental retards." Another third were deemed to be suffering degenerative mental illnesses that were turning them into schizoids, paranoids or psychopaths. Their fall into Marxism was, in turn, exacerbated by the fact that 29% were also considered "social imbeciles." As *The Guardian* of London noted:

> For dictator General Francisco Franco's chief psychiatrist, Dr. Antonio Vallejo Nagera, it must have seemed obvious. If the generalissimo and his fellow right wing rebels in the Spanish civil war were crusaders for justice, God and the truth, then their leftwing opponents had to be mad, psychotic or at least congenitally subnormal.

Dr. Vallejo concluded: "Once more we see confirmed that social resentment, frustrated aspirations, and envy are the sources of Marxism."[26]

Also in 2002, it was reported that:

> In an attempt to divine the terrorist impulse, German officials authorized the removal and study of the brains of four Red Army Faction leaders following their deaths in the 1970s, according to news reports in Germany, but scientists apparently came up with no physiological explanation for the leaders' political violence.[27]

Anything for officials to avoid facing up to social and political realities.

NOTES

1. *Miami Herald*, September 12, 2001
2. *Agence France Presse*, November 19, 2002
3. *Washington Post*, August 1, 2003, p.4
4. *New York Times*, August 22, 1998, p.15
5. *Washington Post*, June 23, 2004
6. Jim Dwyer, et al., *Two Seconds Under the World* (New York, 1994), p.196; see also the statement made in court by Ramzi Ahmed Yousef, who planned the attack, *New York Times*, January 9, 1998, p.B4
7. *Washington Post*, October 3, 2002, p.6
8. *Agence France Press*, December 23, 2002; *Washington Post*, November 9, 2002
9. *Los Angeles Times*, November 13, 2002, p.6
10. *Associated Press*, November 7, 2002
11. Ibid.
12. Voice of America News, April 21, 2003
13. *Washington Post*, June 15, 2002
14. US Department of Defense, Defense Science Board 1997 Summer Study Task Force on DOD Responses to Transnational Threats, October 1997, Final Report, vol.1 http://www.acq.osd.mil/dsb/trans.pdf , p.31
15. *New York Times*, March 26, 1989, p.16
16. Colin Powell with Joseph E. Persico, *My American Journey* (New York, 1995), p.291
17. *Boston Globe*, October 12, 2001, p.28
18. *Washington Post*, March 27, 2003
19. Ibid., June 4, 2003, p.18
20. Pentagon briefing, June 30, 2003
21. *Washington Post*, June 29, 2003
22. Ibid., July 24, 2003, p.7
23. Ibid., August 8, 2003
24. Ibid., June 17, 2004, p.14
25. *Associated Press*, June 19, 2004
26. *The Guardian* (London), November 1, 2002
27. *Washington Post*, November 19, 2002

9 | Terminology in the Middle East Conflict

NEIL LOWRIE

T HE BATTLE BETWEEN Palestinians and Israelis over the West Bank and Gaza strip is played out nightly on our television sets. This vicious cycle of killing and counter-killing is being complemented by a much less visible but equally important war of words, whose use and misuse play an important part in swaying the impartial observer this way and that. One could venture so far as to say that words written over fifty years ago were the direct cause of the suffering we see today, for it was on the 29th November, 1947, that the United Nations resolution 181 was written partitioning Palestine into Jewish and Arab sections. Words, cleverly used, continue to blind us to the truths of the conflict to the current day.

Listen to a newsreel or read a newspaper and you will find terms that are used over and over again. These include "suicide bomber," "targeted killing," "terrorist," "Israeli Defense Forces" and "settlements" while Israelis will be also familiar with terms such as "Judea and Samaria."

Let us begin by looking at what are generally known as the "occupied territories." These lands include the West Bank, Gaza Strip and the Golan Heights conquered by Israel on the 5th June 1967. The events leading up to what became known as the six day war are disputed by both sides of the conflict, but what cannot be disputed is that on the 22nd November, 1967, the United Nations in resolution 242 called the "Withdrawal of Israeli armed forces from territories occupied in the recent conflict."

Such a clear statement cannot easily be misinterpreted, yet in the aftermath of the 1993 peace deal signed by Yasser Arafat and Isaac Rabin, the Clinton administration began using the term "disputed territories." These terms were specifically used to undermine international efforts to halt the building of illegal Israeli settlements in the West Bank. The argument was that if the ownership of the land was in dispute, then no decisions could be taken as to the legitimacy of these settlements until the ownership was agreed upon. Such terms soon began circulating in the media and served to de-legitimize Palestinian rights. No longer were the territories occupied, they were disputed. Even so, while "disputed" still implies some sort of disagreement over the possession of the land, Israeli newspapers such as the *Jerusalem Post* and Israeli government officials still routinely refer to the West Bank simply as "Judea and Samaria," thereby reducing it to a province of Israel. The Israeli Ministry of Foreign Affairs does not publish a map of the Israel and the occupied territories; it publishes one of Israel to include Judea and Samaria.

The Israeli settlements on the occupied West Bank are regarded as one of the most contentious issues of the second *Intifada* and one that led to the collapse of the Camp David talks in July 2000. Yet again, while these settlements are recognized by UN resolution 446 as having "no legal validity and constituting a serious obstruction to achieving a comprehensive, just and lasting peace in the Middle East," they are often referred to by media outlets such as CNN as "Jewish communities" or "suburbs of Jerusalem" if they happen to be in the vicinity. A community conjures up an image of a small number of people living in a picturesque and sleepy village. One such example is the settlement of Gilo overlooking Beit Jala, often described by CNN as a "Jewish neighborhood." In fact, this settlement was built in 1970 on land expropriated from the Palestinian towns of Beit Jala and Beit Safafa. It currently houses over thirty thousand settlers. Such settlements are connected by highways and are designed to break up the West Bank and destroy any territorial continuity. They are built on hilltops and dominate the surrounding areas and do not blend into the environment as well as traditional Palestinian stone houses do. The media's insistence on downplaying their symbolism and their effect on the politics of the region robs the impartial consumer of news of vital information.

Several misnomers have been widely circulated since the Palestinian uprising, or *Intifada*, began in September 2000. One of the best known must surely be the Israeli Defense Forces. More commonly known as the IDF, these include the army, navy and air force and are by all standards, branches of a modern and efficient military machine. Yet the term "defense" implies a defensive role, one in which the sole purpose of these forces is the defense of the homeland. Such a term is deliberately misleading, as the IDF has routinely shown its deadly offensive capabilities. Regular incursions into Arab land have been commonplace since the 1967 war, while the second *Intifada* has shown graphically that the theatre of operation of the IDF is not limited to internationally recognized borders, but that its main theatre of operations is in the occupied territories. Actions by the IDF are counter to its own doctrine that there is a "desire to avoid war by political means and a credible deterrent posture" while its offensive nature has led to another widely used misnomer, that of "targeted killing."

Using the dictionary definition of each word, a targeted killing implies accurately causing the death of a person or an animal. Such a term conveniently bypasses the moral and legal implications of such actions, and serves to mislead us as to the results of such an action when it occurs. Targeted killings are often undertaken against Palestinian activists on the assumption that they are involved in either political or military action against Israel. The favored instrument of such killing has been the used of air-launched guided missiles and occasionally tank shells or undercover squads. As the victim of such a killing is unsuspecting, a more accurate term would be an "assassination," defined as "to murder (a person, especially a public or political figure), usually by surprise attack." The operative word here is murder, as the victims of such an attack are not afforded the universal right to a fair trail as no evidence is submitted against them in a court of law. The Palestinian Center for Human Rights (PCHR) and LAW, the Palestinian Society for the Protection of Human Rights and the Environment submitted a report to the UN High Commission on Human Rights on the 20th February 2002 stating that fifty-three Palestinians have been assassinated while eighteen bystanders, including four children, were killed during these events. These killings are neither lawful nor are they accurate. It is left to the reader to decide how to label them.

One final term, often used and greatly misused, is the term "terrorist." Hardly an article has been written in recent months about the Middle East conflict without the term being mentioned. Once again, the Collins

English dictionary defines terrorism as the "systematic use of violence and intimidation to achieve some goal," while a terrorist is "a person who employs terror or terrorism, especially as a political weapon." It is here that the dictionary definition falls short of a full description, because it is clear that not only individuals, but organizations and states, can also systematically use violence and intimidation to achieve some goal. It would be a fruitless exercise to define the term in a way that is acceptable to all parties in the Middle East conflict and this essay is not the place to attempt to do so; rather, the use of the word when describing actions undertaken in similar circumstances will be examined. Let us first assume that regardless of the legality or the morality of an action, if it is carried out with the express interest of causing death or injury and to bring about a political goal, it is terrorism.

In Israeli media, the term terrorist is always used to describe a person perpetrating acts of violence against Israeli persons or property. These include Palestinian suicide bombers, those attacking Israeli military targets within and without the occupied territories or Lebanese fighting to free the occupied Shebaa Farms in Southern Lebanon. Such actions are clearly aimed at achieving a political goal. *The New York Times* routinely describes the Palestinian Hamas group as a "terrorist" organization and it members, "terrorists."

Actions by the Israeli armed forces however are routinely described as "targeted killings," "retaliatory" or "accidents." For example, an *Associated Press* report on the 16th April 2001 says that "Israeli helicopters and tanks hammered Palestinian positions in several parts of Gaza late Monday, retaliating for mortar shells fired at an Israeli town for the first time since fighting broke out seven months ago." On Sunday the 10th June 2001, Israeli tank fire killed three Bedouin women in their tent. Later, Israel Radio reported that army chief of staff Shaul Mofaz claimed that the killing of three Palestinian women in the Gaza Strip overnight was "probably a technical error."

Similarly, armed Israeli settlers have frequently attacked Palestinians. In a July 19th 2001, *New York Times* article written by Joel Greenberg, entitled "Three Arabs Slain; Jewish Settlers Claim Responsibility," three Palestinians were described as being killed by "Jewish gunmen" or "militant Jewish settlers." Similarly, a 23rd July 2001 *New York Times* article written by Clyde Haberman "Sharon Booed by Fellow Rightists Who Say He's Too Soft," the killers of the same three Palestinians were described as being "Jewish vigilantes." If we look back further in history at another conflict, during World War Two, the German army was regarded as occupying France and those Frenchmen resisting this occupation are now known a "resistance" or "freedom" fighters.

It is clear from the four examples dealing with terrorism above that actions undertaken by persons of different political affiliations, but that have the express motive of causing political change, are treated differently according to the protagonist. Journalists, who use the power of the pen to influence our views routinely, use specific works to elicit certain emotional responses in their readers or listeners. This is regardless of the fact that the actions themselves, viewed by an impartial observer, appear very similar and have similar results as far as the victim is concerned.

Further examples of skewed terminology exist. Palestinians who survived their ethnic cleansing in 1948 and became holders of the Israeli nationality are described as "Israeli Arabs" even though they have much more in common with Palestinians in the occupied territories than with the European immigrants who make up the majority of Israeli society. "Rubber bullets" are used to describe the steel cylinders coated with a thin layer of rubber fired at Palestinian protesters. This ignores their lethality and is an attempt at making them an acceptable method of controlling Palestinians for the global audience.

For certain, those sympathizing with the Israeli point of view will find articles where a Palestinian bias is detected. In either case, readers who rely on only one source of information are limiting themselves to one point of view, a view that expresses the writer's own opinion. It is important that in an age where vast amounts of information are available to us through different media outlets, that consumers constantly question the truth in what is presented to them as facts. Winston Churchill was quoted as saying that "In wartime [...] truth is so precious that it should always be attended by a bodyguard of lies."

Bear this in mind the next time you read something.

Of War, Islam & Israel

JOHN CHUCKMAN

WAR BETWEEN ISLAM and the nations of the West? There have been a good many careless words printed and broadcast in America touching on this simplistic idea. And an American president who lacks the most superficial knowledge of the world or its history offers no reassurance, as he lurches from one misstatement to another, that this idea is not being incorporated into national policy.

The concept of Islam as an intrinsically violent, anti-progressive opponent in the modern world is both ignorant and dangerous. The new prominence of this idea in America provides a good measure of the distorted information that exists in our political environment. It's almost as though the bloody, parochial views of Ariel Sharon on the nature of Palestinians had been exalted to a world view, worthy of every statesman's consideration.

How easily we forget that the history of organized Christianity provides almost certainly the bloodiest tale in all of human history.

The Crusades, that dark saga of Christianity written in blood and terror, continued sporadically over hundreds of years. They served little other purpose than gathering wealth through spoils and sacking cities and easing the periodic domestic political difficulties of the papacy and major princes of Europe.

We hear of the treatment of women under Islam in certain places, not remembering that Christian women were left locked in iron chastity belts for years while their husbands raped their way across the Near East. And the character of Salah al-din, hard warrior that he was, shines nobly in history compared to the moral shabbiness of Richard the Lionheart.

Europe wove a remarkable tapestry of horrors in the name of

Christianity from the beginning of the modern era. There was the Holy Inquisition, the Expulsion of the Jews from Spain, the Reformation, the Counter-Reformation, the Thirty Years' War, the English Civil War, the St Bartholomew Massacre, Cromwell's slaughter in Ireland, the enslavement and widespread extermination of native peoples in the Americas, the Eighty Years' War in Holland, the expulsion of the Huguenots from France, the pogroms, the burning of witches, and numberless other horrific events right down to the Holocaust itself, which was largely the work of people who considered themselves, as did the slave drivers of America's South, to be Christians.

Over and above the conflicts motivated by religion, European and American history, a history dominated by people calling themselves Christian, runs with rivers, lakes, and whole seas of blood. Just a sampling includes the Hundred Years' War, the War of the Spanish Succession, the Seven Years' War, the slave trade, the French Revolution, the Vendée, the Napoleonic Wars, the Trail of Tears, the Opium War, African slavery in the American South, the American Civil War, the Franco-Prussian War, the massacre in the Belgium Congo, the Crimean War, lynchings, the Mexican War, the Spanish-American War, the Korean War, the Vietnam War, World War I, the Spanish Civil War, and World War II. How anyone with this heritage can describe Islam as notably bloodthirsty plainly tells us that immense ignorance is at work here.

What limited knowledge I have of Islam is enough to know that there is no history, despite bloody characters like Tamerlane, to overtop Europe's excesses, and, in some cases, there has been generosity of spirit exceeding that shown by Christians.

The Moorish kings of Spain tended to follow the same tolerant attitude towards religion that the classical Romans had done. The Romans allowed any religion to flourish, often officially adopting the gods of a conquered people, so long as the religion represented no political threat to Rome's authority.

People today point to a well-publicized excess like the Taliban's destruction of ancient statues, apparently completely oblivious to the fact that the religiously-insane Puritans, direct ancestors of America's Christian fundamentalists, ran through the beautiful, ancient cathedrals of England after the Reformation, smashing stained glass, desecrating ancient tombs, destroying priceless manuscripts, and smashing sculptures.

A remarkably tolerant society flourished under the Moors in Spain for hundreds of years. Jews, Christians, and Muslims were tolerated, and the talented served the state in many high capacities regardless of religion. Learning advanced, trade flourished.

During the centuries of the Jewish Diaspora, the Arab people of the Holy Land looked after the holy places and largely treated Jewish visitors with hospitality and respect. There was none of the bitter hatred we see today. All this changed at the birth of modern Israel and the expulsion of Palestinians from places they had inhabited for centuries.

No reasonable, decent-minded person can deny that the manner of Israel's rebirth did a great injustice to the Palestinians. And the great powers, first Britain and then the United States, had entirely selfish motives in seeing this done.

Under the original UN proposal for Israel, there were to be two roughly equal states carved out of Palestine, and the city of Jerusalem was to have an international status. More than half a century later, what we have is an Israel that covers three-quarters of Palestine and militarily occupies the rest.

Yet somehow, the burden of appropriate behavior, in a fuzzily defined "peace process" leading to some fuzzily-defined Palestinian state at some undefined date, is always placed upon the Palestinians. They are supposed to live patiently, exhibiting the peacefulness of model citizens in Dorothy's Kansas, while under a humiliating occupation, in order just to earn the privilege of talking to Israel about the situation.

I often wonder how Americans, with their Second-Amendment rights and hundreds of millions of guns, would behave under such circumstances. Would they patiently wait decade after decade, watching "settlers" fresh from other places build on what was their land? Watching bulldozers flatten their orchards? Watching their people harassed and often demeaned at checkpoints as they simply travel from one point to another near their homes? Not being able to so much as build a road or a sewer without the almost impossible-to-get permission of the occupying authorities? Being told that only their patient behavior can earn them the right to talk with those who control their lives? Looking at the situation in that hypothetical light may offer a better appreciation for what the

Palestinians have endured with considerable patience.

The simple fact is that it has been the clear policy of Israeli governments over the last half-century to avoid, at all costs, the creation of a Palestinian state. Every effort at delay, every quibble over definitions, every tactical shift that could possibly be made has been made, many times over, in an effort to buy time, hoping that time alone will somehow make the problem of the Palestinians go away.

This policy may have changed, ever-so-slightly, under Mr. Barak from one of preventing the creation of a Palestinian state to one of preventing the creation of a viable Palestinian state, but that is not the same thing as "the great opportunity missed" that has been dramatized, over and over again, in America's press. And even this slight change in policy remains unacceptable to many conservatives in Israel.

And when the Palestinians, morally exhausted by endless waiting that yields no change, resist the occupation they are under with the limited, desperate means they possess, they are regarded as unstable lunatics who don't love their children. A number of apologists for Israel's worst excesses have repeated this theme, an extension of a remark attributed to the late Golda Meir about peace coming "when the Palestinians learn to love their children more than they hate us." The actual quote from Ms. Meir that is most applicable here is one she made to the *Sunday Times* of June 15, 1969, "They [the Palestinians] did not exist."

We are repeatedly told that Israel is the only democracy in the Middle East and it is defending itself against malevolent forces. This vaguely defined image of enlightenment versus darkness appeals to Americans. But democracy has never been a guarantee of fairness or decency. It is only a means of selecting a government.

Under any democracy, a bare majority of people with an ugly prejudice can tyrannize over others almost in perpetuity. Indeed, this very experience is a large part of the history of the United States, even with its much-vaunted Bill of Rights. But Israel has no Bill of Rights, and what's more important for actual day-to-day fairness and decency, the very will to act in a fair manner appears to be absent. What else can one say where assassination, torture, and improper arrest have been management tools of government for decades?

Israel's politics are highly polarized, undoubtedly far worse than those of the United States, and the balance of power needed to form any parliamentary coalition is always in the hands of far-out religious parties. The interests of these people are anything but informed by enlightenment values and democracy, holding to views and ideas, as they do, that predate the existence of democracy or human rights.

It is not an exaggeration to say that killing the Philistines or tearing down the walls of Jericho are regarded as current events by a good many of these fundamentalist party members. A number of their leaders have, time and again, described Palestinians as "vermin."

The extreme conservatives receive many special privileges in Israel that distort the entire political mechanism. For example, their rabbis decide the rules governing who is accepted as a Jew or what are acceptable religious, and religiously-approved social, practices. The students in the fundamentalist religious schools traditionally have been exempt from the army. In effect, they are exempt from the violent results of the very policies they advocate.

These parties generally believe in a greater Israel, that is, an Israel that includes what little is left of Palestine, the West Bank and Gaza, minus its current undesirable inhabitants. It has been the view of Israeli government after Israeli government over the last half century to consider Jordan as the Palestinian's proper home. Thus, when Israeli governments talked of peace, it meant something entirely different than what Palestinians meant.

And when, finally, an offer for a Palestinian state was made by Mr. Barak at Camp David—an offer that, by all reports, was made quite angrily and contemptuously to Mr. Arafat—under any honest, rational analysis, it reduced to one for a giant holding facility for people not wanted in Israel. How surprising that Mr. Arafat left in anger when after days of being subjected to good-cop/bad-cop treatment by Mr. Clinton and Mr. Barak, this was the end result. Surely, this was an immensely frustrating disappointment to the Palestinians after years of effort and compromise trying to achieve and implement the Oslo Accords.

Mr. Bush's War on Terror, a mindless crusade against disagreeable Islamic governments, has had the terrible effect of casting the bloody-minded Mr. Sharon in the role of partner against the forces of terror and darkness. He has received a new mantle of legitimacy for continued destruction and delay, for continued injustice against those too powerless to effectively oppose him.

As Israel's leaders well know, the Palestinian population is growing rapidly. Rapid population growth is the general case for poor people throughout the world. Israel's highly organized and costly efforts to support Jewish immigration reflect awareness of this fact. But a combination of large birth rates on one side and heavy immigration on the other is a certain formula for disaster in the long term. The region's basic resources, especially water, will sustain only a limited population.

A large population, out-sizing its resources, is almost certainly the major underlying reason for the immense slaughters and numerous coups and civil wars of Western Africa in recent years, a region whose population growth has been high but whose usable resources are limited.

And the history of civilization tells us that vast changes and movements of population have been far more decisive in human affairs than atomic weapons.

So it appears that not only in the short term, but over some much longer time horizon, Israel and the Palestinians are on a deadly collision course.

There is hope. Modern societies have all experienced a phenomenon called demographic transition. This term simply means that, faced with a reduced death rate, people's normal response is a reduced birth rate, yielding a net result of slow, or even negative, population growth.

Couples prefer to have only two or three children who are almost certain to survive instead of six or more, at least half of whom die before growing up. This is the reason why modern countries depend entirely on migration for growth, or to avoid actual decline, in population.

Israel, populated largely by people from Europe and North America and being a fairly prosperous society, follows the pattern of advanced nations. The West Bank and Gaza, with some of the world's highest birth rates, do not. Now, the only way to trigger demographic transition is through healthful measures like adequate diet, good public sanitation, and basic health care, especially measures for infant care. These things done, nature takes a predictable path and people stop having large families.

But these are not measures that can be accomplished quickly, and the need to get on with them should add some sense of urgency to ending the occupation and helping the Palestinians achieve a state with some degree of prosperity.

By now, it should be clear that life in Israel, for the foreseeable future, cannot be quite the same as life in Dorothy's Kansas, no matter who leads the government. No one has been more ruthless or bloody-minded than Mr. Sharon, and he has only succeeded in making every problem worse.

Yet life in Israel similar to Dorothy's Kansas—that is, a life lived as though you were not surrounded by people seething over injustice and occupation and steeped in poverty—is a condition that Mr. Sharon insists on as a precondition even for talking about peace. Somehow, Mr. Arafat, with a wave of his hand, is to make all the violence disappear. This is not only unrealistic, it is almost certainly dishonest.

Israel herself, in any of the places she has occupied, and despite having one of the best-equipped armies in the world, has never been able to do that very thing. All those years in Lebanon, and the violence continued at some level for the entire time. Indeed, a new enemy, Hizballah, rose in response to Israel's activities. It is simply a fact that there has always been some level of violence in any place occupied by Israel. How is Mr. Arafat, with his limited resources and in the face of many desperate factions, supposed to be able to accomplish what the Israeli army and secret services cannot?

And were he to try running the kind of quasi-police state one assumes Israel favors, with regular mass arrests of suspects, how long would he remain in power?

Moreover, Mr. Sharon treats Mr. Arafat with utter contempt, dismissing him as insignificant, and has destroyed many of the means and symbols of his authority. How can a leader, treated as contemptible, exercise authority? For all his faults, and he has a number of them, Mr. Arafat has demonstrated through many compromises related to the Oslo Accords that he is a man who sincerely desires peace and a constructive relationship with Israel.

Mr. Sharon's entire adult life has been dedicated to killing. I do believe there is more blood on his hands than any terrorist you care to name. Mr. Sharon first made a name for himself with the Qibya massacre in 1953, when a force under his command blew up forty-five houses and killed sixty-nine people, most of them women and children.

Nearly thirty years later, in 1982, he was still at it when Lebanese militia forces under his control murdered and dumped into mass graves, using Israeli-supplied bulldozers, between two and three thousand civilians in the refugee camps called Sabra and Shatila. Mr. Sharon was responsible for the disastrous invasion of Lebanon which saw hundreds of civilians killed by Israel's shelling of Beirut and precipitated a bloody civil war in which thousands more died.

Mr. Sharon's policies of assassination and bombing have succeeded only in multiplying the suicide bombings beyond anything in recent memory.

It is almost impossible to imagine this man as capable of making a meaningful gesture towards peace. Yes, of course he wants peace, peace on his terms, a cheap peace without giving anything, but by definition that is not peace for the Palestinians.

We always hear about what is required of the Palestinians for peace, but a genuine peace requires some extraordinary things on Israel's part.

First, she must at some point accept a Palestinian state. This condition is a necessary one, but it is far from sufficient, for she must be prepared to generously assist this state towards achieving some prosperity, reducing the causes of both run-away population growth and the dreary hopelessness that causes people to strap bombs to their bodies.

Most difficult of all, it is hard to see how Israel can avoid some level of violence during a period of Palestinian nation-building. This is something no ordinary state would consciously embrace, but then Israel is no ordinary state. The norms of Dorothy's Kansas simply do not apply. The hatreds generated by a half century of aggressive policies are not going to just melt away, but if there is enough genuine, demonstrated goodwill, it does seem likely that such violence would be minimal. It is an unappetizing risk that almost certainly needs to be taken, for no one is going to run a police state on Israel's behalf in the West Bank.

Considering the immense difficulty of these things and political barriers that exist against them in Israel, it does not seem likely that peace is coming any time soon. The prospect seems rather for low-grade, perpetual war, paralleling that Mr. Bush so relishes speaking of. For someone of Mr. Sharon's turn of mind, this may be a wholly acceptable alternative.

11 | The Betrayal of Tradition

Zionism's challenge to Jews & Muslims

AFTAB AHMAD MALIK

O N MAY 14, 1948, the British mandate in Palestine came to an
end and within eleven minutes, President Truman announced
that America recognized the new State of Israel.[1] Since then,
a "special relationship" between the US and Israel has existed, largely
due to the perception of Israel being a US "strategic asset."[2] This "special
relationship," embodies diplomatic, economic, military and ideological
support for Israel.[3] So strong is this support, that despite intense
international protests over violations of international law, scandals[4] and
its poor human rights record in the occupied territories, the US continues
to share with Israel, highly sensitive intelligence and military technology.
It seems that nothing can frustrate the intimacy between these two
countries.[5]

By describing Ariel Sharon as "a man of peace," President Bush has
ignored the fact that many lawyers consider him a war criminal[6] which
demonstrates his administration's state of blindness to Sharon's crimes in
the Sabra and Shatila massacre.[7] This would seem to confirm that Bush
has little or no regard for Israel's long record of human rights violations.

ISRAEL'S "WAR ON TERRORISM"

PHASE ONE: JENIN

Israel wholeheartedly supports the *War on Terrorism* and President
Bush completely supports Israel's right to defend itself from "terrorists."
Soon after George Bush's announcement of a war on terrorism, on
April 3, 2002, Israel proceeded to legitimize its own 'war on terror'

that culminated in the Israeli army launching itself into what was then described as the bloodiest battle in the West Bank since the 1967 Middle East war. There was no shortage of outrage and condemnation from the world community. The UN's top human rights body condemned Israel for "mass killings" of Palestinians and for "gross violations" of humanitarian law, while affirming the "legitimate right of Palestinian people to resist."[8] The devastation was "horrific beyond belief" according to the UN special envoy Terje Roed-Larsen, while Amnesty International's representative at the camp, Javier Zuniga, said "this is one of the worst scenes of devastation that I have ever witnessed."[9] Even the Israeli foreign minister, Shimon Peres, admitted that what occurred was a "massacre."[10]

PHASE TWO: RAFAH

The Israeli army on May 17th 2004 penetrated deep into the Rafah refugee camp, situated in Gaza Strip, under the pretext[11] of searching for tunnels used by Palestinians to smuggle alleged arms from Egypt. Between 17th and 20th May, 43 Palestinians were killed, mostly civilians. Among those killed were nine children, one being five year old Rawan. While playing with her friends, two bullets killed her; one in the head and the other in the neck.[12]

In an operation aimed at crushing armed Palestinian resistance, the Israeli army opened fire on thousands of peaceful demonstrators and bulldozed homes making more than a thousand people homeless. Peter Hansen, the chief of the United Nations agency for refugees in the region confirmed that homes were toppled on their dwellers. While the UN Security Council passed a resolution criticizing Israel for killing Palestinian civilians and demolishing their houses,[13] America abstained, much to the displeasure of Israel who wanted Washington to veto the resolution. Amnesty International noted that Israel's actions constituted "a form of collective punishment" which was "a violation of international humanitarian law."[14]

The scale of the destruction at Rafah was unprecedented, even surpassing the devastation of Jenin. Any criticism of Israel that remained after the carnage soon evaporated amid Israel's insistence that it was part of the "war on terrorism," and President Bush's resolute comment made just a day after the incursion, was that Israel has the "right to self defense."

TRYING TO UNDERSTAND

Since 9/11, many people have attempted to understand the causes of turmoil in the Israeli/Palestinian conflict, but doing so is not so easy. The newly published research by the Glasgow University media group entitled *Bad News from Israel*,[15] concludes that a clear bias exists in television news reportage in favor of Israel. The book details how different language is used to describe Israelis and Palestinians, with the latter often shown as "terrorists" and Israelis as victims of "mass-murder," "brutal murder," "savage cold blooded murder," and the like. A crucial point that the study makes is that most of the people interviewed were actually unaware of the historical context of the conflict. Many television reviewers told researchers that they thought the conflict was about a border dispute between Palestinians and Israelis, as one viewer said: "The impression I got [from the news] was that the Palestinians had lived around about that area and now they were trying to come back and get some more land for themselves."

Many viewers had no idea that the Israelis were *occupying* Palestinian land and saw the Palestinians as "starting" the problems in Israel and the Israelis having to respond. Because of this uncertainty of the cause of the conflict, the researches concluded that many viewers were simply confused by what was reported.

SUICIDE-BOMBERS: ASKING WHY?

The hatred towards the Israelis is not something that is intentionally taught to the Palestinian children, as much as it is derived from the feelings of having lived under a brutal occupation which has created a generation of Palestinian children who suffer from Post Traumatic Disorder.[16]

Homes in Palestinian society represent safety, security and identity. Losing homes leads to losing these feelings. With 1.3 million people hemmed into a tiny strip of land, Gaza Strip is one of the most densely populated areas in the world. Those Palestinians living there are like those living in an open prison: there is limited movement, a lack of freedom, ambulances cannot reach hospitals, sick people might die waiting at Israeli checkpoints, Israeli tanks and bulldozers invade all places in Gaza Strip, bulldozing farms, demolishing homes and killing people. This is the reality which confronts the thousands of Palestinians on a daily basis, something which is hard to truly envisage from our abodes of security, prosperity and peace. As Rachel Corrie explained:

> I have been in Palestine for two weeks and one hour now, and I still have very few words to describe what I see. It is most difficult for me to think about what's going on here when I sit down to write back to the United States—something about the virtual portal into luxury. I don't know if many of the children here have ever existed without tank-shell holes in their walls and the towers of an occupying army surveying them constantly from the near horizons.[17]

TRAUMA AND PALESTINIAN PSYCHE

Trauma in Palestine is real and ongoing, yet there is hardly any discussion upon the psychological state of the Palestinians in relation to suicide-bombings. By turning a blind eye to the atrocities conducted by Israel and the well-defined media coverage, the Palestinians are dehumanized, stripped of any human characteristics and caricatured as mindless savages with a fetish for suicide. However, since Palestinians are humans, the science applied to understand why people commit suicide should also be applied to them. Often referred to as the "Father of modern Suicidology," Edwin Shneidman described ten characteristics of a suicidal person:

1. The common stimulus in suicide is "unendurable psychological pain."

2. The common stress in suicide is "frustrated psychological needs."

3. The common purpose of suicide is "to seek a solution."

4. The common goal of suicide is "cessation of consciousness."

5. The common emotion in suicide is "hopelessness-helplessness."

6. The common internal attitude toward suicide is "ambivalence."

7. The common cognitive state in suicide is "constriction."

8. The common interpersonal act in suicide is "communication of intention."

9. The common action in suicide is "egression" (a way out).

10. The common consistency in suicide is with "life-long coping patterns."[18]

It is remarkable how too few investigative journalists have attempted to make any connection between suicide-bombers and the profile of a suicidal person. Instead, the immediate response to why Palestinians commit suicide-bombings is that in some twisted logic, they simply "hate" Israelis and take happiness in killing themselves and others. Another name that is absent in the discussions on what motivates suicide-bombers is that of Emile Durkheim. Durkheim's seminal work on suicide, written in 1966 argues that suicide is "a consequence of a disturbed social order. Moral codes were disrupted in times of change and affected rich and poor [...] The strain led to suicide and abnormal behavior."[19]

As we look into greater detail to the social-sciences to understand the mind of a suicidal individual, the picture becomes clearer as to how these characteristics apply also to a Palestinian suicide-bomber. Shneidman goes further to state that suicidal victims see suicide as "the only solution to their problems."[20]

Although this research applies to a suicidal individual and not specifically to suicide-bombers, through examination of the characteristics of a suicidal individual, it becomes clear that they also apply to the Palestinian suicide-bomber. These individuals seek to escape unbearable pain, so we must seek from where this pain arises to be able to eliminate the cause of suicide-bombing and its horrific consequence.

"FORCED TO HATE"

While Sharon and his predecessors have always demanded that Arafat to do more to stop the suicide-bombings, in reality, Israel and only Israel can stop these attacks by giving back Palestinians their freedom, dignity and a reason to live. For the Palestinians their future is bleak: all they see is an endless occupation and being made refugees in their own homeland. Zbigniew Brzeziniski (who served as the National Security Advisor to President Carter from 1977 to 1981) alluded to this reality when he said that "the Palestinians are being turned, largely thanks to the efforts of Prime Minister Ariel Sharon, into [. . .] people absolutely determined to wage urban guerrilla warfare brutally, ruthlessly. At any cost and at enormous self-sacrifice."[21]

To understand the rationale of why men, and now women, are willing to blow themselves up, we must question *what drives them* to this violence? To answer this question, we must take the perspective of any ordinary Palestinian. Since the Israeli occupation, young Palestinians have grown up with images and memories of subjugation and humiliation—witnessing family members being beaten (and tortured), and Israeli tanks continually patrolling the streets, which has left them in a "chronic state of helplessness." Observers have often described the humiliating living situation that the Palestinians have found themselves in akin to "an apartheid regime that looks remarkably like the former South African regime—hemming the Palestinians into small, non-contiguous Bantustans, imposing 'closures' and 'curfews' to control where they go [. . .]"[22]

In witnessing the death and destruction of Jenin, a Palestinian nurse exclaimed, "I believe in peace and harmony. I have never hated the Jews. But now, they have forced me to hate them."[23] It is no wonder that the policies of successive Israeli governments have nurtured a population of angry, humiliated and defiant people.[24] It is in this context, of all the suffering that the Palestinians have experienced, that their anger is directed towards Israel. The strength that the Palestinians draw upon is from Israeli oppression. It is this relationship that made Robert Fisk conclude the "Israelis have created their own unconquerable enemy. They have made the Palestinians so crushed, so desperate, so humiliated that they have nothing to lose."[25]

The recent Israeli incursions further demand that we question the difference between state terrorism and individual terrorist acts. When Yasser Arafat was barred from giving live interviews and put under curfew in his own offices, he was constantly pressed into condemning terror. Suicide bombers killing innocent civilians must be unequivocally condemned—but they cannot be compared to state terrorism: the former are individual acts of despair of a people that see no future or hope, whereas the latter, as Dr Lev Grinberg of the Ben Gurion University asserts, comes from "old and rational decisions of a state and a military apparatus of occupation, well-equipped, financed and backed by the only superpower in the world."[26]

IMPLICATIONS FOR AMERICA

The US is seen as continually supporting Israel (despite its unremitting breach of various international laws and UN resolutions) by vetoing any UN resolutions that seek to curb Israel's aggressive and expansionist policies. The value it places on its relationship with Israel is illustrated by the amount of aid which it annually allocates for Israel which is unparalleled in the history of US foreign policy.

For the last quarter of a century, the total amount of direct US aid to Israel has been at around 3 billion dollars per year. That figure accounts only for "direct" aid—Israel receives a further 3 billion dollars per year in "indirect" aid: that is, military support from the US defense budget, for given loans and special grants. Despite the existence of the US Foreign Assistance Act which prohibits military assistance to any country "which engages in a consistent pattern of gross violations of internationally recognized human rights" and to governments that refused to sign the Nuclear Non—Proliferation Treaty, aid still pours forth into Israel while it continues to breach both categories.

While at times the US may indulge in verbal condemnation of Israel for attacking civilian targets, it is seen as hypocritical, since at the same time the very machinery that is used has been provided by the US "gratis or at bargain rates."[27] The US is the very supplier of those tanks, helicopters and rockets which Israel uses to control the West Bank and the very same machinery that killed Rachel Corrie. While this attracts international condemnation, US officials can rarely bring themselves to say that what Israel is doing is wrong. Knowing that America is backing the very entity that has driven them out of their homes and left them defenseless against such a massive military arsenal—the hate that is targeted at Israel then also turns to America. While it may be the Israelis that pull the trigger it is "American missiles smashing into Palestinian homes and US helicopters [that are] firing missiles."[28] This fact doesn't go unnoticed.

ORTHODOX JEWS:
THE RELIGIOUS CRITIQUE

Not only Muslims and those concerned with the crimes being carried out in Israel have marched against Israeli policies—Rabbis have even taken part in similar marches. In February of 2002, several thousand orthodox Jews gathered in front the Israeli Consulate in Canada to denounce the existence of the state of Israel. They were organized by the Central Rabbinical Congress, who stressed that: "the Jewish role [...] is to humbly serve the Creator, remaining always patriotic and seeking peace with all men. Zionism, on the other hand seeks to exacerbate Jewish-Gentile animosity at every opportunity."

Many Jewish organizations have emerged to counter the assertion that all Jewish people blindly support the policies of the State of Israel, as well as asserting the right of Palestinian refugees to return to Palestine.[29] Indeed, most Rabbis and orthodox Jews have condemned the idea of a political Jewish state from its birth. The Philadelphia Conference of November 1869 denounced the very principles of political Zionism—even before they had been articulated by Theodore Herzl. In the 1890s, German Rabbis declared that "attempts to found a Jewish state in Palestine were contrary to the Messianic promises of Judaism."[30] Orthodox Jewish groups, such as the Neturei Karta, repudiate the concept of a sovereign Jewish State as they believe its existence to be contrary to Jewish Law and a number of Judaism's fundamental teachings. Far from having any legitimacy in its Scriptures, such orthodox Jewish groups maintain that the Israeli State was the product of a number of secular Zionists and call Zionism "a rebellion against God."[31]

By referring to the Talmud which teaches that Jews shall not use human force to bring about the establishment of a Jewish State before the coming of the Messiah, orthodox Jews affirm that this can only come about through a divine act and when divine favor is once again upon the Jews. Conveniently forgetting the Jewish prayer "and for our sins have we been exiled from our Lord," orthodox Jews maintain that Zionists ignore the fact that the Torah itself forbids the Jews to end their exile and are required to remain under the rule of the nations of the world and not rebel against them, rather, they should remain loyal citizens. Far from being an expression of faith, Zionism is an expression of nationalism.

In their critique of Zionism, the orthodox Jewish Community points to how in the past two-thousand years, of enduring suffering and the dangers of exile, none of the Sages of Israel ever suggested that they should protect themselves through an establishment of a Jewish State. In fact, you find that they wrote warnings against doing so.

Recognizing immediately its contradictory nature to Judaism, various Jewish organizations were set up to fight Zionism, such as *Agudath Israel* (Union of Israel) established in 1912 to represent Jews around the world. Under its auspices, Jews who were living in Palestine obtained permission from Britain to declare in writing that they *did not* wish to be represented by the Zionists, some fifty years ago. Amongst the thousands of Rabbis that were against the idea of a Jewish State, was Rabbi Amran Blau. An ardent critic of Zionism, and someone who had never left Palestine, he stressed that Jews and Arabs lived in harmony in the Holy-Land until the advent of political Zionism. He fought the "innovations" of the Zionists and was later imprisoned for denouncing the Zionist State.[32]

THE MORAL CASE

Some of the most distinguished Jews in the world protested against the formation of Israel: Albert Einstein, the scientist and philosopher; Martin Buber, the philosopher, theologian, Bible translator and first President of the Hebrew University of Jerusalem and Professor Judah Magnes. A letter sent by a host of Jewish intellectuals, including Albert Einstein, to the *New York Times* in 1948 regarded the emergence of Israel as among "the most disturbing political phenomena of our times."[33] Amongst the prime reasons for their opposition was that the establishment of a Jewish state in Palestine would inevitably result in conflict with the population, which had been living there for centuries. Judah Magnes proclaimed "the Jews have more than a claim upon the world for justice [. . .] But as far as I am concerned, I am not ready to try to achieve justice to the Jew through injustice to the Arab."[34] Albert Einstein wrote that he would "rather see reasonable agreement with the Arabs on the basis of living together in peace than the creation of a Jewish state."[35]

UNLIKELY ALLIES:
CHRISTIAN ZIONISTS

Whereas the idea of a Jewish state may have been heretical in the eyes of orthodox Jews, for Christian Zionists, it was a necessity to ensure the Second Coming of Christ was possible. It has been argued that it could have been possible that the ideas of Herzl's vision of a viable Jewish state may have been inspired by the writings of Christians. Whereas *The Jewish State* was written in 1896, by as early as 1809, a Christian Church had already articulated its commitment for the "physical restoration of the Jewish people to *Eretz Israel*."[36]

Reduced to its simplest meaning, Christian Zionism can be defined as Christian support for Zionism. It is a remarkable example where politics and religion are interwoven and where interpretation of scripture has a profound effect on political action. Christian Zionists see themselves as defenders of the state of Israel, and by implication, arch opponents of critics of Israel. Amongst their principle beliefs, derived from a literal and futuristic reading of the Bible, is that Jews remain God's chosen people. They view the return of the Jews to Israel and the establishment of the state of Israel as a fulfillment of Old Testament prophecies. Thus, Christian Zionists actively encourage Jewish people to move to Israel. They view Jerusalem as the exclusive capital of Jews and so it cannot be shared with Palestinians.

It goes without saying that Christian Zionists have been heavily criticized by many other Christian organizations and denominations for what they see as a heretical interpretation of the Bible. Rather than focusing upon Christ's love today, they have been rebuked for placing their emphasis on events leading up to the end of history. Their uncritical support for Israel has also shown their lack of compassion for the Palestinians and in doing so, other Churches argue that the Christian Zionists have legitimized their oppression by justifying it by using the Gospel.[37]

BETRAYAL OF HISTORY

Thirty years ago, Moshe Dayan, who served as Minister of Foreign Affairs exclaimed to the Cabinet of the Labor Government, "we should tell the Palestinians in the [occupied] territories that 'You shall continue to live like dogs, and whoever wishes, may leave, and we shall see where this process will lead.'"[38] It certainly seems that his words have come true.

When the Jews were a persecuted people throughout the lands of Christian Europe, they found refuge and were welcomed in Muslim lands, where Jewish communities thrived for centuries. These epochs are referred by Jewish historians as being a "golden age." Erwen Rosenthal observed that "The Talmudic age apart, there is perhaps no more formative and positive time in our long and checkered history than that under the empire of Islam."[39] Jews lived in a dignified manner and were amongst the elites of Muslim society. Commemorating the fourth centennial of the settlement of the Jews in Turkey, the *Central Committee* of the *Alliance Israelite Universelle*, wrote to the Caliph, Sultan Abdul Hamid II in 1892, explaining how "[i]n the spring of the year 1492, the Jews expelled from Spain found shelter in Turkey. While they were oppressed in the rest of the world, they enjoyed in the lands of your glorious ancestors a protection that had never ceased."[40]

Amidst intense persecution in Europe following the fall of Spain and over two-hundred and fifty years of *convivencia*,[41] many Jews dispersed to other Muslim lands such as Yemen, North Africa and Turkey. It was to Turkey that most Jews fled. What compelled them to travel and live in Muslim lands was *freedom and the ability to live as Jews*. A letter written by Rabbi Isaac Tzarfati who was residing in Turkey during this exodus shows the freedoms enjoyed by the Jews living under Muslim rule. He urged Jews to:

[...] come to the Turkish land, which is blessed by God and filled with good things. Here I have found rest and happiness [...] Here in the land of the Turks we have nothing to complain of. We are not oppressed with heavy taxes, and our commerce is free and unhindered [...] ever one of us lives in peace and freedom. Here the Jew is not compelled to wear a yellow hat as a badge of shame, as is the case in Germany, where even wealth and great fortune are a curse for the Jew because he therewith arouses jealousy among Christians [...] Arise, my brethren, gird your loins, collect your forces, and come to us here. Here you will be free of your enemies, here you will find rest [...][42]

When Muslims see the pathetic state of the Palestinians, there is no frame of reference for what they see. Most, if not all Muslims ask themselves *what is it that they have done to the Jews to deserve such base treatment?* [43] Muslims have not forgotten history. Most are in full knowledge at how their ancestors continually extended friendship and protection to Jews throughout the centuries, when they were the objects of persecution, humiliation and hatred.[44] Whereas the Jews were welcomed to the lands of Islam where both Jews and Muslims cultivated art, music, science and literature, Muslims who were living in Palestine for generations were suddenly told that they had no rights living there. They were told "[..] there is room only for the Jews," and were commanded to "[g]et out!" If they resisted, they would be "driven out by force."[45]

THE DEMISE OF A TRADITION:
KNOWLEDGE VS IDEOLOGY

Unlike Christianity, where anti-Semitism was institutionalized to the extent that pogroms and massacres were thought to be divinely sanctioned,[46] in the Islamic world, such behavior towards Jews never existed. When violence towards Jews occurred in the Muslim world, it was neither systematic nor justified by Islamic doctrine. Bernard Lewis, in *The Jews of Islam*, writes that:

> Persecution, that is to say, violent and active repression, was rare and atypical. Jews and Christians under Muslim rule were not normally called upon to suffer martyrdom for their faith. They were not often obliged to make the choice, which confronted Muslims and Jews in re-conquered Spain, between exile, apostasy and death. They were not subject to any major territorial or occupational restrictions, such as were the common lot of Jews in pre-modern Europe.[47]

Speaking against the recent bombings carried out against Jewish communities in Turkey, Morocco and Tunisia, the Chief Rabbi of the United Hebrew Congregations of the Commonwealth and leader of

Britain's Jews, Jonathan Sacks, asserted that these crimes were committed in areas where both Jews and Muslims had lived together in "peace and goodwill" for centuries.[48] The attitudes that could legitimately be called anti-Semitic appeared in the Muslim world "from the late nineteenth century," the form and content of which was very much "expressed in the unmistakable language of European Christian anti-Semitism."[49] We cannot fail to forget the Christians had been living amongst Muslims for centuries and where negative attitudes towards Jews formed in Muslim lands, it was in all probably molded by indigenous Christian communities. Arab Catholics are cited by Lewis as having initiated the translation of anti-Semitic tracts into Arabic.[50]

Anti-Semitism in the Muslim world is very much a recent phenomenon. Rather than being ancient and religiously sanctioned, it is with a certain reading of Islam, one that is highly politicized, and emotionally driven, that is leading Muslims to equate all Jews as Zionists, and in effect, dismissing Islam's traditional outlook of the Jews.[51] This vision and outlook has been shaped very much by the events and politics of the nineteenth century. Such groups reject the traditional principles of Islamic jurisprudence, thus in effect, creating an entirely new *Sharia*. In these groups is a noticeable absence of scholarly works or scholars. By adopting a literal understanding of the Qur'an, denouncing jurisprudential differences as heretical and rejecting established theological principles, these groups have given way to a number of sub-groups; each with their own understanding and interpretation of the *Sharia*. The most extreme amongst them are the *Takfiris* who are quick to condemn other Muslims as non-Muslims and who relegate Jews and Christians as non-believers (as opposed to the *Ahl al-Kitab*). They reject political authority and ignore the established juridical rules of military engagement which have led them to wage sacrilegious *Jihads* in the name of Islam.[52]

Most of these groups, which have sprung from the Middle-East have been shaped by, and formed as a reaction to the post-colonial experience. These groups tend to adopt a political approach to most issues and in so doing their approach is neither anchored in Islamic ethics or morality.[53] Rather than being the intellectual fruits of the Islamic tradition, they ignore Islamic culture, heritage and the richness and diversity of the Islamic Civilization. These fringe groups reduce Islam to an ideology concerned with the dynamic of power which is constructed as the antithesis to the West.

Anger within these Muslims, fuels fiery rhetoric whereby a black and white Manichean world-view is constructed. The complexities and nuances of Islamic scholarship vanish as a simple and comforting world is constructed. It is because of this simplistic and erroneous approach to the *Sharia* that we have seen mindless aggression committed against innocent people which constitute grave breaches of *Sharia*. These crimes are in fact an act of *Hiraba*, an Islamic juristic term which means spreading mischief in the earth, the crime of which is extremely severe.[54] Despite Qur'anic injunctions urging the faithful not to allow aggressive acts of other people drive them to react with aggression, nor to allow ill will towards a people prevent them from dealing justly,[55] the anger over Palestine has often been the catalyst for the radicalization of Muslims. Indeed, Osama bin Laden often refers to the plight of the Palestinians and regularly cites the oppressive nature of the Zionists.

OPPRESSOR-OPPRESSED AND THE POLITICS OF ANTI-SEMITISM

Zionism has taken on the attributes and method of oppression that were used to persecute and oppress the Jews throughout most of Europe in the past. It was because of anti-Semitism by Christian states in general and the Holocaust in particular that the Zionist enterprise justifies the dispossession of the Palestinians. David Ben Gurion, Israel's first Prime Minister, remarked:

> If I were an Arab leader, I would never sign an agreement with Israel. It is normal; we have taken their country. It is true God promised it to us, but how could that interest them? Our God is not theirs. There has been Anti-Semitism, the Nazis, Hitler, Auschwitz, but was that their fault? They see but one thing: we have come and we have stolen their country. Why would they accept that?[56]

While UN resolution 3379 was passed in 1975 condemning "Zionism as a form of racism and racial discrimination," its repeal in December

1991 has effectively muted attempts to differentiate between Judaism and Zionism. We are now told that "anti-Semitism" means "opposition to Zionism: sympathy with opponents of the state of Israel," as stated in *Webster's Third New International Dictionary*. The Zionist fathers saw in anti-Semitism the key to their justification for a Jewish State; the stronger and more pervasive anti-Semitism was, the greater the case for asserting a national homeland for Jews becomes. Herzl himself acknowledged the benefits gained by the rise of anti-Semitism, writing that "The anti-Semites will become our most loyal friends, the anti-Semite nations will become our allies."[57] Words were often said that seemed to have no other purpose than to fuel anti-Semitism and feed into existing stereotypes of Jews. Herzl explained that anti-Semitism was "an understandable reaction to Jewish defects," and that Jews carried "the seeds of anti-Semitism" wherever they lived. Chaim Weizmann, who later became president of Israel, remarked "each country can only absorb a limited number of Jews, if she doesn't want disorders in her stomach. Germany has already too many Jews."[58] Weizmann was the head of the World Zionist Organization when he made this statement.

Oppressive and anti-intellectual attempts to silence criticism of Israel, by labeling anyone who dares to discuss honestly and openly the policies of Israel as being anti-Semitic,[59] have only made people bitter, resentful and even more determined to show that they will not fold by such accusatory tactics. The notion that anti-Semitism is now seen to be hidden and disguised as "anti-Israelism" is a further attempt to silence critics of Israel. The fact that it may be a Jew who is criticizing Israeli policies—does not even exclude them from being labeled anti-Semitic.[60]

In his acceptance speech in Jerusalem (May 2004), Daniel Barenboim was awarded the Wolf Prize established to award and honor outstanding artists and scientists who have worked "in the interest of mankind and friendly relations among people." In his speech, Barenhoim who is a Jew, recollected at how as a ten year old boy he arrived in Israel seeing the nation's Declaration of Independence as a source of inspiration. He spoke of the documents commitment to ensure that:

> The state of Israel will devote itself to the development of this country for the benefit of all its people. It will be founded on the principles of freedom,

justice and peace, guided by the visions of the prophets of Israel. It will grant full equal, social and political rights to all its citizens regardless of differences of religious faith, race or sex.

However, Barenboim pointed at the discrepancy between the ideal of Israel and its reality. In his damning critique, speaking before the Knesset, he asked:

Does the condition of occupation and domination over another people fit the Declaration of Independence? Is there any sense in the independence of one at the expense of the fundamental rights of the other? Can the Jewish people, whose history is a record of continued suffering and relentless persecution, allow themselves to be indifferent to the rights and suffering of a neighboring people?[61]

This confusion has grown from anti-Semitism being poorly defined which has blurred the distinction between the vast majority of Jews that have decided not to immigrate to Israel, and those who are responsible for the endorsement of Zionist policies. Continued emphasis by Zionists about Israel being a "Jewish State" creates a real and dangerous confusion between faith and nationality.[62] Jews should be extremely concerned over this confusion. In a poll conducted in 2003, 59% of fifteen European Union countries polled actually saw Israel as "the greatest threat to world peace."[63] The honor and credibility of the Jewish people are seriously at stake, since many people increasingly associate Jews in general with the actions and policies of the Israeli administration. As Yakov M Rabkin, professor of history at the Université de Montréal concludes:

Zionism has brought about a new identity that negates the image and the traditional values of the Diaspora Jew. Zionism has bred a new, muscular Israeli, proud, intrepid and assertive. Zionists have disdained the "old Jew" whom the tradition of Judaism expects "to be bashful, compassionate and charitable." It is the New Israeli, not the old Jew, who built up the army and chased potential enemies from the land. It is the New Israeli, not the old Jew, who has stubbornly weathered decades of conflict that ensued from his daring moves.

CONCLUSION

Ever since its occupation, Israel has remained in violation of international law and numerous UN Security Council and General Assembly resolutions.[64] Israel's occupation is immoral and illegitimate, constituting "war crimes, flagrant violations of international humanitarian law and crimes against humanity."[65] Articulating what many have known for decades, Mary Robinson, former President of Ireland and former UN High Commissioner for Human Rights, asserted that "the root cause of the Arab-Israeli conflict is the occupation."[66] Desmond Tutu remarked that "Israel will never get true security and safety through oppressing another people."[67] Unless these two realities are realized and accepted, there will be no peace in the Middle East. By oppressing the Palestinians, Israel provides the motivation for suicide-bombers. Israel's most influential journalist Nahum Barnea conceded that suicide-bombers were "borne of despair," and as Lord Gilmour of Craigmillar (a former Secretary of State for Defense) explained, despair has been induced through "Israel's continued building of illegal settlements on Palestinian land, military occupation, daily humiliation and economic suffering," and once the Israelis had succeeded in making life unbearable and "not worth living for thousands of Palestinians, there will be no shortage of suicide bombers."[68]

Arthur Koestler defined to perfection what was accomplished by the Balfour Declaration of 1917.[69] It was nothing less than "One nation solemnly" promising "to a second nation the country of a third nation."[70] The myth that the Israeli-Palestinian conflict is one that has continued for 75 years because of "mindless Arab hatred of the Jews" has been repudiated by work mostly carried out by Israeli academics and journalists. They conclude that the dynamics of the conflict is not rooted "in mindless Arab anti-Semitism but in Zionism's insistence that a Jewish state must be created in Palestine, despite the fact that for over 1,300 years it has been overwhelmingly inhabited by Arabs."[71]

When Gandhi reminded Martin Buber that Palestine belongs to the Arabs and that it would be unjust and inhuman to impose Jewish domination upon Arabs, Buber replied "We have no desire to dispossess them: we want to live with them."[72] Unfortunately, history has unfolded to reveal just the opposite. In 1917, the Arabs of Palestine owned 97.5% of the land, of which Israel now occupies over 80%. In 1966, Israel's representative at the United Nations, Michael Comay, announced that "Israel covets no territory of any of its neighbors," then in 1967, the Israeli forces occupied a territory three times as big as that which had been assigned to them in 1947. Between 1993 and 2000, the size of illegal Israeli settlements actually doubled. Since then, Israel has continued its policy of expansion, construction and population of illegal colonies (settlements) on Palestinian land.

JUSTICE FOR ONE nation of people cannot be solved through committing injustice to another. Mahatma Gandhi, the man renowned for his peaceful protests against the British Imperial rule of India, in his editorial of the *Harijan* (November 11 1938), wrote concerning this issue of a homeland for the Jews. He acknowledged that all Jews had been subjected to inhuman treatment and persecution over a long period of time, however, he asserted, "My sympathy does not blind me to the requirement of justice."

Liberty and human rights which the Universal Declaration of Human Rights enjoins upon all people of all races and of all nationalities, is just that: for all. The genocide committed against the Jews forms a major part of European history, and for such crimes, the Palestinians—who had nothing to do with this dark episode—have been made to suffer.

THE NEED FOR TRADITIONAL VALUES

Given the fact that most of the *"Jihadist"* propaganda is directed at Jews, for Muslims, there is an absolute need to be clear that what is shaping the attitude towards the Palestinians is not Judaism, but the skewed vision of the Zionist enterprise. We know that "the entire Torah can be summed up in two statements: love God with all your heart and love your neighbor as yourself,"[73] and when compared with statements of Zionists, the distinction between these two philosophies becomes absolutely clear.[74] Jewish Law embodies the notion of compassion and Justice as well displaying a sense of human honor *(Kavod habriyot)*, which stresses that a society must ensure equal dignity. It also asserts that "God is the parent of humanity" and by extension, the whole of mankind "are all members of a single extended family."[75] This is also very similar to the Islamic tradition which states that because of God's love of humankind, He conferred dignity upon all His Creation. As God confirms in the Qur'an, "We have bestowed dignity on the children of Adam and conferred on them special favors [...]" This divine favor is without qualification, inalienable and applies to the whole of mankind.[76] The *Sharia* actually sets out to preserve life, not take it and is there to protect human dignity. Imam al-Ghazzali,[77] articulates this understanding when he said that:

> In respect of the sanctity of life and the prohibition of aggression against it, Muslims and non-Muslims are equal. Even during military engagements—Muslims cannot destroy civilian life and have strict rules of engagement to the extent that the chopping of trees is prohibited

This understanding is also articulated by Ibn al-Qayyim,[78] who said:

> The *Sharia* is all Justice, kindness, common good and wisdom. Any rule that departs from justice to injustice [...] or departs from common good to harm [...] is not part of *Sharia*, even if it is arrived at by a literal interpretation.[79]

Many non-Muslims suffer from ignorance about Islam, unfortunately, the same ignorance is shared by Muslims themselves about their own tradition. Expressed as an ideology anchored in opposition to the West, and determined to wage a universal *Jihad*, these Muslims reduce Islam to a violent anti-intellectual force. While Islam suffers at their hands, Judaism has been hijacked by the Zionists. It is the Muslim and Jew who are caught between these extremist interpretations and twisted distortions of their faith and it is for the Muslim and the Jew to denounce acts of terror recognizing in the process that "violence is not a religious truth—it never has been, and it never will be."[80]

NOTES

1. The Israeli historian, Michael Stone in his book *Truman and Israel* notes that while serving his first term, Truman was actually "not overly enthusiastic about supporting a Jewish state in Palestine." He attributes this change in direction to well-placed Zionist sympathizers in Washington. Having access to Truman's "inner sanctum," they were able to influence others by virtue of their positions of prestige but also through donations. Finance played a key role in shaping Truman's attitude. His 1944 Vice-Presidential election was largely financed by a wealthy Zionist, Dewey Stone and his 1948 election financed by another pro-Zionist, Abe Feinberg. It wasn't soon after that his Zionist donors were lobbying hard for Truman to recognize the state of Israel, which eventually came in his second inauguration. See Andrew and Leslie Cockburn, *Dangerous Liaison: The Inside Story of the US-Israeli Covert Relationship and the International Activities it has served to Conceal* (London: The Bodley Head, 1992) pp.26-27.

2. It has been argued that Israel's "strategic" relationship with the US has been forged (and protected) by the efforts of those who are sympathetic to Israel. There are many dimensions between the relationship between foreign policy, the government and the American society that can at any one time, yield sufficient influence to affect the way foreign policy is molded. In such a complex society as America, undoubtedly, there are many sources of influence. In one administration alone, the bureaucracy is so large, containing many individuals and organizations each seeking to influence the foreign policy process. The President relies upon close advisors, who themselves may want their organizational interests represented. One such source of influence of interest here is that of interest groups. By definition, interest groups are an organized group which attempts to influence government decisions, without seeking itself to exercise the formal powers of government. Often associated with this aspect of interest groups, are the Political Action Committees (PACs). More associated with Congress, PACs provide large donations to members, but also expect something back, other than good government. One of the most influential lobby groups in the US is AIPAC (the American-Israeli Public Affairs Committee), which has been referred as "the most powerful, best run and effective foreign policy interest group in Washington." *The Wall Street Journal* reported in August 1983 that "[...] the political effort of Jewish PAC money is greater than that of other major lobbies." Pro-Israel PACs tend to focus upon federal elections and on House members

who occupy key foreign policy positions. As a former AIPAC Chairman, I.C Keenan once noted that, "campaign contributions must play a very real part in winning friends in Congress." At one time, Israel was ranked by the vast majority of American's as the second most important country in the world. General US support has consistently remained high. Even though 'fluctuations' may occur, the public tends to have more sympathy towards Israel and her Middle Eastern dilemmas. AIPAC has demonstrated how a powerful, single issue lobby can effectively organize itself to be best suited to influence policy. See Christopher Hitchins, *The trial of Henry Kissinger* (London: Verso Press, 2001); Paul Findley, *They Dare to Speak Out: People and Institutions Confront Israel's Lobby* (Amana Books: Lawrence Hill and Company, 1995); Gabriel Sheffer (ed) *Dynamics of Dependence: US-Israeli Relations* (Boulder, Colorado: Westview Press, 1987); Martin. C Feuerwerger, *Congress and Israel: Foreign Aid Decision Making in the House of Representatives. 1969-1976* (Greenwood Press, 1979); Nimrod Novik, *The United States and Israel: Domestic Determinants of a Changing US Commitment* (Perseus Books, 1986); *The Jewish Chronicle*, November 8, 1996; Andrew Cockburn and Ken Silverstein, *Washington Babylon* (London: Verso, 1996) and Charles W. Kegley & Eugene R. Wittkopf, *American Foreign Policy. Pattern and Process* (New York: St Martin's Press, 1996) 5th edition.

3. For a thorough investigation into the "special relationship" between the US and Israel and its consequences for Palestinians, see Noam Chomsky, *The Fateful Triangle: The United States, Israel and Palestinians* (London: Pluto Press, 2002)

4. Two scandals that would have tried the healthiest of relationships; the sinking of the USS Liberty and the Pollard scandal.

5. Michelle Maraldo, "The US-Israeli Relationship: The past, present and future." http://uwf.edu/govt/studentinfo/maraldoforum1.pdf. A very interesting report that charts the history of the relationship between the two countries, citing that while US Presidents were eager to support the Jews to return to their homeland, amongst some of their motivations was to seek their conversion into Christianity.

6. See Francis A. Boyle, "Barak Appoints War Criminal Yaron." http://www.derechos.org/human-rights/mena/doc/boyle2.html. Ironically, in the very rare instance where an American president used financial support as leverage against Israel was against Sharon, during the Eisenhower administration. As head of the Israeli special unit 101, Ariel Sharon had attacked a Jordanian village, blowing up forty-one houses in the process and one school. The unwarranted attack

killed fifty-three civilians who were all in their homes. See Andrew and Leslie Cockburn, op. cit., p.50

7. In the summer of 1982, the massacre of Sabra and Shatila took place in Lebanon. This was, according to Robert Fisk, "the greatest act of terrorism—using Israel's own definition." Fisk reminds us that it was a time when "Israel's Phalangist militia allies started their three-day orgy of rape and knifing and murder [. . .] that cost 1,800 lives. It followed an Israeli invasion of Lebanon [. . .] which cost the lives of 17,500 Lebanese and Palestinians, almost all of them civilians." Robert Fisk, "Bush is walking into a trap," *The Independent*, September 13, 2001

8. Emma Jane Kirby, "UN Rights Body Condemns Israel." The BBC; http://news.bbc.co.uk/hi/english/world/middle_east/newsid_1930000/1930606.stm

9. "UN Envoy Says Jenin Camp 'Horrific Beyond Belief'"; http://www.islamonline.net/english/News/2002-04/18/articla54.shtml

10. "Peres calls IDF operation in Jenin a 'massacre.'" *Ha'aretz* online June 13, 2002; http://www.adcgeorgia.org/misc/jenin/timeline/peresmassacre.pdf

11. For an interesting article on the possible reasons why this incursion took place, see Uri Avnery, "The Rape of Rafah," *Counterpunch* May 22/23, 2004; http://www.counterpunch.org/avnery05222004.html

12. "Rawan's Innocence Assassinated By Israeli Bullets," IslamOnline May 24, 2004; http://www.islamonline.net/English/News/2004-05/24/article07.shtml

13. United Nations Security Council Resolution 1544 which "[...] calls on Israel to respect international law in particular its obligation not to undertake demolition of homes [...]"

14. Amnesty International; http://web.amnesty.org/library/index/ENGMDE150532004

15. See Greg Philo and Mike Berry, *Bad News from Israel* (London: Pluto Press, 2004)

16. Indeed, a Save the Children survey carried out in the Occupied Territories, revealed that:
• 93% of Palestinian children felt unsafe
• More than half felt that their parents could no longer protect them
• Half the children surveyed had witnessed violence affecting an immediate family member
• 21% had to flee their home for a period due to conflict
• Almost all parents reported traumatic behavior including nightmares,

bedwetting, increased aggression and hyperactivity

John Dugard, the UN's Commissioner on Human Rights exclaimed that the Israeli forces had "inflicted a reign of terror upon innocent Palestinians [...] not to mention the methodical intimidation and humiliation of civilians at checkpoints." After visiting the Occupied Territories, Dugard said that the situation was characterized by "serious violations of general international law, of human rights law and of international humanitarian law." See "United Nations Report: Israeli forces have inflicted a 'reign of terror'"; http://www.wsws.org/articles/2004/mar/2004/occu-m24.shtml

17. See http://www.wsws.org/articles/2003/mar2003/corr-m19_prn.shtml

18. Quoted from Sam Bahour and Leila Bahour, "The Making of a Suicide Bomber: Are Palestinians Human?" *CounterPunch*, http://www.counterpunch.org/sbahour8.html

19. Cf., Akbar S. Ahmed, *Islam Under Siege: Living Dangerously in a Post-Honor World* (Lahore, Pakistan: Vanguard Books, 2003) p. 13

20. See Sam Bahour and Leila Bahour, op cit.

21. Nathan Gardels, "US Wrong To Back Sharon," *New Perspectives Quarterly*, April 12th 2002. http://www.alternet.org/story.html?storyID=12854

22. Matt Bowles, "US Aid: The Lifeblood Of Occupation," *Left Turn Magazine*, March / April issue www.leftturn.org

23. T Christian Miller, "They Forced Me to Hate. Residents of the Jenin refugee camp speak of the viciousness of the Israeli attack," http://ww.latimes.com/news/nationworld/world/la-000026946apr15.story?coll==la%2Dheadlines%2Dworld

24. Dr Eyad El Sarraj, "Wounds and Madness. Why We've Become Suicide Bombers," *Time* magazine, March 31, 2002

25. *The Independent* April 17, 2001

26. Lev Grinberg, "Israel's State Terrorism"; http//www.tikkun.org/TikkunMail/index.cfm/action/current_issue.html

27. Noam Chomsky, op. cit., p.1

28. Robert Fisk, "The Awesome Cruelty of a Doomed People," *The Independent*, September 12, 2001

29. Such organizations include: *Tikkun Magazine*; http://www.tikkun.org; Not in Our Name Coalition: http://www.nimn.org; Jewish Voice for Peace; http://www.jewishvoiceforpeace.org; Gush Shalom; http://www.gush-shalom.org; Jews Against Occupation; http://www.angelcities.com/members/jato; Jewish Peace Fellowship; http://www.jewishpeacefellowship.org; Israeli Committee

Against Home Demolitions; http://www.salam.org/activism/home_demolitions. html; B'Tselem (Israeli Human Rights Group); http://www.btselem.org; Bat Shalom, Israeli Women for Peace; http://www.batshalom.org; Rabbis for Human Rights; http://www.rhr.israel.net; Association for Civil Rights in Israel; http:// www.nif.org/acri; Visions for peace with justice in Israel/Palestine; http://www. vopj.org and Search for Justice and Equality in Palestine/Israel; http://www. searchforjustice.org

30. A. C. Forrest, *The Unholy Land*, (McClelland and Stewart, 1971) p. 53

31. See Appendix I for a summary on the differences between Zionism and orthodox Judaism,

32. See the following websites that aim to distinguish Judaism from Zionism: http://www.jewsnotzionists.org/index.htm; http://www.nkusa.org/index.cfm; http://www.jewsagainstzionism.com

33. See "Prominent Jews' December, 1948 Letter to *New York Times*" http:// www.rense.com/general27/let.htm

34. Norman Bentwich, *For Zion's Sake: A Biography of Judah Magnes* (Philadelphia, 1954) p.188

35. Quoted by Mosche Menuhin, *The Decadence of Judaism in Our Time* (New York: Exposition Press, 1965) p.324

36. Stephen Sizer, unpublished PhD, Christian Zionism, www.sizers.org and Regina Sharif, Non-Jewish Zionism: Its roots in Western History (London: Zed Books, 1983)

37. Donald Wagner, *Anxious for Armageddon* (Pennsylvania: Herald Press, 1995) and Kelvin Crombie, *For the Love of Zion: Christian witness and the restoration of Israel* (London: Hodder and Stoughton, 1991). Also see "The Alliance between Fundamentalist Christians and the Pro-Israel Lobby: Christian Zionism in US Middle-East Policy," in this collection

38. Cf., Noam Chomsky's blog, July 7, 2004; http://blog.zmag.org/ttt/archives/ more

39. Quoted in A. Schleifer, "Jews and Muslims: A Hidden History," in *The Spirit of Palestine* (Barcelona: Zed,1994) p.5

40. Quoted in Avigdor Levy, op.cit., p.3

41. See John L. Esposito, "Islam and the West After September 11: Dialogue or Conflict?" in Aftab Ahmad Malik (ed) *The Empire and the Crescent: Global Implications for A New American Century*, (Bristol: Amal Press, 2003) pp.112-128

42. Quoted in A. Schleifer, op. cit., p.8

43. A tradition by the Prophet Muhammad states that he said, "All Muslims are like a single body: if one part is hurt the whole body feels the pain."

44. The history concerning Jews of the Ottoman Empire is still relatively little known amongst most non-Muslims. Between the sixteenth and seventeenth centuries, more Jews lived in the Ottoman Empire than anywhere else in the world. It was considered by the great Jewish historian, Salo Baron, as another Jewish Golden Age, even surpassing the Jewish experience in Muslim Spain, as the most important place for Jewish scholarship and learning in the world. See Avigdor Levy (ed) *Jews, Turks, Ottomans: A Shared History, Fifteenth Through Twentieth Century* (New York: Syracuse University Press, 2002) and Avigdor Levy, *The Sephardim in the Ottoman Empire* (Princeton: New Jersey, The Darwin Press Inc., 1992).

45. Professor Ben-Zion Dinur (1954), One of Israel's founding Ministers of Education and Culture. Quoted from: http://www.amandashome.com/why. html

46. For a thorough over-view on this matter, see Dan Cohn-Sherbok, *The Crucified Jew: Twenty Centuries of Christian Anti-Semitism* (London: HarperCollins Religious, 1992); Albert S. Lindemann, *Anti-Semitism before the Holocaust* (London: Longman, 2000); Jocelyn Hellig, *The Holocaust and Anti-Semitism: A Short History* (Banbury, Oxford: Oneworld Publications, 2003) and Dan Cohn-Sherbok, *Anti-Semitism* (Sutton Publishing, 2002).

It was only under the leadership of Pope John Paul II, that the Roman Catholic Church has made a number serious efforts to create better understanding between Christianity and Judaism. Perhaps the greatest change came in 1965, at the end of the second Vatican Council, where the Church officially renounced its view of Jews having been responsible for the death of Jesus. The Church also removed all negative references to the Jews in the liturgies and undertook a complete revision of what was taught about Jews in Catholic schools.

47. Bernard Lewis, *The Jews of Islam* (Oxford: Princeton University Press, 1987) p. 8

48. Speaking on BBC Radio 4's *Today Program*, November 17, 2003

49. Bernard Lewis, op. cit., p. 185. It's interesting to note that describing the deterioration the condition and attitudes towards Jews, Lewis describes this under the chapter heading "End of the Tradition." See note 51 on the traditional understanding on relations between Jews and Christians.

50. Ibid.

51. Jews and Christians are known as *Ahl al-Kitab*, or the "People of the Book" in Islam. While Islam contends that these two religions have been abrogated with the advent of Islam, it nonetheless bestows them this dignified status, merely from having been inheritors of a divine tradition. By doing so, Islam provided an environment of religious freedom and tolerance, unprecedented in history. The protection of the lives, properties and honor of non-Muslims residing in Islamic lands was laid down as a religious obligation for Muslims. Such a duty was taken very seriously, as in a tradition of the Prophet Muhammad, it is related that he said that anyone who acted improper against the *Dhimmi*, he would take their case on the Day of Judgment. The *Dhimmi* were non-Muslim citizens who resided in Muslim lands. For this protection, they were levied a tax, which the Prophet said should not "overburden" them.

While conclusions of studies carried out by Muslim and non-Muslim scholars concerning the condition and status of non-Muslim communities under Muslim rulers differ, the Muslim attitude to tolerance and religious freedom was on the whole, genuine and unparalleled. (See William Montgomery Watt, *Islamic Political Thought* (London: Cambridge University Press, 1968) p. 51) While no-one claims that Muslims were free from committing wrong-doing or carrying out injustices against non-Muslims, the point is that Muslims were obliged by the *Sharia* to honor the civil, communal and religious rights of other religious communities. As 'Umar, the second Caliph, articulated to the people of Jerusalem in 639:

> In the name of God, the Merciful the Compassionate. This is the security which 'Umar, the servant of God, the Commander of the faithful, grants to the people of Aelia. He grants to all, whether sick or sound, security for their lives, their possessions, their churches and their crosses, and for all that concerns their religion. Their churches shall not be changed into dwelling places, nor destroyed; neither shall they nor their appurtenances be in any way diminished, nor the crosses of the inhabitants nor aught of their possessions, nor shall any constraint be put upon them in the matter of their faith, nor shall anyone of them be harmed.

—*Quoted from; Thomas W. Arnold, The Preaching of Islam (Lahore: S.M.*
Ashraf, 1961) pp.56-57

This tolerance can be seen in the writings of a seventh century letter, written by the Patriarch Isho'yab concerning how 'Umar's words had been operationalized. He wrote "The Arabs to whom God has given at this time the government of the world [...] do not persecute the Christian religion. Indeed, they favor it, honor our priests and the saints of the Lord and confer benefits on churches and monasteries." Quoted from W.H.C Frend, "Christianity in the Middle East: Survey Down to AD 1800," in *Religion in the Middle East* (ed) A.J Arberry (Cambridge: 1969) vol. II, p.289

'Umar was articulating the message of Islam as laid out in the Qur'an and the Prophet's tradition *(sunna)*. Justice and Mercy are the over-riding qualities that Muslims are commanded to show. The Qur'an exhorts Muslims to show integrity, be just and judge with justice. The Qur'an not only reminds Muslims, but mankind of their common ancestry, namely all being children of Adam (Qur'an 49:13) and the Prophet articulated this on many occasions. He once said that "(all of) you are the children of Adam and Adam is from dust. Let some men cease to take pride in others." (Narrated by Abu Hurayrah; Ahmad and Abu Dawud, 4/331) Rather than being created to "clash" with one another, mankind was created in their diversity to "come to know each other." (Qur'an 49:13). Muslims are prohibited from allowing hatred of a people to commit crimes of aggression against them (Qur'an 5:8) and insists that monasteries, churches and synagogues must be protected (Qur'an 22:40). The Qur'an counts Jews and Christians as "those who believe" and upon whom "will feel no fear and will no sorrow." (Qur'an 2:62) Muslims are told not to force people to convert to Islam (Qur'an 2:256) and rather says "[t]o you your religion, and to me, mine." (Qur'an 109:6) The Qur'an instructs Muslims that so long as they show no hostility to Islam or Muslims, a tolerant and friendly attitude must be maintained towards other religions (Qur'an 60:8-9) and even when hostilities do break out, to abide by strict rules of engagement, as emphasized in the Qur'an by the injunction "[...] but transgress not the limits." (Qur'an 2:190)

The limitations of *Jihad* have been enumerated by many sayings of the Prophet Muhammad and recording in the various authentic *hadith* collections, along with pronouncements made by his successive Caliphs. So we find, as related by al-Tabari in his *al-Jami al-bayan*, that the Prophet's cousin, Ibn Abbas, explained concerning the verse "but transgress not the limits," to mean "do not kill women, or children, or the old, or the one who greets you with peace, or (the one who) restrains his hand (from hurting you)." Malik in his *Muwatta* records that Abu

Bakr, the first Caliph instructed the commander of an army "do not kill women, children, the old or the infirm, do not cut down fruit bearing trees; do not no destroy towns; do not cut the gums of sheep or camels except for the purpose of eating; do not burn down date trees nor submerge them; do not steal from booty and do not be cowardly." There is a great corpus of *hadiths* related to this issue, which largely are ignored by modern *"Jihadist"* groups (including al-Qaʻida and Osama bin Laden) who also use Qur'anic verses grossly out of context to justify their total war against Jews and Christians. Applying specific verses revealed at specific points of Muslim history, these groups have used certain verses as a *carte blanch* to wage a bloody war against everyone as they see at war with Islam and Muslims. See below note for details.

52. In his 1998 fatwa, Osama bin Laden issued a ruling "to kill the Americans and their allies—civilians and military—(which) is an individual duty for every Muslim who can do it in any country in which it is possible [...]" For a translation of the entire fatwa, see Vincenzo Oliveti, *Terror's Source: The Ideology of Wahhabi-Salafism and its Consequences* (Birmingham: Amadeus Books, 2002) p.82. In an attempt to project authority, people like Osama bin Laden use the term "fatwa" to indicate some authenticity to their claim. A fatwa is a juristic legal opinion that is not binding. The key word here is juristic. One needs to be a qualified expert (a *Mufti*) and grounded in all the necessary requisite sciences to be able to present one. As far as we know, Osama bin Laden is not a qualified jurist but someone who has trained in the construction industry. His skills in issuing this fatwa are akin to an "American citizen with a great deal of money but with minimal or no education in law deciding to issue a personal Supreme Court decision." See Hatem Bazian, "Osama Bin Laden's Fatwa: A Question of Legitimacy," in *Islam in the Balance: Toward a Better Understanding of Islam and its Followers* (California: Rumi Bookstore, 2001) pp.9-12.

Bin Laden and other *"Jihadists"* follow an understanding that is dismissive of the dialectical hermeneutic methods of classical jurisprudence and who reject most of the intellectual tradition of Islam. By ignoring a thousand years of scholarly commentary and analysis of the Qur'an as well as a complete disregard for historical settings, injunctions related to *Jihad* have been altogether ignored. Verses that related to specific incidents during the formative period of the Muslim community as well as to a certain grouping of people have now been used indiscriminately to wage "a path of unbounded bloodshed." For a detailed exposition on the implications of the words *"Kuffar"* (non-Muslims),

"Mushrikin" (polytheists) and *"Munafiqin"* (hypocrites) relating to *Jihad* See David Dakake, "The Myth of Militant Islam," in *Islam, Fundamentalism and the Betrayal of Tradition* (Bloomington, Indiana: World Wisdom, 2004) pp.4-29. The essay provides an incisive examination on the historical settings of verses most commonly used from the Qur'an that are used today to apply to the Americans, their allies and Jews. On the concept of *Jihad* its legal meaning and contrasts between traditional and modern understandings as well as legal and moral restrictions see: Khaled Abou El Fadl, "The Rules of Killing in War: An Inquiry into Classical Sources," in *Muslim World*, vol. 89, No. 2, pp.144-157; Zaid Shakir, "Jihad as Perpetual War," in Aftab Ahmad Malik (ed) *The Empire and the Crescent: Global Implications for A New American Century*, (Bristol: Amal Press, 2003) pp.129-141; Sherman Jackson, "Jihad and the Modern World" in *The Journal of Islamic Law and Culture* (Spring/Summer 2002); Sohail H. Hashmi, *"Jihad"* in Robert Wuthnow (ed) *Encyclopedia of Politics and Religion*, 2 vols. (Washington, D.C.: Congressional Quarterly, Inc., 1998) pp. 425-426

53. For a summary on the distinctions between traditional Islam and the radicalized ideals of *Takfiri* groups, see: Vincenzo Oliveti, *Terror's Source: The Ideology of Wahhabi-Salafism and its Consequences* (Birmingham: Amadeus Books: 2002); *Islam and the Theology of Power* in this collection; John L. Esposito, *Unholy War: Terror in the Name of Islam* (Oxford: Oxford University Press, 2002) and 'Abdal Hakim Murad, *Recapturing Islam from the Terrorists*, http://www.masud.co.uk

54. See Khaled Abou El Fadl, *Rebellion in Islamic Law* (Cambridge: Cambridge University Press, 2002) for a comprehensive study on rebellion as understood in the scholastic tradition of Islam.

55. Qur'an: 5:2 and 5:8

56. Quoted by Nahum Goldmann in Le Paraddoxe Juif ("The Jewish Paradox"), pp.121; http://www.whatreallyhappened.com/palestinians.html

57. Cf., Oren Medicks, Israel, Zionism and anti-Semitism; http://www.redress.btinternet.co.uk/omedicks2.htm

58. Cf., Time Wise, Reflections on Zionism from a Dissident Jew, ZNet, September 5, 2001; http://home.mindspring.com/~fontenelles/wise1.htm

59. For an excellent collection of articles concerned with the issue of anti-Semitism and the criticism of the policies of Israel, see Alexander Cockburn and Jeffrey St. Clair (eds) *The Politics of Anti-Semitism* (California: Counterpunch and AK Press, 2003)

60. The female British Rabbi, Alexandra Wright, an outspoken critic of the Israeli government, found herself being accused of being anti-Semitic by the Jewish Board of Deputies. See "What does Britain's Jewish community make of events in Israel?" *The Independent,* May 3, 2002.

61. Daniel Barenboim "On Israel" http://www.thenation.com/doc.mhtml?i=2 0040607&s=barenboim

62. See Noah Efron, *Real Jews* (New York: Basic Books, 2003)

63. After Israel with 59% came Iran, North Korea and the US, each ranking second with 53%. Iraq weighed in with 52%. For a commentary on these findings, see Andrew Kohut, "Anti-Americanism: Causes and Characteristics," The Pew Research Center: http://people-press.org/commentary/display. php3?AnalysisID=77

The director of the Pew Center commenting on the results acknowledged that: "For Muslims, it has become an article of faith that the US unfairly sides with Israel in its conflict with the Palestinians – 99% of Jordanians, 96% of Palestinians and 94% of Moroccans agree. So too do most Europeans. The only dissent comes from Americans, where a 47% plurality sees US policy as fair. Even in Israel, more respondents view US policy as unfair, than say it is fair."

64. See Appendix II "UN Resolutions and US Vetoes"

65. See Appendix III "Israel's Crimes against Palestinians"

66. Cf. Robert Fisk "A Warning to Those Who Dare to Criticize Israel in the Land of Free Speech"; http://www.counterpunch.org/fisk0424004.html

67. Desmond Tutu, "Apartheid in the Holy Land," *The Guardian,* April 29, 2002

68. Ian Gilmour, "Let there be Justice for all, Mr Bush" *The Observer* (on-line edition) March 31, 2002

69. The British Balfour Declaration promised the Jews a national home in Palestine which would not harm the interests of the indigenous inhabitants, whereas Zionists have exploited this to affirm a Jewish homeland of Palestine, in which the indigenous population would be subjected to decades of crimes as noted in this essay. To the Palestinians—this simply provided no legitimacy—since it was a unilateral action taken by colonialist Britain which ignored the wishes of the indigenous peoples.

70. Arthur Koestler, *Promise and Fulfillment: Palestine 1917—1914* (London: MacMillan, 1949) p.4

71. Jerome Slater, "What Went Wrong? The Collapse of the Israeli-Palestinian

Peace Process," *Political Science Quarterly*, volume 116, Number 2, Summer 2001, pp 172-173

72. Martin Buber, *Israel and the World* (New York, 1948) p. 233

73. Hamza Yusuf, "Religion, Violence and the Modern World," *Seasons*, Hayward, California, vol. 1, No. 2, 2003-2004, p.5

74. For examples of hateful speeches made by Zionist leaders, see: http://www.whatreallyhappened.com/palestinians.html How does such rhetoric transform itself into reality? For an appalling example, See http://www.whatreallyhappened.com/apartheid.jpg

75. Rabbi Jonathan Sacs, *The Dignity of Difference: How to Avoid the Clash of Civilizations* (London: Continuum, 2003), see in particular, chapter six

76. For an excellent exposition on this verse as well as a erudite discussion on the Islamic understanding of human rights, see: Mohammad Hashim Kamali, *The Dignity of Man: An Islamic Perspective* (Cambridge: Islamic Texts Society, 2002)

77. Regarded by most Muslim historians and scholars as one of the greatest thinkers in Islamic history and among the foremost theologians, Imam al-Ghazzali (d.1111) is referred to as *Hujjat al-Islam* or the "proof of Islam."

78. A specialist in Qur'anic commentary, *hadith*, *fiqh* and its principles. Probably the greatest student of controversial theologian, Ibn Taymiyya (d. 1328)

79. Cf., Muhammad Khalid Masud, *Shatibi's Philosophy of Islamic Law*, (Islamic Research Institute: Islamabad, Pakistan, 1995) opening quote

80. Hamza Yusuf, op. cit.

Chapter 3 UNHOLY ALLIANCE

We should invade [Muslim] countries, kill their leaders and convert
them to Christianity.
—*Columnist Ann Coulter, National Review Online, Sept. 13, 2001*

[Islam] is a very evil and wicked religion wicked,
violent and not of the same god [as Christianity]
—*Rev. Franklin Graham,*
Head of the Billy Graham Evangelistic Association, November 2001

Islam is a religion in which God requires you to send your son to
die for him. Christianity is a faith where God sent his Son to die for
you.
—*Attorney General John Ashcroft,*
interview on Cal Thomas radio, November 2001

Just turn [the sheriff] loose and have him arrest every Muslim that
crosses the state line.
—*Rep. C. Saxby Chambliss (R-GA),*
Chairman of the House Subcommittee on Terrorism and Homeland
security and Senate candidate, to Georgia law officers, November 2001

[Nuking *Mecca*] seems extreme, of course, but then again few
people would die and it would send a signal.
—*Richard Lowry, editor National Review Online, online forum*
"The Corner" March 7 2002

It is my belief that the Bible Belt in America is Israel's only safety
belt right now [...] There are 70 million of us, and if there's one
thing that brings us together quickly it's whenever we
begin to detect our government becoming a little anti-Israel.
—*Rev. Jerry Falwell, October 6, 2002*

I believe that we are seeing prophecy unfold so rapidly and
dramatically and wonderfully and, without exaggerating,
makes me breathless.
—*Ed McAteer, October 6, 2002*

I think Mohammed was a terrorist. I read enough of the
history of his life, written by both Muslims and non-Muslims,
that he was a violent man, a man of war.
—*Rev. Jerry Fallwell, October 6, 2002*

The war in Iraq was conceived by twenty five neo-conservative
intellectuals [...] who are pushing President Bush to change the
course of history
— *Haaretz, April 5, 2003*

I believe that God wants me to be president.
—*President George W. Bush*

Thinking about Neo-conservatism

KEVIN MACDONALD

Recently there's been another spate of articles on neo-conservatism raising some vexing issues: is neo-conservatism a Jewish movement? Is it "anti-Semitic" to say so? Are neo-conservatives different from other conservatives? My views on these issues are shaped by my research on several other influential Jewish intellectual and political movements, including the Boasian school of anthropology, psychoanalysis, the Frankfurt School of Social Research, the New York Intellectuals, several movements of the radical left, and the movement to change the ethnic balance of the United States by opening up immigration to all the peoples of the world.[1] In the following I will discuss some general features of these movements and try to show how contemporary neo-conservatism fits into the general picture of Jewish intellectual and political activism.[2]

In all of the Jewish intellectual and political movements I studied, there is a strong Jewish identity among the core figures. In the case of neo-cons, the key figures trace their intellectual ancestry to the anti-Stalinist left. This was a diverse group, some of whom clustered around Trotskyite theoretician Max Schactman who gradually changed into a social democrat and labor leader whose followers became influential in the Democratic Party in the 1970s; their descendants include figures like Carl Gershman (head of the National Endowment for Democracy), and former Reagan administration officials Max Kampelman and Joshua Muravchik, all of whom are affiliated with the Social Democrats/USA. The other strand was centered around influential journals like *Partisan Review* and *Commentary*, the latter published by the American Jewish Committee. The central figures in these movements—people like Sydney

Hook, Irving Kristol, Norman Podhoretz, Clement Greenberg, Nathan Glazer, Saul Bellow, Seymour Martin Lipset, Daniel Bell, and Edward Shils—were deeply concerned about anti-Semitism and other Jewish issues; many of them worked closely with Jewish activist organizations. Since the 1950s, they became increasingly disenchanted with leftism and their overriding concern has been the welfare of Israel.

More recently, the core figures of the movement by all accounts include a long list of Jews prominently placed in the government (Paul Wolfowitz, Richard Perle, Douglas Feith, I. Lewis Libby, Elliott Abrams, David Wurmser), interlocking media and thinktankdom (Bill Kristol, Michael Ledeen, Stephen Bryen, John Podhoretz, Daniel Pipes), and the academic world (Richard Pipes, Donald Kagan). As with the other Jewish intellectual movements I have studied, this group has a history of mutual admiration, close, mutually supportive personal, professional and familial relationships, and focused cooperation in pursuit of common goals.

As the neo-conservatives lost faith in radical leftism as a vehicle for attaining Jewish interests, a new influence was Leo Strauss, a classicist and political philosopher at the University of Chicago. Strauss had a very strong Jewish identity and viewed his philosophy as a means of ensuring Jewish survival in the Diaspora.[3] As Strauss himself noted, "I believe I can say, without any exaggeration, that since a very, very early time the main theme of my reflections has been what is called the 'Jewish 'Question.'"[4] Strauss believed that liberal, individualistic modern Western societies were best for Judaism because the illiberal alternatives of both the left (communism) and right (Nazism) were anti-Jewish. (By the 1950s, anti-Semitism had become an important force in the Soviet Union.) However, Strauss believed that liberal societies were not ideal because they tended to break down group loyalties and group distinctiveness—both qualities essential to the survival of Judaism. And he thought that there was a danger that, like the Weimar Republic, liberal societies could give way to fascism, especially if traditional religious and cultural forms were overturned; hence the neo-conservative attitude that traditional religious forms are a good thing.[5] (Although Strauss believed in the importance of Israel for Jewish survival, his philosophy is not a defense of Israel but a blueprint for Jewish survival in a Diaspora in Western societies.) The fate of the Weimar Republic combined with the emergence of anti-

Semitism in the Soviet Union seems to have had a formative influence on his thinking. As Stephen Holmes writes, "Strauss made his young Jewish-American students gulp by informing them that toleration [secular humanism] was dangerous and that the Enlightenment—rather than the failure of the Enlightenment—led directly to Adolph Hitler."[6]

Although not all neo-conservatives are Straussians, Strauss has become a cult figure for some—the quintessential rabbinical guru with devoted disciples.[7] Strauss relished his role as a guru to worshiping disciples, once writing of "the love of the mature philosopher for the puppies of his race, by whom he wants to be loved in turn."[8] In turn, Strauss was a disciple of Hermann Cohen, a philosopher at the University of Marburg, who ended his career teaching in a rabbinical school; Cohen was a central figure in a school of neo-Kantian intellectuals whose main concern was to rationalize Jewish non-assimilation into German society.

Strauss understood that inequalities among humans were inevitable and advocated rule by an aristocratic elite of philosopher kings forced to publicly respect the traditional religious and political beliefs of the great mass of people while not really believing them.[9] The elite should pursue its vision of the common good but must reach out to others using deception and manipulation to achieve its goals. As Strauss's disciple, Bill Kristol described how elites have the duty to guide public opinion, but "one of the main teachings [of Strauss] is that all politics are limited and none of them is really based on the truth."[10] Strauss based his philosophy on his interpretation of classical Greek political philosophy: "I really believe [...] that the perfect political order, as Plato and Aristotle have sketched it, *is* the perfect political order."[11] Given Strauss's belief that classical political theory sketched the perfect political order and his central concern that an acceptable political order be compatible with Jewish survival, it is reasonable to assume that Strauss believed that the aristocracy would serve Jewish interests.

While Strauss and his followers have come to be known as neo-conservatives or even simply "conservatives," there is nothing conservative about their goals. This is not only the case in foreign policy where Straussians are attempting to rearrange the entire Middle East in the interests of Israel; it is also the case with domestic policy where acceptance of rule by an aristocratic elite would require a complete political transformation in order to create a society that was "as just as possible":

> Nothing short of a *total transformation* of imbedded custom must be undertaken. To secure this inversion of the traditional hierarchies, the political, social and educational system must be subjected to a radical reformation. For justice to be possible the founders have to 'wipe clean the dispositions of men,' that is, justice is possible only if the city and its citizens are *not* what they *are*: the weakest [i.e., the philosophic elite] is supposed to rule the strongest [the masses], the irrational is supposed to submit to the rule of the rational.[12] [emphasis in original]

Strauss described the need for an external *exoteric* language directed at outsiders, and an internal *esoteric* language directed at ingroup members.[13] A general feature of the movements I have studied is that this Straussian prescription has been followed: Issues are framed in language that appeal to non-Jews rather than explicitly in terms of Jewish interests, although Jewish interests always remain in the background if one cares to look a little deeper.

The most common rhetoric used by Jewish intellectual and political movements has been the language of moral universalism and the language of science—languages that appeal to the educated elites of the modern Western world. But beneath the rhetoric it is easy to find statements describing the Jewish agendas of the principle actors. And the language of moral universalism often went hand in hand with a narrow Jewish moral particularism, as in the case of the earlier generation of American Jewish Trotskyites who ignored the horrors of the Soviet Union until the fall of Trotsky and the gradual emergence of official, state-sponsored anti-Semitism.

The movements I studied have been advocated with great intellectual passion and moral fervor and with a very high level of theoretical sophistication. Each movement promised its own often overlapping and complementary version of utopia: a society composed of people with the same biological potential for accomplishment and able to be easily molded by culture into ideal citizens as imagined by a morally and intellectually superior elite (Boasian anthropology, Marxism); a classless society in which there would be no conflicts of interest and people would altruistically work for the good of the group (Marxism); a society in which people would be free of neuroses and aggression toward outgroups and in tune with their biological urges (psychoanalysis); a multicultural paradise in which different racial and ethnic groups would live in harmony and cooperation, and the peoples of European descent would have no ethnic consciousness or sense of group identity (Boasian anthropology; the Frankfurt School).

Neo-conservatives have certainly used a utopian vision and appeals to American platitudes in their advocacy of war throughout the Middle East—gushing about spreading American democracy and freedom to the area, while their strong ethnic and family ties to Israel have remained submerged and are never a part of their public rhetoric. Michael Lind calls attention to the neo-conservatives' "odd bursts of ideological enthusiasm for 'democracy'"[14]—odd not the least because Leo Strauss, the guru of the movement, viewed democracy as requiring management by an elite able to manipulate popular attitudes—hardly the advertised future of Iraq. Odd also because these ringing calls for democracy and freedom do not fit well with Richard Perle et al's original call for the installation of a Hashemite monarchy in Baghdad as part of its plan to secure Israeli interests in the region[15] or for the neo-con promotion of Reza Pahlavi, the son of the former Shah, as the new leader of a post-regime-change Iran.[16] Nor are they compatible with Wolfowitz's complaints that the Turkish military did not take a leadership role in modifying the democratic will of the Turkish Parliament when it rejected the use of Turkey as a staging area for the war in Iraq.[17] Neo-conservative calls for democracy and freedom throughout the Middle East are also coupled with support for the Likud Party and other like-minded groups in Israel that are driven by a vision of an apartheid-like, expansionist Israel where democracy is little more than an instrument of ethnic warfare rather than an expression of Western universalism. Indeed, the movement for expelling the Palestinians is alive and well, with Binyamin Elon and similar minded people playing important roles in Ariel Sharon's cabinet.

Actually, the inconsistencies of the neo-conservatives are not odd or surprising. The Straussian idea is to achieve the aims of the elite ingroup by using language designed for mass appeal—a war for "democracy and freedom" sells much better than a war to achieve the foreign policy aims of Israel. For Straussians, deception is a big part of the game. The director of the Office of Special Plans in the Department of Defense—the origin of much of the disinformation on Iraq's WMD and its ties to al-Qaʻida—is Abram Shulsky who received his Ph.D. under Strauss.[18] (Recently Wolfowitz acknowledged that claims that Iraq had WMD's were deception.[19]) The Office of Special Plans is overseen by Douglas Feith, third ranking civilian in the Pentagon, and longtime associate of JINSA and the Zionist Organization of America, both of which oppose territorial concessions by Israel.[20] The ZOA is a strong supporter of Israeli settlers on the West Bank and in Gaza.

It is an extraordinary comment on the current state of US foreign policy that Richard Perle, a major architect of that policy, was the main force behind a 1996 report to the Israeli government by an Israeli think tank advocating the overthrow of the Iraqi regime and thereby securing Israeli interests.[21] (Also signing that report were other prominent Jewish-American neo-conservatives: Douglas Feith, and David and Meyrav Wurmser. Feith and David Wurmser have influential foreign policy positions in the current Bush Administration.) Little noted these days is that in 1970, Perle was recorded by the FBI discussing classified information with the Israeli embassy or that he was on the payroll of an Israeli defense contractor.[22] It is also extraordinary but little commented on that Paul Wolfowitz has close family ties to Israel and is friendly with Israel's generals and diplomats.[23]

As with the other Jewish intellectual and political movements I reviewed, non-Jews have been welcomed into the movement and often given highly visible roles as the public face of the movement. This of course lessens the perception that the movement is indeed a Jewish movement, and it makes excellent psychological sense to have the spokespeople for any movement resemble the people they are trying to convince. That's why Ahmed Chalabi (a Shi'ite Iraqi, student of Wohlstetter, and close personal associate of prominent neo-cons, including Richard Perle) and not Douglas Feith has been the neo-cons' choice for leading postwar Iraq. (Feith remains in the background as head of the Defense Department's Office of Reconstruction and Humanitarian Assistance for Iraq.) There are lots of examples—including Freud's famous comments on needing a non-Jew to represent psychoanalysis (he got Karl Jung for a time until he balked at the role, and then Ernest Jones), Margaret Mead and Ruth Benedict as the most recognized Boasian anthropologists, and a great many examples of non-Jewish leftists and pro-immigration advocates being promoted to visible positions in Jewish dominated movements— and sometimes resenting their role.[24] Albert Lindemann describes non-Jews among the leaders of the Bolshevik revolution as "jewified non-Jews"—"a term, freed of its ugly connotations, [that] might be used to underline an often overlooked point: Even in Russia there were some non-Jews, whether Bolsheviks or not, who respected Jews, praised them abundantly, imitated them, cared about their welfare, and established intimate friendships or romantic liaisons with them."[25]

There was a smattering of non-Jews among the New York Intellectuals who were the forerunners of the neo-cons in the 1940s, most notably Dwight MacDonald (labeled by Michael Wrezin "a distinguished goy among the Partisanskies"[26]—i.e., the *Partisan Review* crowd), James T. Farrell, and Mary McCarthy. John Dewey also had close links to the New York Intellectuals and was lavishly promoted by them.[27] Among the current crop in this intellectual lineage, the most important non-Jews are Dick Cheney and Donald Rumsfeld, both of whom have close professional and personal relationships with neo-cons that long pre-date their present power and visibility. Both Cheney and Rumsfeld have been associated with Bill Kristol's Project for a New American Century (PNAC), which advocated a unilateral war for regime change in Iraq at least as early as 1998,[28] and the Center for Security Policy (CSP), two neo-con think tanks. Cheney was also a member of the Jewish Institute for National Security Affairs (JINSA) until assuming his office as Vice-President. Both Cheney and Rumsfeld have close personal relationships with Kenneth Adelman, former Ford and Reagan administration official and a member of the inner circle of neo-cons.[29] Rumsfeld has also had a long association with Robert A. Goldwin, a student of Strauss and Rumsfeld's deputy both at NATO and at the Gerald Ford White House. Goldwin is now Resident Scholar of the American Enterprise Institute, another important neo-con think tank.

PNAC, CSP, JINSA, and the AEI are prototypical neo-con institutions and strong advocates of rearranging the politics of the Middle East in the interests of Israel. Cheney's role in the ascendancy of the neo-cons in the Bush Administration is particularly important: As head of the transition team, he and Lewis Libby, his Chief of Staff, were able to staff the sub-cabinet levels of the State Department (John Bolton) and the Defense Department (Wolfowitz, Douglas Feith) with key figures who had long-term personal, political, and family ties. Libby is Jewish and has a long history of involvement in Zionist causes and as the attorney for the notorious Marc Rich. Libby and Cheney were involved in pressuring the CIA to color intelligence reports to fit with their desire for a war with Iraq.[30]

JINSA is a good example of a Jewish organization designed to appeal to non-Jews. In addition to a core of prominent neo-conservative Jews (Michael Ledeen, Stephen D. Bryen, Joshua Muravchik, Richard Perle), JINSA's Advisory Board includes a bevy of non-Jewish retired US military officers who are staunch supporters of Israel. Former Iraq pro-consul General Jay Garner signed a JINSA letter stating that "the Israel Defense Forces have exercised remarkable restraint in the face of lethal violence orchestrated by the leadership of [the] Palestinian Authority."

Similarly, the PNAC has a large core of Jewish members sprinkled with some non-Jews. PNAC was founded by Bill Kristol and foreign policy analyst Robert Kagan and has links with all of the prominent Jewish neo-conservatives. However, PNAC's statements and letters have also included as signatories prominent non-Jews such as William J. Bennett, Dick Cheney, Francis Fukuyama, Frank Gaffney, and Donald Rumsfeld. The ability to recruit prominent non-Jews while nevertheless maintaining a Jewish core and a commitment to Jewish interests has been a hallmark—perhaps *the* hallmark—of influential Jewish intellectual and political movements throughout the 20th century into the present.

The Jewish intellectual and political movements I have studied are typified by a deep sense of orthodoxy—a sense of "us versus them" that has been typical of Jewish society throughout the ages. Dissenters are expelled, usually amid character assassination and other recriminations. This has certainly been a feature of the neo-con movement, beginning with Leo Strauss's belief that politics was fundamentally about creating ingroups versus outgroups with a double standard of morality for ingroup members versus outgroup members.[31] The quintessential recent example of this "We vs. They" world is David Frum's recent attack on "unpatriotic conservatives" as anti-Semites.[32] Any conservative who opposes the war as being against US interests and who notes the pro-Israeli motivation of many of the most important players in the pro-war movement is liable to such a charge.

Another feature of the Jewish intellectual and political movements I have studied has been that they were associated with prestigious universities and media sources. The university most closely associated with the current crop of neo-conservatives is the University of Chicago, the academic home not only of Leo Strauss, but also of Albert Wohlstetter, a mathematician turned foreign policy strategist, who was mentor to both Perle and Wolfowitz. The University of Chicago was also home to Allan Bloom, Edward Shils, and Saul Bellow, the latter two among the earlier generation of neo-conservatives.

Jewish intellectual and political movements also have typically had ready access to prestigious mainstream media outlets, and this is certainly true for the neo-cons. Most notable are Bill Kristol's *The Weekly Standard*, *The Wall Street Journal, Commentary, The Public Interest, Basic Books* (book publishing), and Rupert Murdoch's media empire, especially the Fox News Channel. Perle is on the board of the Boards of Directors of the pro-Likud *Jerusalem Post* and Conrad Black's Hollinger Corporation and Co-Director of Hollinger Digital, a subsidiary of Hollinger Corporation. Neo-conservatives under Jonah Goldberg have also managed to dominate *The National Review*, formerly a bastion of traditional conservative thought in the US. Neo-con think tanks such as the AEI have a great deal of cross-membership with Jewish activist organizations such as AIPAC and the Washington Institute for Near East Policy. (When President George W. Bush addressed the AEI on Iraq policy recently, it was appropriate that the event was held in the Albert Wohlstetter Conference Center.) A major goal of the AEI is to maintain a high profile as pundits in the mainstream media. For example, AEI fellow Michael Ledeen, who is extreme in his lust for war against the entire Middle East even among the neo-cons, is "resident scholar in the Freedom Chair at AEI," writes op-ed articles for *The Scripps Howard News Service* and *The Wall Street Journal*, and appears on the Fox News Channel. Michael Rubin, visiting scholar at AEI, writes for *The New Republic* (controlled by staunchly pro-Israel Martin Peretz),

The New York Times, and *The Daily Telegraph*. Reuel Marc Gerecht, a resident fellow at AEI and Director of the Middle East Initiative at PNAC, writes for the *Weekly Standard* and *The New York Times*.

Finally, another common theme of Jewish intellectual and political movements has been the involvement and clout of the wider Jewish community. While the prominent neo-conservatives represent a small fraction of the American Jewish community, there is little doubt that the organized Jewish community shares their commitment to the Likud Party in Israel and, one might reasonably infer, Likud's desire to see the United States conquer and occupy virtually the entire Arab world.[33] Recently we are seeing the same coalition for regime change in Iran that accomplished the destruction of Iraq: Jewish organizations, neo-con hawks in the Bush administration, and foreign exile groups on friendly terms with Israel and the American Jewish establishment.[34] As mentioned above, the neo-con choice for the leader of the new regime in Iran is Reza Pahlavi, son of the former Shah. As is also the case with Ahmed Chalabi, who has been promoted by the neo-cons as the leader of post-Saddam Iraq, Pahlavi has good relations with several Jewish groups. He has addressed the board of JINSA, given a public speech at the Simon Wiesenthal Center's Museum of Tolerance in Los Angeles, met with American Jewish communal leaders, and is on friendly terms with Likud Party officials in Israel.[35]

Moreover, the main Jewish defense organizations have been quick to condemn those who have noted the Jewish commitments of the neo-conservative activists in the Bush administration or seen a hand of the Jewish community in pushing for the present policy. (Of course, neo-cons in the media—most notably David Frum, Max Boot, Jonah Goldberg, and Alan Wald[36]—have been busy on this front as well.) For example, the ADL's Abraham Foxman singled out Pat Buchanan, Joe Sobran, Rep. James Moran, Chris Mathews of MSNBC, *San Diego Union-Tribune* columnist James O. Goldsborough columnist Robert Novak, and writer Ian Burama as subscribers to "a canard that America's going to war has little to do with disarming Saddam, but everything to do with Jews, the 'Jewish lobby' and the hawkish Jewish members of the Bush Administration who, according to this chorus, will favor any war that benefits Israel."[37] These mainstream media and political figures stand accused of anti-Semitism—the most deadly charge that can be imagined in the contemporary world—by the most powerful Jewish activist organization in the US. The Simon Wiesenthal Center has also charged Buchanan and Moran with anti-Semitism for their comments on this issue.[38] While Foxman feels no need to provide any argument at all, the SWC feels it is sufficient to note that Jews have varying opinions on the war. This of course is a non-issue. The real issue is whether it is legitimate to open up to debate the question of whether the neo-con activists in the Bush administration are motivated by their long ties to the Likud Party in Israel and whether the organized Jewish community in the US similarly supports the Likud Party and its desire to enmesh the United States in wars that are in Israel's interest. (There's not much doubt about how the SWC viewed the war with Iraq; Rumsfeld invited Rabbi Marvin Hier, dean of the Center, to briefings on the war.[39])

The wider Jewish community also provides financial support for intellectual and political movements, as in the case of psychoanalysis, where the Jewish community signed on as patients and as consumers of psychoanalytic literature.[40] This has also been the case with neo-conservatism, as noted by Gary North:

> With respect to the close connection between Jews and neo-conservatism, it is worth citing [Robert] Nisbet's assessment of the revival of his academic career after 1965. His only book, *The Quest for Community* (Oxford UP, 1953), had come back into print in paperback in 1962 as *Community and Power*. He then began to write for the neo-conservative journals. Immediately, there were contracts for him to write a series of books on conservatism, history, and culture, beginning with *The Sociological Tradition*, published in 1966 by Basic Books, the newly created neo-conservative publishing house. Sometime in the late 1960's, he told me: "I became an in-house sociologist for the *Commentary-Public Interest* crowd. Jews buy lots of academic books in America." Some things are obvious but unstated. He could follow the money: book royalties. So could his publishers.[41]

The support of the wider Jewish community and the elaborate neo-conservative infrastructure in the media and thinktankdom provide irresistible professional opportunities for Jews and non-Jews alike. I am not saying the people like Nisbet don't believe what they write in neo-conservative publications. I am simply saying that having opinions that are attractive to neo-conservatives can be very lucrative and professionally rewarding.

As always, when discussing Jewish involvement in intellectual movements, there is no implication that all or even most Jews are involved in these movements. As discussed below, the organized Jewish community shares the neo-con commitment to the Likud Party in Israel. However, neo-conservatism has never been a majority viewpoint in the American Jewish community, at least if being a neo-conservative implies voting for the Republican Party. In the 2000 election, 80 percent of Jews voted for Al Gore.[42]

These percentages may be misleading, since it was not widely known during the 2000 election that the top advisors of George W. Bush had very powerful Jewish connections, pro-Likud sympathies, and positive attitudes toward regime change in Arab countries in the Middle East. Republican strategists are hoping for 35 percent of the Jewish vote in 2004.[43] President Bush's May 18, 2004 speech to the national convention of AIPAC

> [...] received a wild and sustained standing ovation in response to an audience member's call for 'four more years.' The majority of some 4,500 delegates at the national conference of the American Israel Public Affairs Committee leaped to their feet in support of the president [...] Anecdotal evidence points to a sea of change among Jewish voters, who historically have trended toward the Democratic Party but may be heading to Bush's camp due to his stance on a single issue: his staunch support of Israel.[44]

Nevertheless, Democrats may not lose many Jewish voters because John Kerry has a "100% record" for Israel and has promised to increase troop strength and retain the commitment to Iraq.[45]

The critical issue is to determine the extent to which neo-conservatism is a Jewish movement—the extent to which Jews dominate the movement and are a critical component of its success. One must then document the fact that the Jews involved in the movement have a Jewish identity and that they are Jewishly motivated—that is, that they see their participation as aimed at achieving specific Jewish goals. In the case of neo-conservatives, an important line of evidence is to show their deep connections to Israel—their "passionate attachment to a nation not their own," as Pat Buchanan terms it,[46] and especially to the Likud Party. As indicated above, I will argue that the main motivation for Jewish neo-conservatives has been to further the cause of Israel; however, even if that statement is true, it does not imply that all Jews are neo-conservatives. I therefore reject the sort of arguments made by Richard Perle, who responded to charges that neo-conservatives were predominantly Jews by noting that Jews always tend to be disproportionately involved in intellectual undertakings, and that many Jews oppose the neo-conservatives.[47] This is indeed the case, but leaves open the question of whether neo-conservative Jews perceive their ideas as advancing Jewish interests and whether the movement itself is influential. An important point of the following, however, is that the organized Jewish community has played a critical role in the success of neo-conservatism and in preventing public discussion of its Jewish roots and Jewish agendas.

Count me among those who accept the idea that the Jewish commitment of the main actors is a critical component of US foreign policy and that the effectiveness of the neo-conservative activists is greatly facilitated by involvement of the organized Jewish community. In my opinion, these conclusions are based on solid data and reasonable inferences. Like any other theory, theories that imply Jewish motivation, Jewish collusion, and Jewish recruitment of non-Jews are subject to disproof and reasoned discussion.

Finally, the dispute between the neo-cons and more traditional conservatives (paleocons) is important because the latter now find themselves on the outside looking in on the conservative power structure. The neo-cons' foreign policy fits well with a common perception of Jewish interests but is at best tenuously related to the interests of the United States and is opposed to the strong strand of isolationism in important wings of traditional American conservatism. In the same way, neo-con attitudes on issues like race and immigration differ profoundly from those of traditional mainstream conservatives and resemble quite closely attitudes that are common throughout the wider American Jewish community.[48] The neo-con/paleocon division is therefore of great significance and will continue to be a lively and divisive issue on the right.

Indeed, one might note that US immigration policy since 1965 fits well with a Straussian analysis because it is a policy that has been advocated by elites despite opposition by the great majority of Americans. Jewish elites were the main force behind the immigration law of 1965,[49] and since 1965 other elites, particularly businesses eager to employ cheap labor, and other ethnic groups advancing their ethnic interests—particularly Latino groups, have also been important.

When, in the middle 1990s an immigration reform movement arose amongst American conservatives, the reaction of the neo-conservatives ranged from cold to hostile. No positive voice was permitted on the op-ed page of the *Wall Street Journal*, by then a neo-conservative domain. The main vehicle of immigration reform sentiment, *National Review*, once the bastion of traditional conservative thought in the US, was quite quickly captured by neo-conservatives and its opposition to immigration quickly reduced to nominal.

Jewish neo-cons have taken the lead in attacking immigration restrictionists on the right in conservative publications.[50] Jewish groups have had several reasons for favoring open immigration, including the idea that Judaism is safer in a more diverse society. Recently, the "diversity as safety" argument was made by Leonard S. Glickman, president and CEO of the Hebrew Immigrant Aid Society, a Jewish group that has advocated open immigration to the United States for over a century. Glickman stated, "The more diverse American society is the safer [Jews] are."[51] At the present time, the HIAS is deeply involved in recruiting refugees from Africa to emigrate to the US

We shouldn't be surprised by the importance of ethnicity in human affairs, nor should we be intimidated by charges of anti-Semitism. We should be able to discuss ethnic issues openly and honestly, but, for well over half a century, with rare exceptions, Jewish interests and activities have been off limits for rational discussion.[52] Ethnic politics in the US is scarcely limited to Jewish activism; it is certainly an all-too-human phenomenon throughout history and around the world.

NOTES

1. K. B. MacDonald, *The Culture of Critique: Toward an Evolutionary Analysis of Twentieth-Century Intellectual and Political Movements* (Bloomington, IN: Author House, 1998), see also;

http://www.csulb.edu/~kmacd/books.htm and

http://www.amazon.com/exec/obidos/tg/detail/-/0759672229/ref=ase_ kevinmacdonal-20/102-7190051-8383323?v=glance&s=books

2. A longer, more detailed version of this paper appeared as "Understanding Jewish Activism III: Neo-conservatism as a Jewish Movement," in *Occidental Quarterly*, 4(2), Summer, 2004. The long version will also appear in K. MacDonald, *Understanding Jewish Influence: A Study in Ethic Activism* (Raleigh, NC: Washington Summit Publishers, Fall, 2004)

3. L. Strauss, "Why we remain Jews: Can Jewish faith and history still speak to us?" in K. L. Deutsch & W. Nicgorski (eds.) *Leo Strauss: Political Philosopher and Jewish Thinker* (Lanham, MD: Rowman & Littlefield Publishers, Inc., 1994), pp. 43–79. Based on a lecture given on February 4, 1962 at the Hillel Foundation, University of Chicago.

4. Ibid, p. 44.

5. Strauss, ibid.; Tarcov, N., & Pangle, T. L., "Epilogue: Leo Strauss and the History of Political Philosophy," in *History of Political Philosophy*, 3rd edn., (ed.) L. Strauss & J. Cropsey. (Chicago: University of Chicago Press, 1987) pp. 909–910. See also Holmes, S., *The Anatomy of Anti-Liberalism* (Cambridge, MA: Harvard University Press, 1993) pp. 61–87.

6. Holmes, ibid., p. 63.

7. M. Himmelfarb (1974, August), On Leo Strauss, *Commentary*, 58, pp. 60–66:"There are many excellent teachers. They have students. Strauss had disciples." See also Holmes, ibid.; N. J. Easton, Gang of Five: *Leaders at the Center of the Conservative Crusade* (Simon & Schuster, 2000) p. 38; S. Drury, *Leo Strauss and the American Right* (New York: St. Martin's Press, 1997) p. 2. D. L. Levine (1994), *Without malice but with forethought*, in Deutsch & Nicgorski (eds.), ibid., p. 354: "This group has the trappings of a cult. After all, there is a secret teaching and the extreme seriousness of those who are 'initiates.'"

8. L. Strauss, *Persecution and the Art of Writing* (Westport, CT: Greenwood, 1952) p. 36.

9. Drury, ibid.; Holmes, ibid.; Tarcov & Pangle, ibid., p. 915. Holmes

summarizes this thesis as follows: "The good society, on this model, consists of the sedated masses, the gentlemen rulers, the promising puppies, and the philosophers who pursue knowledge, manipulate the gentlemen, anesthetize the people, and housebreak the most talented young" (p. 74).

10. N. J. Easton, op cit., pp. 45, 183.

11. K. L. Deutsch & W. Nicgorski (1994), *Introduction.* In Deutsch & Nicgorski, ibid, pp.1–40. The quotation from Strauss is on p. 9. See also, Holmes, op cit., p. 71.

12. Levine, op cit., p. 366.

13. L. Strauss, *Persecution and the Art of Writing*, Ch. 2 op cit.

14. Michael Lind, "How neo-conservatives conquered Washington—and launched a war." *New Statesman*, April 7, 2003;

http://www.newstatesman.com/site.php3?newTemplate=NSTemplate_NS&n ewTop=Section%3A+Front+Page&newDisplayURN=Section%3A+Front+Page

15. "A Clean Break: A New Strategy for Securing the Realm."http://www. israeleconomy.org/strat1.htm This report was prepared by Richard Perle, James Colbert, Charles Fairbanks, Jr., Douglas Feith, Robert Loewenberg, David Wurmser, and Meyrav Wurmser for The Institute for Advanced Strategic and Political Studies' "Study Group on a New Israeli Strategy Toward 2000."

16. J. Lobe, "Neo-cons move quickly on Iran." *Asian Times*, May 28, 2003.

http://www.atimes.com/atimes/Middle_East/EE28Ak01.html

M. Perelman, "New Front Sets Sights On Toppling Iran Regime." *Forward*, May 16, 2003. http://www.forward.com/issues/2003/03.05.16/news2.html

17. H. D. S. Greenway, "The neo-cons style of democracy." *Boston Globe*, May 16, 2003.

18. S. M. Hersh, "Selective Intelligence," *New Yorker*, May 6, 2003. J. Wolf, "US Insiders Say Iraq Intel Deliberately Skewed"; *Reuters*, May 30, 2003. P. Seale, "A Costly Friendship," *The Nation*, July 21, 2003. http://www.thenation.com/doc. mhtml?i=20030721&s=seale

19. Wolfowitz stated that the WMD rationale was adopted "for bureaucratic reasons": *Washington Post*, May 30, 2003 http://www.washingtonpost.com/wp-dyn/articles/A57988-2003May30.html.

20. O. Nir, Feith Seen as War-Plans Fall Guy. *Forward*, June 20, 2003.http:// www.forward.com/issues/2003/03.06.20/news6.html

21. "A Clean Break: A New Strategy for Securing the Realm."op cit.

22. P. Findley, *They Dare to Speak Out: People and Institutions Confront Israel's*

Lobby, 2nd ed. (Chicago: Lawrence Hill Books, 1989) p. 160.

23. B. Keller, "The Sunshine Warrior." *New York Times* Magazine, September 23, 2002.

24. MacDonald, 1998/2002, ibid., Chs. 3, 7; see also H. Klehr (1978). *Communist Cadre: The Social Background of the American Communist Party Elite* (Stanford, CA: Hoover Institution Press) p. 40; A. Liebman (1979), *Jews and the Left* (New York: John Wiley & Sons) pp. 527ff; S. M. Neuringer, S. M. (1980). *American Jewry and United States Immigration Policy, 1881–1953* (Arno Press, 1980) p. 92; S. Rothman & S. R.Lichter, *Roots of Radicalism: Jews, Christians, and the New Left* (New York: Oxford University Press, 1982) p. 99; S. Svonkin, *Jews Against Prejudice: American Jews and the Fight for Civil Liberties* (New York: Columbia University Press, 1997) pp. 45, 51, 65, 71–72.

25. A. Lindemann, *Esau's Tears: Modern Anti-Semitism and the Rise of the Jews* (New York, Cambridge University Press, 1997) p. 433.

26. M. Wrezin, *A Rebel in Defense of Tradition: The Life and Politics of Dwight Macdonald* (New York: Basic Books, 1994)

27. MacDonald, 1998/2002, op.cit, Ch. 7; D. A. Hollinger, *Science, Jews, and Secular Culture: Studies in Mid-Twentieth—Century American Intellectual History* (Princeton, NJ: Princeton University Press, 1996) p. 158.

28. PNAC Letter to President Clinton, Jan. 26, 1998 http://www.newamericancentury.org/iraqclintonletter.htm;PNAC Letter to Speaker of the House Newt Gingrich and Senate Majority Leader Trent Lott, May 29, 1998 http://www.newamericancentury.org/iraqletter1998.htm .

29. Elizabeth Drew, "The Neo-cons in Power," *The New York Review of Books*, 50(10), June 12, 2003; http://www.nybooks.com/articles/16378; see also: http://www.defensecentralstation.com/1051/indexwrapper.jsp?PID=1051-155&CID=1051-BIOADELMANKEN

30. W. Pincus and D. Priest, "Some Iraq Analysts Felt Pressure From Cheney Visits," *Washington Post*, June 5, 2003.

31. See Drury, op cit., p. 23; Holmes, op cit., p. 68; Levine, op cit., p. 368.

32. David Frum, "Unpatriotic Conservatives," *National Review*, March 19, 2003. http://www.nationalreview.com/frum/frum031903.asp

33. Massing, M. (2002). "Deal Breakers", *American Prospect*, March 11.http://www.prospect.org/print/V13/5/massing-m.html

34. M. Perelman, "New Front Sets Sights On Toppling Iran Regime." *Forward*, May 16, 2003. http://www.forward.com/issues/2003/03.05.16/news2.html

35. Ibid.

36. Jonah Goldberg, "Jews and the war." *National Review* Online, March 13, 2003. http://www.nationalreview.com/goldberg/goldberg031303.asp; Alan Wald, "Are Trotskyites running the Pentagon?" History News Network, 6/23/03 http://hnn.us/articles/1514.html ; see also Michael Lind, "I was smeared" History News Network, 6/30/03 http://hnn.us/articles/1530.html

37. *Jerusalem Report*, May 5. 2003. http://www.adl.org/anti%5Fsemitism/as%5Fsimple.asp

38. http://www.wiesenthal.com/social/press/pr_item.cfm?itemID=7323

39. S. L. Morris, "Shipwrecked: Swimming with sharks in a sea of arts funding," *LA Weekly*, June 27–July 3, 2003. http://www.laweekly.com/ink/03/32/news-morris.php

40. See K. MacDonald, *The Culture of Critique*, op cit., Ch. 4.

41.Gary North, An Introduction to Neo-conservatism. http://www.lewrockwell.com/north/north180.html

42.Friedman 2002; Young Jewish Leadership Political Action Committee http://yjlpac.org/dc/fyi.htm

43. Kessler 2004.

44. M. Horrigan, "Bush increases margins with AIPAC." *United Press International*, May 18, 2004. http://www.washingtontimes.com/upi-breaking/20040518-015208-9372r.htm

45. See Buchanan 2004.

46. Buchanan 2004.

47. B. Wattenberg interview with Richard Perle, PBS, November 14, 2002. http://www.pbs.org/thinktank/transcript1017.html. The entire relevant passage from the interview follows. Note Perle's odd argument that it was not in Israel's interest that the US invade Iraq because Saddam Hussein posed a much greater threat to Israel than the US.

Ben Wattenberg: As this argument has gotten rancorous, there is also an undertone that says that these neo-cons hawks, that so many of them are Jewish. Is that valid and how do you handle that?

Richard Perle: Well, a number are. I see Trent Lott there and maybe that's Newt Gingrich, I'm not sure, but by no means uniformly.

Ben Wattenberg: Well, and of course the people who are executing policy, President Bush, Vice President Cheney, Don Rumsfeld, Colin Powell, Connie Rice, they are not Jewish as last report.

Richard Perle: No, they're not. Well, you're going to find a disproportionate number of Jews in any sort of intellectual undertaking.

Ben Wattenberg: On both sides.

Richard Perle: On both sides. Jews gravitate toward that and I'll tell you if you balance out the hawkish Jews against the dovish ones, then we are badly outnumbered, badly outnumbered. But look, there's clearly an undertone of anti-Semitism about it. There's no doubt.

Ben Wattenberg: Well, and the linkage is that this war on Iraq if it comes about would help Israel and that that's the hidden agenda, and that's sort of the way that works.

Richard Perle: Well, sometimes there's an out and out accusation that if you take the view that I take and some others take towards Saddam Hussein, we are somehow motivated not by the best interest of the United States but by Israel's best interest. There's not a logical argument underpinning that. In fact, Israel is probably more exposed and vulnerable in the context of a war with Saddam than we are because they're right next door. Weapons that Saddam cannot today deliver against us could potentially be delivered against Israel. And for a long time the Israelis themselves were very reluctant to take on Saddam Hussein. I've argued this issue with Israelis. But it's a nasty line of argument to suggest that somehow we're confused about where our loyalties are.

Ben Wattenberg: It's the old dual loyalty argument.

48. K. MacDonald, *The Culture of Critique*, Ch. 7. See also: http://www.csulb. edu/~kmacd/paper/ABERNET3.PDF

49. MacDonald, 1998/2002, Ch. 7; Hugh Davis Graham, *Collision Course: The Strange Convergence of Affirmative Action and Immigration Policy in America* (New York, Oxford University Press, 2002) pp. 56–57.

50. MacDonald, 1998/2002, Preface to the paperback edition, 2002, Ch. 7.

51. *Forward,* November 29, 2002.

52. MacDonald, 1998/2002, Preface to the paperback edition, 2002.

13 | Neo-conservative Designs on Saudi Arabia

TANYA C. HSU

Hijacking planes, terrorizing innocent people and shedding blood, constitute a form of injustice that cannot be tolerated by Islam, which views them as gross crimes and sinful acts [...] Any Muslim who is aware of his teachings of his religion and who adheres to the directives of the Qur'an and the *Sunna* will never involve himself in such acts because they will invoke the anger of God Almighty and lead to harm and corruption on earth.

—*Grand Mufti of Saudi Arabia, Sheikh 'Abdul-'Aziz. September 15th, 2001*

THERE IS A growing assumption on the part of members of the US Congress, US-Saudi diplomats, and the American public that the Bush administration is making a "turnaround" in US policy towards the Kingdom of Saudi Arabia because of neo-conservative and domestic interest group pressure. Those opposed to the current administration accuse the White House of maintaining ties to an enemy of America in exchange for lucrative business deals. In contrast, those who support ties with Saudi Arabia maintain that the US has no intention of severing relations with a regional stabilizing force and with long term friends in the House of Saud. Who is correct?

Neither.

The US has not had wholly "friendly" intentions towards the Kingdom for the past thirty years. Any appearance of such is only the visible veneer of real US military policy. Declassified documents reveal that there has been a constant drumbeat to invade Saudi Arabia that has sounded behind the closed doors of our government. The Pentagon, for three decades, has formulated and updated secret plans to seize Saudi oil wells and rid the Kingdom of the ruling House of Saud. This is not only a neo-conservative cabal. Time and again plans have been made for an invasion of Saudi Arabia for a larger purpose: US control of the global oil supply thereby dominating global economic markets.

The most recent wave of charges that Saudi Arabia supports, condones, and aids terrorism signify a secondary and more public attempt to gain support to finally execute a thirty year old plan to occupy Saudi Arabia. Other regional players' objectives, (securing oil supplies; the rationale of a "war on terror") may add synergy and an unstoppable impetus for an American invasion. This essay discloses and evaluates the motives and actions of those behind the new drive to occupy Saudi oil fields.

CLASSIFIED PLANS BROUGHT TO LIGHT

In 1973, the Nixon administration described a plan of attack against Saudi Arabia to seize its oil fields in a classified Joint Intelligence Report entitled "UK Eyes Alpha." British MI5 and MI6 were informed, and under British National Archive rules the document was declassified in December of 2003. The oil embargo had been over for only three weeks but "Eyes Alpha" suggested that the "US could guarantee sufficient oil supplies for themselves and their allies by taking the oil fields in Saudi Arabia, Kuwait, and the Gulf State of Abu Dhabi." It followed that "pre-emptive" action would be considered, and that two brigades could seize the Saudi oilfields and one brigade each could take Kuwait and Abu Dhabi.

In February of 1975 the London *Sunday Times* revealed information from a leaked and classified US Department of Defense plan.[1] The plan, drawn up by the Pentagon, was code named "Dhahran Option Four" and provided for an invasion of the world's largest oil reserves, namely Saudi Arabia.

Also in 1975, Robert Tucker, US intelligence and military analyst, wrote an article for "Commentary" magazine, owned by the Jewish American Committee, entitled "Oil: The Issue of American Intervention." Tucker stated that, "Without intervention there is a distinct possibility of an economic and political disaster bearing [...] resemblance to the disaster of 1930s [...] The Arab shoreline of the Gulf is a new El Dorado waiting for its conquistadors." And this was followed in February of the same year by an article in *Harper's Magazine* by a Pentagon analyst using a pseudonym, Miles Ignotus, emphasizing the need for the US to seize Saudi oil fields, installations and airports entitled "Seizing Arab Oil."[2] According to James Akins, former US diplomat, the author was probably Henry Kissinger, Secretary of State at the time. Kissinger has neither confirmed nor ever denied the charge.

Further, in August of 1975, a report entitled, "Oil Fields as Military Objectives: A Feasibility Study," was produced for the Committee on Foreign Relations. In this report, the CRS stated that potential targets for the US included Saudi Arabia, Kuwait, Venezuela, Libya, and Nigeria. "Analysis indicates ... [that military forces of OPEC countries were] quantitatively and qualitatively inferior [and] could be swiftly crushed."

The real premise of an attack against the Kingdom of Saudi Arabia has been around since the Cold War. The idea was, however, revived under the aegis of a new "war against terrorism" on the charge that the Saudi state supported such terrorism against the west. One nexus of this drive is Richard Perle.

NEO-CONSERVATIVE DESIGNS ON SAUDI ARABIA

Richard Perle is an outspoken critic of any Americans doing business with the Kingdom, despite his own attempt to secure $100 million in Saudi investment for his private venture capital firm. His ill-fated attempt to become a power-broker with one foot on in the door of the US Defense Policy board of the Department of Defense and another foot in the door of Trimeme capital investments is well documented.[3] He has since become more hard-line, telling the *National Review*, "I think it's a disgrace. The Saudis are a major source of the problem we face with terrorism." (Perle had to resign from the Defense Policy Board when his secret and extortive fundraising meetings with Saudi Arabian businessmen became public.)

Perle's efforts to rearrange the dynamics of the region, including Saudi Arabia, have gone on for many years. Incoming Israeli Likud

Prime Minister Benjamin Netanyahu asked Perle to draft a regional strategy paper for Israel. The Institute for Advanced Strategic & Political Studies, a think tank based in Washington DC and Jerusalem published the completed paper, "A Clean Break: A New Strategy for Securing the Realm,"[4] emphasized the need to overturn the Oslo Accords and Middle East peace process. It demanded that Chairman Yasser Arafat be blamed for every act of Palestinian terror; required the overthrow of Saddam Hussein and the Ba'athist regime in Iraq and Syria; and the force of democracy foisted upon the entire Arab world plus Iran. One senior Israeli intelligence officer stated the goal was to make Israel the dominant power in the region and expel the Palestinians. Perle's efforts to neutralize international funding for the Palestinian resistance and support of Palestinians have driven his policy recommendations ever since.

Another author of "A Clean Break" was David Wurmser. In September of 2003, Wurmser was moved to the US State Department to work directly under Vice President Dick Cheney and his Chief of Staff Lewis Libby. David Wurmser's wife, Meyrav, ran MEMRI (Middle East Media Research Institute) alongside Colonel Yigal Carmon, of Israeli Army Intelligence. MEMRI specializes in selective retrieval, searching and translating especially plucked Arab language documents that confirm MEMRI's bias that the Arab world despises the West. Meyrav Wurmser received her doctorate at George Washington University on the life of Vladimir Jabotinsky, founder of Revisionist Zionism and declared fascist, and hero of Prime Minister Ariel Sharon and the Likud Party.

Saudi Arabia was again declared an enemy of the United States on July 10th, 2002, when RAND Corporation's Laurent Murawiec gave a PowerPoint presentation to the Defense Policy Board at the invitation of Perle. Like Meyrav Wurmser, Murawiec is also from George Washington University and listed as a past faculty member. He was also a follower of the Lyndon LaRouche cultist organization. This group indoctrinates its members to abandon their homes because "family values are really immoral," according to those who left the group.

Entitled "Taking Saudi Out Of Arabia" the PowerPoint presentation states "Saudi Arabia the strategic pivot" and declared that the Kingdom is an enemy of the USA. It advocated the US seize the Kingdom and its oil fields, invade Mecca and Medina, and confiscate Saudi Arabian financial assets unless the Kingdom stop supporting anti-Western terrorist activities.

Saudi Arabia was declared as the "kernel of evil, the prime mover, the most dangerous opponent" in the Middle East. Murawiec claimed, "Since independence, wars have been the principal output of the Arab world" and that "plot, riot, murder, coup are the only available means to bring about change [...] Violence is politics, politics is violence. This culture of violence is the prime enabler of terrorism. Terror as an accepted, legitimate means of carrying out politics has been incubated for 30 years [...]" James Akins explained the overall plans thus: "It'll be easier once we have Iraq. Kuwait, we already have. Qatar and Bahrain too. So it's only Saudi Arabia we're talking about, and the United Arab Emirates falls into place."

The connections between individuals pressing for a US invasion of Saudi Arabia run deep. Richard Perle's lifelong mentor was the RAND Corporation's late Albert Wohlstetter, the grandfather of neo-conservative analysts. Wohlstetter, also, was Ahmed Chalabi's classmate at the University of Chicago. Chalabi, the leader of the Iraqi National Congress and the protagonist of the information provided to the US government regarding the thus far non-existent Iraqi weapons of mass destruction, is an indicted criminal in Jordan where he has been sentenced to more than 20 years' hard labor for currency manipulation and embezzlement through Jordanian Petra Bank.

The analytical and populist groundswell of denunciation against Saudi Arabia as a state sponsor of terrorism from progressive and conservative circles alike may culminate in an invasion sooner rather than later. Supporters within the current US administration can use this unity to execute another "blueprint" for US policy. It can follow as easily as Saddam Hussein's "imminent threat towards America" and Iraq's WMDs served as the principle rationale for the US invasion of Iraq.

TARGET SAUDI ARABIA: TAKING
THE CASE FROM THINK TANK TO THEATER

In reality there has been no hard evidence linking Saudi Arabian leaders and officials to terrorism, little evidence of Saudi subjects playing a mindful role, and far less financial ties to terrorism than could be found in most nations with a banking system. In fact, the US State Department lists the Netherlands, Switzerland, Italy, Germany, Australia and indeed the United States itself as having al-Qa'ida financial ties and connections. However, facts may not be enough to stem rising anti-Saudi sentiment among policy makers and average Americans.

Stating that Saudi Arabia is "[a]n instable group," the Murawiec PowerPoint indictment continued, "[...] Wahhabism loathes modernity, capitalism, human rights, religious freedom, democracy, republics, an open society" and that "Wahhabism is spreading world-wide" [sic] based upon Iran's Revolution led by Shi'ite Ayatollah Khomeini; that "Wahhabism moves from Islam's lunatic fringe", and that there was a "[s]hift from pragmatic oil policy to promotion of radical Islam.... [Saudi Arabians are] treasurers of radical fundamentalists, terrorist groups." Saudi Arabia is then charged with being "the chief vector of the Arab crisis [...] active at every level of the terror chain...[it] supports [US] enemies [and has] virulent hatred against US [...] There is an "Arabia" but it need not be "Saudi"...[US must] stop any funding and support for any fundamentalist *madrasa*, mosque, *ulama*, predicator anywhere in the world [...] Dismantle, ban all the kingdom's 'Islamic charities,' confiscate their assets... [and] What the House of Saud holds dear can be targeted— Oil [...] the Holy Places [...] Saudi Arabia [is] the strategic pivot."

Were these presentations not heard by top-level Bush administration officials, they would be dismissed as simplistic absurdity. However, the sparks of a mass movement to demonize Saudi Arabia had already begun to ignite, and on June 6th 2002 the right wing Hudson Institute held a seminar called "Discourses on Democracy: Saudi Arabia, Friend or Foe?" Laurent Murewiec and Richard Perle in attendance.

Of even further interest is the ironic and direct link between Richard Perle and terrorism. A recent fundraiser in support of the victims of the Iranian earthquake in Bam, sponsored by the Mujahedin-e-Khalq, asked Richard Perle to be their keynote speaker. Despite rejections by other groups to speak at the event, based upon the US state department's official designation that the MEK is an officially designated "foreign terrorist organization," Richard Perle knew of the designation, ignored it, and was happy to oblige and raise monies—monies which were immediately seized after the event by US Treasury agents. The MEK is the same terrorist organization that attempted to assassinate Richard Nixon in 1972.

Two weeks after the PowerPoint presentation to the Pentagon's Defense Policy Board, the American Enterprise Institute held yet another seminar by Dore Gold, former UN Ambassador from Israel to promote his new book, *Hatred's Kingdom: How Saudi Arabia Supports the New Global Terrorism.* Having never visited the country, Gold has been promoted on broadcast television networks as an "expert" on Saudi Arabia when not introduced as "an advisor of Israeli Prime Minister Ariel Sharon."

Gold claims that the al-Haramain group has channeled massive funding to al-Qa'ida whilst omitting that Saudi Arabia shut down the organization and froze its assets. Gold's strongest claim is an Israeli document claiming funds to Hamas come from Saudi Arabia. Hamas has strongly denied the charge of any Saudi government involvement and Saudi Arabia also dismissed the charges as false. Gold uses the book to promote the Netanyahu/Perle/Bush agenda to pursue Saudi Arabia "far more aggressively if Middle Eastern security is to be protected" and argues that Israel has only a "minor role" in al-Qa'ida related acts of terrorism because Saudi Arabia is to blame for funding the "global *jihad* of al-Qa'ida." Gold then testified before the United States' Congress about the inherent evil of Saudi Arabia. Yet throughout the book Gold only confirms that terrorism connections come from foreigners who infiltrate the country, and non-Saudi governments. The book provides no proof of official or unofficial support.

Hudson Institute co-founder and neo-conservative Max Singer wrote a paper sent to the Pentagon's Office of Net Assessment in May 2002 urging the outside break up of Saudi Arabia. On October 7th 2003 fellow arch conservative William Kristol, editor of the *Weekly Standard,* stated that he was upset that the US had not gone beyond the war on Iraq to the "next regime change" of the "next horrible" Middle East dictator Bashar Assad of Syria.

Before publication of his book *Sleeping with the Devil,* Robert Baer, ex-CIA officer, was ordered by the CIA to remove multiple passages claiming special CIA knowledge of Saudi royals having funneled money to al-Qa'ida for terrorist funding, assassination plots, and even Chechen rebels. He asserts that Saudi Arabia is a "powder keg waiting to explode," the royal family is "corrupt," "hanging on by a thread" and "as violent and vengeful as any Mafia family." Baer, filled with loathing towards the Saudis, relies upon a tacit, yet rejected CIA stamp of approval, but also shows little hard evidence. Baer refused to comply with the CIA's request "just [to] defy them." The CIA is considering filing a lawsuit against Baer, who, like Gold, has also never personally visited Saudi Arabia.

Another author who has made the best-seller list is Gerald Posner, who wrote *Why America Slept*, which implicates Osama bin Laden and the Saudi government. In Posner's opinion the rulers have been paying hush money to bin Laden for years in order to prevent terrorist attacks upon the Kingdom. One might consider it strange that there have been multiple fatal attacks upon civilians in Saudi Arabia if bin Laden receives such bribes. And how was Posner able to create a book with such a detailed indictment within a few months when US intelligence has taken years? Posner presents no clarifications.

The US government itself not only unknowingly harbored and sponsored terrorists (9/11 al-Qa'ida members, IRA, al-Haramain Islamic Foundation etc.) it consciously negotiated with Iranian terrorist groups to secure US troop safety from attack in Iraq from Iranians in exchange for Iraqi weapons. Up until 2001 and since the mid-nineties the US dealt directly with the Taliban for oil pipeline rights, agreeing to pay the Taliban tax on every one of the million cubic feet of fuel that would have passed through Afghanistan daily. Vice President Dick Cheney, Halliburton CEO at the time, stated, "Occasionally we have to operate in places where, all things considered, one would not normally choose to go. But we go where the business is." During this timeframe, Hamid Karzai was the Taliban's deputy foreign minister and a former UNOCAL consultant (UNOCAL leading these negotiations along with Paul Wolfowitz aide Zalmay Khalilzad).

On November 9th 2003, Israel confirmed that it had failed in secret negotiations with Hezbollah, sleeping with their own devil. (In January 2004 the Israeli negotiations with their designated terrorist group Hezbollah bore fruit, when a prisoner swap became actuality.) Gerald Posner writes in his book that terrorists had been set up by the US posing as Saudi interrogators, releasing a flood of information under excess cruelty. This charge would mean that the US was in violation of international law by using torture on terror suspects.

Whatever inconsistencies exist between US public relations and the "war on terror," the efforts to tie the Saudi government or "Saudis" in general to terrorism is taking effect. Merit or evidence is not the issue. Passion and mobilization is.

THE APPROACHING DECISION

On June 25, 2004, Michael Moore's film, "Fahrenheit 9/11" opened to 500 screens and insatiable crowds. The film's message to audiences is clear and simple: the US-Saudi relationship must end. However, Americans should take time to go beyond the film, books, and talk-show pundits to re-examine the complicated history between the US and Saudi Arabia and real motives of parties pushing for war. By understanding the motives and histories of the driving personalities, new and old, we can uncover and more fully comprehend a growing case for war in Arabia.

Americans will soon be asked to make a decision about whether invasion is the proper course for American policy. But unlike the build up to a war in Iraq, an informed decision will serve America in a way that hidden plans, rationales and one-sided messages on sale at the box-office cannot.

NOTES

1. See http://www.irmep.org/images/2_9_2004_Sunday_Times.jpg for a jpg image of the original article

2. See Miles Ognotus, "Seizing Arab Oil: How the U.S. can break the oil cartel's stranglehold on the world" *Harper's Magazine* http://www.harpers.org/SeizingArabOil.html

3. See Seymour M. Hersh, "Why was Richard Perle meeting with Adnan Khashoggi?" *The New Yorker*, http://www.newyorker.com/fact/content/?030317fa_fact

4. See appendix iv "Clean Beak or Dirty War?"

14 | When US Foreign Policy Meets Biblical Prophecy

PAUL S. BOYER

D OES THE BIBLE foretell regime change in Iraq? Did God establish Israel's boundaries millennia ago? Is the United Nations a forerunner of a satanic world order?

For millions of Americans, the answer to all those questions is a resounding yes. For many believers in Biblical prophecy, the Bush administration's go-it-alone foreign policy, hands-off attitude toward the Israeli-Palestinian conflict, and invasion of Iraq are not simply actions in the national self-interest or an extension of the war on terrorism, but part of an unfolding divine plan.

Evangelical Christians have long complained that "people of faith" do not get sufficient respect, and that religious belief is trivialized in our public discourse. So argues Stephen L. Carter, a Yale University law professor and an evangelical Christian, in his 1993 *The Culture of Disbelief.* Carter has a point, at least with reference to my own field of American history. With notable exceptions, cultural historians have long underplayed the importance of religion in the United States, particularly in the modern era. Church historians have produced good work, but somewhat in isolation, cut off from the larger currents of cultural and intellectual history. That is changing, as evidenced by Mark A. Noll's magisterial *America's God: From Jonathan Edwards to Abraham Lincoln* (2002). But, over all, the critics are on target.

However, I would vigorously challenge Carter's related complaint that religious belief plays little role in shaping public policy. In fact, religion has always had an enormous, if indirect and under-recognized, role in policy formation.

And that is especially true today, as is illustrated by the shadowy but vital way that belief in Biblical prophecy is helping mold grassroots attitudes toward current US foreign policy. All of us would do well to pay attention to the beliefs of the vast company of Americans who read the headlines and watch the news through a filter of prophetic belief.

Abundant evidence makes clear that millions of Americans—upwards of forty percent, according to some widely publicized national polls—do, indeed, believe that Biblical prophecies detail a specific sequence of end-times events. According to the most popular prophetic system, pre-millennial dispensationalism formulated by the 19th century British churchman John Darby, a series of last-day signs will signal the approaching end. Those will include wars, natural disasters, rampant immorality, the rise of a world political and economic order, and the return of the Jews to the land promised by God to Abraham.

In Darby's system, the present "dispensation" will end with the Rapture, when all true believers will join Christ in the air. Next comes the Tribulation, when a charismatic but satanic figure, the Antichrist, will arise in Europe, seize world power, and impose his universal tyranny under the dread sign "666," mentioned in Revelation. After seven years, Christ and the saints will return to vanquish the Antichrist and his armies at *Har-Megiddo* (the biblical Armageddon), an ancient battle site near Haifa. From a restored Temple in Jerusalem, Christ will then inaugurate a thousand-year reign of peace and justice—the Millennium.

That scenario, which Darby ingeniously cobbled together from apocalyptic passages throughout the Bible, was popularized in America by expositors like Cyrus Scofield, whose 1909 Scofield Reference Bible became a best seller. More recently, dispensationalism has been promulgated by radio evangelists; paperback popularizers; fundamentalist and Pentecostal pastors; and TV luminaries like Jerry Falwell, Jack Van Impe, and John Hagee.

Hal Lindsey's *The Late Great Planet Earth* (1970), a slangy update of Darby's teachings, became the non-fiction best seller in the 1970s. Today's *Left Behind* series, a multivolume fictional treatment of dispensationalism by Tim LaHaye and Jerry Jenkins, has sold 50 million copies since the first volume appeared, in 1995. Volume 10, *The Remnant*, topped the *New York Times's* bestseller list for several weeks last summer.

During the cold war, Lindsey and other prophecy gurus focused on the Soviet Union, citing a passage in Ezekiel foretelling the destruction of a northern kingdom, Gog, which they interpreted as Russia. Today's popularizers, however, spotlight the Middle East and the rise of a New World Order led by their own "axis of evil": the United Nations and other international bodies; global media conglomerates; and multinational corporations, trading alliances, and financial institutions. This interlocking system, they preach, is laying the groundwork for the Antichrist's prophesied dictatorship.

As for the Middle East, the popularizers view Israel's founding in 1948, and its recapture of Jerusalem's Old City in 1967, as key end-times signs. They also see the Jewish settlements in the West Bank and Gaza, and a future rebuilding of the Jerusalem Temple on a site sacred to Muslims as steps in God's unfolding plan. The most hard-line and expansionist groups in Israel today, including Likud Party leaders, have gratefully welcomed this unwavering support. When Prime Minister Benjamin Netanyahu visited the United States in 1998, he called first on Falwell, and only then met with President Clinton. (Dispensationalist dogma also foretells the mass slaughter of Jews by the Antichrist and the conversion of the surviving remnant to Christianity, but those themes are played down by most current popularizers.)

On the basis of such beliefs, dispensationalists denounce any proposals for shared governance of Jerusalem. As Hagee writes in *Final Dawn Over Jerusalem* (Thomas Nelson, 1998):

> Christians and Jews, let us stand united and indivisible on this issue: There can be no compromise regarding the city of Jerusalem, not now, not ever. We are racing toward the end of time, and Israel lies in the eye of the storm [...] Israel is the only nation created by a sovereign act of God, and He has sworn by His holiness to defend Jerusalem, His Holy City. If God created and defends Israel, those nations that fight against it fight against God.

Dispensationalists also oppose any scaling back of Jewish settlements in the West Bank or Gaza, since those areas lie well within God's grant to Abraham, recorded in Genesis 15:18, of all of the land from "the river of Egypt" to the Euphrates.

In this scenario, the Islamic world is allied against God and faces annihilation in the last days. That view is actually a very ancient one in Christian eschatology. Medieval prophecy expounders saw Islam as the demonic force whose doom is foretold in Scripture. As Richard the Lionhearted prepared for the Third Crusade in 1190, the famed prophecy interpreter Joachim of Fiore assured him that the Islamic ruler Saladin, who held Jerusalem, was the Antichrist, and that Richard would defeat him and recapture the Holy City. (Joachim's prophecy failed: Richard returned to Europe in 1192 with Saladin still in power.) Later interpreters cast the Ottoman Empire in the Antichrist role.

That theme faded after 1920 with the Ottoman collapse and the rise of the Soviet Union, but it surged back in the later 20th century, as prophecy popularizers began not only to support the most hard-line groups in Israel, but also to demonize Islam as irredeemably evil and destined for destruction. "The Arab world is an Antichrist-world," wrote Guy Dury in *Escape From the Coming Tribulation* (1975). "God says he will lay the land of the Arabs waste and it will be desolate," Arthur Bloomfield wrote in *Before the Last Battle—Armageddon,* published in 1971 and reprinted in 1999. "This may seem like a severe punishment, but [...] the terms of the covenant must be carried out to the letter."

The anti-Islamic rhetoric is at fever pitch today. Last June, the prophecy magazine *Midnight Call* warmly endorsed a fierce attack on Islam by Franklin Graham (son of Billy) and summed up Graham's case in stark terms: "Islam is an evil religion." In Lindsey's 1996 prophecy novel, *Blood Moon,* Israel, in retaliation for a planned nuclear attack by an Arab extremist, launches a massive thermonuclear assault on the entire Arab world. Genocide, in short, becomes the ultimate means of prophetic fulfillment.

Anticipating George W. Bush, prophecy writers in the late 20th century also quickly zeroed in on Saddam Hussein. If not the Antichrist himself, they suggested, Saddam could well be a forerunner of the Evil One. In full-page newspaper advertisements during the Persian Gulf war of 1991, the organization Jews for Jesus declared that Saddam "represents the spirit of Antichrist about which the Bible warns us."

Prophecy believers found particular significance in Saddam's grandiose plan, launched in the 1970s, to rebuild Babylon on its ancient ruins. The fabled city on the Euphrates, south of Baghdad, which included one of the seven wonders of the ancient world, owed its splendor to King Nebuchadnezzar, the same wicked ruler who warred against Israel and destroyed Jerusalem in 586 B.C., for which impiety, according to the Book of Daniel, he went mad and ended his days eating grass in the fields.

In the Book of Revelation, Babylon embodies all that is corrupt, "a great whore [...] with whom the kings of the earth have committed fornication." It stands as the antithesis of Jerusalem, the city of righteousness, and Revelation prophesies its annihilation by fire. Since Babylon cannot be destroyed unless it exists, Saddam's ambitious public-works project is seen as an essential step toward prophetic fulfillment.

Charles Dyer's *The Rise of Babylon: Sign of the End Times* (1991) elaborates the theme. Along with the emergence of modern Israel and the European Union (as forerunner of the Antichrist's world system), writes Dyer, Saddam's restoration of Babylon signals the approaching end and offers "thrilling proof that Bible prophecies are infallible." "When Babylon is ultimately destroyed," he continues, "Israel will finally be at peace and will dwell in safety."

Hal Lindsey's Web site featured a cartoon of a military aircraft emblazoned with a US flag and a Star of David and carrying a missile with a label targeting "Saddam." The caption quoted the prophet Zechariah: "It shall be that day I will seek to destroy all nations that come against Israel."

All of these themes converge in the *Left Behind* novels. As the plot unfolds, the Antichrist, Nicolae Carpathia, becomes secretary general of the United Nations. ("I've opposed the United Nations for fifty years," boasts one of the authors, Tim LaHaye, a veteran activist on the religious right.) Carpathia moves the UN from New York to a rebuilt Babylon, laying the groundwork for the simultaneous destruction of both the city that, in the grammar of dispensationalism, represents absolute evil and defiance of God's prophetic plan, and the organization that more than any other prefigures the Antichrist's satanic world order.

To be sure, some current Bush-administration policies trouble prophecy believers. For example, the expansion of Washington's surveillance powers after 9/11 (led, ironically, by Attorney General John Ashcroft, darling of the religious right) strikes some as another step toward the Antichrist's global dictatorship. Counterbalancing that, however, are other key administration positions—its hostility to multinational cooperation and international agreements, its downgrading of the Israeli-Palestinian conflict, its muted response to growing Jewish settlement in Palestinian territory, and its unrelenting focus on Saddam Hussein—strike prophecy believers as perfectly in harmony with God's prophetic plan: a plan that will bring human history to its apocalyptic denouement and usher in the longed-for epoch of righteousness, justice, and peace.

Academics do need to pay more attention to the role of religious belief in American public life, not only in the past, but also today. Without close attention to the prophetic scenario embraced by millions of American citizens, the current political climate in the United States cannot be fully understood.

Leaders have always invoked God's blessing on their wars, and, in this respect, the Bush administration is simply carrying on a familiar tradition. But when our born-again president describes the nation's foreign-policy objective in theological terms as a global struggle against "evildoers," and when, in his State of the Union address, he cast Saddam Hussein as a demonic, quasi-supernatural figure who could unleash "a day of horror like none we have ever known," he is not only playing upon our still-raw memories of 9/11. He is also invoking a powerful and ancient apocalyptic vocabulary that for millions of prophecy believers conveys a specific and thrilling message of an approaching end—not just of Saddam, but of human history as we know it.

15 | Apocalypse Now

Why the Book of Revelation is Must Reading

GARY LEUPP

> Then I saw a new heaven and a new earth; the first heaven and the first earth had disappeared now, and there was no longer any sea. I saw the holy city, and the New Jerusalem, coming down from God out of heaven, as beautiful as a bride all dressed for her husband
>
> —*Revelation 21:1-2*

REVELATION IS MUST reading nowadays, *especially* for the non-believer. I have returned to it many years after abandoning my childhood faith, not because I think it is inspired prophecy, but because many other people think that it is. And, because some of them think this piece of Holy Scripture somehow justifies ongoing imperialist war, which they (with their commander-in-chief) conceptualize religiously as a war of Good versus Evil. And because that conviction causes believers to support, on faith, Bush's efforts to remold the Middle East in the way the neo-cons (who are overwhelmingly not fundamentalist Christians, but who assiduously court them) want to do it. One should read Revelation to see how it can be used, and to see what sort of worldview the book encourages.

That a considerable portion of the US population consists of persons who take the book seriously is truly a godsend to those in the administration who want to transform the Muslim world, acquiring strategic control over Southwest Asia while enhancing Israel's security situation. The neo-cons and patrons manipulate the Christian devout who adulate Ariel Sharon like a rock star, believe Israel[1] can do no wrong, have little concern about Arabs' rights, and think Islam is a teaching of the Devil. Rev. Jerry

Falwell calls the Prophet Muhammad a "terrorist." Rev. Franklin Graham calls Islam "a wicked, evil religion" and says its God is not the Christians' God. These reverends' followers are very useful supporters of the war on the human mind that is the "war on terrorism," the focus of which shifted so swiftly from al-Qa'ida to Iraq (alike in little save their 'Muslimness'), and could shift to Syria or Iran or Pakistan suddenly tomorrow. When you mix the anti-Islam pronouncements with Bush policy decisions and millenarian faith, you have an explosive combination.

APOCALYPSES

> But fire will come down from heaven and consume them. Then the devil, who misled them, will be thrown into the lake of fire and sulfur, where the beast and false prophet are, and their torture will not stop, day or night, for ever and ever. (20:10)

This ancient, mysterious Book of Revelation is itself incendiary. It's one example of a popular type of literature (*apocalypse* in Greek) which, using richly symbolic language encouraging multiple interpretations, reveals that which is hidden, including events in the future. There are many other examples of such works written between 300 BCE and 200 CE; Jewish ones include the Book of Enoch and the Apocalypse of Ezra, Christian ones include the Apocalypse of Paul and the Apocalypse of Peter.[2] The Apocalypse of Peter was very popular in Rome as of the third century, but didn't make it into the Bible. The present canon of twenty-seven New Testament books was fixed at a synod at Rome in 382, where the Apocalypse of Peter as well as numerous gospels and letters were denounced as "false" and subsequently burned.

Authorities differ on the dating of Revelation, some favoring the late 60s, soon after Nero's persecution of the Christians, but more favoring ca. 95, after the dispersion of the Jews from Roman Palestine. It is of unknown authorship; although traditionally attributed to Jesus' disciple John, its language is so different from the Gospel of John and that of the three letters attributed to John in the New Testament that most serious scholars doubt it was written by the apostle. Authored by a Jewish Christian who had spent time on Patmos (a tiny Aegean island used as a penal colony by the Romans), it expresses great rage at the Roman Empire, referred to here as "Babylon," the name of the empire that had conquered the kingdoms of Israel and Judah and dispersed their populations centuries earlier.

Biblical prophecy, a cousin of Zoroastrian and Buddhist and other prophecy, and a harbinger of prophetic writing from Mani to Nostradamus to Jeanne Dixon, rests on the assumption that the future is pre-determined as part of God's plan, and can be foretold by those whom God decides shall do so. Some Biblical prophecy was in fact composed after the events the prophet is purported to have predicted; the Old Testament Book of Daniel, which predicts the fall of Babylon to the Persians, and Persia's fall to the Greeks, was written around 167 BCE, after all these things had already happened.

Unless it's demystified, prophecy is one of the spookiest and most powerful elements in religion, and can be deftly deployed to play upon fears and earnest expectations alike. James Warren Jones, architect of the Jonestown Massacre, convinced his followers that he was the Second Coming of Christ. Aum Shinrikyo guru Asahara Shoko could persuade very sophisticated, intelligent Japanese people to randomly gas others in the Tokyo subway by manipulating bits and pieces of Christian, Buddhist and Hindu prophecy about the end of the world. Far more sophisticated and well-funded religious leaders can draw upon faith in a foregone future to get people to abet that future's fulfillment—for example, by supporting administration actions in the Middle East believing they portend the Second Coming.

The Book of Revelation is filled with kabbalism, symbolic use of numbers, such as the number seven[3] and that number which strikes fear into some hearts: 666. Revelation makes no reference to the Trinity, but rather to "seven spirits of God" and to Jesus as an emanation of God, subordinate to him although present from the dawn of time. Jesus in Revelation is not meek and mild but brutally vengeful upon his return— the second earthly appearance predicted in Matthew 25, Luke 21, John 16 etc.

SUMMARY OF JOHN'S VISIONS

The Book of Revelation is a long, confusing sequence of visions, but can be summarized as follows. John of Patmos first transmits divine wisdom to seven churches in Asia Minor. These were not necessarily the most important Christian communities of the time, just ones whose problems he was apparently familiar with; and again, the number seven is special. Then John conveys the content of a vision in which the door of Heaven opens and he sees God (who "looked like a diamond and a ruby") surrounded by twenty-four elders in white robes and four fantastic animals giving praise. In the right hand of God is a scroll "sealed with seven seals." A Lamb (that is, Jesus Christ) who appears to have been sacrificed, with seven horns and seven eyes "which are the seven Spirits God has sent out all over the world," steps forward to accept the scroll while the twenty-four sing a hymn. The Lamb breaks the seals, and as he does so, a rider on a white horse appears to accept a victor's crown; another rider, on a red horse, comes to receive a huge sword and "set people killing one another;" another, on a black horse, arrives with scales while the four animals shout about daily wages, barley, oil and wine; another, on a deathly pale horse, arrives representing Plague. These Four Horsemen of the Apocalypse are given authority over a quarter of the earth, "to kill by the sword, by famine, by plague and wild beasts."

When the fifth seal is broken, John sees underneath the heavenly altar the souls of all those killed for witnessing to the word of God. They ask why God does not immediately pass sentence and take vengeance on the inhabitants of the earth for their deaths (6:10-11). They are given white robes and told to wait a bit longer until the prophesized number of Christians are killed. Then the sixth seal is broken and the sky disappears, and the people of the world flee to mountains and caves, begging the rocks to fall on them to protect them from the wrath of God. Four avenging angels appear to destroy humankind, but are restrained by another who asks them to wait until seals have been placed on the heads of one hundred and forty-four thousand persons "out of all the tribes of Israel" who are servants of God.[4] That's the twelve tribes of Israel times twelve thousand; there's no mention here of the non-Jewish converts to Christianity.

The opening of the seventh seal produces silence in heaven for half an hour. Thereupon seven trumpets are given to seven angels standing before God. One angel throws fire from a golden censer to earth, and the earth shakes. One by one the angels blow their trumpets, bringing punitive devastation to the earth. These events do not seem to represent happenings that chronologically succeed one another (and the whole narrative is filled with logical puzzles); rather, the trumpet events expand upon those events associated with the opening of the seals. Between the sixth and seventh trumpet blasts, John is told to go to the Temple in Jerusalem with a measuring rod, and to measure the sanctuary and altar and people worshipping there—but not the outer court, which has been given over to pagans for forty-two months. God sends two sackcloth-clad witnesses with special powers, such as the ability to turn water into blood, to prophesy in Jerusalem. But the serpent, after those forty-two months, makes war on them and kills them. Their corpses lie in the Great City (not Jerusalem but evil Rome), as people rejoice at the troublemakers' deaths. But they are revived after three and a half days, while a great earthquake occurs, killing seven thousand.

John meanwhile sees a vision of a pregnant woman, "adorned with the sun, standing on the moon" who as she gives birth is confronted by a huge red dragon (Satan) who tries to eat the child as it is born.[5] But God takes the baby (destined "to rule all the nations with an iron scepter") up into heaven while the woman escapes to the desert for one thousand two hundred and sixty days. War breaks out in Heaven between the dragon and the archangel Michael and other angels; the dragon, defeated, is thrown down to earth, where he unsuccessfully attacks the woman and "the rest of her children, that is, all who obey God's commandments and bear witness to Jesus."

The dragon delegates his power to a seven-headed beast emerging from the sea (who appears to be a political ruler, and is often associated with the Antichrist[6]). Then another beast (a religious ruler, a false prophet) emerges as slave to this beast from the sea. He makes the world worship the first beast, and makes everyone worship his statue. The number of the second beast is 666.[7]

Next, John in his vision sees the Lamb standing on Mt. Zion with the one hundred and forty-four thousand, all with the Father's name on their foreheads. These are the ones who have kept their virginity[8] and have never lied. No fault can be found with them. Flying overhead, angels call upon all to worship God and announce "Babylon has fallen!" They declare that they will torture all who worship the statue of the beast. One of the four animals gives the seven angels seven golden bowls filled with God's wrath; these are emptied over the world, producing disease and turning rivers and oceans to blood. Again, the disasters described overlap and amplify the first two sequences of seven.

Now here is where it starts to get especially "relevant." The sixth angel empties his bowl over the Euphrates River (that is to say, in present day Iraq), drying up the water so that the "kings of the East" are able to come in. From the jaws of the dragon and two aforementioned beasts appear three "foul spirits" looking like frogs; they are in fact demon spirits able to work miracles. Their job is to organize the kings of the world to war against the Almighty. They call the kings together at Armageddon.[9]

The seventh angel empties his bowl into the air, producing the greatest earthquake the world has ever known and destroying the Great City, all islands, and all mountains. But this isn't yet the end, and the vision is not over. One of the seven angels with a bowl shows John a "famous prostitute," a woman riding a scarlet beast with seven heads and ten horns (that is, the beast from the sea, the political ruler); on her forehead is written "Babylon the Great, the mother of all prostitutes and all the filthy practices of the earth."[10] She is drunk with the blood of the Christian martyrs. The heads of the beasts she rides, John learns, are "seven emperors," five of who have gone (the Roman emperors Augustus, Tiberius, Caligula, Claudius, and Nero?), while one lives now (Galba?) and one is yet to come. This last will rule for only a short time; the beast and him will go to their destruction.[11]

The beast's ten heads represent ten kings who will rule "for only an hour," going to war with the Lamb and meeting defeat at the hands of the faithful. Then the prostitute will be stripped naked, the faithful will eat her flesh and burn the remains in a fire.[12] All the merchants, traders and sea captains who profited from trading with her will be punished, while victory songs resound in heaven. Another great battle begins, between the beast and the kings of the earth and a rider called the Word of God who rides on a white horse. The beast from the sea and the false prophet are thrown into a fiery lake of burning sulfur, while the dragon ("which is the devil and Satan") who had appeared at the outset of the narrative is chained up for a thousand years. Those Christians who died in persecutions are now resurrected, and reign with Christ for those thousand years.[13]

One is tempted to stop the summary here, since, one might expect, those who accept this text as prophecy are just thinking about events up to this millennium moment. But some Christian thinkers (notably St. Augustine of Hippo, 354-430) came to interpret all the foregoing as pre-fourth century, past events, symbolically portrayed, preceding Emperor Constantine's Edict of Toleration (313) and soon thereafter, the establishment of Christianity as the Empire's official and only tolerated faith. Augustine thought he lived at the inception of the thousand years mentioned above. There are logical problems here, since the "Great City" and "Babylon" are Rome, and Rome didn't in fact meet with the predicted fire and brimstone but rather become thoroughly and aggressively Christianized. But if one says all the foregoing is a symbolic representation of the past, what comes next[14] is of key importance.

Satan is for some reason released from prison after a thousand years, and deceives the leaders of all the nations, led by Gog and Magog, to attack Jerusalem, "the camp of the saints."[15] But fire comes down from heaven to consume them (20:9). God opens the book of life and judges all the dead; those already in Hades and anyone not listed in the book are thrown into a second death in a burning lake. A new heaven and new earth appear, their precedents having passed away; the new Jerusalem comes down from Heaven, and there is universal joy. Curiously, there are still pagan nations, but they "will live by the light" of the New Jerusalem (22:24).

REVELATION AND BUSH'S WAR

This is the basic presentation in Revelation, presented, I hope, with fairness.[16] Many supplement it with material from Old Testament prophecy (such as Ezekiel and Daniel) and other New Testament material, such as the Antichrist concept and the notion of the "Rapture."[17] Obviously in its vagueness, it can be applied to many times and places, rather like the dire predictions of the Buddhist Lotus Sutra have been employed to explain calamities in Asian societies over centuries. Eugene Gallagher, Professor of Religious Studies at Connecticut College, writes that "the lush imagery and the complicated imagery of Revelation, has been one of the things that has kept people reading it. Because it can always be renewed. It can always be applied to a new situation."[18]

Indeed, surfing the web, you find the Pope, Russian President Putin, even President Bush, all identified as the beast/Antichrist, on sites creatively combining New Age trends, kabbalism, astrology, Nostradamus cultism and Biblical literalism.

So how can Revelation be politically applied today? Well, let's say we forget the scholarly analysis that interprets the whole thing as a statement of Christian hatred for Rome, and of passionate belief in an imminent Second Coming that will bring ruin to the Roman Empire and glory to the Christian oppressed. Let us say it indeed refers to the future, while noting that there are some people out there very disappointed that the year 2000 went by with nary a trace of a Second Coming. They long for that Coming, understandably, as we all pine for utopia, and they want to apply Revelation to current events.

Let us say that Babylon really means Babylon, the city along the Euphrates, in modern-day Iraq, noting that it suffers terrible ruin at the hand of God. Let us note that the sixth angel allows the "kings of the East" to attack the dried-up Euphrates, and that thereafter apocalyptic battles take place in Armageddon and Jerusalem, resulting in Christ's return and the establishment of a new Jerusalem on earth. Let's note that earthly rulers mentioned in general fight against God and Jerusalem, including "ten kings" who some in the past have identified as the leaders of the European Union.[19] Gog and Magog have been identified in the past with the Soviet Union, but that doesn't work well nowadays. As for the beast (Antichrist), there have been and are many candidates, and something as random as a US political scandal could throw up more.

Well, it doesn't take too much a stretch of the fevered imagination to see in this narrative a divine plan for a righteous attack on Iraq, followed by continued disorder in Iraq involving kings from the east,[20] triggering war in Israel, pitting the good souls of Jerusalem (aided for a time by two divinely-sent witnesses) against the whole world arrayed against them, including "pagans" (Palestinians?) who occupy the outer court of the Temple in Jerusalem for forty-two months, but after fire comes down from heaven to consume armies whose soldiers are as numerous as grains of sand, the chosen will remain, to rule with Jesus forever, headquartered in Jerusalem. It's an affecting, and at the end, even beautiful vision for some believing Christians, whose view of the contemporary Middle East might be deeply influenced by this text.

But there must be, according to the prophecy, a war of unprecedented horror in the Middle East before Jesus returns and renders judgment, and finally solves all the problems of the world.

So the current war, undertaken by godly men, might be good. Forget the moral qualms of the bleeding heart non-believers. If righteous cruelty is prophesied, can we not condone it in the here and now? Have thousands of Afghans and Iraqis died? Well, divine fire rains from the sky in Revelation. God wills this. Torture at Abu Ghuraib and elsewhere? Why, angels torture in Revelation 18:7. Why should this be a problem?

SECURING THE REALM

Let us say you embrace this general Lucy in the Sky with Diamonds scenario. Do Bush's reasons for attacking Iraq make any difference? No. The nonexistent weapons of mass destruction aside, the unsubstantiated al-Qaʻida links, all pale against the argument that God's chosen president expressed to Palestinian President Mahmoud Abbas: "God told me to strike at al-Qaʻida and I struck them, and then he instructed me to strike at Saddam, which I did, and now I am determined to solve the problem in the Middle East." The problem of the credibly of his Iraq claims recedes in importance when you read, in *Christianity Today*, Bush's heartfelt statement of political philosophy: "when you're trying to lead the world in a war that I view as really between the forces of good and the forces of evil, you got [sic] to speak clearly. There can't be any doubt." Bush is working God's will, following his Plan, swaggering towards Armageddon. It's undoubtedly as simple as Good and Evil.

One wants to think, of course, that logical analysis and methodical exposure of the accelerated moves towards unchallenged global control the Bush administration has undertaken since 9/11 might slowly but surely disabuse the most benighted of their support for continued US military aggression. Skepticism increases in the wake of disasters in Iraq, journalistic exposés, and official investigations, but much of this flies over the heads of those most vulnerable to a kind of neo-fascist, deliberately non-rational appeal.

Revelation, like most scriptures, is what Marx said of religion in general: an expression of, and protest against, suffering. As such it holds great appeal, and is of interest even to the non-believer. It contains powerful images; the Four Horsemen of the Apocalypse, for example, is an often-encountered literary trope. It has a beauty analogous to a Wagnerian opera, but just as (and I say this as a great admirer) such art held a particularly dangerous content in Germany in the 1930s, so at present this text's message dovetails so smoothly with the war plans of this administration that it may be *dangerous.*

Of course Revelation is read differently by different people. The Rastafarians believe that the Second Coming it describes refers to Emperor Haile Selassie, and for them, "Babylon" means any oppressive society. Bob Marley could draw upon Revelation to write about liberation. Folksongs and Negro spirituals pining for a "New Jerusalem" don't urge military aggression to create it. Like so much scripture, Revelation lends itself to interpretation. Hong Houxiu, head of the *Taiping* Rebellion in China in the mid-nineteenth century, believed he was the younger brother of Jesus Christ, sent to establish the Taiping or Kingdom of Heaven. His fanatic followers, ruling from 1853 in Nanjing until their defeat in 1860, drew upon the Book of Revelation. In the 1890s the Paiute Indian Wavoka, also influenced by the Book of Revelation and claiming to be Christ, taught the Ghost Dance[21] to his followers so that they could dance up into the air while a new earth was being established.[22]

Revelation does not instruct its believing reader to favor this or that policy option. I assume there are believers who are thoroughly against the war on Iraq. But believers energized by anticipation of a glorious new world on the horizon and by the belief that they are participating in prophesized events, may become particularly apt to place blind faith in an aggressive Good vs. Evil foreign policy. They should be informed that beneath the simplistic religious justification for the "war on terrorism"[23] there is a layer of carefully researched and presented strategy papers authored by the prophetic neo-cons. These neo-conservatives have led the administration in producing regime change in Afghanistan, invading and occupying Iraq, deferring in unprecedented fashion to Israeli policy while demanding changes in the Palestinian Authority and severing ties with Yassir Arafat.

They have imposed sanctions on Syria, indicated approval of an Israeli air strike, and have been preparing a case to justify military action against Damascus. They have stepped-up efforts to influence the unstable political situation in Iran, with Radio Farda, and have depicted the Iranian nuclear program currently under UN inspection as a serious threat, hinting that they would support an Israeli strike *à la Osiraq* 1981. They've put the onus for Arab backwardness on Arab culture, pronouncing the democratization of the Middle East a US policy priority. Meanwhile they've established US military bases throughout Muslim Central Asia and set up new ones throughout the Persian Gulf region to compensate for the withdrawal of forces from Saudi Arabia. Plainly they have big plans for the region. You get some inkling of those plans are in the 1996 strategy paper "A Clean Break: A New Project for Securing the Realm,"[24] authored by Richard Perle, Douglas Feith, David Wurmser and other neo-cons that have shaped and articulated current US Middle East policy. It was written for the Israeli government, but the authors see the interests of Israel and the US as nearly identical and have in their capacity as American officials pursued the goals indicated in this document. The authors of the position papers of the unabashedly imperialist Project for a New American Century[25] also indicate neo-con goals for the region. These gentlemen and women by and large do not believe in the Book of Revelation, but I'll bet they believe in its utility.

This is the problem. Leo Strauss's thought divides humanity into three types: the wise, the gentlemen, and the vulgar. The wise use deception (noble lies) to attain their ends, using gentlemen (who are not wise but who are powerful) to control the masses. Religion is a vital tool in controlling the masses ("as lambs to the slaughter"), and the non-believing wise can also use it to manipulate "gentlemen." Revelation, at the hands of the wise, gentle or vulgar, is among the world's most easily manipulated of books; the wise can do it best.

Hal Lindsey, best-selling author of *The Late Great Planet Earth* (1970) identified the beast of Revelation (the Antichrist) with the Soviet Union. But later, with the European Union. Now, perhaps, global Islam. His most recent book, *The Everlasting Hatred: The Roots of Jihad,* traces Arab-Israeli enmity back to the days of Abraham, depicting Islam itself as the problem, and concludes with a chapter on "Armageddon: The Climax of Hate." Many are being influenced by this book, and its association of the Muslim fighter with the Serpent, the Beast, the False Prophet, etc. Those persuaded by its message might be more inclined to support more troops in Iraq, or the expansion of the war into Syria, or restoration of a draft, because prophesy supports it. Very dangerous indeed.

Friedrich Engels wrote in one of his last substantial works[26] that the Book of Revelation was both the "most obscure book in the Bible" and "the most comprehensible and the clearest." Drawing upon recent German scholarship, he emphasized that the work should be clearly comprehended as an expression of rage against Rome (that republic led by a senate that had morphed over time into an empire oppressing people from Britain to Mesopotamia, meeting with particularly fierce resistance in the lands of the Middle East) and its persecution of Christians, who were overwhelmingly drawn from the humblest classes throughout the empire. As such, it commands respect as an expression of resistance to oppression. But in the hands of evangelical commentators, who (thoroughly at peace with contemporary imperialism) line up chronological charts about the near-term future, with authoritative pomposity linking prophecy with current Middle Eastern events,[27] it becomes something quite different: a validation for ongoing war.

Luther in no way detected the Holy Spirit in it. But Bush, committed to an Armageddon-like war between the forces of good and those of evil, no doubt sees forces of good throughout this scripture, which may speak to him directly. We should all study this particular weapon, if only to better understand the minds of the president and his dead-ender followers.

NOTES

---

1. Miraculously reconstituted half a century ago, in fulfillment of Ezekiel 37:12-14

2. For translations, see Willis Barnstone (ed), *The Other Bible* (HarperSanFrancisco, 1984)

3. As in, the seven hills of Rome, the seven Roman emperors from Augustus, the seven churches of Asia to whom the work is addressed

4. The Jehovah's Witnesses especially emphasize this passage, Revelation 7:4.

5. Commentators differ on whether this woman is Israel giving birth to the Messiah, or the Virgin Mary doing so. Catholic commentary favors the first interpretation.

6. Although that term does not occur in this text, but only in 1 John 2:18, 4:2-3 and 2 John 1:7

7. The kabbalist association of numbers with the Roman letters "Nero Caesar" produces this figure.

8. Sexual abstinence being a requisite for membership in some Christian Gnostic sects before the emergence of an orthodox form of Christianity

9. This refers to the Megiddo mountains, near the modern Israeli town of Megiddo, about 15 miles from the Palestinian town of Jenin. In the seventh century BC, King Josiah was defeated here by the Egyptian pharaoh. The name became synonymous with military disaster.

10. Most commentators think this means Rome.

11. Obviously the writer thought the end of the world was very near.

12. (17:16)

13. There are different opinions as to whether these Christians are limited to the aforementioned one hundred and forty-four thousand

14. 20:7 through 22:25

15. Some conflate this with the Battle of Armageddon only hinted at in 16:16.

16. The true believer often resents dispassionate presentation of material he or she thinks obviously holy more than the mere contemptuous dismissal of the same.

17. Based on 1 Thessalonians 4:13-18

18. See "James Tabor, Apocalypticism Explained: The Book of Revelation,"; http://www.pbs.org/wgbh/pages/frontline/shows/apocalypse/explanation/

brevelation.html

19. That's gotten harder with the expansion of the EU

20. East from Iraq you have Iran, Afghanistan, Pakistan

21. See: Robert A. Toledo, "The Paiute Messiah," http://www.viewzone.com/wovoka.html

22. Many of his dancers perished at Wounded Knee

23. Including the war in Iraq, which the Bush administration sees as the central battlefield of the "war on terrorism," but which many scholars and officials regard as an entirely separate phenomenon

24. See http://www.cooperativeresearch.org/archive/1990s/instituteforadvancedstrategicandpoliticalstudies.htmas well as "Clean-Break or Dirty War?" in the Appendix.

25. See: http://www.newamericancentury.org/publicationsreports.htm

26. See Federick Engels, On the History of Early Christianity; http://csf.colorado.edu/psn/marx/Archive/1894-Christ/

27. See http://jesus-is-the-way.com/PostWar.html for examples

16 | Christian Zionism in US Middle-East Policy

DONALD WAGNER

AFTER 11 SEPTEMBER 2001, considerable attention turned to what many media analysts called a new force in US politics: the Christian Right.[1] Most reports in the mainstream Western media saw the political influence of the Christian Right as a new and surprising phenomenon. Forgotten is the important role that the Moral Majority and similar organizations have played in US politics since the late 1970s. Moreover, there is abundant evidence that there have been interludes of political advocacy by the Christian Right in England and the US for more than one hundred years. However, the current influence of the movement has been unprecedented, particularly in shaping US Middle East policy.

A number of political and religious trends have converged in the US since September 11, 2001 to bring about a powerful, and often surprising, political alliance between pro-Israeli think-tanks and lobby organizations with fundamentalist Christians. It would, however, be simplistic to trace to that tragic date the beginning of the alliance, as it would also be to conclude that the recent prominence of the Christian Right was a direct result of the events of that tragic day. Careful analysis indicates that a series of political and religious dynamics had been in motion for more than a decade and were awaiting an opportunity to enter the political mainstream.

The election of George W. Bush in 2000 enabled several political currents to converge and move into high positions of power in the new administration, and, within a very short time, to exercise their dominance in shaping the policies of the new administration during a period of national crisis. Neo-conservative ideologues, such as Paul Wolfowitz and Richard Perle, were among the personalities which emerged.[2] Added to that were multinational construction firms, such as Bechtel and Halliburton (the latter associated with Vice-president Dick Cheney), the petroleum industry, and the arms industry. These alliances were followed by the close collaboration of the pro-Israel lobby with the Christian Right. Both the President and Defense Secretary Donald Rumsfeld seemed to have been influenced by all of these elements. The alignment of these constituencies, personalities, and ideologies immediately after September 11 provided a new ideological and political direction for the US in what many called the New American Empire. This essay will examine the emergence of one of these important influences, the Christian Zionist movement's theological and historical origins in England[3] and the US from 1800 to the present, including their potential impact on future negotiations on the "Roadmap" to Israeli-Palestinian peace.

BACK TO THE FUTURE:
THE ROOTS OF CHRISTIAN ZIONISM

Christian fascination with the idea of Israel and its central role in shaping how people interpret Biblical prophecy has its roots in the Hebrew and Christian scriptures. The primary genre of literature that inspired this theology is "apocalypticism" or the apocalyptic form of eschatology. Specialists in the field of Biblical apocalypticism, such as Bernard McGinn of the University of Chicago, claim that the first generation of Christians were significantly influenced by Jewish apocalypticism.[4] Many theologians trace apocalyptic thought to Persian religious influences on the Jewish community during the Babylonian Exile (587-538 BC). The book of Daniel, and Ezekiel 37-38, along with several non-canonical works, such as the Dead Sea Scrolls, reflect the spirit of apocalyptic thought as it developed in Judaism during the postexilic period. The literature blossomed during the Maccabean Revolt (167161 BC) and continued to influence Palestinian Judaism during the period of Second Temple Judaism and the Zealot revolts of 66-70 and 131-35 AD. The New Testament incorporates apocalyptic thought as reflected in such passages as Matthew 24, Mark 13, Luke 21, Acts 1.6-9, 1 Thessalonians 4-5, and the Book of Revelation.

McGinn argues that apocalypticism is a complex phenomenon that developed over a long period of time. In its Jewish form apocalypticism is "a species of the genus eschatology [...] a peculiar kind of belief about last things-the end of history and what lies beyond it."[5] He adds that theologians often use the terms eschatology and apocalyptic interchangeably, which is confusing and essentially inaccurate. Apocalyptic thought is a particular type of eschatology that generally emphasizes the predictive and climactic aspects of Biblical prophecy, employing specific categories and a heightened sense of urgency concerning the final clash between the forces of good and evil. Biblical scholar, Gerhard von Rad, says:

> The characteristic of apocalyptic theology is its eschatological dualism, the clear-cut differentiation of the two aeons, the present one and the one to come. A further characteristic is its sheer transcendentalism-the saving blessings of the coming aeon are already pre-existent in the world above and come down to earth. The early idea that the final events were determined far back in the past and foretold in detail to certain chosen men many centuries before they were to occur is also characteristic [...] The last things can be known; indeed, they can be exactly calculated, but this is only possible for the initiated.[6]

Christian apocalypticism incorporated the thought-forms of Jewish apocalyptic theology, and adjusted it to incorporate the return of Jesus and his ultimate clash and victory over the forces of the Antichrist, as well as the establishment of Jesus' millennial kingdom.

As Christian apocalypticism evolved it began to take different forms. One type that gained popularity in the early church was "historic pre-millennialism," which taught that Jesus would return to earth prior to his establishment of a thousand-year rule on earth (the "millennium"). This view is intimated in the early letters of Paul (1 Thessalonians 4 and 5), but such "pre-millennial" symbolism is absent from the later letters of Paul. Historic pre-millennial eschatology is also evident in several documents of the early church such as the Didache, Epistle of Barnabas, and Shepherd of Hernias (all dated in the 100-160 AD period). Several of the great Church Fathers such as Justin Martyr (160 AD), Irenaeus of Lyon (c. 130-200 AD) and Tertullian (c. 160-220 AD) articulated these views, indicating the early Christians derived hope and comfort from these beliefs during periods of intense persecution under the Roman Empire.

Once persecution subsided under Constantine (c. 312 AD), however, historic pre-millennialism declined in influence, although the symbols remained, and would be invoked again during periods of crisis and persecution. Most theologians in the post-Constantinian period were decidedly anti-apocalyptic, best exemplified by the influential Augustine of Hippo (364-430 AD) who interpreted eschatological symbols allegorically. His influence remained dominant in Roman Catholic and Western Christian theology with the few exceptions that emerged during the Crusades.

Periods of crisis such as the perceived threat of Islam, the Crusades, the Mongol invasions, and the Spanish Inquisition inspired some Christian thinkers to return to apocalyptic eschatology. Joachim de Fiore (1135-1202), the Abbot of the monastery at Fiore, was one of the most influential medieval apocalyptic writers. Fiore developed an early form of dispensationalism. This interpreted the whole of history according to eras that were designated by God's method of judging humanity (i.e. "Paradise, The Law, Grace," and so on). Fiore's teachings inspired speculation concerning the date of Jesus' return, as well as the identity of the Antichrist, which he assigned to the great Muslim leader, Saladin (Salah al-Din), who liberated Jerusalem from the Crusaders in 1187 AD.[7]

Fiore's influence lasted well into the sixteenth century as various apocalyptic movements drew upon his eschatology, including the Spanish Inquisition and radical currents in the Protestant Reformation. His endorsement of the Crusades and his denigration of Islam finds parallels in contemporary dispensationalists such as US televangelists Pat Robertson, Jerry Falwell and Franklin Graham, whose recent demonization of Islam has drawn international notoriety.

THE BRITISH DIMENSION: PROTO-CHRISTIAN ZIONISM

By the late sixteenth century a distinct form of pre-millennial eschatology emerged within Protestant Christianity. Among its early advocates was the Rev. Thomas Brightman, an Anglican clergyman, whose controversial treatise *Apocalypsis Apocalypseos* (Revelation of the Revelation) called for a literal and futuristic interpretation of the prophetic texts in the Bible concerning Israel and the restoration of the Jews. Brightman was forced to withdraw his treatise and publicly reject these controversial teachings which were viewed by the authorities as anti-monarchical. A generation later, a prominent British lawyer and Member of Parliament, Sir Henry Finch, wrote a treatise calling for Jewish restoration in Palestine, based on his literal and dispensationalist interpretation of the prophetic texts:

> Where Israel, Judah, Zion and Jerusalem are named [in the Bible] the Holy Ghost meant not the spiritual Israel, or the Church of God collected of the Gentiles or of the Jews and Gentiles both [...] but Israel properly descended out of Jacob's loynes [...] these and such like are not allegories, setting forth on terrene similitudes or deliverance through Christ but meant literally and really the Jews.[8]

Finch's essential argument merged the concept of Jewish restoration in Palestine with pre-millennialism.[9] Finch was perhaps the first person to call upon a Western government to support the restoration of the Jews in Palestine in conformity with the prophetic scriptures, as he interpreted them. He wrote: "(the Jewes) shall repair to their own country-shall inhabit all parts of the land as before, shall live in safety, and shall continue in it forever."[10] Brightman and Finch might be categorized as proto-Christian Zionists in that they were solitary voices advocating that the Jews return to Palestine in order to fulfill the prophetic scriptures, but at this early stage there was no such organized Christian or Jewish political movement. Events at the end of the eighteenth century brought insecurity and a sense of impending doom across Europe and North America. Gradually, postmillennial optimism shifted to pre-millennial visions of catastrophe, much of which has been ascribed to the anxiety generated by the American and French Revolutions, plus the Napoleonic Wars of 1809-15. Historian, LeRoy Froom, captured the shift in eschatological expectation:

> After the troublous times of the American Revolution and its aftermath, and especially after the devastating effects of the infidelic French philosophy, men turned again to the Bible for light, especially the prophecies of Daniel and Revelation. They were seeking a satisfying explanation of the prevailing irreligion of the time and to find God's way out of the situation.[11]

One of the important movements of the early nineteenth century that signaled the shift from postmillennial eschatology to pre-millennialism was the revival of the floundering London-based missionary organization, the London Society for Promoting Christianity Among the Jews (LSPCJ). By 1804, LSPCJ had professed postmillennial missionary motivations in relation to the Jews, and established a college to train missionaries who would convert Jews to Christianity. Under a new director, Louis Way, its orientation gradually shifted toward pre-millennialism but with a new ingredient: a call for the political resolution to the Jewish question. Way became one of the first Christian leaders in the nineteenth century to advocate a clear Christian Zionist position, including advocacy for a resolution of the Jewish question, based on his reading of the prophetic scriptures. He called upon Christians to urge the British Parliament to settle Jews in Palestine. Way held meetings with Tsar Alexander I of Russia and several European heads of state to solicit their support for the project. In 1818, he spoke in favor of a Jewish state before the Congress of Aix la Chapelle, which involved the heads of England, Prussia, Russia, Austria, and France.[12] His writings, the influential *Jewish Expositor* and the pamphlet *The Latter Rain*, focused on the imminent return of Christ. *The Jewish Expositor* became popular among many clergy, academics, and such literary figures as Samuel Taylor Coleridge. Like Brightman and Finch, Way taught that the Old Testament prophecies concerning the Jews were to be taken literally, and that in the scheme of God's plan they would have a future political fulfillment.

The most influential advocate of pre-millennialism during this period was the renegade Church of Ireland (Anglican-Episcopalian) priest, the Rev. John Nelson Darby (1800-82). Darby made six missionary journeys to North America between 1840 and 1880, where he became an influential leader in the Bible and Prophecy Conference movement. Among those who adopted his version of pre-millennialism were the Chicago-based evangelist Dwight L. Moody, best-selling evangelical author William E. Blackstone, and C.E. Scofield, whose Scofield Bible of 1909, with its dispensationalist interpretations of the Biblical texts, would influence millions for the next ninety years. These Christian leaders would be pivotal in advancing pre-millennial theology, and laying the foundations of Christian Zionism in North America.

Darby's approach is best called futurist dispensationalism, an adaptation of earlier forms of historic pre-millennial theology with various novel doctrines, including the assertion that:

• the prophetic texts and most of the Bible must be interpreted within a literalist and predictive hermeneutic;

• while there are two separate covenants between God and the "chosen people" (Israel and the Church), the covenant with Israel (and all of its components such as land, nation, etc.) should be interpreted as being eternal and exclusively for Jews.

• "the true Church" (those born again in Jesus Christ) will be raptured ("translated") out of history when Jesus will return to meet it in the clouds (1 Thessalonians 5.1-11). At that point, the nation Israel will become the primary covenantal body in history, but only Jews who accept Christ as Savior will be spared in the final battle.

• there were seven "dispensations" or historical epochs that marked the entirety of history from Creation to Christ's millennial reign on earth.

The doctrines of the "rapture" of the true Church and the restoration of the covenant to Israel (generally interpreted as a modern political nation-state) constitute radical departures from historic pre-millennialism, and for that matter from all branches of Catholicism, Eastern Orthodoxy, and Protestantism. Darby's pre-millennial dispensationalism is, in fact, a modern theological invention with innovative doctrines drawn from the margins of apocalyptic eschatology. Evangelical historian, Timothy Weber, has summarized the futurist pre-millennialist worldview and its pessimistic orientation:

Pre-millennialists reject popular notions of human progress and believe that history is a game that the righteous cannot win. For them, the historical process is a never ending battle between good and evil, whose course God has already conceded to the Devil. people may be redeemed in history but history itself is doomed. History's only hope lies in its own destruction [...] At the end of the present age, the forces of evil will be marshaled by Satan's emissary, the Antichrist, who will attempt to destroy God's purposes. After an intense period of tribulation, Christ will return to earth, resurrect the righteous death, defeat Antichrist and his legions at Armageddon, bind Satan, and establish his millennial rule.[13]

These elements of Darbyism became the foundation upon which the movement of Christian Zionism would be built. Moreover, the Bible would increasingly be used as a predictive book that could be decoded so as to provide believers with an understanding of the signs pointing to the end of history.

Christian Zionism can be defined as a theo-political movement primarily within Protestant Christian fundamentalism that advocates the political platform of modern Jewish Zionism. Its political character and advocacy of Jewish Zionist aspirations distinguishes Christian Zionism from pre-millennial dispensationalism, yet the latter theology is essentially the stepfather of the political movement. Christian Zionists believe the State of Israel is the fulfillment of divine promises in the Bible pertaining to the Jewish people, thus granting them exclusive land claims to the entirety of historic Palestine, and the right to a Jewish nation-state there. Early Christian Zionists in England and the US either anticipated, or intentionally advocated a political program of Jewish Zionists in their quest for political sovereignty, settlement, and military conquest of the land and control of its indigenous Palestinian population (Christian and majority Muslim). Christian Zionists advanced the claim that the Jewish people had moral, religious and political rights to settle and occupy the entirety of the land of Palestine, despite the fact that the indigenous population constituted over 94 per cent of the population when the Zionist political program was formally launched in August 1897. Based on their literal interpretation of Genesis 12.3 ("1 will bless those who bless you and curse those who curse you..."), Christian Zionists oblige themselves to be involved in the programs to advance the cause of a Jewish state in Palestine, not only religiously, but also by way of providing political and economic assistance.

LORD SHAFTSBURY'S (CHRISTIAN) ZIONISM

In fusing both elements, political and religious, Lord Shaftesbury (1801-85), the British evangelical social reformer, merited the later designation "Christian Zionist." In 1839, he published an extensive essay, "State and Restauration of the Jews," in the literary journal *Quarterly Review*. He wrote: "The Jews must be encouraged to return [to Palestine] in yet greater numbers and become once more the husbandman of Judea and Galilee."[14] Shaftsbury's essay set forth two important propositions with significant political implications. Firstly, he outlined the role that England must play in facilitating the return of Jews to political power and residence in Palestine. Secondly, he called upon the British Parliament to help finance and facilitate an Anglican Bishopric in Jerusalem. Shaftesbury believed that through the work of the bishopric, larger numbers of Jews would be converted to Christianity, and hence would become part of the end-time scenario. If Parliament advanced this double-phased program, the Empire would, according to Genesis 12.3, be blessed. In the following year (1840), Shaftesbury gained increased access to leadership in the British Foreign Office and mounted a persistent campaign designed to achieve these goals. On 4 November, he paid for the following advertisement in *The Times* (London), which brought his campaign to further public attention:

Restauration of the jews: A memorandum has been addressed to the Protestant monarchs of Europe on the subject of the restauration of the Jewish people to the land of Palestine. The document in question, dictated by a particular conjunction of affairs in the East and other striking "signs of the times," reverts to the original covenant which secures the land to the descendants of Abraham.[15]

Although Shaftsbury did not live to see an organized Jewish movement of Zionism he did see his vision for the Anglican Bishopric come to fruition in 1843. Moreover, the first British colonial office in Palestine can be attributed at least in part to his lobbying Members of Parliament. Shaftsbury's agenda was assisted by his close political connection to Lord Palmerston, the Foreign Secretary, who was married to the widowed mother of Shaftsbury's wife. Shaftesbury convinced Palmerston and others in the Foreign Office to support the Jerusalem bishopric, the colonial office in Palestine, and Jewish return to Palestine in order to outflank French interests in the region. Shaftesbury, more than anyone prior to the emergence of the formal Zionist movement in 1897, prepared the British Parliament and the religious establishment for their eventual embrace of political Zionism, well in advance of Zionism's appearance some fifty years later.

Shaftesbury was the originator of the Zionist phrase, "A land of no people for a people with no land," used by Max Nordau, Israel Zangwill, and Theodor Herzl.[16] In his 1839 essay in *Quarterly Review*, Shaftesbury's exact phrase was "a people with no country for a country with no people." Another British pre-millennialist who played a strategic political role in preparing the way for the Zionist movement was the Rev. William Hechler (1845-1931), Anglican Chaplain to the British Embassy in Vienna. His assignment to Vienna enabled him to meet Theodor Herzl and assist him with important political contacts that Herzl was still unable to execute. Hechler was passionately committed to futurist pre-millennialist dispensationalism, so much so, that he used the prophetic text Daniel 7-9 to calculate the return of the Jews to Palestine. Herzl pointed this out in his diary entry of 10 March 1896, after first meeting the Chaplain:

> He [Hechler] is enthusiastic about my solution to the Jewish Question.
> He also considers my movement a prophetic turning-point-which he had
> foretold two years before. From a prophecy in the time of Omar (637 AD)
> he had reckoned that at the end of forty-two prophetic months (total 1260
> years) the Jews would get Palestine back. This figure he arrived at was
> 1897-8.[17]

Even more impressive to the secular Herzl were the political connections of the elderly Chaplain. At a time when Herzl was trying unsuccessfully to meet Kaiser Wilhelm and other European leaders, Hechler was able to open doors previously closed to the Zionists. He organized the initial meeting between the German Kaiser and Herzl, then with the Grand Duke of Baden, and eventually with representatives of the British Foreign Office.

Shaftesbury and Hechler provided a political legacy that would bear additional fruit when two high-ranking British political leaders, the Secretary of State for Foreign Affairs, Arthur Balfour and Prime Minister David Lloyd-George facilitated the political processes that gave the Zionist movement its initial international legitimacy. Both Lloyd-George and Balfour were predisposed to support the Zionist cause due to their Christian Zionist background. Balfour embraced a vision that was similar to Shaftsbury's, a union of British imperialism and Christian Zionism, believing the British Empire would be blessed if it facilitated a Jewish state in Palestine. Balfour and Lloyd-George saw Palestine also as an important land bridge to India where a Jewish colony sympathetic to England would be a strategic asset in the colonial competition with France. Balfour stated as much in an important speech in 1919:

> For in Palestine we do not propose even to go through the form of consulting the wishes of the present inhabitants of the country [...] The four great powers are committed to Zionism. And Zionism, be it right or wrong, good or bad, is rooted in age-long traditions, in present needs, in future hopes, of far profounder import than the desires and prejudices of 700,000 Arabs who now inhabit that ancient Land.[18]

The statement reflects a fusion of British imperial designs with Christian Zionist doctrines ("age-long traditions, future hopes") and betrays the British bias towards the Zionist movement.

David Lloyd-George was also committed to the Zionists' political aspirations and, like Balfour, Hechler and Shaftesbury before him, the Prime Minister was predisposed to Zionism due to his pre-millennialist Christian teachings absorbed as a youth. Christopher Sykes, son of Sir Mark Sykes of the Sykes-Picot Agreement, noted that Lloyd-George was unable to grasp present names of nations and cities in the Middle East, but kept slipping back to the Biblical cities and districts of ancient Palestine that he learned in Sunday School during his youth. Moreover, in a 1925 speech before the Jewish Historical Society, Lloyd-George admitted as much and added that he was more acquainted with the Biblical geography of ancient Palestine than even of England:

I was brought up in a school where I was taught far more about the history of the Jews than about the history of my own land. I could tell you all the kings of Israel. But I doubt whether I could have named half a dozen of the kings of England, and not more of the kings of Wales [...] We were thoroughly imbued with the history of your race in the days of its greatest glory, when it founded that great literature which will echo to the very last days of this old world, influencing, molding, fashioning human character, inspiring and sustaining human motive, for not only Jews, but Gentiles as well.[19]

Clearly, British imperial designs directed its support of Zionism, but the decades of preparation by Christian leaders such as Way, Darby, Hechler, and Lord Shaftesbury are usually overlooked. Their pioneering work would be fulfilled initially by the Balfour Declaration of 1917 and the British Mandate over Palestine (1922), both instrumental in paving the way for legitimizing the Zionist cause and Jewish settlement in Palestine.

EARLY CHRISTIAN ZIONISM IN THE UNITED STATES

In the United States, like Britain, theological support for Christian Zionist concepts prepared the way for eventual adoption of the Zionist project. John Nelson Darby's missionary journeys to North America and his prominence at the aforementioned Bible and Prophecy Conferences enabled him to display his unique version of futurist pre-millennial dispensationalism, which became the preferred eschatology of most Protestant evangelicals and fundamentalists by World War 1.[20] Among the many evangelical leaders to be influenced by Darby was best-selling author William E. Blackstone (1841-1935). His *Jesus is Coming* (1878) brought pre-millennial dispensationalism to millions of US Christians, and was translated into over a dozen languages and reached an international audience.

Blackstone organized what appears to have been the first Zionist lobbying effort in the US which occurred in 1891, six years before Theodor Herzl convened the inaugural World Zionist Congress in Basle (August 1897). The initiative was launched in response to the massive numbers of

Jews who were fleeing Eastern Europe and coming to New York following the outbreak of pogroms during the 1880-90s. Blackstone was able to enlist major US financiers such as multi-millionaire industrialists John D. Rockefeller and J.P. Morgan, as well as publisher Charles B. Scribner to underwrite a massive newspaper campaign with a petition that was signed by over 400 prominent personalities. The petition called for President Benjamin Harrison to support the creation of a Jewish state in Palestine. Moreover it was signed by the Chief Justice of the US Supreme Court, several members of the US Congress, and in total over 400 prominent Jewish and Christian leaders. The petition (which Blackstone called a "memorial") stated in part:

> Why not give Palestine back to them again? According to God's distribution of nations it is their home, an inalienable possession from which they were expelled by force. Under their cultivation, it was a remarkably fruitful land, sustaining millions of Israelites, who industriously tilled its hillsides and valleys.[21]

President Harrison did not support the petition but the evangelist made his mark on US politics while gaining a foothold of support for secular Jewish Zionists in the United States. Justice Louis Brandeis, the first Jew to serve as a member of the US Supreme Court, was the leader of the Zionist movement in the US after 1915. Brandeis and Blackstone became close friends and the Zionist movement received significant financial support from Blackstone, as did various Christian agencies that Blackstone directed to support Jewish colonization in Palestine. Brandeis once said of Blackstone: "you are the father of Zionism as your work antedates Herzl."[22]

CHRISTIAN ZIONISM IN THE UNITED STATES: WORLD WAR II—THE REAGAN ERA

There is little evidence of the Christian Right or Christian Zionists having any political influence on US Middle East policy after the 1890s, and certainly not during the pivotal World War I or II periods, nor during President Harry S. Truman's support for the UN vote to partition

Palestine (1947). Christian fundamentalism was largely during retreat from political involvement after the fundamentalist controversies after World War I, resulting in an extended period of isolation from the political mainstream. During the post-World War II period, support for Zionism came from mainstream Protestant churches and those theologians who saw Zionism as the answer to the Holocaust.

However, Israel's creation in 1948 was a pivotal moment in the revitalization of pre-millennial dispensationalism, and in due course, Christian Zionism would follow within two decades. For the dispensationalist school of eschatology, Israel's birth as a state in 1948 was crucial in that it was a sign that the latter-day events predicted in the Bible were about to be fulfilled. The June War of 1967 served as further confirmation that the pre-millennial dispensationalist interpretation of history would guide believers in the countdown to Jesus' return. Politically, the 1967 War marked a turning point in US-Israeli relations, as Israel was increasingly seen as a "strategically" and guardian of US interests in the Middle East. During this period of "Cold War" politics the pro-Israel lobby gradually elevated its profile and became one of the most powerful lobbies in Washington, DC.[23]

During the 1970s several important developments led American Jewish leaders to re-examine their historic alliance with the liberal Protestant and Roman Catholic establishments and turn to the fundamentalist Christians for support. At least five trends converged in the late 1970s that forged the new partnership of the American Jewish establishment with the Christian Right.[24]

First, by the late 1960-70s the fastest growing sectors of American Christianity were the Charismatic, Pentecostal, and fundamentalist churches, where pre-millennialist dispensationalism was the dominant theological orientation. Roman Catholic and mainstream Protestant churches were on the decline, both in terms of membership and annual budgets. Secondly, an evangelical Christian was elected President of the US in 1976, drawing considerable support from conservative Christians. President Jimmy Carter's initial popularity gave positive energy and significant encouragement for conservative Christians to be involved more directly in the political process. During the same period, Christian fundamentalist organizations such as the Moral Majority appeared to capture the new conservative Christian engagement in politics. Their impact was augmented by televangelists such as Pat Robertson, Jimmy Swaggert and Jerry Falwell.

Thirdly, Jewish leaders took note of increased criticism of Israel's human rights record from the National Council of Churches and several mainstream Protestant denominations, particularly the Lutherans, the United Church of Christ, Presbyterians, United Methodists, and Episcopalians. Rabbi Marc Tannenbaum of the American Jewish Community summarized the change:

> The evangelical community is the largest and fastest growing block of pro-Israel sentiment in this country. Since the 1967 War, the Jewish community has felt abandoned by Protestants, the groups clustered around the National Council of Churches, which because of sympathy with third world causes, gave the impression of support for the PLO. There was a vacuum of public support for Israel that began to be filled by the fundamentalist and evangelical Christians.[25]

The fourth development occurred in Israel when Menachem Begin of the conservative and more extreme Likud Party was elected Prime Minister in 1977. Begin adopted more maximalist policies concerning negotiating land and boundaries with the Palestinians while simultaneously accelerating the construction of settlements in Palestinian areas. Seeking support from new sources, Begin and the Likud leaders courted the Christian Right to a higher degree than their more secular Labor Party predecessors and soon the Israeli Tourism Bureau offered fundamentalist Christian pastors from the Bible Belt attractive financial incentives for bringing their congregations to the Holy Land. Within a short time the conservative Christians became a significant source of revenue and political support for Israel.

The fifth and final development occurred in March 1977, when President Jimmy Carter inserted into a speech in New England that the Palestinians must have full human rights and have a right to a "homeland." No US President had so clearly stated this position. The Israeli lobby and its new friends in the Christian Right commenced joint political action for the remainder of the year in opposition to Carter's policies. Full-page advertisements appeared across the US in the secular and Christian press. The advertisement took direct aim at Carter's statement when it stated: "We affirm as evangelicals our belief in the Promised Land to the Jewish people [...] We would view with grave concern any effort to carve out of the Jewish homeland another nation or political entity."[26] The ad campaign was organized by Jerry Strober, a former employee of the American Jewish Committee, who told *Newsweek* magazine: "[the Christian Right] is Carter's constituency and he had better listen to them. The real source of strength the Jews have in this country is from the evangelicals."[27] These developments marked the initial political alignment of the Christian Zionist "Right" and the pro-Israel lobby. It is well known that when the 1980 election came, the Iran hostage crisis dogged Carter. What is less discussed, however, was the shift of well over 80 per cent of the Christian "Right" to the candidacy of Ronald Reagan, himself a supporter of Christian Zionism and pre-millennial dispensational theology.

The Rev. Jerry Falwell quickly became a favored person for Menachem Begin and various Likud organizers. According to an investigative report by the *Washington Post*, Falwell was given a Lear jet by the Israeli government and later received the Jabotinsky Award, named after Begin's mentor and chief ideologue of the Likud movement.[28] In the mid 1980s, Falwell made his most significant contribution to the Israeli cause as he embarked upon the project of influencing North Carolina Senator Jesse Helms in favor of Israel. Helms had been a critic of Israel's policies for several years, but Falwell and the pro-Israel lobby were able to bring significant funding and voting support from the Christian Right to re-elect Helms in a remarkably close election. The Senator instantaneously muted his fierce criticism of Israel and became one of the strongest voices for Israel in the history of the US Senate, especially on assuming the Chair of the Senate Foreign Relations Committee with oversight of the foreign assistance budget and foreign policy.

Ronald Reagan's own Christian Zionist perspective facilitated his alliance with the pro-Israel lobby which lent its support to his 1980 Presidential election. It also contributed to his becoming the most pro-Israel President in US history, at least until the Presidency of George W. Bush. During his years as Governor of California, Reagan had been influenced by a cadre of Charismatic Christian leaders, including Pat

Boone and evangelists Harald Bredesen, George Otis, and later the best-selling pre-millennial dispensationalist author, Hal Lindsay (*Late, Great Planet Earth*).[29] Reagan adopted their dispensationalist theology and never retreated from it. He uttered at least seven public references to "Armageddon" during his Presidency and seemed to blend his political analysis with his Armageddon theology quite naturally. One of the most revealing statements by the President occurred during a private telephone conversation with Tom Dine, Executive Director of the powerful pro-Israel lobby AIPAC (America-Israel Public Affairs Committee). Reagan stated:

> You know, I turn back to your ancient prophets in the Old Testament and the signs foretelling Armageddon, and 1 find myself wondering if-if we're the generation that is going to see that come about. I don't know if you've noted any of these prophecies lately, but believe me, they certainly describe the times we're going through.

The President's statement was published in the *Jerusalem Post*[30] and received coverage across the US by the *Associated Press* wire service. Several of Reagan's close associates held similar views, such as Secretary of the Interior James Watt, Legal Counsel Edwin Meese, and Secretary of Defense Cap Weinberger and many others. Indeed, James Watt encouraged the sale of massive tracks of environmentally sensitive land in California, the Pacific Northwest, and Alaska to corporations for industrial and commercial development, because, according to his dispensationalist theology, saving the environment was a low priority due to Jesus' imminent return. Moreover, Reagan encouraged pro-Israel briefings in the White House for pro-Israel fundamentalist Christian leaders, a project that was co-ordinated by the US State Department and the pro-Israel lobby AIPAC with assistance from the Christian Zionist leadership. During the course of these "Christian" briefings, not a single mainstream Protestant, Eastern Orthodox, or Roman Catholic leader was invited, whereas the list was a "Who's Who" of the Christian Zionists: Jim and Tammy Bakker, Pat Robertson, Hal Lindsay, Jimmy Swaggert, Tim and Bev LeHaye, political strategist and Moral Majority architect Ed McAteer, James Dobson of Focus on the Family, and countless others. Among those who provided the briefings were Israeli diplomats and Republican staff, such as Oliver North and Bud McFarlane, later of the Iran-Contra scandals.[31] Both North and McFarlane were devoted Christian Zionists.

DECLINE AND REVIVAL, 1988-2000

While the Christian Zionist/pro-Israel lobby alliance remained active during the Bush and Clinton administrations it was not at centre stage. The Bush Senior administration's Middle East policy was led by Secretary of State James Baker and colleagues in the Department of State who were considerably better informed by the CIA and the US embassies across the Middle East and Islamic world. The administration had grown impatient with Israeli Prime Minister Yitzhak Shamir's refusal to end settlement construction and his rejection of direct negotiations with Palestinians during the Madrid Conferences which commenced in November 1991. The Christian Zionists and the Christian "Right" in general had fallen into disarray following the humiliating defeat of Presidential candidate Pat Robertson in 1988. The Jim and Tammy Bakker and Jimmy Swaggert sex and financial scandals were also factors in their "fall from grace."

With the Clinton era came a different approach to the Israeli-Palestinian conflict, one that eclipsed the power and perspectives of both the Christian Zionists and Likud rejectionists. Although his background was Southern Baptist evangelicalism, Bill Clinton's religious views were as much an enigma as were his personal ethics. He quickly became the target of the Republican Right and of such conservative talk-show hosts as Rush Limbaugh, Jerry Falwell, Pat Robertson, and a recycled Oliver North. The Clinton administration developed a close alliance with the secular Labor Party in Israel, but Likud (and the Christian Zionists) remained steadfast in its opposition to Oslo and any demand for Israel to return occupied land to the Palestinians.

Not long after Prime Minister Rabin was assassinated by an Israeli extremist on 4 November 1995, Benyamin Netanyahu became Prime Minister after the 29 May 1996 elections, and the Oslo process stagnated with a Knesset dominated by Likud policies. Netanyahu had long been a close ally of Christian Zionist organizations, speaking regularly at such events as the National Prayer Breakfast for Israel and conferences organized by the Jerusalem-based Christian Zionist organization, the International Christian Embassy-Jerusalem. Within months of his election, Netanyahu convened the Israel Christian Advocacy Council, bringing 17 US-based fundamentalists to Israel for a publicity tour of the Holy Land and a conference whose statement clearly reflected the Likud political platform. The Christian leaders signed a pledge that stated in part: "America will never, never desert Israel."[32] Among the points of the declaration was a blanket rejection of pressure on Israel to abandon the illegal settlements in the West Bank, East Jerusalem, the Gaza Strip, and the Golan Heights. The statement supported a united Jerusalem under Israeli sovereignty, rather than a Jerusalem shared between Palestinians and Israelis.

The Christian leaders returned to the US and launched a campaign with full-page advertisements in major newspapers and Christian journals under the heading "Christians Call for a United Jerusalem." The text of the advertisement carried several of the familiar Christian Zionist themes, claiming: "Jerusalem has been the spiritual and political capital of only the Jewish people for 3000 years." Citing Genesis 12.17, Leviticus 26.44-45 and Deuteronomy 7.7-8, it stated that "Israel's Biblical claim to the land was an eternal covenant from God."[33] Among the signatories were several familiar and also new Christian Zionists: Pat Robertson (CBN); Ralph Reed (then Director of the Christian Coalition); Jerry Falwell; Brandt Gustafson (President of the National Religious Broadcasters); Rev. Don Argue (President of the National Association of Evangelicals); and Ed McAteer of the Religious Roundtable, one of the first Christian Zionist organizations in North America. The campaign was a direct response to the "Churches for a Shared Jerusalem" advertisements of 6th March 1995, from the mainstream US Protestant, Orthodox, and Catholic Churches.

Likud also turned to the Christian Zionists for help with Israel's financial woes in the late 1990s to replace revenue lost from North American Jews due to the hostile debate between the Orthodox and Reform-Conservative branches of Judaism. When the Jewish groups reduced their generous contributions to the Jewish National Fund several Christian Zionist organizations and sympathetic churches worked to offset the difference. The campaign was led by the International Fellowship of Christians and Jews, headed by former Anti-Defamation

League employee and Orthodox Rabbi, Yechiel Eckstein. In 1997, the organization claimed to have raised over $5 million from fundamentalist Christian sources. Rev. John Hagee's Cornerstone Church in San Antonio, Texas, presented Eckstein with more than $1 million, stating that the funds would be used to resettle Jews from the Soviet Union into the West Bank and Jerusalem. When asked if support of the illegal settlements was at cross purposes with US policy, Hagee responded: "I am a Bible scholar and a theologian, and from my perspective the law of God transcends the laws of the US Government and the US State Department."[34]

BACK TO THE FUTURE:
2000 AND BEYOND

Several factors converged after the 2000 Presidential elections to signal a dramatic shift to the right in US policy regarding not only the Israeli-Palestinian conflict, but domestic and foreign policy issues as well. First, the secular and religious media had saturated the public for two years with anxiety-ridden speculation on the various tragedies that might befall the public when the clock struck midnight 2000. Sales of Christian books on Bible prophecy skyrocketed, an additional sign of the anxiety that captured the public. Food and water shortages were predicted, and people began to stockpile goods in their cupboards. Terrorist attacks were predicted on the eve of the millennium. Capturing the spirit of the millennial build-up, several dispensationalist books and films were released such as the *Left Behind* series, which provided the old dispensationalist symbols in an attractive new form, reaching the *New York Times* best-selling list.

Secondly, with the collapse of the Soviet Union more than a decade earlier, the Christian Zionists and Christian "Right" were in search of a new enemy. Israel, which had no shortage of enemies, continued to need new arguments to justify the $6 billion it received annually from US taxpayers. The rise of Islamic extremism and the second Palestinian *Intifada* provided Israel and the dispensationalists with their opponents: militant Islam and the Palestinians.

Thirdly, the neo-conservative movement had been awaiting an opportunity to advance its ideology and leadership. Led by a number of pro-Israeli advocates such as William Kristol of the *American Standard*, syndicated journalists William Safire of the *New York Times* and Charles Krauthammer of the *Washington Post*, and Reagan ideologues Paul Wolfowitz, Elliot Abrams, Douglas Feith and Richard Perle, they advanced their agendas within the conservative wing of the Republican Party where they found a warm reception. Many were placed in high positions in the Department of Defense and offices dealing with Middle East policy formation. The Christian fundamentalist and Christian Zionist worldviews converged with neo-conservative doctrines, enabling them to take control of Middle East policy. Some of the neo-conservative ideologues were former employees of the pro-Israel lobby AIPAC and various Pro-Israel think-tanks. Indeed, Perle had narrowly escaped conviction of trading intelligence secrets with Israel in the late 1970s[35] and Abrams had been convicted (and pardoned by President Ronald Reagan) in the Iran-Israel-Contra triangular weapons and financial scandal.

Fourthly, it should not have been a surprise that the Christian "Right" and Christian Zionist-Likud policies would be a major influence in the George W. Bush administration. As early as 1987, polls indicated that the "Christian Right" represented 26 per cent of the total membership of the Republican Party. However, by 1999, the percentage increased to 33 per cent and was steadily on the rise.[36] The pro-Israel political action committees and the Christian Zionist influence in such vital swing states as Texas, California, and the all-important Florida elections, may have been the deciding factor in favor of George W. Bush. The new president was aware that he owed a political debt to the pro-Israel lobby.

Fifthly, the collapse of the Oslo peace process at the Camp David II meetings of July 2000 were followed by Ariel Sharon's provocative entry into the tense *Haram al-Sharif* (Temple Mount) under the cover of 1,100 Israeli police, helicopters, and military forces. The ensuing clashes led to violent demonstrations that would later be known as Al-Aqsa *Intifada*. The violent nature of this second *Intifada* played directly into the hands of Ariel Sharon's message of security and aggressive retaliation against the Palestinians. Sharon had campaigned on a pledge to oppose the peace process, expand settlements, and break-off all negotiations with the Palestine Liberation Organization (PLO). Each Palestinian suicide bombing provided additional support for Sharon's policies.

The new Bush administration had delayed a clear declaration of its position on the Israeli-Palestinian conflict, stating initially that the two sides needed to work out a peace settlement between them. Bush issued conflicting messages, calling for a Palestinian state one day and then denouncing the Palestinian leadership the next. Gradually, the pro-Israel hawks (Rumsfeld, Cheney, Perle, Wolfowitz, Feith, Abrams et al.) came to dominate the Bush administration's approach to Middle East policy. Now buttressed by the significant popular vote of the Christian Zionists and the clout of the pro-Israel lobby in Congress, the Zionist-neo-conservative control over US Middle East policy appears to be in the dominant position for the immediate future.

To illustrate the point, one need only turn to the period immediately after September 11, 2001. When support for Israel began to waver in the mind of President George W. Bush and Secretary of State Colin Powell, the pro-Israel lobby and the Christian Right began to close ranks. Several initiatives culminated in the "2002 Washington Rally for Israel." According to some accounts, well over 100,000 people made their way into the Washington Mall on 15 April 2002. An impressive line-up of US politicians was joined by leading voices from the Christian "Right," Israel, and the American Jewish community, to address the predominantly Jewish audience. The list included former Israeli Prime Minister Benyamin Netanyahu; Israeli parliamentarian and former activist for Soviet Jews, Natan Sharansky; Deputy Secretary of Defense, Paul Wolfowitz; Holocaust writer Elie Weisel; NewYork Governor George Pataki; former Mayor of New York Rudolf Guliani; US Senators Arlen Specter (RPA[37]) and Barbara Mikulski (D-MD[38]); leading Members of Congress Dick Gebhart (D-MO[39]), and House Majority Leader Dick Armey (R-TX13[40]), a Christian Zionist.[41]

CONCLUSION:
THEO-POLITICAL IMPLICATIONS OF
THE CHRISTIAN ZIONIST-JEWISH ALLIANCE

There are many contradictions in the Christian Zionist Jewish partnership that have been analyzed convincingly by the Israeli writer Gershom Gorenberg, in his *The End of Days*.[42] Gorenberg points out one of the central concerns in the new alliance of Jews and the Christian "Right," that is, Jews are given only two options in the dispensationalist scenario: either you convert to Christianity or you are incinerated at the Armageddon holocaust. Although the leaders of the movements choose not to discuss these significant points of tension one can be sure that serious problems will arise, since avoidance strategies eventually lead to serious conflicts. Unless the progressive wings of the Jewish community face the challenges of these contradictions the short-term gains may eventually become a nightmare.

A related problem arises from the anti-Semitism that is often just beneath the surface of many Christian Zionists and fundamentalist Christians. Only short term memories will forget that former Southern Baptist President Rev. Bailey Smith once stated: "God does not hear the prayers of the Jews." After the pro-Israel lobby sent him on a quick indoctrination tour of the Holy Land he returned as a strong Christian Zionist. Even the leading Christian Zionist, Jerry Falwell, indicated his insensitivity to the Jewish community when he stated: "God told me that the Antichrist is alive and is indeed a Jew living in Romania." Falwell apologized repeatedly to his Jewish friends in major Jewish organizations but the "slip" is symbolic of the problem. Related is the fact that the Christian Right's primary agenda for the US is the creation of a "Christian" America, which would undoubtedly impose severe restrictions on every religious minority. Jews once were in the forefront of opposing threats to civil liberties in the United States. The civil liberties community and Jewish organizations, including many Reform rabbis, who are normally vigilant on these matters, have been strangely silent. Even the major Jewish watchdog agencies such as the Anti-Defamation League, the American Jewish Committee, the American Jewish Congress, and the Jewish Federation are under a veil of silence as they enjoy the political support from the more numerous Christian Right.

Equally disturbing is the silence of the mainstream Protestant, Roman Catholic, and Eastern Orthodox Churches on the issues of Christian Zionism and the pro-Israel lobby alliance with the Christian Right. Serious theological analysis, the equipping of pastors, seminarians, and the laity for the task of deconstructing Christian Zionist arguments should be on the agenda of mainstream denominations, seminaries, and church-related universities. It is already clear that pre-millennial dispensationalist doctrines are creeping into the churches and the youth culture across the United States, particularly in the Bible Belt and south-western regions. Moreover, the serious matter of the theological program of Christian Zionism and its underlying assumptions must be addressed as a theological heresy that challenges the churches as well as the conduct of foreign policy in the United States.

Since the pro-Israel lobby is not exclusively Jewish it is important that analysts designate it as such. Indeed, the largest bloc of pro-Israel sentiment is found within Christian fundamentalist circles, whose numbers dwarf the Jewish voting population in the US (approximately 25 million Christian fundamentalists to 4 million Jews). The pro-Israel lobby and influence, then, is Christian as well as Jewish, and that reality should always be reflected. Not only does this avoid the canard that criticism of Israel and Zionist political activity equals anti-Semitism, but it accurately describes the contemporary political reality.

The theological program and doctrinal system of the Christian Zionists introduce novel doctrines and distortions of historic evangelical theology that must be debated and confronted across the broader evangelical movement, especially in North America. The broad evangelical centre, whose numbers may exceed 100 million in the United States, is generally not dispensationalist in its orientation and is often open-minded on the issue of Christian Zionism. However, as the culture gives rise to an outpouring of Christian Zionist literature, film, television and radio programming, one senses a continued growth of these views among current and future voters. Based as it is on a literal and futurist Biblical hermeneutic, Christian Zionism reduces the Bible to several distortions that should concern the evangelical mainstream, which itself insists on the correct interpretation of the Bible. For example, evangelicals ought to address the fact that the Christian Zionist worldview elevates Israel to the level of being a political entity that is above the Torah, let alone outside the norms of international law and the rule of law. In its justification of Israel's illegal program of land confiscation, demolition of homes, targeted assassinations, and continued transfer of Palestinians from their homeland, the Christian Right encourages the breaking of the Ten Commandments and the Levitical codes. As such the Christian Zionists have traded the prophetic mantle of the Biblical prophets for an idolatry of the nation-state against which the prophets consistently warned in advance of impending doom. Evangelical scholars, journals, theological seminaries and universities should be addressing the dangerous doctrines and consequences of Christian Zionist teachings and practices.

Christian Zionism, like its theological stepfather, pre-millennialist dispensationalism, is grounded in a reductionist ecclesiology, having itself a weak sense of the Church of Jesus Christ, and in the end elevates the nation-state Israel above the Church. Such a view is inconsistent with the New Testament message and plays itself out in practices that are both practically as well as theologically inconsistent with Scripture. Darby's doctrine that the church is a "mere parenthesis," and will soon vanish in the pre-millennial rapture is but one of the theological presuppositions that under-gird the movement's hostility to the Church universal, and its rejection of Palestinian Christians. Opposition to Christian Zionist views is more than ever necessary in the light of the cries for help by many Palestinian Christian leaders as they endure a brutal Israeli military assault on their communities, and not least against the background of the fact that the Palestinian Christian community has shrunk from having been 13 per cent of the Palestinian population in the Occupied Territories in 1967 to under 2 per cent today.

Research on emigration patterns shows that Palestinian Christians are fleeing their homeland not due to Islamic fundamentalism, as many Israelis and Christian Zionists would have us believe, but because their lives, livelihood, and future are doomed by the continued Israeli occupation.[43] The mere fact that Christian Zionists provide political and economic support for Israeli militancy against Palestinian Christians and Muslims, leading to the near end of Christianity in the Holy Land, should not be tolerated. That Christian Zionists can perpetuate the destruction of Palestinian Christianity through their considerable support of Israel's militant policies seems to be anti-Christian behavior.

The general Christian Zionist view of God is that of a vindictive tribal deity and a god of war, a perspective that seriously undermines the theological foundation of the entire Christian Zionist project, and renders it incompatible with the life and teachings of Jesus. Also, the Christian Zionist political position is oppositional to US policy on the

Israeli-Palestinian conflict. It is no accident that Christian Zionists, in concert with the Likud Party in Israel, have opposed the previous two peace proposals (the Oslo Accords and the Roadmap) while they have also supported Israel's accelerated militarization of the Israeli-Palestinian conflict. Moreover, the Christian Zionist community supported the war in Iraq and seems willing to live with the "perpetual conflict" scenario for the Middle East rather than curb Israel's aggression.

Finally, the pendulum of political support often swings far in every decade. While the Bush administration, intimately allied with the Christian Right, the pro-Israeli lobby, and the neo-conservative ideologues, is in the zenith of power and influence, such power could diminish if certain economic, political and military developments turn against it. Perhaps of highest importance is the fact that the period between late 2003 through most of 2004 will involve a US Presidential election wherein the economy will be a primary issue. If the economy does not improve-and there are few signs that it will-the popular tide of support in the wake of the victory over Iraq will be short-lived. There are looming problems also at the political level. At the time of writing, preliminary investigations are underway in Britain concerning the possible distortion of intelligence data concerning Iraq's alleged weapons of mass destruction and other justifications for the 2003 war on Iraq. Questions are being asked in the US also. If the inquiries reveal that British Prime Minister Tony Blair and the Bush administration misled the public and Parliament/Congress, their base of support will begin to erode. There is a further ongoing problem deriving from not only the drain on the US economy brought about by the US occupation of Iraq and Afghanistan but also by the increase in the number of US troops killed or wounded by resistance forces: history indicates that Americans have limited tolerance for their own casualties.

Worse still, if there is another, or several, terrorist attacks on the United States, the public's tolerance of the current Bush policies and those who support them will decrease. Already on 29 May 2003, the respected Amnesty International (US) released a report that indicated that the world was less secure, and that clearly US citizens also were less secure, after the war in Iraq.

FURTHER READING

Brightman, Thomas, *Apocalypsis Apocalypseos* (London: self-published, 1585).

Darby, John Nelson, *The Works of John Nelson Darby*, vol. I, no. I (Kingston-on-Thames: Stow Hill Bible and Trust Depot, 1962).

Hurewitz J.C., *The Struggle for Palestine* (New York: Schocken Books, 1976).

Wagner, Donald, *Dying in the Land of Promise: Palestine and Palestinian Christianity from Pentecost-2000* (London: Melisende, 2nd edn., 2003).

Wagner, Donald with Hassan Haddad, *All in the Name of the Bible* (Brattleboro, VT: Amana Press, 1985).

Weber, Timothy P., *Living in the Shadow of the Second Coming: American Premillennialism, 1875-1925* (New York: Oxford University Press, 1979).

NOTES

1. Since early 2002 there has been a surge of popular articles analyzing the influence of the Christian Right in US domestic and foreign policy. See Matthew Engel, "War in the Gulf Bringing Aid and the Bible," *The Guardian*, 4th April 2003, p. 6; *Time* Magazine, 24th February, p.19; Margot Patterson, "Will Fundamentalist Christians and Jews Ignite Apocalypse?" *National Catholic Reporter*, 3rd March 2003: "A Very Mixed Marriage," *Newsweek*, 2nd June 2003: Ken Silverstein and Michael Scherer, "Born Again Zionists," *Mother Jones*, September 2002, pp. 56-61.

2. For a rich source of analysis and articles on the neo-conservatives, see www. newamericancentury.org, particularly articles by William Kristol, Paul Wolfowitz, Richard Perle, Douglas Feith, Frank Gaffney, Robert Kagan and Donald Rumsfeld.

3. For further discussion of pre-millennialism see Paul Boyer, *When Time Shall Be No More: Prophecy Belief in Modern Culture* (Cambridge, MA: Harvard University Press, 1992), Timothy P. Weber, *Living in the Shadow of the Second Coming: American Premillennialism, 1875-1925* (New York: Oxford University Press, 1979) and Ernest R. Sandeen, *The Roots of Fundamentalism: British and American Millenarianism, 1800-1930* (Chicago: University of Chicago Press, 1970).

4. Bernard McGinn, *Visions of the End: Apocalyptic Traditions in the Middle Ages* (New York: Columbia University Press, 1979) pp.3-27

5. Ibid., p.3

6. Gerhard von Rad, *Old Testament Theology*, vol. 2 (Westminster: John Knox Press, 1965) pp.301-302

7. Paul Boyer, op cit., pp. 52-55 and Bernard McGinn, op cit., pp.126-41

8. Henry Finch, *The World's Great Restauration or Calling of the Jewes* (London: Edward Grifen for William Bladen, 1621) pp.126-41

9. For a more detailed account, see Donald Wagner, *Anxious for Armageddon* (Scottsboro, PA: Herald Press, 1995) pp.85-95

10. Henry Finch, op cit., p.3

11. LeRoy Froom, *The Prophetic Faith of Our Fathers* (Washington, DC: Washington Review and Herald Press, 1954) p. 137

12. Stephen Sizer, "The Promised Land: A Critical Investigation of Christian Zionism in Britain and the United States of America Since 1800" (unpublished PhD dissertation; London: Middlesex University and Oak Hill Theological College, 2003) p.26

13. Timothy P. Weber, *Living in the Shadow of the Second Coming: American Premillennialism, 1875-1925* (New York: Oxford University Press, 1979) p.6

14. Nahum Sokolow, *History of Zionism* (London: Longman, Green & Co., 1919) p.127

15. Ibid.

16. Albert M. Hyamson, *Palestine Under the Mandate* (London: Methuen, 1950) p.10 and Regina Sharif, *Non Jewish Zionism* (London: Zed Press, 1983) p.42

17. Theodor Herzl, *The Complete Diaries of Theodore Herzl* (ed. Raphael Patai; trans. Harry Zohn; 5 vols.; New York: Herzl Press, 1960) p.71

18. Doreen Igrams, *Palestine Papers, 1917-22, Seeds of Conflict* (London: John Murray, 1972) p. 73

19. Christopher Sykes, *Two Studies in Virtue* (New York: Alfred A. Knopf, 1953) p.239

20. I use the term "evangelical" as the movement of conservative Christians, constituting approximately 125 million Americans. Fundamentalists are approximately 25 per cent of evangelicals, yet many of its spokespersons (e.g. Jerry Falwell and Pat Robertson) tend to inflate their numbers, or claim they represent all evangelicals.

21. Regina Sharif, op cit., p.92

22. Stephen Sizer, op cit., p.66

23. See Fred J. Khouri, *The Arab-Israeli Dilemma* (Syracuse, NY: Syracuse University Press, 1985) pp.382-83; Edward W. Said, *Peace and Its Discontents* (New York: Vintage Books, 1996) pp.244-66 and Kathleen Christison, *Perceptions of Palestine* (Berkeley and Los Angeles: University of California Press, 2000) pp.136-56

24. For a more detailed discussion see Donald Wagner, "Evangelicals and Israel," *Christian Century*, 4th November, 1998, pp. 1020-26

25. William Claibourne, "Israelis Look on US Evangelical Christians as Potent Ally," *Washington Post* 23rd March 1981

26. *Chicago Sun-Times*, 9th November 1977

27. Quoted in *Washington Post*, 23rd March 1981

28. Grace Halsell, *Prophecy and Politics* (Westpott, CT: Lawrence Hill, 1986) p.74

29. See Larry Jones and Gerald T. Sheppard, "Ronald Reagan's Theology of Armageddon," *TSF Bulletin* (September/October, 1984) pp.16-19

30. 12th October 1983

31. Author's personal copy of the White House invitation and guest list.

32. *United Methodist Review*, November 1996

33. *New York Times*, 10th April 1997

34. Religious News Service, 23rd February 1998

35. See Michael Saba, *The Armageddon Network* (Brattleboro, VT: Amana Press, 1984),where the author witnessed the exchange of US intelligence by Richard Perle and Israeli agents at the Madison Hotel in Washington, DC.

36. Matthew Engel, "Meet the New Zionists," *The Guardian* 28th October, 2002, p.2

37. Republican from Pennsylvania.

38. Democrat from Maryland

39. Democrat from Missouri

40. Republican from Texas

41. See Maureen Dowd, "Perle's Plunder Blunder," *New York Times*, 23rd March, 2003, p.13; Seymour Hersh, "Lunch with the Chairman," *New Yorker*, 17th March, 2003, pp. 76-81;Robert Fisk, "The Case Against War," *The Independent*,15th February 2003;Eric Alterman, "Perle Interrupted," *The Nation*, 7th April, 2003 and Gary Dorrien, "Axis of One," *Christian Century*, 8th March, 2003, pp.30-35.

42. Gershom Gorenberg, 2000 *The End of Days: Fundamentalism and the Struggle for the Temple Mount* (New York: Oxford University Press, 2000) pp.232-50

43. See, for example, Bernard Sabella, "Socio-Economic Characteristics and the Challenges to Palestinian *Christians in the Holy Land*," in Michael Prior and William Taylor (eds.), *Christians in the Holy Land* (London: WIFT/Scorpion Press, 1994) pp.31-44 and Sami Geraisy, "Socio-Demographic Characteristics: Reality, Problems and Aspirations within Israel," in Michael Prior and William Taylor (eds.), *Christians in the Holy Land* (London: WIFT/Scorpion Press, 1994) pp. 45-55.

16 | Dangerous Religion

George W. Bush's Theology of Empire

JIM WALLIS

Religion is the most dangerous energy source known to humankind. The moment a person (or government or religion or organization) is convinced that God is either ordering or sanctioning a cause or project, anything goes. The history, worldwide, of religion-fueled hate, killing, and oppression is staggering.

—Eugene Peterson (from the introduction to the book of Amos in the Bible paraphrase The Message)

"THE MILITARY VICTORY in Iraq seems to have confirmed a new world order," Joseph Nye, dean of Harvard's Kennedy School of Government, wrote recently in *The Washington Post*. "Not since Rome has one nation loomed so large above the others. Indeed, the word 'empire' has come out of the closet."

The use of the word "empire" in relation to American power in the world was once controversial, often restricted to left-wing critiques of US hegemony. But now, on op-ed pages and in the nation's political discourse, the concepts of empire and even the phrase *Pax Americana* are increasingly referred to in unapologetic ways.

William Kristol, editor of the influential *Weekly Standard*, admits the aspiration to empire. "If people want to say we're an imperial power, fine," Kristol wrote. Kristol is chair of the Project for the New American Century, a group of conservative political figures that began in 1997 to chart a much more aggressive American foreign policy. The Project's papers lay out the vision of an "American peace" based on "unquestioned US military pre-eminence." These imperial visionaries write, "America's grand strategy should aim to preserve and extend this advantageous position as far into the future as possible." It is imperative, in their view, for the United States to "accept responsibility for America's unique role in preserving and extending an international order friendly to our security, our prosperity, and our principles." That, indeed, is empire.

There is nothing secret about all this; on the contrary, the views and plans of these powerful men have been quite open. These are Far Right American political leaders and commentators who have ascended to governing power and, after the trauma of September 11, 2001, have been emboldened to carry out their agenda.

In the run-up to the war with Iraq, Kristol told me that Europe was now unfit to lead because it was "corrupted by secularism," as was the developing world, which was "corrupted by poverty." Only the United States could provide the "moral framework" to govern a new world order, according to Kristol, who recently and candidly wrote, "Well, what is wrong with dominance, in the service of sound principles and high ideals?" Whose ideals? The American right wing's definition of "American ideals," presumably.

BUSH ADDS GOD

To this aggressive extension of American power in the world, President George W. Bush adds God—and that changes the picture dramatically. It's one thing for a nation to assert its raw dominance in the world; it's quite another to suggest, as this president does, that the success of American military and foreign policy is connected to a religiously inspired "mission," and even that his presidency may be a divine appointment for a time such as this.

Many of the president's critics make the mistake of charging that his faith is insincere at best, hypocrisy at worst, and mostly a political cover for his right-wing agenda. I don't doubt that George W. Bush's faith is sincere and deeply held. The real question is the content and meaning of that faith and how it impacts his administration's domestic and foreign policies.

George Bush reports a life-changing conversion around the age of 40 from being a nominal Christian to a born-again believer—a personal transformation that ended his drinking problems, solidified his family life, and gave him a sense of direction. He changed his denominational affiliation from his parents' Episcopal faith to his wife's Methodism. Bush's personal faith helped prompt his interest in promoting his "compassionate conservatism" and the faith-based initiative as part of his new administration.

The real theological question about George W. Bush was whether he would make a pilgrimage from being essentially a self-help Methodist to a social reform Methodist. God had changed his life in real ways, but' would his faith deepen to embrace the social activism of John Wesley, the founder of Methodism, who said poverty was not only a matter of personal choices but also of social oppression and injustice? Would Bush's God of the 12-step program also become the God who required social justice and challenged the status quo of the wealthy and powerful, the God of whom the biblical prophets spoke?

Then came September 11, 2001. Bush's compassionate conservatism and faith-based initiative rapidly gave way to his newfound vocation as the commander-in-chief of the "war against terrorism." Close friends say that after 9/11 Bush found "his mission in life." The self-help Methodist slowly became a messianic Calvinist promoting America's mission to "rid the world of evil." The Bush theology was undergoing a critical transformation.

In an October 2000 presidential debate, candidate Bush warned against an over-active American foreign policy and the negative reception it would receive around the world. Bush cautioned restraint. "If we are an arrogant nation, they will resent us," he said. "If we're a humble nation, but strong, they'll welcome us."

The president has come a long way since then. His administration has launched a new doctrine of pre-emptive war, has fought two wars (in Afghanistan and Iraq), and now issues regular demands and threats against other potential enemies. After September 11, nations around the world responded to America's pain—even the French newspaper *Le Monde* carried the headline "We are all Americans now." But the new pre-emptive and—most critically—*unilateral* foreign policy America now pursues has squandered much of that international support.

The Bush policy has become one of potentially endless wars abroad and a domestic agenda that mostly consists of tax cuts, primarily for the rich. "Bush promised us a foreign policy of humility and a domestic policy of compassion," Joe Klein wrote in *Time* magazine. "He has given us a foreign policy of arrogance and a domestic policy that is cynical, myopic, and cruel." What happened?

A MISSION AND AN APPOINTMENT

Former Bush speechwriter David Frum says of the president, "War had made him [...] a crusader after all." At the outset of the war in Iraq, George Bush entreated, "God bless our troops." In his State of the Union speech, he vowed that America would lead the war against terrorism "because this call of history has come to the right country." Bush's autobiography is titled *A Charge to Keep*, which is a quote from his favorite hymn.

In Frum's book *The Right Man*, he recounts a conversation between the president and his top speechwriter, Mike Gerson, a graduate of evangelical Wheaton College. After Bush's speech to Congress following the September 11 attacks, Frum writes that Gerson called up his boss and said, "Mr. President, when I saw you on television, I thought—God wanted you there." According to Frum, the president replied, "He wants us all here, Gerson."

Bush has made numerous references to his belief that he could not be president if he did not believe in a "divine plan that supersedes all human plans." As he gained political power, Bush has increasingly seen his presidency as part of that divine plan. Richard Land, of the Southern Baptist Convention, recalls Bush once saying, "I believe God wants me to be president." After September 11, Michael Duffy wrote in *Time* magazine, the president spoke of "being chosen by the grace of God to lead at that moment."

Every Christian hopes to find a vocation and calling that is faithful to Christ, but a president who believes that the nation is fulfilling a God-given righteous mission and that he serves with a divine appointment can become quite theologically unsettling. Theologian Martin Marty voices the concern of many when he says, "The problem isn't with Bush's sincerity, but with his evident conviction that he's doing God's will." As *Christianity Today* put it, "Some worry that Bush is confusing genuine faith with national ideology." The president's faith, wrote Klein, "does not give him pause or force him to reflect. It is a source of comfort and strength but not of wisdom."

The Bush theology deserves to be examined on Biblical grounds. Is it really Christian, or merely American? Does it take a global view of God's world or just assert American nationalism in the latest update of "manifest destiny"? How does the rest of the world—and, more important, the rest of the church worldwide—view America's imperial ambitions?

GETTING THE WORDS WRONG

President Bush uses religious language more than any president in US history, and some of his key speechwriters come right out of the evangelical community. Sometimes he draws on Biblical language, other times old gospel hymns that cause deep resonance among the faithful in his own electoral base. The problem is that the quotes from the Bible and hymnals are too often either taken out of context or, worse yet, employed in ways quite different from their original meaning. For example, in the 2003 State of the Union, the president evoked an easily recognized and quite famous line from an old gospel hymn. Speaking of America's deepest problems, Bush said, "The need is great. Yet there's power, wonder-working power, in the goodness and idealism and faith of the American people." But that's not what the song is about. The hymn says there is "power, power, wonder-working power *in the blood of the Lamb*" (emphasis added). The hymn is about the power of Christ in salvation, not the power of "the American people," or any people, or any country. Bush's citation was a complete misuse.

On the first anniversary of the 2001 terrorist attacks, President Bush said at Ellis Island, "This ideal of America is the hope of all mankind [...] That hope still lights our way. And the light shines in the darkness. And the darkness has not overcome it." Those last two sentences are straight out of John's gospel. But in the gospel the light shining in the darkness is the Word of God, and the light is the light of Christ. It's not about America and its values. Even his favorite hymn, "A Charge to Keep," speaks of that charge as "a God to glorify"—not to "do everything we can to protect the American homeland," as Bush has named our charge to keep.

Bush seems to make this mistake over and over again—confusing nation, church, and God. The resulting theology is more American civil religion than Christian faith.

THE PROBLEM OF EVIL

Since September 11, President Bush has turned the White House "bully pulpit" into a pulpit indeed, replete with "calls," "missions," and "charges to keep" regarding America's role in the world. George Bush is convinced that we are engaged in a moral battle between good and evil, and that those who are not with us are on the wrong side in that divine confrontation.

But who is "we," and does no evil reside with "us"? The problem of evil is a classic one in Christian theology. Indeed, anyone who cannot see the real face of evil in the terrorist attacks of September 11, 2001, is suffering from a bad case of post-modern relativism. To fail to speak of evil in the world today is to engage in bad theology. But to speak of "they" being evil and "we" being good, to say that evil is all out there and that in the warfare between good and evil others are either with us or against us—that is also bad theology. Unfortunately, it has become the Bush theology.

After the September 11 attacks, the White House carefully scripted the religious service in which the president declared war on terrorism from the pulpit of the National Cathedral. The president declared to the nation, "Our responsibility to history is already clear: to answer these attacks and rid the world of evil." With most members of the Cabinet and the Congress present, along with the nation's religious leaders, it became a televised national liturgy affirming the divine character of the nation's new war against terrorism, ending triumphantly with the "Battle Hymn of the Republic." War against evil would confer moral legitimacy on the nation's foreign policy and even on a contested presidency.

What is most missing in the Bush theology is acknowledgement of the truth of this passage from the gospel of Matthew: "Why do you see the speck in your neighbor's eye, but do not notice the log in your own eye? Or how can you say to your neighbor, 'Let me take the speck out of your eye,' while the log is in your eye? You hypocrite, first take the log out of your own eye, and then you will see clearly to take the speck out of your neighbor's eye." A simplistic "we are right and they are wrong" theology rules out self-reflection and correction. It also covers over the crimes America has committed, which lead to widespread global resentment against us.

Theologian Reinhold Niebuhr wrote that every nation, political system, and politician falls short of God's justice, because we are all sinners. He specifically argued that even Adolf Hitler—to whom Saddam Hussein was often compared by Bush—did not embody absolute evil any more than the Allies represented absolute good. Niebuhr's sense of ambiguity and irony in history does not preclude action, but counsel the recognition of limitations and prescribes both humility and self-reflection.

And what of Bush's tendency to go it alone, even against the expressed will of much of the world? A foreign government leader said to me at the beginning of the Iraq war, "The world is waiting to see if America will listen to the rest of us, or if we will all just have to listen to America." American unilateralism is not just bad political policy, it is bad theology as well. C.S. Lewis wrote that he supported democracy not because people were good, but rather because they often were not. Democracy provides a system of checks and balances against any human beings getting too much power. If that is true of nations, it must also be true of international relations. The vital questions of diplomacy, intervention, war, and peace are, in this theological view, best left to the collective judgment of many nations, not just one—especially not the richest and most powerful one.

In Christian theology, it is not nations that rid the world of evil—they are too often caught up in complicated webs of political power, economic interests, cultural clashes, and nationalist dreams. The confrontation with evil is a role reserved for God, and for the people of God when they faithfully exercise moral conscience. But God has not given the responsibility for overcoming evil to a nation-state, much less to a superpower with enormous wealth and particular national interests. To confuse the role of God with that of the American nation, as George Bush seems to do, is a serious theological error that some might say borders on idolatry or blasphemy.

It's easy to demonize the enemy and claim that we are on the side of God and good. But repentance is better. As the *Christian Science Monitor* put it, paraphrasing Alexander Solzhenitzyn. "The gospel, some evangelicals are quick to point out, teaches that the line separating good and evil runs not between nations, but inside every human heart."

A BETTER WAY

America's foreign policy is more than pre-emptive, it is theologically presumptuous; not only unilateral, but dangerously messianic; not just arrogant, but bordering on the idolatrous and blasphemous. George Bush's personal faith has prompted a profound self-confidence in his "mission" to fight the "axis of evil," his "call" to be commander-in-chief in the war against terrorism, and his definition of America's "responsibility" to "defend the [...] hopes of all mankind." This is a dangerous mix of bad foreign policy and bad theology.

But the answer to bad theology is not secularism; it is, rather, good theology. It is not always wrong to invoke the name of God and the claims of religion in the public life of a nation, as some secularists say. Where would we be without the prophetic moral leadership of Martin Luther King Jr., Desmond Tutu, and Oscar Romero?

In our own American history, religion has been lifted up for public life in two very different ways. One invokes the name of God and faith in order to hold us accountable to *God's intentions*—to call us to justice, compassion, humility, repentance, and reconciliation. Abraham Lincoln, Thomas Jefferson, and Martin Luther King perhaps best exemplify that way. Lincoln regularly used the language of scripture, but in a way that called both sides in the Civil War to contrition and repentance. Jefferson said famously, "I tremble for my country when I reflect that God is just."

The other way invokes God's blessing on *our activities*, agendas, and purposes. Many presidents and political leaders have used the language of religion like this, and George W. Bush is falling prey to that same temptation.

Christians should always live uneasily with empire, which constantly threatens to become idolatrous and substitute secular purposes for God's. As we reflect on our response to the American empire and what it stands for, a reflection on the early church and empire is instructive.

The Book of Revelation, while written in apocalyptic language and imagery, is seen by most Biblical expositors as a commentary on the Roman Empire, its domination of the world, and its persecution of the church. In Revelation 13, a "beast" and its power is described. Eugene Peterson's *The Message* puts it in vivid language: "The whole earth was agog, gaping at the Beast. They worshiped the Dragon who gave the Beast authority, and they worshiped the Beast, exclaiming: 'There's never been anything like the Beast! No one would dare to go to war with the Beast!' It held absolute sway over all tribes and peoples, tongues, and races." But the vision of John of Patmos also foresaw the defeat of the Beast. In Revelation 19, a white horse, with a rider whose "name is called The Word of God" and "King of kings and Lord of lords," captures the beast and its false prophet.

As with the early church, our response to an empire holding "absolute sway," against which "no one would dare to go to war," is the ancient confession of "Jesus is Lord." And to live in the promise that empires do not last, that the Word of God will ultimately survive the *Pax Americana* as it did the *Pax Romana*.

In the meantime, American Christians will have to make some difficult choices. Will we stand in solidarity with the worldwide church, the international body of Christ—or with our own American government? It's not a surprise to note that the global church does not generally support the foreign policy goals of the Bush administration—whether in Iraq, the Middle East, or the wider "war on terrorism." Only from inside some of our US churches does one find religious voices consonant with the visions of American empire.

Once there was Rome; now there is a new Rome. Once there were barbarians; now there are many barbarians who are the Saddams of this world. And then there were the Christians who were loyal not to Rome, but to the kingdom of God. To whom will the Christians be loyal today?

18 | The Christian Zionists Distortion

CORRINE WHITLATCH

HERE ARE MANY sources for news and views about what's going on in the Middle East and what's ahead. Some followers of Pat Robertson's 700 Club are looking at weather patterns. The Christian Broadcasting Network reported that May's damaging tornados were a repercussion of US pressure on Israel that put the "covenant lands of Israel at risk." According to CBN, a researcher has proven that "when Israeli settlements are touched, there are also occurrences of hurricanes, tornados, and major problems in the American economy."

This forecast may seem foolish to most Americans and irrelevant to the serious business of crafting foreign policy. However, the Christian-evangelical community along with its Christian Zionist wing is a significant constituency for the Bush Administration and Republican-majority Congress. Joining with some hard-line Jewish groups, Christian Zionists have launched "The Committee for a One-State Solution" with an eight-state billboard campaign to stop the Roadmap and its goal of a two-state resolution of the conflict. The locations for the billboards were selected (according to the chair of Americans for a Safe Israel) in states where the Republican presidential win was slim, in order to make President Bush aware "that a disaffected Christian Community can adversely affect" the coming presidential campaign.

It is crucial for all advocates of a political and diplomatic solution—based on applying the rational elements of international law and negotiation—to counter the message of the Christian Right. For those of us, including Churches for Middle East Peace, whose political activism is also grounded in a faith-based commitment to justice and peacemaking as Christians, there is an additional responsibility to say publicly that there is an alternate Christian perspective to that of Christian Zionists.

"THE BIBLE IS MY ROADMAP"

This is the title of an internet petition circulated by Pat Robertson, Jerry Falwell, and Tim LaHaye opposing the Roadmap and a political solution to the Israeli-Palestinian conflict. Beginning with "Save the Settlements," the text asserts that the "peace plan rewards terrorists," talks about "tiny Israel giving its Bible land to terrorist regimes," and "dividing Jerusalem and giving a portion of the city and our holy sites to an Islamic terrorist organization that has killed Americans."

Unashamedly playing on internal Administration disputes, the petition asserts: "The State Department has been giving Israel's land to the PLO for more than a decade." Another example comes from television preacher Pat Robertson. In May, he asked his supporters to mount a nationwide protest against the State Department and demand the dismissal of William Burns, the Assistant Secretary of State for the Near East. Some State Department officials believe there is a campaign by conservatives to accuse the diplomatic corps of being disloyal to Bush.

SELLING THE ROADMAP TO CONGRESS

Also seeking to discredit the State Department was House Majority Leader Tom DeLay. In his April 2 remarks at the gathering of Ralph Reed's Stand for Israel, he said, "The moral ambiguities of our diplomatic elites notwithstanding, Israel is not the problem; Israel is the solution."

The diplomatic problems of implementing the Roadmap will be compounded for the President by domestic politics. The Christian conservatives, a core constituency for President Bush, are passionately pro-Israel and deeply distrustful of the European Union and the UN who are part of the "Quartet" sponsors of the Roadmap. On Capitol Hill, the religious right has joined forces with the neo-conservative wing of the Republican party and pro-Israel Democrats to form a broad coalition of lawmakers who don't want Israel pressured to make concessions.

As Secretary of State Powell headed to the Middle East in May, Representative Mike Pence (R-IN), who sits on the House International

Relation's Middle East subcommittee, said "America is not a neutral party in the negotiations in the Middle East. We are not, nor do we aspire to be, an honest broker. America stands with Israel."

According to *CQ Weekly*, a reputable Capitol Hill publication, one of AIPAC's (American-Israel Public Affairs Committee) legislative priorities is Congress' "codification" of the major changes that Israel seeks in the Roadmap. Such legislation could be in the form of a non-binding resolution or attached to an appropriations bill that would restrict the Administration's ability to fund peace-related initiatives.

WHAT'S IN A NAME?

News reports often use the political terms "Christian Right," and "Christian fundamentalists," or refer generally to "conservative Christians" or "Evangelicals." Yet, not all who fall within those groupings hold to Biblically-mandated support for Israel.

The term "Christian Zionist" is probably most accurate, even though "Zionism" itself is a concept that emerged in the late 19th century among Jewish intellectuals out of the ferment of nationalist, socialist and utopian ideas that swept through Europe at the time. The Zionist movement sought and achieved the founding and development of a Jewish homeland (now Israel) in Palestine, then a part of the Ottoman Empire. Now, many Zionists, both Israeli and American-Jewish, support ending Israel's occupation and establishing a Palestinian state. Not so with Christian Zionists. Central to Christian Zionism is the belief in the abiding relevance of the promise God made to Abraham in Genesis 12:3, "I will bless those who bless you, and whoever curses you I will curse; and all peoples on earth will be blessed through you."

Some of the organizations associated with Christian Zionism are: the Christian Coalition of America, the International Fellowship of Christians and Jews, National Unity Coalition for Israel, Christian Broadcasting Network, Christians for Israel-US, Gary Bauer's American Values and The International Christian Embassy in Jerusalem.

EVANGELICALS WHO DO SUPPORT PEACE

Christian Zionists may identify themselves as evangelical Christians, but not all evangelical Christians agree with their uncritical support of Israel. In July of 2002, nearly 60 prominent evangelical theologians and heads of organizations wrote to the President, voicing an even-handed policy towards Israelis and Palestinians that affirms two states, "free, economically viable and secure." They asked that the President vigorously "oppose injustice, including the continued unlawful and degrading Israeli settlement movement," which they characterized as "the theft of Palestinian land."

Regarding theology, they wrote, "Significant numbers of American evangelicals reject the way some have distorted Biblical passages as their rationale for uncritical support for every policy and action of the Israeli government instead of judging all actions—of both Israelis and Palestinians—on the basis of Biblical standards of justice. The great Hebrew prophets, Isaiah and Jeremiah, declared in the Old Testament that 'God calls all nations and all people to do justice one to another, and to protect the oppressed, the alien, the fatherless and the widow.'"

IGNORING THE PALESTINIAN CHRISTIANS

American Christians travel to the Holy Land as pilgrims and are a major segment of the tourism industry. They visit the holy sites but most have virtually no contact with Arab Christians themselves. Arab Christians hold strongly negative views of Christian Zionism, which is considered by some to be an instrument of Western colonialism and American imperialism. The zealous support given to Israel's claim of sovereignty over all of Jerusalem and the building of settlements in "Judea and Samaria" by these Western Christians angers both Christian and Muslim Palestinians. Some evangelical churches have supportive relationships with settlements.

Among Palestinians, there are the traditional churches—Greek Orthodox, Armenian Orthodox and Roman Catholic—and the so-called "reform" churches established in the 19th century—Lutherans and Episcopalians or Anglicans. They work ecumenically through the Middle

East Council of Churches. These Christians consider themselves, and are considered by the Muslims, to be an integral part of the Palestinian community, even though they are a minority of less than two percent.

From his Jerusalem office, Bishop Munib Younan, of the Evangelical Lutheran Church, has written that "Christian Zionism is the enemy of peace in the Middle East." The Rev. Naim Ateek, director of Jerusalem's Sabeel Ecumenical Liberation Theological Center, has called pre-millenialism a "heresy" and Christian Zionism a "menace."

THEOLOGY, POPULAR FICTION AND
THE CHURCH IN SOCIETY

When the *Washington Post* commits a full page of its Sunday opinion section to a religious topic, it clearly has political significance. On February 2, the headline was "It's the Dawning of the Age of Apocalypse." American Studies professor Melani McAlister wrote about the very popular "Left Behind" fictional series—the last four have topped the best-seller lists. She writes of the "stark political spirituality at the heart of the stories, which can fairly be described as Christian *Jihadist.* It is the obligation of the "Left Behind" Christians both to evangelize as many potential converts as possible and to join in battle on behalf of Israel against the armies of the Antichrist."

The term "Left Behind," along with "the rapture", "pre-millennialism", "end-times" and "Armageddon" are parts of the terminology associated with this strain of eschatology - which is the study of the "last things," the culmination of history and the second coming of Jesus Christ.

It is the political implications of these beliefs that troubles Churches for Middle East Peace. McAlister writes that "Left Behind" authors Tim LaHaye and Jerry Jenkins undercut the very notion of Middle East peace, from Israel to Iraq. With the Antichrist posing as a peacemaker and campaigning for world disarmament, such things as arms control or peace processes are fig leaves for those planning world domination. That Israel is the epicenter of Armageddon, the final battle, is made clear to the "Left Behind" readers.

With a theology that calls us to be peacemakers, the approach of Churches for Middle East Peace is grounded in the National Council of

Churches policy statement that was approved in 1980. This "calls upon American Christians to recognize the moral dimensions of political action, to give witness to God's justice, love and mercy, to build peace upon the foundation of justice."

The deep religious significance and spiritual value of the Middle East is affirmed for Jews and Muslims as well as for Christians. "Affirming the need for mutual respect and understanding, it [the NCC statement] acknowledges the reality of strife; it seeks to identify the sources of mistrust and prejudice and to lay the basis for reconciliation."

Catholic Biblical scholar, Ronald Witherup, SS, in an article titled "Whose Land Is It?" wrote that:

> We should acknowledge the perennial value of the Bible's teachings without asserting that the Bible applies directly to every moral situation in our own world. This approach is both thoroughly Catholic and consistent with many other interpretive traditions, Protestant and Jewish [...] We must begin with reality as it now exists. The situation 'on the ground' is what we must now confront. There is no going back to an idyllic, premodern vision.

And it was the situation on the ground that compelled the statement of a delegation of American Church leaders who visited Jerusalem, Jenin, Bethlehem and Beit Jala in May of 2002:

> The word of the Spirit in our day is a call to all people of faith to be witnesses to the way of peace. That witness begins with unceasing prayer. It calls us to be reconcilers, to stand for truth, forgiveness, and justice in every place. Only thus may we sing to the Lord a new song.

Chapter 4 SHATTERING ILLUSIONS

The Servants of the God of Mercy are those who walk
upon the earth humbly, and when the ignorant address
them, they reply "peace."
—*Qur'an 25:63*

On those who show compassion, God is the most Compassionate.
—*Qur'an 12:64*

People who show mercy to others will be shown
mercy by the All-Merciful.
—*Saying of Prophet Muhammad (Tirmidhi)*

Whoever shows no mercy will be shown no mercy.
—*Saying of Prophet Muhammad (Bukhari and Muslim)*

19 | Shattering Illusions

AS'AD ABU KHALIL

WESTERN EPISTEMOLOGY OF the Middle East has been riddled with illusions and misconceptions since the early traffic between the West and the world of Islam. Historically, the interest in learning about the Middle East was scant; the public did not care to learn about a people that were first seen as heathen, and later seen as inferior savages. In the era of the crusades, the Arabs were superior technologically, civilizationally, and scientifically to the invading westerners. But they were non-Christians, and Muslims at that. In later eras, the Arabs were characterized with whatever was found to afflict colonized people. They had to be afflicted with primitiveness, barbarity, and savagery in order to rationalize the colonization and subjugation of the people.

September 11 came to reveal the persistence of Islamophobia and of the ignorance of things Arab. September 11 came about partly in response to a history of American (mis)dealings with the Middle East. When the president of the US referred to his war "on terrorism" as a crusade, a strong reaction followed among Muslims. He had to be alerted to the meaning; he never uttered it again. His advisors must have appreciated the repercussions. Ignorance of the Middle East and Islam in the West is partly ignorance and partly malfeasance.

When Edward Said published his book *Orientalism* in 1978, some critics thought that he overstated his case; that he went too far in criticizing the legacy of Western scholarly and literary production dealing with the Middle East and Islam. Now we know: Said was right and he did not exaggerate. The pitfalls of Orientalist productions remain with the US today, and they influence generation after generation, and they shape public opinion leaders and policy makers. What else would explain the strong association between Islam and terrorism? And what would explain the tendency to explain all behavior of Muslims by exclusive references to religion, implying that Muslims only respond to the calls of the minarets. Whether in the Gulf War or in the current (unending) war: Americans rush to bookstores to buy the Qur'an, as if it contains the answers to Muslim political behavior, or more accurately, to the political behavior of Muslims. Furthermore, we have to concede that ignorance about Islam and Arabs is institutionalized in some parts of the US as part of the propaganda efforts of various institutions and research centers, some of which dabble in the art "terrorism study" while others focus on "strategic studies."

The highly influential Washington Institute for Near East Policy, which supplies staffers who are "Middle East experts" to Democratic and Republican administrations alike, produces "studies" and policy papers at a frenzied pace. No establishment foreign policy maker can earn a reputation without passing through its ranks or boards. It is now customary that Secretaries of State retire to one of its boards once they end their services. The message of the Washington Institute, which is perhaps the most quoted of its kind on the Middle East in US newspapers, is unwaveringly pro-Israel: for its Staff and "senior fellows," Israel can do no wrong, no matter who is running the country. The Arabs are always posing a danger, and Arafat always has to do more, and the Palestinians always have to show more "reason" and more "moderation." The rest is predictable. The Washington Institute was initially founded as an arm of the pro-Israeli lobby, but is now insisting on a façade of independence.

Orientalist academia is not dead, as evidenced by the revival of the retired octogenarian Princeton professor Bernard Lewis. Lewis has had the most effect in Middle East studies in the US in the last fifty years. Students of the region could not, and cannot, escape his books and readings. He was brought back to the talk shows, and Sunday "news shows," and was invited to the White House although he remains coy over whether he had a tete-a-tete with the president of the US. His writings (always recycled) were in demand by liberal and conservative publications alike. He asked the US to act "toughly" with the Arabs in an article in *National Review*. While Lewis is a specialist in medieval Islamic history, he never avoids offering opinion on the present-day Arab world, perhaps because he feels strongly against the Palestinians (and Arabs), and because he is more an advocate for Israel and Turkey's General. But the public remains unaware of Middle East academic debates, and his selection by the mainstream media as the doyen of Middle East experts helped propel his books to the best-seller list. His book *What Went Wrong* (which has nothing to say about the crisis or even about the Arab world) remains high on the *New York Times* best-seller list.

In the world of Bernard Lewis, the Arabs are prisoners of Islam, and their world is stifled by their religion in culture. The Muslims (especially Arab Muslims) are fanatic people bent on threatening the West and Israel. And while Lewis is knowledgeable about the ancient world, his views on the modern world are uninformed. His basis for an Iranian-PLO (which was very brief) was the mere exchange of kisses between Arafat and Khomeni. How could it possibly escape the notice of this esteemed expert that Arabs routinely exchange kisses, even if they are rivals or enemies?

Orientalist knowledge of the Middle East is a field of production where a few select experts of the Middle East (those with the convenient opinions and views) are exposed to the public through the mainstream media, and their writings then shape the political and popular cultures of the US. Thus, what the public knows of the Middle East—the little that it knows—has to be filtered through the prism of accepted representatives of pro-Israeli experts. To be sure, some representatives of Arab American and Muslim American organizations are invited; but they always are asked to express "the other point of view," the one that is less reasonable from that expressed by American supporters of Israel. And in the age of the "war on terrorism," nobody is reasonable who does not join "us" against "them." The Arabs are always "them" of course, especially as they refuse to reduce the Palestinian national struggle to terrorism, while Israel is a member of the "Free World" struggle for freedom and democracy. Such obfuscations of Middle East realities have lasted for the entire duration of Israel's existence; its brutal aggression and expansionism have been made into a heroic campaign of self-defense against fanatic enemies.

WHAT THE PUBLIC SHOULD NOT
KNOW ABOUT SEPTEMBER 11

A consensus was formed—if not imposed—after September 11. The Mayor of New York City kept repeating that any reference to any cause, especially that of the Palestinians of whom he has always been an enemy, is simply a service to terrorism. Dissent has been largely and successfully muzzled, and some ninety three percent of all Americans supported this glorious "war on terrorism." Any mention of the civilian casualties in Afghanistan (which exceeded the number of the civilian casualties of September 11) was considered an acceptable distraction, or worse a service to the enemy. The President of CNN had to remind his staff that footage of the civilian suffering in Afghanistan had to be contextualized; viewers had to be constantly reminded that those are being killed in Afghanistan (presumably including the women and children) are responsible for the horrific bombings in the US.

The coverage of post-September 11, America and post-September 11 Middle East has to conform to the government's interests and intentions. Disagreements with the violations of civil liberties (juridically enshrined in the draconian Patriot Act) are tantamount to support for terrorism, according to the Attorney General of the US. The Middle East has to be re-represented. Images from Arab TV cannot be trusted; Israeli experts are always preferable to Arab ones. Israelis speak unaccented English and they have been dealing with Arab "terrorism" since Israel's creation. Arab grievances have to be dismissed, and Islam has to be presented as the religion of violence and fanaticism. Thomas Friedman assured Muslims that he does not believe in launching a war "against Islam." He wanted a war "within Islam," perhaps implying that we should use Muslims to kill other Muslims, instead of using US troops. It worked with the US use of Northern Alliance forces in the front lines, while the US pilots bombed the country from the air, unleashing a total of some twenty-three thousand bombs and missiles, twenty-five percent of which missed their targets, according to US Central Command

The war against Islam, statements from US officials to the contrary notwithstanding, continues: both at home with the whole sale arrest and detention of hundreds of Arabs and Muslims, and abroad with the expansive "war on terrorism," which seems to always pick enemies with dark skins and Islamic faith. The relationship between Muslims and the US have worsened and the US public is enthusiastically supporting (to the tune of some ninety-three percent) a war intended for the eradication of terrorism.

But while we should categorically condemn the September 11 attacks (which caused the deaths of innocent people from some ninety countries), the event was not unique in contemporary history, or even in the present-day world. Hundreds of people sometimes die daily in the Congo, and the US has caused the death of hundreds of innocent people in Afghanistan itself, all in the name of fighting "terrorism." Are the innocent people who die from US bombs less innocent than the victims of September 11 because they happen to be poor, Muslim, and non-Western? Certainly one can draw a picture of (im)moral equivalence between the actions of bin Laden, and US actions around the world. One can mention the death of thousands (not members of Saddam's family of course or his high command) in Iraq, or the needless death of children in the Sudan due to US 1998 bombing of a medicine factory that we now know has no links to bin Laden.

The US is also responsible for the perpetuation of highly unpopular, dictatorial rule in much of the Middle East, especially in the Gulf region. The resentment against the US role is not due to local opposition to democracy, as some US columnists would have it, but due to the opposition to democracy by the US. The US favors the oppression of dissent and opposition especially as democratization brings about anti-US forces and groups. And the opposition to the US does not stem from fundamentalist, anti-Christian impulses, nor from civilizational rejection of the West, but is based on the bloody and oppressive record of the US in the Middle East region. The recent American endorsement of Israeli militancy and brutality is only one example; and the US has continued to play the role of the benefactor for militant Zionism since the 1950s.

The US would also like us erase the long record of American embrace of fundamentalist Islam, which was a staple of the Cold War. The US and Saudi Arabia both played important roles in cultivating and arming the most reactionary and fundamentalist forces in the region as an alternative to the then popular forces of the left and Arab nationalism. Saudi Arabia faced serious threats to its survival in the 1950s and 1960s, and to the survival of other principalities, kingdoms, and princedoms in the Gulf region. Nasser and his allies put a lot of pressures on those regimes, and dubbed them the "tails of colonialism." The rise of anti-American feelings and sentiments only exposed those regimes further as allies of the enemy of the Arabs. Saudi opposition to communism—and to any semblance of progressive thought and practice—made them natural allies to the West in the Cold War. All sorts of "Islamic" bodies and organizations were formed to combat communism and leftism. Those groups failed in attracting popular appeal and were marginalized during the Nasserist era.

The death of Nasser, and the successive Arab defeats vis-à-vis Israel, energized Islamic fundamentalist thought; Nasser's successor, Anwar Sadat, also funded fundamentalist groups to create rivals to leftist groups in Egypt. Similarly, Jordan and Israel sponsored fundamentalist groups and organizations to ostensibly cultivate ideological allies. What those regimes did not anticipate was the radicalization of those groups, and the proliferation of splinter groups that preached armed struggle against Arab regimes and Israel.

It was in the context of the Cold War that the US and Saudi Arabia created the haven or the so-called Arab Afghans: the reference being to those Arab volunteers throughout the region who wanted to join the fight against atheist communism. Bin Laden was one of many volunteers and he came to organize the ranks of the Arab volunteers, and later after the death of `Abdullah `Azzam (the spiritual guide of the group) emerged as the ultimate leader. But bin Laden continued to be an ally of the Saudi government (and presumably of the US, his past patron during the anti-Soviet struggle) up until the Iraqi invasion of Kuwait in 1990.

But the most important factor that the Mayor of New York City did not want to hear about was the persistence of the Palestinian problem. Decades of Israeli brutality and of US sponsorship of militant Zionism, produced generations of angry Arab youths, who were bent on taking revenge for their brothers and sisters in Palestine. Of course, the actions that resulted in the death of innocent civilians in the US in no way helped the people of Palestine, and bin Laden has not been known to have contributed money or weapons to Palestinian struggle. Members of al-

Qa'ida have not even thrown a stone against an Israeli target. Such is the grotesque vision of bin Laden, that the killing of innocent Americans was a priority for him. But the youths from whose ranks bin Laden recruited were the Arabs who were outraged by the injustices committed against the Arabs by Israel and the US.

We are told that one should not even engage in any analysis of the political situation after September 11. Analysts may be quickly accused of aiding terrorism. The Attorney General of the US unabashedly equates critics of the government with terrorists, and the nation supports a "war against terrorism." The Palestinian problem has become the lightening rod for Arab opposition to US interests. It reveals the deep-seated bias of the US government (and public) against Palestinian and Arab interests. Only the US stands alone in this glaring endorsement of Israeli militancy and brutality. The events of March 2002 (and their aftermath) when Israel invaded Palestinian areas in the West Bank (which it never left to begin with) revealed that European public opinion is far more sympathetic to Palestinian interests than the US public (according the a study by the Pew foundation). The US sees in Israel a fulfillment of Biblical prophecies. And the "war on terrorism" is more often than not a license by the US for governments to oppress their dissidents and critics in the name of fighting terrorism, provided that links to bin Laden are alleged. Lo and behold, China also revealed links to bin Laden among its Muslim dissident movement, as has the republic of Georgia. Of course, Israel has been milking this ostensible "war on terrorism" for decades: but Israel always goes to extremes in this regard. For Israel the Palestinian people and their society are all terrorists; this enables Israel to kill terrorist children, women, and innocent people.

The war in Afghanistan went according to the plan from the US perspective. Victories were declared and the menacing regime was toppled. The true background US allies and their ethnic and political unrepresentativeness are mere details that the US press does not want to bother with. The nation was not in the mood for self-critical reflection, especially when the leaders assured the public that the voices that are heard around the world against the US are due to anger at US "freedoms," or to the American "way of life".

In the context, the war on terrorism has been a success for the current administration. Its domestic programs are being passed; the huge increase in the defense budget went through smoothly. The sick, the elderly, the homeless, all have to wait. A "war on terrorism" has to be fought and won.

Of course, the "war on terrorism" will expand, and the ambition of the administration will ensure that it will be prolonged. It will know no end: new groups, individuals, and states will continuously be added to the list of "evil." The "axis of evil" may spiral out of control. The popular Arab reaction to the brutal Israeli invasion of the West Bank manifested strong and unprecedented rejection of US economic, political, and military interests in the Middle East. But in the age of "the war on terrorism," critics of the US can be easily dismissed as supporters of terrorism.

20 | Islam & the Question of Violence

SEYYED HOSSEIN NASR

D
ESPITE THE PRESENCE of violence in many regions of the world, ranging from Ireland to Lebanon to the Pacific Basin and involving many religions from Christianity to Hinduism, the Western world associates Islam more than any other religion with violence. The Muslim conquest of Spain, the Crusades (which were not begun by Muslims) and the Ottoman domination of Eastern Europe have provided a historical memory of Islam as being related to force and power. Moreover, the upheavals of the past few decades in the Middle East, and especially movements using the name of Islam and seeking to solve problems of the Muslim world created by conditions and causes beyond the control of Muslims, have only reinforced the idea prevalent in the West that in some special way Islam is related to violence.

To understand the nature of Islam and the truth about the assertion often made of Islam's espousal of violence, it is important to analyze this question clearly, remembering that the word Islam itself means peace, and that the history of Islam has certainly not been witness to any more violence than one finds in other civilizations, particularly that of the West. In what follows, however, it is the Islamic religion in its principles and ideals with which we are especially concerned and not particular events or facts relating to the domain of historical contingency belonging to the unfolding of Islam in the plane of human history.

First of all, it is necessary to define what we mean by violence. There are several dictionary definitions that can be taken into account such as "swift and intense force," "rough or injurious physical force or action," "unjust or unwarranted exertion of force especially against the rights of others," "rough or immediate vehemence" and finally "injury resulting from the distortion of meaning or fact." If these definitions are accepted for violence, then the question can be asked as to how Islam is related to these definitions. As far as "force" is concerned, Islam is not completely opposed to its use, but rather seeks to control it in the light of the divine Law (*al-Sharia*). This world is one in which force is to be found everywhere, in nature as well as in human society, among men as well as within the human soul. The goal of Islam is to establish equilibrium in this field of tension of various forces. The Islamic concept of justice itself is related to equilibrium, the word for justice (*al-'Adl*) in Arabic being related in its etymology to the word for equilibrium (*Ta'adul*). All force used under the guidance of the divine Law with the aim of re-establishing an equilibrium that has been destroyed is accepted and in fact necessary, for it is a means to carry out and establish justice. Moreover, not to use force in such a way is to fall prey to other forces, which cannot but increase dis-equilibrium and disorder and result in greater injustice. Whether the use of force in this manner is swift and intense or gentle and mild depends upon the circumstances, but in all cases force can only be used with the aim of establishing equilibrium and harmony and not for personal or sectarian reasons identified with the interests of a person or a particular group and not the whole.

By embracing the "world" and not shunning the "kingdom of Caesar," Islam took upon itself responsibility for the world in which force is present. But by virtue of the same fact it limited the use of force, and despite all the wars, invasions, and attacks which it experienced, it was able to create an ambiance of peace and tranquility which can still be felt whenever something of the traditional Islamic world survives. The peace that dominates the courtyard of a mosque or a garden, whether it be in Marrakech or Lahore, is not accidental but the result of the control of force with the aim of establishing that harmony which results from equilibrium of forces, whether those forces be natural, social or psychological.

As for the meaning of violence as "rough or injurious physical force or action," Islamic Law opposes all uses of force in this sense except in the case of war or for punishment of criminals in accordance with the *Sharia*. Even in war, however, the inflicting of any injury to women and children is forbidden, as is the use of force against civilians. Only fighters in the field of battle must be confronted with force and it is only against them that injurious physical force can be used. Inflicting injuries outside of this context or in the punishment of criminals according to the dictum of the *Sharia* and the view of a judge is completely forbidden by Islamic Law.

As far as violence in the sense of the use of unjust force against the rights of others and laws is concerned, Islam stands totally opposed to it. Rights of human beings are defined by Islamic Law and are protected by this Law which embraces not only Muslims but also followers of other religions who are considered as "People of the Book"(*ahl al-kitab*). If there is nevertheless violation in Islamic society, it is due not to the teachings of Islam but the imperfection of the human recipients of the Divine Message. Man is man wherever he might be and no religion can neutralize completely the imperfections inherent in the nature of fallen man. What is remarkable, however, is not that some violence in this sense of the word does exist in Muslim societies, but that despite so many negative social and economic factors, aggravated by the advent of colonialism, overpopulation, industrialization, modernization resulting in cultural dislocation, and so many other elements, there is less violence as unjust exertion of force against others in most Islamic countries than in the industrialized West.

If one understands by violence "rough or immoderate vehemence," then Islam is totally opposed to it. The perspective of Islam is based upon moderation and its morality is grounded upon the principle of avoiding extremes and keeping to the golden mean. Nothing is more alien to the Islamic perspective than vehemence, not to say immoderate vehemence. Even if force is to be used, it must be on the basis of moderation.

Finally, if by violence is meant "distortion of meaning or fact resulting in injury to others," Islam is completely opposed to it. Islam is based on the Truth which saves and which finds its supreme expression in the testimony of the faith, *la ilaha illa 'Llah* (there is no divinity but the Divine). Any distortion of truth is against the basic teachings of the religion even if no one were to be affected by it. How much more would distortion resulting in injury be against the teachings of the Qur'an and the tradition of the Prophet!

In conclusion it must be emphasized that since Islam embraces the whole of life and does not distinguish between the sacred and the secular, it must concern itself with force and power which characterize this world as such. But Islam, in controlling the use of force in the direction of creating equilibrium and harmony, limits it and opposes violence as aggression to the rights of both God and His creatures as defined by the divine Law. The goal of Islam is the attainment of peace, but this peace can only be experienced through of ourselves and leads to living in the world in accordance with the dicta of the *Sharia*. Islam seeks to enable man to live according to his theomorphic nature and not to violate that nature. Islam condones the use of force only to the extent of opposing that centripetal tendency which turns man against what he is in his inner reality. The use of force can only be condoned in the sense of undoing the violation of our own nature and the chaos which has resulted from the loss of equilibrium. But such a use of force is not in reality violence as usually understood. It is the exertion of human will and effort in the direction of conforming to the Will of God and in surrendering the human will to the divine Will. From this surrender (*taslim*) comes peace (*salam*), hence Islam, and only through this Islam can the violence inbred within the nature of fallen man be controlled and the beast within subdued so that man lives at peace with himself and the world because he lives at peace with God.

21 | American Muslims, Human Rights & the Challenge of 9/11

ZAID SHAKIR

T HE TRAGIC EVENTS of September 11, 2001, have called into question many fundamental Islamic principles, values, and beliefs. The ensuing discourse in many critical areas reveals the weakness of Muslims in making meaningful and substantive contributions towards a clear understanding of the Islamic position on a number of critical issues. The purpose of this paper is to examine one of those issues, human rights, in an effort to identify:

1. How human rights are defined in the Western and Islamic intellectual traditions;
2. Why human rights issues are of central importance to Islamic propagation efforts in North America;
3. What are the implications of the tragic events of September 11, 2001 for prevailing Muslim views of human rights.

This essay is not designed to respond the attacks of those authors who assail the philosophy, conceptualization, formulation, and application of human rights policy among Muslims. Such a response would be quite lengthy, and owing to the complexity of the project, would probably raise as many questions as it resolved. Nor is it an attempt to call attention to the increasingly problematic indifference of the United States government towards respecting the civil liberties and other basic rights of its Muslim and Arab citizens. We do hope that this essay will help American Muslims identify and better understand some of the relevant issues shaping our thought and action in the critical area of human rights. Hopefully, that enhanced understanding will help lead to the creation of a vibrant, sober, relevant Islamic call in the United States.

DEFINING HUMAN RIGHTS

A review of the relevant literature reveals a wealth of definitions for human rights. Some of these definitions are quite brief, others quite elaborate.[1] However, few of these definitions deviate far from the principles delineated by the Universal Declaration of Human Rights (UDHR), issued by the UN General Assembly in 1948. That landmark document emphasizes, among other things:

> The right to life, liberty, and security of person; the right to freedom of thought, speech, and communication of information and ideas; freedom of assembly and religion; the right to government through free elections; the right to free movement within the state and free exit from it; the right to asylum in another state; the right to nationality; freedom from arbitrary arrest and interference with the privacy of home and family; and the prohibition of slavery and torture.

This declaration was followed by the International Covenant on Economic, Social, and Cultural Rights (ICESCR) in 1966. In the same year, the International Covenant of Civil and Political Rights (ICCPR), was also drafted. These arrangements, collectively known as the International Bill of Human Rights, were reaffirmed in the Helsinki Accords of 1975 and buttressed by the threat of international sanctions against offending nations. When we examine these and other international agreements governing human rights, we find a closely related set of ideas, which collectively delineate a system of fundamental or inalienable, universally accepted rights.

These rights are not strictly political, as the UDHR mentions:

> The right to work, to protection against unemployment, and to join trade unions; the right to a standard of living adequate for health and well-being; the right to education; and the right to rest and leisure

In summary, we can say that human rights are the inalienable social, economic and political rights, which human beings accrue by virtue of their belonging to the human family.

Defining human rights from an Islamic perspective is a bit more problematic. The reason for this is that there is no exact equivalent for the English term, "human rights," in the traditional Islamic lexicon. The frequently used Arabic term, *al-Huquq al-Insaniyya*, is simply a literal Arabic translation for the modern term. However, our understanding of the modern term, when looked at from the abstract particulars which comprise its definition, gives us insight into what Islam says in this critical area. For example, if we consider the word "right" (*Haqq*), we find an array of concepts in Islam, which cover the range of rights mentioned in the UDHR.

If we begin with the right to life, Islam clearly and unequivocally guarantees that right. The Qur'an states, *Do not unjustly take the life which God has sanctified.*[2] Similarly, in the context of discussing the consequences of the first murder in human history, *For that reason [Cain murdering Abel], we ordained for the Children of Israel that whoever kills a human being for other than murder, or spreading corruption on Earth, it is as if he has killed all of humanity. And whoever saves a life, it is as if he has saved all of humanity.*[3]

It should be noted in this regard, as the first verse points out, Islam doesn't view humanity as a mere biological advancement of lower life forms. Were this the case, there would be little fundamental distinction between human and animal rights, other than those arising from the advancement and complexity of the human mind. However, Islam views human life as a biological reality, which has been sanctified by a special quality that has been instilled into the human being –the spirit (*Ruh*).[4] The Qur'an relates, [...]*then He fashioned him [the human being] and breathed into him of His spirit.*[5]

It is interesting to note that this spiritual quality is shared by all human beings, and precedes our division into nations, tribes, and religious collectivities. An illustration of this unifying spiritual bond can be gained from considering a brief exchange, which occurred between the Prophet Muhammad (Peace and Blessings of God be upon him), and a group of his companions (May God be pleased with them). Once a funeral procession passed in front of the Prophet (Peace and Blessings of God be upon him) and a group of his companions. The Prophet (Peace and Blessings of God be upon him) reverently stood up. One of his companions mentioned that the deceased was a Jew, to which the Prophet (Peace and Blessings of God be upon him) responded, "Is he not a human soul?"[6]

Possession of this shared spiritual quality is one of the ways our Creator has ennobled the human being. God says in this regard, *We have truly ennobled the human being* [...][7] This ennoblement articulates itself in many different ways, all of which serve to highlight the ascendancy of the spiritual and intellectual faculties in man. It provides one of the basis for forbidding anything, which would belittle, debase, or demean the human being, and its implications extend far beyond the mere preservation of his life.[8] It guarantees his rights before birth, by forbidding abortion, except in certain well-defined instances; and after death, it guarantees the right of the body to be properly washed, shrouded, and buried. It also forbids the intentional mutilation of a cadaver,[9] even in times of war, and forbids insulting or verbally abusing the dead, even deceased non-Muslims. While these latter points may be deemed trivial to some, they help create a healthy attitude towards humanity, an attitude that must be present if acknowledged rights are to be actually extended to their possessors.

If we examine other critical areas identified by the UDHR for protection as inalienable rights, we can see that Islam presents a very positive framework for the safeguarding of those rights. In the controversial area of religious freedom, where Islam is identified by many in the West as a religion which was spread by forced conversion, we find that Islam has never advocated the forced acceptance of its creed, in fact, the Qur'an unequivocally rejects this idea, *Let there be no compulsion in [accepting] Religion, truth clearly distinguishes itself from error.*[10] God further warns His Prophet (Peace and Blessings of God be upon Him) against forced conversions, *If your Lord had willed, everyone on Earth would have believed [in this message]; will you then compel people to believe?*[11]

In this context, every human being is free to participate in the unrestricted worship of his Lord. As for those who refuse to do so according to the standards established by Islam, they are free to worship as they please. During the Ottoman epoch, this freedom evolved into sophisticated system of minority rights known as the *Millet* System. Bernard Lewis comments on that system:

> Surely, the Ottomans did not offer equal rights to their subjects—a

meaningless anachronism in the context of that time and place. They did however offer a degree of tolerance without precedence or parallel in Christian Europe. Each community—the Ottoman term was *Millet*—was allowed the free practice of its religion. More remarkably, they had their own communal organizations, subject to the authority of their own religious chiefs, controlling their own education and social life, and enforcing their own laws, to the extent that they did not conflict with the basic laws of the Empire.[12]

Similarly positive Islamic positions can be found in the areas of personal liberties, within the parameters provided by the Islamic legal code. We will return to a brief discussion of those parameters, and their implications for an Islamic human rights regime. However, it isn't the purpose of this paper to engage in an exhaustive treatment of this particular subject.

Stating that, we do not propose that Islamic formulations in this regard are an exact replica of contemporary Western constitutional guarantees governing human rights policy. Muslims and non-Muslims alike, when examining the issue of human rights within an Islamic legal or philosophical framework, should realize that human rights regimes, as we know them, are a contemporary political phenomenon, which have no ancient parallel. A particularly relevant distinction between contemporary human rights regimes, and any scheme which could arise from Islamic principles, lies in the fact that the ultimate concern of Islam is protecting human beings from eternal damnation. Hence, the greatest right we owe to each other as members of a human family is helping to eliminate the worldly obstacles to salvation.

Leaving this strictly Islamic consideration aside, we are still prepared to defend the thesis that Islam has historically presented a framework for protecting basic human rights, and that it presents a system of jurisprudential principles that allow for the creation of a viable modern human rights regime, totally consistent with the letter and spirit of Islam.

THE RELEVANCE OF HUMAN RIGHTS FOR
ISLAM IN AMERICA

Islam in America has historically been characterized by a strong advocacy of human rights and social justice issues. This is so because it has been associated with people who would be identified as ethnic minorities. The first significant Muslim population in this country, the enslaved believers of African origin, would certainly fit that description.[13] The various Islamic movements, which arose amongst their descendents, appeared in a social and political context characterized by severe oppression. That socio-political context shaped the way Islam was understood by the people embracing it. It was a religion, in of all its variant understandings, which was seen as a source of liberation, justice, and redemption.[14]

When the ethnic composition of the Muslim community began to change due to immigration in the 1970s, 1980s, and into the 1990s, the minority composition of the Muslim community remained. These newly arriving non-European immigrant Muslims were generally upwardly mobile, however, their brown and olive complexions, along with their accents, and the vestiges of their original cultures, served to reinforce the reality of their minority status. This fact, combined with the fact that the most religiously active among them were affiliated with Islamic movements in the Muslim World, movements whose agenda were dominated by strong human rights and social justice concerns, affected the nature of the Islamic call in this country, keeping human rights concerns to the fore.

Illustrative of this human rights imperative is the stated mission of the *Ahmadiyya* Movement when it began active propagation in America. Mufti Muhammad Sadiq, the first significant *Ahmadi* missionary to America, consciously called to a multicultural view of Islam, which challenged the entrenched racism prevalent in early 20th Century American society.[15] This message presented Islam as a just social force, capable of extending to the racial minorities of this country their full human rights. However, there were strong anti-white overtones of the *Ahmadi* message, shaped by Mufti Muhammad Sadiq's personal experience, and the widespread persecution of people of Indian descent (so-called Hindus) in America, which dampened the broader appeal of the *Ahmadi* message. Those overtones were subsequently replaced by the overtly racist proclamations of the Nation of Islam, which declared whites to be devils. In the formulation of the Nation of Islam, Islam came to be viewed as a means for the restoration of the lost pre-eminence of the "Asiatic" Blackman. This restoration would be effected by a just religion, Islam, which addressed the social, economic and psychological vestiges of American race-based slavery. In other words, Islam was the agent that would grant the Muslims their usurped human rights.[16]

The pivotal figure who was able to synthesize these various formulations into a tangible, well-defined human rights agenda was Malcolm X.[17] By continuing to emphasize the failure of American society to effectively work to eliminate the vestiges of slavery, he was an implicit advocate of the justice-driven agenda of the Nation of Islam, even after departing from that movement. His brutal criticism of the racist nature of American society, which he often contrasted with the perceived racial harmony of Islam, highlighted by his famous letter from Mecca[18] in which he envisioned Islam as a possible cure for this country's inherent racism, was the continuation of the original multi-cultural message of the *Ahmadiyya* Movement. Finally, his evolving thinking on the true nature of the struggle of the African American people, and his situating that struggle in the context of the Third World human rights struggle, reflected the human rights imperative which figured so prominently in the call of Middle Eastern groups such as Egypt's Muslim Brotherhood, and the Indian Subcontinent's *Jamati Islami*, groups which had a strong influence on the founders of this country's Muslim Students Association (MSA) in 1963.[19]

These various groupings, along with the *Dar al-Islam* Movement, the Islamic Party of North America, and Sheikh Tawfiq's Mosque of Islamic Brotherhood,[20] which would develop in many urban centers during the 1960s and 1970s as the purveyors of an emerging African American "Sunni" tradition, a tradition consolidated by the conversion of Malcolm X to the orthodox faith, represented in their various agendas, the crystallization of the sort of human rights agenda which Malcolm was hammering out during the last phase of his life. These groups all saw Islam as the key to liberation from the stultifying weight of racial, social, and economic inequality in America.

The Iranian Revolution of 1979 further strengthened this human rights imperative. The revolution was presented by its advocates in America, who were quite influential at the time, as an uprising of the oppressed Muslim masses, the "Mustad'afin," to secure their usurped rights from the Shah, an oppressive "Taghut." This message, conveyed strongly and forcefully through the call of the Muslim Students Association: Persian Speaking Group (MSA-PSG), was extremely influential in shaping the human rights imperative in American Islam, not only because of its direct influence, but also because of the vernacular of struggle it introduced into the conceptual universe of many America Muslims, and the way it shaped the message of contending "Sunni" groups. The combined influence of these forces worked to insure that human rights issues were prominent in the call of Islamic organizations and individuals prior to the tragic events of September 11, 2001.

THE CHALLENGE OF SEPTEMBER 11, 2001

The tragic events of September 11, 2001 present a clear challenge to the human rights/social justice imperative of Muslims in North America. The reasons for this are many and complex. The apocalyptic nature of the attacks of September 11, 2001, particularly the assault on, and subsequent collapse of the World Trade Center towers, led many observers to question the humaneness of a religion which could encourage such senseless, barbaric slaughter. Islam, the religion identified as providing the motivation for those horrific attacks, was brought into the public spotlight as being, in the view of many of its harshest critics, an anti-intellectual, nihilistic, violent and chauvinistic atavism.[21]

The atavistic nature of Islam, in their view, leads to its inability to realistically accommodate the basic elements of modern human rights philosophy.[22] This inability was highlighted by the September 11, 2001 attacks in a number of ways. First of all, the massive and indiscriminate slaughter of civilians belied, in the view of many critics, any claims that Islam respects the right to life. If so, how could so many innocent, unsuspecting souls be so wantonly sacrificed? Secondly, "Islam's" refusal to allow for the peaceful existence of even remote populations of "infidels," the faceless dehumanized "other," calls into question its respect for the rights of non-Muslims within its socio-political framework. It also highlights its inability to define that "other" in human terms.

As a link between the accused perpetrators of the attacks, Osama bin Laden, and the Taliban rulers of Afghanistan was developed by both the United States government and news media, the human rights position of Islam was called into further question. The Taliban, by any standards of assessment, presided over a regime that showed little consideration for the norms governing international human rights. Much evidence exists which implicates the Taliban in violating the basic rights of women, ethnic minorities (non-Pashtun), the Shi'ite religious minority, detainees, artists, and others, using in some instances, extremely draconian measures. Many of these violations occurred under the rubric of applying what the regime identified as Islamic law. The news of Taliban excesses, coupled with the shock of the events of September 11, 2001, combined to create tremendous apprehension towards the ability and willingness of Islam to accommodate a meaningful human rights regime.[23]

The political climate existing in America in the aftermath of September 11, 2001 has been exploited by certain elements in American society to call into question any humanitarian tendencies being associated with Islam. For example, in the aftermath of the brutal murder of Daniel Pearle, an act whose implications are as chilling as the attacks of September 11, 2001, Mr. Pearle's bosses at the *Wall Street Journal*, Peter Kann and Paul Steiger remarked, "His murder is an act of barbarism that makes a mockery of everything that Danny's kidnappers claimed to believe in." Responding to those comments, Leon Wieseltier, of the *New Republic*, stated, "The murder of Daniel Pearle did not make a mockery of what his slaughterers believe. It was the perfect expression, the inevitable consequence, of what his slaughterers believe."[24] This, and similar indictments of Islam, challenge the ability of American Muslims to effectively speak on human rights issues in obvious ways.

If we examine the actual nature of the American Muslim human rights discourse prior to September 11, 2001, we find that it was based in large part on Muslims contrasting the generalities of the *Sharia*, with the specific shortcomings of American society and history in relevant areas of domestic and international policy and practice.[25] This discourse ignored the positive human rights strictures contained in sections of the American constitution, the Bill of Rights, and the UDHR, to which the United States is a signatory.

As in other areas, this inadequate approach produced a false sense of moral superiority among Muslims in America. This sense was shattered by the attacks of September 11, 2001, in that many Americans were suddenly pointing to what they viewed as the inadequacy of Islamic human rights regimes, their inadequate philosophical basis, and their failure to guarantee basic human rights protection, especially for women and religious, racial, and ethnic minorities living in Muslim lands.

Responding adequately to these charges will require a radical restructuring of current Islamic human rights discourse, and the regimes that discourse informs. The generalities, which formerly sufficed in that discourse will have to be replaced by concrete, developed policy prescriptions, which stipulate in well-defined, legal terms, how viable human rights protections will be extended to groups identified as systematically suffering from human rights abuses in Muslim realms.

An example of the dangerous and inadequate generalities alluded to above, can be glimpsed from a brief examination of the Cairo Declaration on Human Rights in Islam (CDHRI). Article 24 of that document states, "All the rights and freedoms stipulated in this Declaration are subject to the Islamic *Sharia*."[26] Such a statement is meaningless, considering the vast corpus of subjectively understood literature that could be identified as comprising the *Sharia*, unless the relevant rulings and principles of the *Sharia* are spelled out in exacting detail.

While this paper has consciously avoided mention of those features of Islam, which would be antithetical to the Western concept of personal liberty, such as the lack of freedom to choose one's "sexual orientation," there are major civil liberties issues, which must be addressed, in clear and unequivocal terms, if Islam's human rights discourse is to have any credence. Hiding behind Islam's cultural, or religious specificity to avoid providing answers to difficult questions will not advance a deeper understanding of our faith amongst enlightened circles in the West. Islam indeed has much to say in the area of human rights. However, much foundational work has to be done before we can speak clearly and authoritatively, especially in the changed political climate following September 11, 2001.

In *Islam and Human Rights*, Ann Elizabeth Mayer, whose work has been previously cited,[27] acknowledges,

> [...] the Islamic heritage comprises rationalist and humanistic currents and that it is replete with values that complement modern human rights such as concern for human welfare, justice, tolerance, and equalitarianism. These could provide the basis for constructing a viable synthesis of Islamic principles and international human rights [...][28]

Perhaps the greatest challenge before us in this regard is successfully identifying those rationalist and humanitarian "currents" and riding them to a new, more enlightened shore. Doing this will require, among other things, a bold, but mature assessment of the proper relationship between creed and action in the social and political realms. A serious attempt to engage in a rational application of legal principles to contemporary social and political problems in no way implies adopting the methodology of the *Mu'tazila*, medieval Muslim legal and theological rationalists. Using human reasoning as the standard to assess the veracity of revelation, and using such reasoning as the basis for discovering meaningful Islamic solutions to pressing social or political problems, in areas where revelation provides no articulated guidance, constitute two entirely different projects.

That being said, our attempts at solving novel contemporary socio-political problems must be guided by well-defined methodologies. Applicable methodologies have been expounded on by Muslim scholars of jurisprudential principles, and those who have assessed those methodologies, and the rulings they inform in light of the great overarching objectives of Islamic law. These scholars include the likes of Imam al-Shatibi, author of the groundbreaking work, *al-Muwafaqat*,[29] and Imam 'Izz al-Din bin 'Abd al-Salam, author of *Qawa'id al-Ahkam*,[30] and many others. These writings are part of a rich heritage of scholarship and thought, which allowed Muslims to adequately respond to a succession of civilizational challenges throughout our long and illustrious past. If we are able to master that rich heritage, and use the best of it to address the burning issues of our day, we will be able to meaningfully discuss human rights, and the full array of issues that currently vex and perplex us. By so doing, we will be able to step confidently into the future.

NOTES

1. One such concise definition of human rights is mentioned in Paul E. McGhee, "Human Rights," in *The Social Science Encyclopedia*, ed. Adam and Jessica Kuper (London, New York: Routledge, 1985), p. 369. He states, "Human rights are the rights and freedoms of all human beings." Cyrus Vance presents a much more elaborate definition in which he envisions human rights encompassing the security of the person, meeting his vital needs, civil and political liberties, and freedom from discrimination. Abridged from Cyrus Vance, "The Human Rights Imperative," in *Taking Sides: Clashing Views on Controversial Issues in World Politics*, ed. John T. Rourke (Guilford, CT: The Dushkin Publishing Group, Inc., 1992), pp. 254-255.

2. Qur'an 6:151

3. Qur'an 5:32

4. Islamic scholars have defined the spirit (*Ruh*) in various ways. Perhaps the best translation would be "life-spirit." Its true nature is unknown to any human being, although there has been much speculation as to what exactly it is. It is created before the creation of the bodies, which will house it. Worldly life begins with its entrance into the body, and ends with its extraction from the body.

5. Qur'an 32:9

6. This incident is based on a rigorously authenticated tradition, which has been conveyed by al-Bukhari, no. 1312; Muslim, no. 2222; and al-Nasa'i, no. 1920.

7. Qur'an 17:70

8. A beautiful discussion of the ways the human being has been ennobled by God can be found in Imam Fakr al-Din al-Razi's commentary of the relevant Qur'anic verse, 17:70. See, Fakhr al-Din al-Razi, *al-Tafsir al-Kabir* (Beirut: Dar Ihya al-Turath al-'Arabi, 1997), vol. 7, pp. 372-374.

9. This practice is condemned based on a tradition related by Imam Ahmad, Abu Dawud, and Ibn Majah.

10. Qur'an 2:256

11. Qur'an 10:99

12. Bernard Lewis, *What Went Wrong: Western Impact and Middle Eastern Response* (Oxford, New York: Oxford University Press, 2002), pp. 33-34

13. For a moving, well-document description of the history, lives, institutions, struggles, and legacy of the Africans enslaved in the America, see, Sylviaane A. Diouf, *Servants of Allah: African Muslims Enslaved in the Americas* (New York, London: SUNY Press, 1998).

14. See, Robert Dannin, *Black Pilgrimage to Islam* (Oxford, New York: Oxford University Press, 2002). Dannin presents a good summary of the evolution of Islam among African-Americans. His book is especially valuable for its detailed treatment of the evolution of the African-American Sunni Muslim community. See, also Richard Brent Turner, *Islam in the African American Experience* (Bloomington: Indiana University Press, 1997).

15. Turner, op cit., pp. 121-131.

16. For a detailed introduction to the racist ideology of the Nation of Islam, see, Elijah Muhammad, *Message to the Black Man* (Chicago: Muhammad's Temple No. 2, 1965). Especially insightful in this regard is a chapter entitled, "The Devil," pp. 100-122.

17. The theme of human rights figured prominently in the political oratory of Malcolm X during the last two years of his life. At the time of his assassination, he was in final stages of a campaign to charge the United States—in the United Nations—with violating the human rights of the then 20,000,000 African Americans in this country. Many observers feel that campaign, a source of great embarrassment for the United States, may have resulted in his death. His views on this subject are presented, among other places, in a speech entitled, "The Ballot or the Bullet" in George Breitman, (ed.) *By Any Means Necessary* (New York: Pathfinder Press, 1970), pp. 21-22. See, also, "Interview with Harry Ring Over Station WBAI, January 28, 1965," in *Two Speeches by Malcolm X* (New York: Pathfinder Press, 1965), pp. 28-29.

18. Alex Haley with Malcolm X, *The Autobiography of Malcolm X* (New York: Ballentine Books, 1964) pp. 338-342.

19. The Muslim Students Association (MSA) was formed in 1963 among immigrant Muslims. It would eventually evolve into the Islamic Society of North America (ISNA). Formed in 1982, ISNA is the largest Islamic organization in North America. See, Dannin, p. 73; and Turner, p. 236.

20. For a summary of the inter-group dynamics between the Islamic Party of North America, *Dar al-Islam*, and Sheikh Tawfiq's Muslim Islamic Brotherhood,

see Dannin, pp. 65-73.

21. For example, The New Republic's Jonah Goldberg refers to Islam as,"[...] anti-capitalist, alien, sometimes medieval, and often corrupt theocratic fascism." Jonah Goldberg, "The Goldberg File," *The New Republic*, 1 October 2001.

22. Perhaps the most thorough assessment of Islam and human rights is Ann Elizabeth Mayer, *Islam and Human Rights: Tradition and Politics* (Boulder: Westview Press, 1999). Although simplistically lauded by many critics of Islam as "an understated and powerful repudiation of the notion of 'Islamic Human Rights,'" Mayer's argument is far more involved. While identifying many of the problems plaguing contemporary Islamic human rights regimes, Mayer sees Islam's rich tradition as being capable of producing an effective, modern human rights movement.

23. For an indication of the extent of the reported human rights abuses of the Taliban, see Ahmad Rashid, *Taliban* (London, New York: I.B. Tauris Publishers, 2000), chs. 4, 5 and 8. Also, see Michael Griffin, *Reaping the Whirlwinds:The Taliban Movement in Afghanistan* (London: Pluto Press, 2001), ch. 12.

24. Leon Wiesiltier, "The Murder of Daniel Pearl," *The New Republic*, 25 February 2002

25. A widely circulated pamphlet, among Muslims, which illustrates this approach is, Mawlana Abu'l 'Ala Mawdudi, *Human Rights in Islam* (Leicester, England: Islamic Foundation, 1980).

26. This declaration was submitted to the World Conference on Human Rights, Preparatory Committee, Fourth Session. Geneva, April 19 – May 7, 1993.

27. See note 16.

28. Mayer, op cit., p. 192.

29. Imam Ibrahim bin Musa Abi Ishaq al-Shatibi, *al-Muwafaqat* (Beirut: Dar al-Ma'rifa, 1997).

30. 'Izz al-Din 'Abd al-'Aziz bin 'Abd al-Salam, *Qawa'id al-Ahkam* (Damascus: Dar al-Tiba'a, 1996).

22 | The Origins of Extremism Theory or Reality?

SOUMAYYA GHANOUSHI

ANGUAGE IS NOT a transparent medium or a neutral instrument, but is overwhelmed with power strategies. Language not only reflects worldviews and modes of life, it articulates and dictates them so as to preclude any possibility of separating terminologies from their contexts. This is most evident in the bulk of Western intellectual and political discourse on Islam. Indeed much can be read into the deceivingly simple words President Bush or Prime Minister Blair use to characterize the blood-chilling and catastrophic events of September 11; "the attacks" we are told "are an assault on the free civilized world." Before such a world stands its antithesis, an enslaved barbaric world, one that encapsulates all that "we" are not. The far stretching lands of Islam loom largely in this bleak uncivilized sphere. If the modern West is dynamic, the world of Islam is stagnant, if it is governed democratically and honors self-ownership, Islam is plagued by a despotism that crushes the individual altogether out of existence. If it is rigorously rational, the world of Islam is the embodiment of raving instincts and wild emotionalism.

The practice is also popular amongst a great many Western intellectuals, journalists and academics who, reminiscent of 18th century Christian missionaries, urge us to promote "our" Western "values everywhere from Burma to Saudi Arabia, Iraq to Chechnya" as a leading columnist in the *Guardian* daily newspaper vehemently proclaims. Islam is thus transformed into a silent passive object laid bare before their gaze, stigmatized, categorized and tried, a "world-picture" to use the words of the well-known German philosopher Martin Heidegger. In this vortex of comments and analyses, Islam's voice remains unheard.

Throughout the nineteenth century, in the general context of western imperialism, the non-European world—including the world of Islam—was banned from raising its own voice, from defining its own self-image, and was rendered into a mere exhibit, an object of contemplation, of modulation and categorization.

Three principle elements have been responsible for shaping the modern Western world's conception of Islam;

Firstly, a recycled Christian memory of Islam that has remained active even in the era of secularization. The medieval Christian view of Islam as a deviant non-rational religion continues to survive in a 'secularized' framework, for although Christian apologetic theology has lost its vanguard role, its content has been swallowed in a modern essentialist philosophy.

Secondly, the shift in the balance of power in favor of the modern west, followed by an international order that gave the upper hand to the European powers over the rest of the globe, mainly in the south Mediterranean hemisphere.

Thirdly, the deep crises and high level of political disintegration that accompanied the accelerated regress of the Ottoman Empire, and which, since the beginning of the nineteenth century, have come to characterize the whole Muslim world. These three interconnected factors gave the modern west leave to silence Islam's voice and impose itself as the unique power of *logos*, of understanding, revealing, categorizing, modulating Islam and its societies.

The so-called "Orient," "East," "Islam" has been transformed into a silent and passive object standing powerless before a European gaze that saw it as a chaotic, deformed scene to be rationalized, organized and made sense of. Only a western intellectual, ethnologist, traveler, sociologist, artist, writer or statesman is apt to reveal the hidden reality of the Islamic picture. In the atmosphere of European military expansion, the world of Islam turned into a theatrical exhibit and the western "spectator" became this external world's provider of meaning and value. Everything seemed to stand before the European as an appearance behind which hides some reality. Thus the "orient," or more precisely the world of Islam, turned into the great "external reality" of modern Europe and the most common object of its "metaphysics of representation." The modern West's bid to distinguish itself from the Muslim world, or the so called East, conferred legitimacy on its representations of its inhabitants' strangeness and quest to separate itself from this "external world" and transform it into a world picture. This required a "fixed cognito" as a force of rationalization, an active and "rational" subject set apart from and outside of the passive object. To represent a geographical and cultural hemisphere called the "Orient" or "Islam" is after all to "orientalize" and "Islamize" it, to impose a set of features upon it. But the act of representing Islam is never detachable from that of defining the "occident" itself. It was not only about one culture portraying another; it was essentially an internal cultural strategy with a view to shaping its own image and strategies. In order for Europe to determine itself as the seat of reason, civilization and order, it had to represent all that it saw outside itself as irrational, disorderly and libidinous. Any intellectual distinction requires the invitation of a homogenous-different other. The uniqueness of Europe could only be properly assessed by reference to another uniqueness. And it was precisely to fulfill such a role that Islam was invited.

The 19th century European traveler's distant detached observations of the strange ways of the Muslim other, the Christian missionary, colonial administrator and military general's representations of the remote world of Islam are now replaced by those of journalists, Islamologists and so-called experts. And while medieval Christians dissociated the historical success of Islam from its doctrinal and philological sources, which were deemed false and indeed fraudulent, modern and present day Western intellectuals almost unanimously attribute the decadent historical condition of Islam to its beliefs and value system. While Medieval theologians insisted that Islam's historical accomplishments did not validate its claim as a true revelation—Christianity being the one and only right path to God—their modern secularist heirs fervently insist that the roots of the backwardness of the Muslim world are to be traced back to its religious texts. Intensely intricate labyrinthine social and political phenomena are thus uprooted from their historical contexts in a bid to consolidate a portrayal of Islam as a "deficient," "stagnant" religion, a warrior blood-thirsty religion that glorifies slaughter and aggression against its enemies on the outside, while oppressing minorities and subordinating women internally.

Since culture is an easy target, ready-made postulates and categories are constantly invoked to explain all the ills plaguing the Muslim world. And it is precisely through this gate that thinkers with little acquaintance with Islam and its world, of the likes of Francis Fukuyama, have engaged in a polemical discourse on Islam overwhelmed with superficiality, generalization and distortion. Such narratives enjoy great currency for two reasons essentially: firstly, since they stand in line with and are at the service of the establishment (it is indeed no secret that such thinkers as Fukuyama and Samuel Huntington have held official positions in the American administration). Secondly, this mode of discourse is in harmony with the deeply entrenched and constantly revived and regenerated Western consciousness of Islam, that sees this religion as the embodiment of fanaticism, theological deficiency, political stagnation, despotism, extremism and violence. Indeed, the words of the most "liberal" of westerners often echo those of their medieval Christian forefathers, stretching as far back as the 9th century, when the last of the Eastern Church's Fathers, John the Damascene, outlined the "heresy of the Ismaelites" in his *Fount of Knowledge*, continuing down the ages with the words of Peter the Venerable Abbot of Cluny in his *Cluniac Corpus* in the 12th century, or indeed those of Martin Luther and Philip Melanchthon the Fathers of the Reformation six centuries ago.

Certain sectors of the Islamic intelligentsia and political class like to blame the tension marking the difficult relations between the world of Islam and the West on ignorance and misunderstanding, which, it is claimed, may be remedied through round table discussions and tranquil dialogue. This appears to be too simplistic an analysis to account for an entrenched widespread stereotypical portrayal of a religion that has become intrinsic to the West itself and not a merely distant other. True, crude generalizations on the subject of Islam are all too frequent, but what underlies these is a will to power that moulds the Western discourse on Islam. Such a will to power both generates and legitimizes hegemony so as to make it impossible to draw a line of distinction between the will to hegemony and the will to knowledge as we encounter it in relation to Islam and its world.

Even those with little if any knowledge of Islam and its intensely complex historical condition movements and traditions have now entered the unrestricted open market on Islam. Thus on the basis of translated scattered fragments pulled out of their interpretive contexts, with no knowledge of any of the great languages of Islam, and no awareness of the complexities of Muslim society, many do not hesitate to declare that Islam is an "intolerant" barbaric religion. With no concern for the most elementary requirements of responsible objective scientific research, parts of verses are extricated from their contexts and combined with other fragments to distort the general meaning, Qur'anic verses are confused with sayings of the prophet, talk of otherworldly punishment and reward is represented as rules determining treatment of non-believers in this world. And daily we witness the hideous spectacle of ignorance and prejudice parading freely across many of the columns and articles on Islam and its world that stretch across countless pages of newspapers, glossy magazines and academic reviews.

Verses are quoted selectively with no mention of the exhortations to peace, which almost always follow teachings on conduct in armed struggle. *Thus, if they let you be, and do not make war on you, and offer you peace, God does not allow you to harm them* (Qur'an 4: 90). Nor indeed is there any mention of the verses which form the bulk of the Qur'an that enjoin Muslims to treat with respect those of other faiths. *Let there be no coercion in religion* is the rule it lays down for the treatment of those of other convictions. A special status is reserved for Jews and Christians, whom it refers to as "the People of the Book." Judaism and Christianity are not regarded as other religions but as intrinsic to Islam itself. Their God is its God, their prophets its prophets. In fact, not only is Islam tolerant to these religions, since tolerance implies dualism and a fundamental difference between the subject and object of tolerance, it identifies itself with Judaism and Christianity and enjoins upon its adherents religious respect and devotion to the Prophets and revelations of these two great religions. It is indeed striking that while no religion preserved the shrines of another in its own base and enabled them to flourish in its midst except Islam, none has been so deeply misrepresented and cruelly disfigured as Islam has been.

Difference according to the Qur'an is not only to be tolerated and accepted, it is to be celebrated as the object of creation itself. The Qur'an emphatically notes, *And had your Lord so willed, He could surely have made the whole mankind one single community, but He willed it otherwise, and so they continue to differ save among those on whom God has bestowed his grace and for this He has created them.*

The principle governing relations between humans is, the Qur'an tells us, (*atta'aruf*) or acquaintance. Addressing humankind it insists: *O people! We have formed you into nations and tribes so that you may know one another* (49:13)—not to conquer, convert or subjugate, but to reach out toward others.

If such is Islam's conception of relations between human beings, why then must we ask do many extremist tendencies manifest themselves on its surface?

If we are to gain insight into the grave phenomena emerging in the Islamic world, we must free ourselves of the blind naïve essentialism characteristic of a great many analyses of the problem, which seek theological explanations for highly complex historical phenomena. The intensely intricate nature of the Islamic socio-political situation, marked by striking contradictions and strong tensions, is better understood when viewed within the context of the waves of Western imperialist expansion, of the crises of the post-colonial state and the reality of social deprivation, economic dependence and decadent educational systems unable to fill the vacuum generated by the erosion of traditional learning centers, along with the marginalization of the Muslim masses from the political system. The situation has been further complicated by American foreign policies in the Middle East, its backing of Israel's military occupation of Palestinian land and insistence on an increasingly painful embargo on Iraq, which according to Columbia University researcher Richard Garfield, led to the death of sixty-thousand to two hundred and twenty thousand children between 1991 and 1998. The West's support of despotic totalitarian regimes that annihilate all margins of freedom and stifle all voices of dissent proves to be another principal source of frustration. The US is widely regarded by many in the Middle East as a crucial obstacle in their struggle for freedom from oppression. It is indeed interesting that the most despotic states in the Middle East region are those who have the closest ties with the United States and its Western allies. One indeed may legitimately ask if such totalitarianism is the product of Islam, or whether it is the creation of Western policies themselves.

It is to the West's hegemonic self-engrossed policies in the region that we should turn if we are to understand the causes of the great turmoil shaking Muslim societies to their very depths. Much to the horror of the journalists and intellectuals acting as the "enlightened missionaries" of new colonialism, it is America's statesmen, generals and money men that hold the key to our search for the origins of so-called Islamic fanaticism and extremism, not the texts of the Qur'an or the tradition of Islam's Prophet as they never tire of repeating.

Even if we chose to accept Bush and Blair's rhetoric that places the "enlightened free world" above and in opposition to the rest of humanity staggering under the weight of fanaticism and extremism, and if we were to see bin Laden and the Taliban as a natural product of an Islamic culture in need of remolding through educational reforms, we would still be faced with the following question: What of the expressions of fanaticism in the Western "free" world itself? Where are we to classify yesterday's brutal totalitarianisms of the likes of Nazism and Fascism and today's ascending extreme political right? Could Le Pen of France, Berlescuni of Italy, Heider of the Netherlands or the deceased Dutch right wing politician Pim Fortuyn be described as by-products of the mighty western modernity and its sublime cultural values? If that is the case, then a process of cultural reform would seem to be more urgently needed in the west, since unlike the elements emerging from the shadowy impoverished and powerless Muslim world, these rising forces will have at the service of their fanaticism, once in power, a staggeringly potent military machine threatening to bring death and destruction to the entire world. Once more the keys to world peace and stability it seems are in the hands of the "enlightened free world," not in the realm of darkness and decadence stretching throughout much of the globe; in Washington and London not in Kabul or Gaza.

23 | Islam & the Theology of Power

KHALED ABOU EL FADL

SINCE THE EARLY 1980s, commentators have argued that Islam is suffering a crisis of identity, as the crumbling of Islamic civilization in the modern age has left Muslims with a profound sense of alienation and injury. Challenges confronting Muslim nations—failures of development projects, entrenched authoritarian regimes and the inability to respond effectively to Israeli belligerence—have induced deep-seated frustration and anger that, in turn, contributed to the rise of fundamentalist movements, or as most commentators have preferred to say, political Islam. But most commentators have been caught off guard by the ferocity of the acts of mass murder committed in New York and Washington. The basic cruelty and moral depravity of these attacks came as a shock not only to non-Muslims, but to Muslims as well.

The extreme political violence we call terrorism is not a simple aberration unrelated to the political dynamics of a society. Generally, terrorism is the quintessential crime of those who feel powerless seeking to undermine the perceived power of a targeted group. Like many crimes of power, terrorism is also a hate crime, for it relies on a polarized rhetoric of belligerence toward a particular group that is demonized to the point of being denied any moral worth. To recruit and communicate effectively, this rhetoric of belligerence needs to tap into and exploit an already radicalized discourse with the expectation of resonating with the social and political frustrations of a people. If acts of terrorism find little resonance within a society, such acts and their ideological defenders are marginalized. But if these acts do find a degree of resonance, terrorism becomes incrementally more acute and severe, and its ideological justifications become progressively more radical.

ASKING WHY?

To what extent are the September 11 attacks in the US symptomatic of more pervasive ideological undercurrents in the Muslim world today? Obviously, not all social or political frustrations lead to the use of violence. While national liberation movements often resort to violence, the recent attacks are set apart from such movements. The perpetrators did not seem to be acting on behalf of an ethnic group or nation. They presented no specific territorial claims or political agenda, and were not keen to claim responsibility for their acts. One can speculate that the perpetrators' list of grievances included persistent Israeli abuses of Palestinians, near daily bombings of Iraq and the presence of American troops in the Gulf, but the fact remains that the attacks were not followed by a list of demands or even a set of articulated goals. The attacks exhibit a profound sense of frustration and extreme despair, rather than a struggle to achieve clear-cut objectives.

Some commentators have viewed the underpinnings of the recent attacks as part of a "clash of civilizations" between Western values and Islamic culture. According to these commentators, the issue is not religious fundamentalism or political Islam, but an essential conflict between competing visions of morality and ethics. From this perspective, it is hardly surprising that the terrorists do not present concrete demands, do not have specific territorial objectives and do not rush to take responsibility. The September 11 attacks aimed to strike at the symbols of Western civilization, and to challenge its perceived hegemony, in the hope of empowering and reinvigorating Islamic civilization.

The "clash of civilizations" approach assumes, in deeply prejudiced fashion, that puritanism and terrorism are somehow authentic expressions of the predominant values of the Islamic tradition, and hence is a dangerous interpretation of the present moment. But the common responses to this interpretation, focusing on either the crisis of identity or acute social frustration in the Muslim world, do not adequately explain the theological positions adopted by radical Islamist groups, or how extreme violence can be legitimated in the modern age. Further, none of these perspectives engage the classical tradition in Islamic thought regarding the employment of political violence, and how contemporary

Muslims reconstruct the classical tradition. How might the classical or contemporary doctrines of Islamic theology contribute to the use of terrorism by modern Islamic movements?

CLASSICAL ISLAMIC LAW AND POLITICAL VIOLENCE

By the eleventh century, Muslim jurists had developed a sophisticated discourse on the proper limits on the conduct of warfare, political violence and terrorism. The Qur'an exhorted Muslims in general terms to perform *jihad* by waging war against their enemies. The Qur'anic prescriptions simply call upon Muslims to fight in the way of God, establish justice and refrain from exceeding the limits of justice in fighting their enemies. Muslim jurists, reflecting their historical circumstances and context, tended to divide the world into three conceptual categories: the abode of Islam, the abode of war and the abode of peace or non-belligerence. These were not clear or precise categories, but generally they connoted territories belonging to Muslims, territories belonging to enemies and territories considered neutral or non-hostile for one reason or another. But Muslim jurists could not agree on exactly how to define the abode of Muslims versus the abode of others, especially when sectarian divisions within Islam were involved, and when dealing with conquered Muslim territories or territories where sizable Muslim minorities resided.[1] Furthermore, Muslim jurists disagreed on the legal cause for fighting non-Muslims. Some contended that non-Muslims are to be fought because they are infidels, while the majority argued that non-Muslims should be fought only if they pose a danger to Muslims. The majority of early jurists argued that a treaty of non-aggression between Muslims and non-Muslims ought to be limited to a ten-year term. Nonetheless, after the tenth century an increasing number of jurists argued that such treaties could be renewed indefinitely, or be of permanent or indefinite duration.[2]

Importantly, Muslim jurists did not focus on the idea of just cause for war. Other than emphasizing that if Muslim territory is attacked, Muslims must fight back, the jurists seemed to relegate the decision to make war or peace to political authorities. There is a considerable body of legal writing prohibiting Muslim rulers from violating treaties, indulging in treachery, or attacking an enemy without first giving notice, but the literature on the conditions that warrant a *jihad* is sparse. It is not that the classical jurists believed that war is always justified or appropriate; rather, they seemed to assume that the decision to wage war is fundamentally political. However, the methods of war were the subject of a substantial jurisprudential discourse.

Building upon the proscriptions of the Prophet Muhammad, may God bless him and grant him peace, Muslim jurists insisted that there are legal restrictions upon the conduct of war. In general, Muslim armies may not kill women, children, seniors, hermits, pacifists, peasants or slaves unless they are combatants. Vegetation and property may not be destroyed, water holes may not be poisoned, and flame-throwers may not be used unless out of necessity, and even then only to a limited extent. Torture, mutilation and murder of hostages were forbidden under all circumstances. Importantly, the classical jurists reached these determinations not simply as a matter of textual interpretation, but as moral or ethical assertions. The classical jurists spoke from the vantage point of a moral civilization, in other words, from a perspective that betrayed a strong sense of confidence in the normative message of Islam. In contrast to their pragmatism regarding whether a war should be waged, the classical jurists accepted the necessity of moral constraints upon the way war is conducted.

AN OFFENSE AGAINST GOD AND SOCIETY

Muslim jurists exhibited a remarkable tolerance toward the idea of political rebellion. Because of historical circumstances in the first three centuries of Islam, Muslim jurists, in principle, prohibited rebellions even against unjust rulers. At the same time, they refused to give the government unfettered discretion against rebels. The classical jurists argued that the law of God prohibited the execution of rebels or needless destruction or confiscation of their property. Rebels should not be tortured or even imprisoned if they take an oath promising to abandon their rebellion. Most importantly, according to the majority point of view, rebellion, for a plausible cause, is not a sin or moral infraction, but merely a political wrong because of the chaos and civil strife that result. This approach effectively made political rebellion a civil, and not a religious, infraction.

The classical juristic approach to terrorism was quite different. Since the very first century of Islam, Muslims suffered from extremist theologies that not only rejected the political institutions of the Islamic empire, but also refused to concede legitimacy to the juristic class. Although not organized in a church or a single institutional structure, the juristic class in Islam had clear and distinctive insignia of investiture. They attended particular colleges, received training in a particular methodology of juristic inquiry, and developed a specialized technical language, the mastery of which became the gateway to inclusion.

Significantly, the juristic class engaged as a rule in discussion and debate. On each point of law, there are ten different opinions and a considerable amount of debate among the various legal schools of thought. Various puritan theological movements in Islamic history resolutely rejected this juristic tradition, which reveled in indeterminacy. The hallmark of these puritan movements was an intolerant theology displaying extreme hostility not only to non-Muslims but also to Muslims who belonged to different schools of thought or even remained neutral. These movements considered opponents and indifferent Muslims to have exited the fold of Islam, and therefore legitimate targets of violence. These groups preferred methods of violence were stealth attacks and the dissemination of terror in the general population.

Muslim jurists reacted sharply to these groups, considering them enemies of humankind. They were designated as *muharibs* (literally, those who fight society). A *muharib* was defined as someone who attacks defenseless victims by stealth, and spreads terror in society. They were not to be given quarter or refuge by anyone or at any place. In fact, Muslim jurists argued that any Muslim or non-Muslim territory sheltering such a group is hostile territory that may be attacked by the mainstream Islamic forces. Although the classical jurists agreed on the definition of a *muharib*, they disagreed about which types of criminal acts should be considered crimes of terror. Many jurists classified rape, armed robbery, assassinations, arson and murder by poisoning as crimes of terror and argued that such crimes must be punished vigorously regardless of the motivations of the criminal. Most importantly, these doctrines were asserted as religious imperatives. Regardless of the desired goals or ideological justifications, the terrorizing of the defenseless was recognized as a moral wrong and an offense against society and God.

DEMISE OF THE CLASSICAL TRADITION

It is often stated that terrorism is the weapon of the weak. Notably, classical juristic discourse was developed when Islamic civilization was supreme, and this supremacy was reflected in the benevolent attitude of the juristic class. Pre-modern Muslim juristic discourses navigated a course between principled thinking and real-life pragmatic concerns and demands. Ultimately, these jurists spoke with a sense of urgency, but not desperation. Power and political supremacy were not their sole pursuits.

Much has changed in the modern age. Islamic civilization has crumbled, and the traditional institutions that once sustained the juristic discourse have all but vanished. The moral foundations that once mapped out Islamic law and theology have disintegrated, leaving an unsettling vacuum. More to the point, the juristic discourses on tolerance towards rebellion and hostility to the use of terror are no longer part of the normative categories of contemporary Muslims. Contemporary Muslim discourses either give lip service to the classical doctrines without a sense of commitment or ignore and neglect them.

There are many factors that contributed to this modern reality. Among the pertinent factors is the undeniably traumatic experience of colonialism, which dismantled the traditional institutions of civil society. The emergence of highly centralized, despotic and often corrupt governments, and the nationalization of the institutions of religious learning undermined the mediating role of jurists in Muslim societies. Nearly all charitable religious endowments became state controlled entities, and Muslim jurists in most Muslim nations became salaried state employees, effectively transforming them into what may be called "court priests." The establishment of the state of Israel, the expulsion of the Palestinians and the persistent military conflicts in which Arab states suffered heavy losses, all contributed to a widespread siege mentality and a highly polarized and belligerent political discourse. Perhaps most importantly, Western cultural symbols, modes of production and social values aggressively penetrated the Muslim world, seriously challenging inherited values and practices, and adding to a profound sense of alienation.

Two developments became particularly relevant to the withering away of Islamic jurisprudence. Most Muslim nations experienced the wholesale borrowing of civil law concepts. Instead of the dialectical and indeterminate methodology of traditional Islamic jurisprudence, Muslim nations opted for more centralized and often code-based systems of law. Even Muslim modernists who attempted to reform Islamic jurisprudence were heavily influenced by the civil law system, and sought to resist the fluidity of Islamic law and increase its unitary and centralized character. Not only were the concepts of law heavily influenced by the European legal tradition, the ideologies of resistance employed by Muslims were laden with Third World notions of national liberation and self-determination. For instance, modern nationalistic thought exercised a greater influence on the resistance ideologies of Muslim and Arab national liberation movements than anything in the Islamic tradition. The Islamic tradition was reconstructed to fit Third World nationalistic ideologies of anti-colonialism and anti-imperialism rather than the other way around.

While national liberation movements—such as the Palestinian or Algerian resistance—resorted to guerrilla or non-conventional warfare, modern day terrorism of the variety promoted by Osama bin Laden is rooted in a different ideological paradigm. There is little doubt that organizations such as the *Jihad, al-Qaʻida, Hizb al-Tahrir* and *Jamaʼat al-Muslimin* were influenced by national liberation and anti-colonialist ideologies, but they have anchored themselves in a theology that can be described as puritan, supremacist and thoroughly opportunistic. This theology is the byproduct of the emergence and eventual dominance of Wahhabism, Salafism and apologetic discourses in modern Islam.

CONTEMPORARY PURITAN ISLAM

The foundations of Wahhabi theology were put in place by the eighteenth-century evangelist Muhammad ibn ʻAbd al-Wahhab in the Arabian Peninsula. With a puritanical zeal, ʻAbd al-Wahhab sought to rid Islam of corruptions that he believed had crept into the religion. Wahhabism resisted the indeterminacy of the modern age by escaping to a strict literalism in which the text became the sole source of legitimacy. In this context, Wahhabism exhibited extreme hostility to intellectualism, mysticism and any sectarian divisions within Islam. The Wahhabi creed also considered any form of moral thought that was not entirely dependent on the text as a form of self-idolatry, and treated humanistic fields of knowledge, especially philosophy, as "the sciences of the devil." According to the Wahhabi creed, it was imperative to return to a presumed pristine, simple and straightforward Islam, which could be entirely reclaimed by literal implementation of the commands of the Prophet, and by strict adherence to correct ritual practice. Importantly, Wahhabism rejected any attempt to interpret the divine law from a historical, contextual perspective, and treated the vast majority of Islamic history as a corruption of the true and authentic Islam. The classical jurisprudential tradition was considered at best to be mere sophistry. Wahhabism became very intolerant of the long-established Islamic practice of considering a variety of schools of thought to be equally orthodox. Orthodoxy was narrowly defined, and 'Abd al-Wahhab himself was fond of creating long lists of beliefs and acts which he considered hypocritical, the adoption or commission of which immediately rendered a Muslim an unbeliever.

In the late eighteenth century, the Al Sa'ud family united with the Wahhabi movement and rebelled against Ottoman rule in Arabia. Egyptian forces quashed this rebellion in 1818. Nevertheless, Wahhabi ideology was resuscitated in the early twentieth century under the leadership of 'Abd al-'Aziz ibn Sa'ud who allied himself with the tribes of Najd, in the beginnings of what would become Saudi Arabia. The Wahhabi rebellions of the nineteenth and twentieth centuries were very bloody because the Wahhabis indiscriminately slaughtered and terrorized Muslims and non-Muslims alike. Mainstream jurists writing at the time, such as the *Hanafi* Ibn 'Abidin and the *Maliki* al-Sawi, described the Wahhabis as a fanatic fringe group.[3]

WAHHABISM ASCENDANT

Nevertheless, Wahhabism survived and, in fact, thrived in contemporary Islam for several reasons. By treating Muslim Ottoman rule as a foreign occupying power, Wahhabism set a powerful precedent for notions of Arab self-determination and autonomy. In advocating a return to the pristine and pure origins of Islam, Wahhabism rejected the cumulative weight of historical baggage. This idea was intuitively liberating for Muslim reformers since it meant the rebirth of *ijtihad*, or the return to *de novo* examination and determination of legal issues unencumbered by the accretions of precedents and inherited doctrines. Most importantly, the discovery and exploitation of oil provided Saudi Arabia with high liquidity. Especially after 1975, with the sharp rise in oil prices, Saudi Arabia aggressively promoted Wahhabi thought around the Muslim world. Even a cursory examination of predominant ideas and practices reveals the widespread influence of Wahhabi thought on the Muslim world today.

But Wahhabism did not spread in the modern Muslim world under its own banner. Even the term "Wahhabism" is considered derogatory by its adherents, since Wahhabis prefer to see themselves as the representatives of Islamic orthodoxy. To them, Wahhabism is not a school of thought within Islam, but *is* Islam. The fact that Wahhabism rejected a label gave it a diffuse quality, making many of its doctrines and methodologies eminently transferable. Wahhabi thought exercised its greatest influence not under its own label, but under the rubric of Salafism. In their literature, Wahhabi clerics have consistently described themselves as Salafis, and not Wahhabis.

BESET WITH CONTRADICTIONS

Salafism is a creed founded in the late nineteenth century by Muslim reformers such as Muhammad 'Abduh, al-Afghani and Rashid Rida. Salafism appealed to a very basic concept in Islam: Muslims ought to follow the precedent of the Prophet and his companions (*al-salaf al-salih*). Methodologically, Salafism was nearly identical to Wahhabism except that Wahhabism is far less tolerant of diversity and differences of opinion. The founders of Salafism maintained that on all issues Muslims ought to return to the Qur'an and the *sunna* (precedent) of the Prophet. In doing so, Muslims ought to reinterpret the original sources in light of modern needs and demands, without being slavishly bound to the interpretations of earlier Muslim generations.

As originally conceived, Salafism was not necessarily anti-intellectual, but like Wahhabism, it did tend to be uninterested in history. By emphasizing a presumed golden age in Islam, the adherents of Salafism idealized the time of the Prophet and his companions, and ignored or demonized the balance of Islamic history. By rejecting juristic precedents and undervaluing tradition, Salafism adopted a form of egalitarianism that deconstructed any notions of established authority within Islam. Effectively, anyone was considered qualified to return to the original sources and speak for the divine will. By liberating Muslims from the tradition of the jurists, Salafism contributed to a real vacuum of authority in contemporary Islam. Importantly, Salafism was founded by Muslim nationalists who were eager to read the values of modernism into the original sources of Islam. Hence, Salafism was not necessarily anti-Western. In fact, its founders strove to project contemporary institutions such as democracy, constitutions or socialism into the foundational texts, and to justify the modern nation-state within Islam.

The liberal age of Salafism came to an end in the 1960s. After 1975, Wahhabism was able to rid itself of its extreme intolerance, and proceeded to co-opt Salafism until the two became practically indistinguishable. Both theologies imagined a golden age within Islam, entailing a belief in a historical utopia that can be reproduced in contemporary Islam. Both remained uninterested in critical historical inquiry and responded to the challenge of modernity by escaping to the secure haven of the text. Both advocated a form of egalitarianism and anti-elitism to the point that they came to consider intellectualism and rational moral insight to be inaccessible and, thus, corruptions of the purity of the Islamic message. Wahhabism and Salafism were beset with contradictions that made them simultaneously idealistic and pragmatic and infested both creeds (especially in the 1980s and 1990s) with a kind of supremacist thinking that prevails until today.

BETWEEN APOLOGETICS AND SUPREMACY

The predominant intellectual response to the challenge of modernity in Islam has been apologetics. Apologetics consisted of an effort by a large number of commentators to defend the Islamic system of beliefs from the onslaught of Orientalism, Westernization and modernity by simultaneously emphasizing the compatibility and supremacy of Islam. Apologists responded to the intellectual challenges coming from the West by adopting pietistic fictions about the Islamic traditions. Such fictions eschewed any critical evaluation of Islamic doctrines, and celebrated the presumed perfection of Islam. A common apologist argument was that any meritorious or worth-while modern institution was first invented by Muslims. According to the apologists, Islam liberated women, created a democracy, endorsed pluralism, protected human rights and guaranteed social security long before these institutions ever existed in the West. These concepts were not asserted out of critical understanding or ideological commitment, but primarily as a means of resisting Western hegemony and affirming self-worth. The main effect of apologetics, however, was to contribute to a sense of intellectual self-sufficiency that often descended into moral arrogance. To the extent that apologetics were habit-forming, it produced a culture that eschewed self-critical and introspective insight, and embraced the projection of blame and a fantasy-like level of confidence.

In many ways, the apologetic response was fundamentally centered on power. Its main purpose was not to integrate particular values within Islamic culture, but to empower Islam against its civilizational rival. Muslim apologetics tended to be opportunistic and rather unprincipled, and, in fact, they lent support to the tendency among many intellectuals and activists to give precedence to the logic of pragmatism over any other competing demands. Invoking the logic of necessity or public interest to justify courses of action, at the expense of moral imperatives, became common practice. Effectively, apologists got into the habit of paying homage to the presumed superiority of the Islamic tradition, but marginalized this idealistic image in everyday life.

Post-1970s Salafism adopted many of the premises of the apologetic discourse, but it also took these premises to their logical extreme. Instead of simple apologetics, Salafism responded to feelings of powerlessness and defeat with uncompromising and arrogant symbolic displays of power, not only against non-Muslims, but also against Muslim women. Fundamentally, Salafism, which by the 1970s had become a virulent puritan theology, further anchored itself in the confident security of texts. Nonetheless, contrary to the assertions of its proponents, Salafism did not necessarily pursue objective or balanced interpretations of Islamic texts, but primarily projected its own frustrations and aspirations upon the text. Its proponents no longer concerned themselves with co-opting or claiming Western institutions as their own, but defined Islam as the exact antithesis of the West, under the guise of reclaiming the true and real Islam. Whatever the West was perceived to be, Islam was understood to be the exact opposite.

ALIENATION FROM TRADITION

Of course, neither Wahhabism nor Salafism is represented by some formal institution. They are theological orientations and not structured schools of thought. Nevertheless, the lapsing and bonding of the theologies of Wahhabism and Salafism produced a contemporary orientation that is anchored in profound feelings of defeat, frustration and alienation, not only from modern institutions of power, but also from the Islamic heritage and tradition. The outcome of the apologist, Wahhabi and Salafi legacies is a supremacist puritanism that compensates for feelings of defeat, disempowerment and alienation with a distinct sense of self-righteous arrogance vis-à-vis the nondescript "other"—whether the other is the West, non-believers in general or even Muslims of a different sect and Muslim women. In this sense, it is accurate to describe this widespread modern trend as supremacist, for it sees the world from the perspective of stations of merit and extreme polarization.

In the wake of the September 11 attacks, several commentators posed the question of whether Islam somehow encourages violence and terrorism. Some commentators argued that the Islamic concept of *jihad* or the notion of the *dar al-harb* (the abode of war) is to blame for the contemporary violence. These arguments are anachronistic and Orientalist. They project Western categories and historical experiences upon a situation that is very particular and fairly complex. One can easily locate an ethical discourse within the Islamic tradition that is uncompromisingly hostile to acts of terrorism. One can also locate a discourse that is tolerant toward the other, and mindful of the dignity and worth of all human beings. But one must also come to terms with the fact that supremacist Puritanism in contemporary Islam is dismissive of all moral norms or ethical values, regardless of the identity of their origins or foundations. The prime and nearly singular concern is power and its symbols. Somehow, all other values are made subservient.

NOTES

1. Khaled Abou El Fadl, "Islamic Law and Muslim Minorities: The Juristic Discourse on Muslim Minorities from the Second/Eighth to the Eleventh/ Seventeenth Centuries," *Journal of Islamic Law and Society* 22/1 (1994).

2. Khaled Abou El Fadl, "The Rules of Killing at War: An Inquiry into Classical Sources," *The Muslim World* #89 (1999).

3. Muhammad Amin Ibn 'Abidin, *Hashiyat Radd al-Muhtar*, vol. VI (Cairo: Mustafa al-Babi, 1966), p. 413; Ahmad al-Sawi, *Hashiyat al-Sawi 'ala Tafsir al-Jalalayn*, vol. III (Beirut: Dar Ihya' al-Turath al-Arabi, n.d.), pp. 307-308. See also Ahmad Dallal, "The Origins and Objectives of Islamic Revivalist Thought, 1750-1850," *Journal of the American Oriental Society* 113/3 (1993).

Summary of Differences between Orthodox Judaism & Zionism

W HILE ZIONISM AND 'Jewishness' are very inter-related, the differences between Zionism in its current political expression and traditional Judaism exist even if reduced to a textual reading. Below, I have tried to highlight some of the basic differences between Judaism and Zionism

SACRED OATHS

• Judaism considers Sacred, 'Three Talmudic Oaths':

1. Jewish people should not rebel against the nations of the world
2. Jewish people should not engage in any actions which will accelerate the coming of the End of Days
3. Jewish people should not go *en masse* to Israel

• Zionism is in conflict with all three Oaths[1]

EXILE

• Judaism views Jewish exile as punishment for sin. Redemption may be achieved solely through prayer and penance.
• Zionism rejects the concept of a divinely imposed exile.
• Zionism believes that Jewish exile can be ended by military strength

PALESTINIANS

• According to the Torah, the Jews are against dispossessing the Arabs of their land and homes, which should be returned

• Zionism has been dispossessing the Palestinian people, subjecting them to persecution and have ignored their just claims

• Thousands of Torah scholars, saints and sages have condemned the Zionist movement since its inception. They knew that pre-existing good relations between the Jews and Muslims was bound to suffer as Zionism advanced

• Jews are called upon to live in peace and harmony with all of humanity. They are exhorted to be law-abiding and patriotic citizens in all lands

STATE OF ISRAEL

• The Jewish people are forbidden to have their own state while awaiting the Messianic era (according to the Jewish faith and Torah Laws).

• Biblical verses quoted by Zionist scholars to affirm that God gave the Children of Israel the Holy-Land, overlook the verses that state God took it away from them due to the sins of the Jewish people. They further ignore those prophecies which explicitly describe the current exile as a divine, not human process

• The people of Israel have existed for thousands of years, whereas Zionism is a relatively new phenomenon

• Jews believe that salvation is occupation in divine service

• Zionists believe salvation is possession of a state and army

JUDAISM, ZIONISM & CHRISTIAN-ZIONISTS

• Zionism and Judaism are two distinct philosophies and should not be confused

• The Zionist State is not a Jewish State

• Not all Jews are Zionists and not all Zionists are Jews.

• Some of the most fervent Zionists have been Christians, who believe that Zionism is an important movement and welcome it as a fulfillment of prophecy that will ultimately usher in the Second coming of Christ and Armageddon. Referred to as Christian-Zionists, they fundamentally believe:

1. *The Covenant.* God's covenant with Israel is eternal and unconditional,

and therefore, the promises of land given to Abraham will never be overturned. This means that the Church has not replaced Israel and that Israel's privileges have never been revoked despite their unfaithfulness

2. *The Church.* God's plan has always been for the redemption of Israel. Yet when Israel failed to follow Jesus, the church was born as an afterthought, or "parenthesis." Thus, at the Second Coming, the church will be removed and Israel will once again become God's primary agent in the world. We now live in the "time of the Gentiles" which will conclude soon. This means that there are two covenants now at work: one given through Moses and the other covenant of Christ. But the new covenant in no way makes the older covenant obsolete

3. *Blessing Modern Israel.* Genesis 12:3 must be taken literally ("I will bless those who bless you and curse those who curse you") therefore, Christian Zionists believe that they have a spiritual obligation to bless Israel and "pray for the peace of Jerusalem." (Psalm 122:6) To fail to bless Israel, defined as a failure to support Israel's political survival today, will incur divine judgment

4. *Prophecy.* The prophetic books of the Bible are describing events of today and do not principally refer to events in Biblical times. Therefore, when Christian-Zionists read, for example, Daniel 7, they believe that they can understand how modern history is unfolding

5. *Modern Israel and Eschatology.* The modern State of Israel is a catalyst for the prophetic countdown. If these are the last days, then we should expect an unraveling of civilization, the rise of evil, the loss of international peace and equilibrium, a coming antichrist and tests of faithfulness to Israel. Above all, political alignments today will determine Christian's position on the fateful day of Armageddon.[2]

NOTES

1. For examples of writings of Rabbis spanning from the fifteenth century who warned against violating these three oaths, see "Words of the Rabbis" http://www.jewsagainstzionism.com/rabbis.htm

2. See Gary Burge, *Christian Zionism, Evangelicals and Israel,* The Holy Land Christian Ecumenical Foundation (HCEF) available at; http://www.hcef.org/hcef/index.cfm/ID/159

UN Resolutions & US Vetoes

THE FOLLOWING UN resolutions have been passed against Israel between 1955 and 1992. No other country in the world, whether member of the United Nations or non-member, has been so frequently condemned by the United Nations.

Resolution 106: condemns Israel for Gaza raid.

Resolution 111: condemns Israel for raid on Syria that killed fifty-six people.

Resolution 127: recommends Israel suspend its no-man's zone in Jerusalem.

Resolution 162: urges Israel to comply with UN decisions.

Resolution 171: determines flagrant violations by Israel in its attack on Syria.

Resolution 228: censures Israel for its attack on Samu in the West Bank, then under Jordanian control.

Resolution 237: urges Israel to allow return of new 1967 Palestinian refugees.

Resolution 248: condemns Israel for its massive attack on Karameh in Jordan.

Resolution 250: calls on Israel to refrain from holding military parade in Jerusalem.

Resolution 251: deeply deplores Israeli military parade in Jerusalem in defiance of Resolution 250.

Resolution 252: declares invalid Israel's acts to unify Jerusalem as Jewish capital.

Resolution 256: condemns Israeli raids on Jordan as flagrant violation.

Resolution 259: deplores Israel's refusal to accept UN mission to probe occupation.

Resolution 262: condemns Israel for attack on Beirut airport.

Resolution 265: condemns Israel for air attacks for Salt in Jordan.

Resolution 267: censures Israel for administrative acts to change the status of Jerusalem.

Resolution 270: condemns Israel for air attacks on villages in southern Lebanon.

Resolution 271: condemns Israel's failure to obey UN resolutions on Jerusalem.

Resolution 279: demands withdrawal of Israeli forces from Lebanon.

Resolution 280: condemns Israeli's attacks against Lebanon.

Resolution 285: demands immediate Israeli withdrawal from Lebanon.

Resolution 298: deplores Israel's changing of the status of Jerusalem.

Resolution 313: demands that Israel stop attacks against Lebanon.

Resolution 316: condemns Israel for repeated attacks on Lebanon.

Resolution 317: deplores Israel's refusal to release Arabs abducted in Lebanon.

Resolution 332: condemns Israel's repeated attacks against Lebanon.

Resolution 337: condemns Israel for violating Lebanon's sovereignty.

Resolution 347: condemns Israeli attacks on Lebanon.

Resolution 425: calls on Israel to withdraw its forces from Lebanon.

Resolution 427: calls on Israel to complete its withdrawal from Lebanon.

Resolution 444: deplores Israel's lack of cooperation with UN peace-keeping forces.

Resolution 446: determines that Israeli settlements are a serious obstruction to peace and calls on Israel to abide by the Fourth Geneva Convention

Resolution 450: calls on Israel to stop attacking Lebanon.

Resolution 452: calls on Israel to cease building settlements in occupied territories.

Resolution 465: deplores Israel's settlements and asks all member states not to assist its settlements program.

Resolution 467: strongly deplores Israel's military intervention in Lebanon.

Resolution 468: calls on Israel to rescind illegal expulsions of two Palestinian mayors and a judge and to facilitate their return.

Resolution 469: strongly deplores Israel's failure to observe the council's order not to deport Palestinians.

Resolution 471: expresses deep concern at Israel's failure to abide by the Fourth Geneva Convention.

Resolution 476: reiterates that Israel's claim to Jerusalem are null and void.

Resolution 478: censures (Israel) in the strongest terms for its claim to Jerusalem in its Basic Law.

Resolution 484: declares it imperative that Israel re-admit two deported Palestinian mayors.

Resolution 487: strongly condemns Israel for its attack on Iraq's nuclear facility.

Resolution 497: decides that Israel's annexation of Syria's Golan Heights is null and void and demands that Israel rescinds its decision forthwith.

Resolution 498: calls on Israel to withdraw from Lebanon.

Resolution 501: calls on Israel to stop attacks against Lebanon and withdraw its troops.

Resolution 509: demands that Israel withdraw its forces forthwith and unconditionally from Lebanon.

Resolution 515: demands that Israel lift its siege of Beirut and allow food supplies to be brought in.

Resolution 517: censures Israel for failing to obey UN resolutions and demands that Israel withdraw its forces from Lebanon.

Resolution 518: demands that Israel cooperate fully with UN forces in Lebanon.

Resolution 520: condemns Israel's attack into West Beirut.

Resolution 573: condemns Israel vigorously for bombing Tunisia in attack on PLO headquarters.

Resolution 587: takes note of previous calls on Israel to withdraw its forces from Lebanon and urges all parties to withdraw.

Resolution 592: strongly deplores the killing of Palestinian students at Bir Zeit University by Israeli troops.

Resolution 605: strongly deplores Israel's policies and practices denying the human rights of Palestinians.

Resolution 607: calls on Israel not to deport Palestinians and strongly requests it to abide by the Fourth Geneva Convention.

Resolution 608: deeply regrets that Israel has defied the United Nations and deported Palestinian civilians.

Resolution 636: deeply regrets Israeli deportation of Palestinian civilians.

Resolution 641: deplores Israel's continuing deportation of Palestinians.

Resolution 672: condemns Israel for violence against Palestinians at the Haram Al-Sharif/Temple Mount.

Resolution 673: deplores Israel's refusal to cooperate with the United Nations.

Resolution 681: deplores Israel's resumption of the deportation of Palestinians.

Resolution 694: deplores Israel's deportation of Palestinians and calls on it to ensure their safe and immediate return.

Resolution 726: strongly condemns Israel's deportation of Palestinians.

Resolution 799: strongly condemns Israel's deportation of 413 Palestinians and calls for their immediate return.

US VETOES OF UN RESOLUTIONS CRITICAL OF ISRAEL

VETOES: 1972-1982

Subject	Date & Meeting	US Rep Casting Veto	Vote
Palestine: Syrian-Lebanese Complaint. 3 power draft resolution 2/10784	10/9/72	Bush	13-1, 1
Palestine: Examination of Middle East Situation. 8-power draft resolution (S/10974)	2/7/73	Scali	13-1, 0 (China not partic.)
Palestine: Egyptian-Lebanese Complaint. 5-power draft power resolution (S/11898)	8/12/75	Moynihan	13-1, 1
Palestine: Middle East Problem, including Palestinian question. 6-power draft resolution (S/11940)	1/26/1976	Moynihan	9-1,3 (China & Libya not partic.)
Palestine: Situation in Occupied Arab Territories. 5-power draft resolution (S/12022)	3/25/1976	Scranton	14-1,0
Palestine: Report on Committee on Rights of Palestinian People. 4-power draft resolution (S/121119)	6/29/1976	Sherer	10-1,4
Palestine: Palestinian Rights. Tunisian draft resolution. (S/13911)	4/30/1980	McHenry	10-1,4
Palestine: Golan Heights. Jordan draft resolution. (S/14832/Rev. 2)	1/20/1982	Kirkpatrick	9-1,5
Palestine: Situation in Occupied Territories, Jordan draft resolution (S/14943)	2/4/82	Lichenstein	13-1,1

Subject	Date & Meeting	US Rep Casting Veto	Vote
Palestine: Incident at the Dome of the Rock in Jerusalem. 4-power draft resolution	4/20/1982	Kirpatrick	14-1, 0
Palestine: Conflict in Lebanon. Spain draft resolution. (S/15185)	8/6/82	Kirpatrick	14-1,0
Palestine: Conflict in Lebanon. France draft resolution. (S/15255/Rev. 2)	6/26/1982	Lichenstein	14-Jan
Palestine: Conflict in Lebanon. USSR draft resolution. (S/15347/Rev. 1, as orally amended)	6/8/82	Lichenstein	11-1,3
Palestine: Situation in Occupied Territories, 20-power draft resolution (S/15895)	2/8/83	Lichenstein	13-1,1

Source: http://www.us-israel.org/jsource/UN/usvetoes.html

Israel's Crimes against Palestinians:
War Crimes, Crimes against Humanity & Genocide

FRANCIS A. BOYLE

ELLIGERENT OCCUPATION IS governed by The Hague
Regulations of 1907, as well as by the Fourth Geneva Convention
of 1949, and the customary laws of belligerent occupation.
Security Council Resolution 1322 (2000), paragraph 3 "Calls upon Israel,
the occupying Power, to abide scrupulously by its legal obligations and
its responsibilities under the Fourth Geneva Convention relative to the
Protection of Civilian Persons in a Time of War of 12 August 1949;..."
Again, the Security Council vote was 14 to 0, becoming obligatory
international law.

The Fourth Geneva Convention applies to the West Bank, to the
Gaza Strip, and to the entire City of Jerusalem, in order to protect the
Palestinians living there. The Palestinian People living in this Palestinian
Land are "protected persons" within the meaning of the Fourth Geneva
Convention. All of their rights are sacred under international law.

There are 149 substantive articles of the Fourth Geneva Convention
that protect the rights of every one of these Palestinians living in occupied
Palestine. The Israeli Government is currently violating, and has since
1967 been violating, almost each and every one of these sacred rights
of the Palestinian People recognized by the Fourth Geneva Convention.
Indeed, violations of the Fourth Geneva Convention are war crimes.

So this is not a symmetrical situation. As matters of fact and of law,
the gross and repeated violations of Palestinian rights by the Israeli army
and Israeli settlers living illegally in occupied Palestine constitute war
crimes. Conversely, the Palestinian People are defending themselves and
their Land and their Homes against Israeli war crimes and Israeli war
criminals, both military and civilian.

THE UN HUMAN RIGHTS COMMISSION

Indeed, it is far more serious than that. On 19th October 2000, a Special Session of the UN Commission on Human Rights adopted a Resolution set forth in UN Document E/CN.4/S-5/L.2/Rev. 1, "Condemning the provocative visit to Al-Haram Al-Sharif on 28th September 2000 by Ariel Sharon, the Likud party leader, which triggered the tragic events that followed in occupied East Jerusalem and the other occupied Palestinian territories, resulting in a high number of deaths and injuries among Palestinian civilians." The UN Human Rights Commission then said it was "[g]ravely concerned" about several different types of atrocities inflicted by Israel upon the Palestinian People, which it denominated "war crimes, flagrant violations of international humanitarian law and crimes against humanity."

In operative paragraph 1 of its 19th October 2000 Resolution, the UN Human Rights Commission then: "Strongly condemns the disproportionate and indiscriminate use of force in violation of international humanitarian law by the Israeli occupying Power against innocent and unarmed Palestinian civilians...including many children, in the occupied territories, which constitutes a war crime and a crime against humanity;..." And in paragraph 5 of its 19th October 2000 Resolution, the UN Human Rights Commission: "Also affirms that the deliberate and systematic killing of civilians and children by the Israeli occupying authorities constitutes a flagrant and grave violation of the right to life and also constitutes a crime against humanity;..." Article 68 of the United Nations Charter had expressly required the UN's Economic and Social Council to "set up" this Commission "for the promotion of human rights."

ISRAEL'S WAR CRIMES AGAINST PALESTINIANS

We all have a general idea of what a war crime is, so I am not going to elaborate upon that term here. But there are different degrees of heinousness for war crimes. In particular are the more serious war crimes denominated "grave breaches" of the Fourth Geneva Convention. Since the start of the Al Aqsa *Intifada*, the world has seen those inflicted every day by Israel against the Palestinian People living in occupied Palestine: e.g., willful killing of Palestinian civilians by the Israeli army and Israel's illegal paramilitary settlers. These Israeli "grave breaches" of the Fourth Geneva Convention mandate universal prosecution for their perpetrators, whether military or civilian, as well as prosecution for their commanders, whether military or civilian, including Israel's political leaders.

ISRAEL'S CRIMES AGAINST HUMANITY
AGAINST PALESTINIANS

But I want to focus for a moment on Israel's "crime against humanity" against the Palestinian People—as determined by the UN Human Rights Commission itself, set up pursuant to the requirements of the United Nations Charter. What is a "crime against humanity?" This concept goes all the way back to the Nuremberg Charter of 1945 for the trial of the major Nazi war criminals. And in the Nuremberg Charter of 1945, drafted by the United States Government, there was created and inserted a new type of international crime specifically intended to deal with the Nazi persecution of the Jewish People.

The paradigmatic example of a "crime against humanity" is what Hitler and the Nazis did to the Jewish People. This is where the concept of crime against humanity came from. And this is what the UN Human Rights Commission determined that Israel is currently doing to the Palestinian People: Crimes against humanity. Legally, just like what Hitler and the Nazis did to the Jews.

THE PRECURSOR TO GENOCIDE

Moreover, a crime against humanity is the direct historical and legal precursor to the international crime of genocide as defined by the 1948 Convention on the Prevention and Punishment of the Crime of Genocide. The theory here was that what Hitler and the Nazis did to the Jewish People required a special international treaty that would codify and universalize the Nuremberg concept of "crime against humanity." And that treaty ultimately became the 1948 Genocide Convention.

In fairness, you will note that the UN Human Rights Commission did not go so far as to condemn Israel for committing genocide against the Palestinian People. But it has condemned Israel for committing crimes against humanity, which is the direct precursor to genocide. And I submit that if something is not done quite soon by the American People and the International Community to stop Israeli war crimes and crimes against humanity against the Palestinian People, it could very well degenerate into genocide, if Israel is not there already. And in this regard, Israeli Prime Minister Ariel Sharon is what international lawyers call a *genocidaire*—one who has already committed genocide in the past.

Clean Break or Dirty War?
Israel's Foreign Policy Directive to the United States[1]

EXECUTIVE SUMMARY

G REAT CHANGES ARE seldom achieved without a plan. The Israeli policy paper "A Clean Break: A New Strategy for Securing the Realm" (ACB) was authored by a group of policy advisors to Israel. Subsequently, nearly all members ascended to influential policy making positions within US government, media, and academic circles. Many of the ACB policies such as toppling the government of Iraq are now in full implementation and present new challenges to the global community. Others, such as the reform of Israel's economy have been abysmal failures, but generate little visibility or impact outside of Israel.

This paper provides an overview of the policy implementation of "A Clean Break: A New Strategy for Securing the Realm."[2] Some of the events and trends that contribute to success or failure of the plan predate ACB by many years. And although many ACB authors ascended to new heights of political power in the US, the success or failure of the policies cannot be solely ascribed to them. *However, ACB policies are, for the most part, extremely damaging to US interests.* The ACB framework is useful for explaining the motives driving the complete failure of US interests in the Middle East and the triumph of politics and lobbies over statecraft.

SECURING THE REALM: BACKGROUND

"A Clean Break: A New Strategy for Securing the Realm" (ACB) contains six pages of policy recommendations for Benjamin Netanyahu. In 1996, Israel's newly elected Prime Minister relied upon opinion makers, thinkers and researchers to craft the paper. This Institute for Advanced Strategic and Political Studies' "Study Group on a New Israeli Strategy Toward 2000" included Richard Perle, James Colbert, Charles Fairbanks, Douglas Feith, Robert Loewenberg, David Wurmser, and

Meyrav Wurmser.

The paper's call for a "break" from failed policies of the past such as "land for peace" and a new concentration on the realities of "balance of power" in the region are striking for their *realpolitik* approaches and high dependence on actions and resources of the US government.

EXHIBIT 1: ACB POLICY INITIATIVES (SOURCE: IRMEP 2003)

Increase US Congressional Support	"Electrify and find support" of key US congressional members
	Strategic cooperation with US on missile defense
	Gain more support among members of Congress with little knowledge of Israel
	Harness support to move the US embassy to Jerusalem from Tel Aviv
	Identify Israel with the US and "western values"
	Utilize Cold War rhetoric to make Israel's case to the American people
"Peace for Peace" Palestinian Solution	Eliminate movements toward a "comprehensive peace" and substitute with the "Peace for Peace" strategy
	Stress "balance of power" as sole test of legitimacy, enforce agreements
	Nurture alternatives to Arafat
	Seek legitimization of "hot pursuit" of Palestinian militants
	Eliminate "land for peace" concept, use negotiations only as a forum for communicating resolve
	Establish a joint monitoring committee with the US for measuring Palestinian compliance
	Withhold US aid to Palestinians
	Promote Human Rights among Arabs to isolate Palestinians in Arab Constituencies
	Legitimize 2000 year old historical land claim
	Foment Arab recognition of Israel in exchange for peace

Contain, Destabilize, and Roll Back Regional Challengers	Challenge Arab countries as "police states" lacking in legitimacy.
	Fortify regional alliances. Work with Turkey and Jordan to insert hostile Arab tribes into Syria
Syria	Publicly question Syrian legitimacy, assume treaties with Damascus are in bad faith
	Contain Syria, strike select targets
	Reject "land for peace" concept on the Golan Heights
Iraq	Install a Hashemite monarchy in Iraq
	Isolate and surround Syria with a friendly regime in Iraq
Lebanon	Engage Syria, Iran and Iraq in Lebanon
	"Wean" Lebanese Shiites from Iraq toward Jordan
Economic Reform	Eliminate Social Zionism from the economy.
	Reform the overall economy, cut taxes
	Show maturity and economic self reliance from the United States
	Eliminate need for defense by US military forces
	Remove US aid leverage over Israel
	Re-legislate a free trade zone, sell off public lands and enterprises
Zionism	Rebuild Zionism, rejuvenate the national ideal
	"Shape the regional environment" in favor of Israel, "transcend foes" rather than contain them
	Pre-emption as the preferred national defense strategy

Although ACB readers can identify nearly 34 distinct and actionable goals eloquently stated within the document, they may be summarized in five overarching policy goals:

1. Increase US Congressional Support
2. "Peace for Peace" Palestinian Strategy
3. Contain, Destabilize, and Roll Back Regional Challengers
4. Economic Reform
5. Rejuvenation of Zionism

In this paper, we evaluate the level of implementation of these five summary goals, and their effect on the interests of the United States. However, *no set of policies ever come to fruition without an active and vocal distribution and implementation network.* ACB's legions of American shock troops are many. At its core, key operatives working within the Bush Administration (called the Neo-cons), policy research "think tanks," specialty press, and opinion columns have achieved amazing success at seasoning and baking ACB policy agenda items into a tenuous mold as "vital interests" of the United States itself. (See Exhibit 2)

The need for "crime scene" levels of evidence linking ACB followers' complicity in the actions of the US Government at Israel's behest is unnecessary. Many US actions are simply so inexplicable that consideration of their chief benefactor, Israel, is the only reasonable explanation. And as Americans dismiss Arab government charges that Israel is attacking them by proxy across the region, the evidence shows that the Arabs are correct. "A Clean Break" is, at heart, an Israeli proclamation of "Dirty War."

EXHIBIT 2: (NEXT PAGE) THE NEO-CON POLICY
DISTRIBUTION & IMPLEMENTATION NETWORK
(SOURCE: IRMEP 2003)

GROUPS	MESSAGES	MEDIUM	MEMBERS
Defense Cabal	Preemption/ Remaking the Middle East Aid for Israel/ Joint Weapons Development New Homeland Security Business Opportunities Legitimization of Israeli occupation of Palestinian territories	Think-Tanks Defense Policy Board Defense Department Defense Contractors Talk Shows Investment Banks	Paul Wolfowitz Richard Perle Douglas Feith Elliot Abrams David Wurmser
Neo-con Specialty Press	Danger of Islam Illegitimacy of all Arab governments Illegitimacy of "land for peace" initiatives Primacy of the defense of Israel	American Enterprise Institute, JINSA, and Heritage Foundation Reports *The Weekly Standard* *The New Republic* *Commentary* (American Jewish Committee)	David Brooks Lawrence Kaplan William Kristol Norman Podhoretz
Columnists	Palestinian militants as "terrorists" Linkage between 9/11 and all Arab governments Israelis as "heroes" Critics of Israel as "anti-Semites"	*Wall Street Journal* *New York Times* *Washington Post* Editorial pages	Robert Kagan Charles Krauthammer Max Boot William Safire

Core members of the group have been able to raise the primacy of Israeli issues to a level that Americans would find absurd if the group were promoting the interests of any other state, (such as Italy or Mexico). Their level of vitriol, hubris and war-mongering by power of the pen and influence over American policy has been stunning. Many have personally engaged in activities that derailed official US foreign policy initiatives in the interest of improving Israel's power. Others have systematically chipped away at the US constitution by supplanting Israeli interests for legitimate US interests in the Defense Department and Executive branch of the US government.

The gaping divide that separates this group's lobbying on behalf of Israel and the true interests of the United States also defines this group with the very label they so frequently hurl at others: traitors to the United States of America.

II. ACB IMPLEMENTATION ASSESSMENT

The level of implementation of ACB policy objectives is not uniform. Nor are the resources, Israeli and American, which have been rallied and deployed in their support. In this section, we consider the level of implementation success of each ACB policy summary.

A. INCREASE SUPPORT IN THE US CONGRESS

It is political suicide for a member of the US Congress to strongly oppose policy positions of Zionist lobbies operating in the United States. Former president George W. W. Bush put it best when he declared that opposing the Zionist lobby in favor of a Palestinian State was the right thing to do, but came "at a hell of price."

The defining demonstration of this power predates ACB. The lobby converted its most powerful aid opponent by rallying massive campaign contributions to defeat North Carolina senator Jesse Helms. Pro-Israel political action committees poured an awe inspiring $222,342 into the campaign of Helms' opponent, North Carolina Governor James Hunt. Hunt's campaign secretary proclaimed that "Senator Helms has the worst anti-Israel record in the United States Senate and supporters of Israel throughout the country know it."

After the scare of almost losing reelection, Helms announced that he would exempt from cuts the more than one-third of total US foreign aid going to Israel since such aid was "in the strategic interest of the US." He also became an ardent and comical supporter of moving the US embassy from Tel Aviv to Jerusalem and worked diligently to increase the appropriations for Israel from the Defense Department, the State Department and half a dozen other different federal agency budgets.

A survey of recently introduced legislation indicates that Congress is repaying the debt to Israel by internalizing Israel's conflicts and putting US resources at Israel's disposal. (See Exhibit 3)

EXHIBIT 3: RECENT PRO-ISRAEL LEGISLATION INTRODUCED IN THE US CONGRESS (SOURCE: LIBRARY OF CONGRESS AND IRMEP 2003)

LEGISLATION	SUMMARY	ANALYSIS
Koby Mandell Act of 2003	To create an office within the Department of Justice to undertake specific steps to ensure that all American citizens harmed by terrorism overseas receive equal treatment by the United States government regardless of the terrorists' country of origin or residence, and to ensure that all terrorists involved in such attacks are pursued, prosecuted, and punished with equal vigor, regardless of the terrorists' country of origin or residence.	Demonize the Palestinian Authority by labeling dual citizen Israeli deaths in the ongoing Israeli-Palestinian conflict as "acts of terrorism" that the US Department of Justice can pursue. Understandably, the legislation does not address the summary arrest and torture of Arab American citizens by the Israeli Shin-Bet

LEGISLATION	SUMMARY	ANALYSIS
Whereas the United States and Israel are close allies whose people share a deep and abiding friendship based on a shared commitment to democratic values H.RES.61	Commends the people of Israel for conducting free and fair elections, reaffirming the friendship between the Governments and peoples of the United States and Israel, and for other purposes.	Seeks to coerce the Palestinian leadership to censor official media in opposition to Israel and take responsibility for the security of Israel by controlling many radical groups essentially beyond its control.
HR 167 IH	To take certain steps toward recognition by the United States of Jerusalem as the capital of Israel.	Seeks to create another set of "facts on the ground" by eliminating resistance to moving US diplomatic facilities to the contested city of Jerusalem from Tel Aviv. Also seeks recognition of births in Jerusalem as being births in Israel and identification in all US government documents of Jerusalem as the capital in spite of international opposition to legitimizing the issue.

LEGISLATION	SUMMARY	ANALYSIS
International School Curriculum Monitoring Act (Introduced in House) HR 1358 IH	Seeks to monitor all international curriculums for "Anti-Semitic" material and tie US aid to official US approval of such educational material.	Would codify McCarthy type independent monitoring groups tied to Zionist organizations such as Daniel Pipe's infamous "Campus Watch." Legitimizes yet another lever for Israeli operatives to influence and deny aid to countries that legitimately oppose Israel.
Senator Lindsey Graham and Congressman Joe Wilson Resolution to protect and open up all holy sites in the state of Israel and nearby territory SCON 32 IS	Expresses the sense of Congress regarding the protection of religious sites and the freedom of access and worship "in the state of Israel and nearby territories." The resolution states that the holy sites currently under the sovereignty of the state of Israel should remain under Israeli protection and that all holy sites in the region remain open to visitors of all faiths.	Seeks to solidify 1967 borders and Israeli occupied territories by putting their religious sites under Congressionally legitimized protection mirroring Israel's "Israeli Protection of Holy Places Law of 1967" which states that freedom of access and worship is ensured at all places of worship and religious significance."

Other than the repetitious and almost desperate rhetoric about the unity of vision and purpose between the US and Israel, and fawning approval of all things Israeli, another common strand runs through this legislation. None of it would be introduced by Congress members preoccupied exclusively with promoting US interests. Most of the legislation is costly to the United States in constraining American civil liberties and foreign policy initiatives in the Middle East while legitimizing even the most despicable Israeli actions much of the rest of the world community and UN consider to be crimes. The gestures create enmity with nations and states with which the US should have steadily improving relationships.

As an ACB policy goal, IRMEP applies a score of "5 out of 5" to demonstrated Israeli influence over the US Congress.

B. "PEACE FOR PEACE" APPROACH TO THE PALESTINIAN QUESTION

Israel has adopted all of the appearances of promoting a "peace for peace" strategy with the Palestinians. Under this policy, Palestinians have no land claims on territory within the borders of Israel or territory occupied by Israel. Palestinians and future enemies under this policy must be content only with avoiding their own destruction by Israel.

One aggressive approach promoted by Richard Perle, former chairman of the US Defense Policy Board, labels Jordan as Palestine, implying relocation or "ethnic cleansing" of Palestinian peoples. "Land for Peace" as a strategy, is widely discredited by pro-Israel agents as being unworkable and lacking in security for Israel. Current efforts to derail remnants of "Land for Peace" include:

1. *Israeli Security Time Limits.* On March 31, 2003, Israeli foreign Minister Silvan Shalom indicated that Israel will only give the Palestinian prime minister designate two months to crack down on terrorism. By placing the prime minister in charge of Israeli security against forces entirely outside his circle of influence, Israel creates ideal conditions for rejecting land for peace movements while accelerating settlement activity.

2. *Legitimizing Israeli Delays through Amendments to the Roadmap.* The

roadmap for peace proposed by the European Union, Russia, the United Nations and United States was originally designed to be non-negotiable for both Israel and Palestine. Intense lobbying pressure has produced cracks that open the possibility for endless Israeli negotiations and delays of the roadmap as Israel proposes 12 major changes to this seven page document. On March 14, 2003, President Bush gave Israel license to pursue the amendment strategy in a Rose Garden announcement. "The United States has developed this plan over the last several months in close cooperation with Russia, the European Union, and the United Nations. Once this road map is delivered, we will expect and welcome contributions from Israel and the Palestinians to this document that will advance true peace."

3. *Discrediting Roadmap Architects.* Prime Minister Ariel Sharon and network members have worked diligently to discredit roadmap architects, particularly European nations. While Israel was unsuccessful in blocking some conferences and Palestinian contributions to the roadmap, the current political climate in the US after traditional allies and the UN failed to support the US invasion of Iraq has boosted Israel's chances of creating schisms in the quartet.

Because Israel has not yet been able to completely derail the roadmap, IRMEP assigns a score of only "3 out of 5" for promotion of the "peace for peace" strategy.

C. CONTAIN, DESTABILIZE AND
ROLL BACK REGIONAL CHALLENGERS

The US invasion of Iraq is such a singular success for Israel that pro-Israel leaders and pundits in the United States have had to restrain their glee that a long and arduous effort to topple Iraq's government and neutralize the state has finally borne fruit. Although Iraq is only one challenger to Israel, an accelerated Israeli effort to discredit, disrupt, and undermine other Arab governments, many in the midst of democratic reform, is moving forward rapidly.

EXHIBIT 4: "CLEAN BREAK" CONTAINMENT & DESTABILIZATION POLICY IMPLEMENTATION (IRMEP 2003)

TARGET	TACTIC	RESULT
Syria	Threats of Invasion. In secretary of State Colin Powell's speech to a conference of AIPAC members, he spoke of the "critical choice" facing Damascus. "Syria can continue to direct support for terrorist groups and the dying regime of Saddam Hussein, or it can embark on a different and more hopeful course. Either way, Syria bears the responsibility for its choices, and the consequences," he declared to loud applause.	The redirection of US forces to Syria after toppling Saddam Hussein is a high priority for Israel. An increase in allegations of Syrian transshipments of war materiel, and use as an entry point for regional Muslims answering a call for *Jihad* could quickly be aggrandized into support for use of force by the massive US military force already in the region
Syria	Simmering Conflict. Violence in and around Golan Heights has flared. Hezbollah guerrillas on the border zone, who have been fighting to force the Israelis to withdraw, have killed seven Israeli soldiers.	Israel responded with air strikes that destroyed three Lebanese power stations and injured 20 civilians. Israel has continued its campaign to label all branches of Hezbollah as terrorists.

TARGET	TACTIC	RESULT
Iran	Linking Free-Lancers to Iran. Defense Secretary Rumsfeld accused hundreds of Iraqi Shiite militia fighters based in Iran have crossed back into Iraq, complicating the military mission for the US-led coalition seeking to oust Iraqi leader Saddam Hussein. He has rushed to classify them as "combatants" even though the forces could be channeled onto the American side. Undersecretary of State John Bolton, a leading hawk, was quoted last month as telling Israeli officials that Iran would be "dealt with" after the war with Iraq.	By immediately rejecting the possibility of Shiite militia as allies and moving quickly implicate the government of Iran for what are probably freelance operatives, the Bush administration advances another step down the ACB regional challenger path. Although the UK has rejected any support for Syrian and Iranian fronts, the mass of US forces could be immediately redeployed to attack Iran.
Saudi Arabia	Smearing and Defame. Former Defense Policy board Chairman Richard Perle spearheaded an intense smear campaign against Saudi Arabia at the Pentagon, laying the foundations for future US military action.	Perle contracted Rand Corporation analyst Laurent Muraweic on July 10, 2002. Rand's briefing declared Saudi Arabia an "enemy of the United States" and advocated that the US invade the country, seize its oil fields and confiscate its financial assets unless the Saudis "stop supporting the anti-Western terror network."
Egypt	Conditioning and Cutting Foreign Aid Condition aid to Egypt on increased support for Israel	Legislation to engage in social engineering in Egypt by tying US foreign aid to rewriting curriculum to proselytize a better image of Israel. Media watch campaigns and scoring are also conditions of aid.

IRMEP assigns an overall score of "4" to Israeli efforts to destabilize and roll back regional rivals. While large successes have been scored in Iraq and Saudi Arabia, it is not yet clear that Israel will be able to motivate the US into armed conflict with Syria and Iran. Also, it is increasingly apparent that Arab nations are "on to" the architects of Middle Eastern conflict, and strategizing to both expose and resist ACB proxy activities.

D. ECONOMIC REFORM

Israel's efforts at economic reform have not yielded positive results. Although ACB calls for increased economic independence from the US which would allow freer reign for Israeli policies the US directly opposes, efforts at reform have been too little, too late. *Israel has mismanaged its economy and continues to export the negative consequences to the United States.*

1. *Israeli Economic Mismanagement.* Hitting 103% of GDP in 2002, Israel maintains one of the highest government debt ratios in the world; a higher debt ratio to GDP than most OECD countries, surpassing Canada. The Bank of Israel predicts the ratio will balloon to at least 106% in 2003. Interest payments on the government debt, under international standards, amount to 8.1% of GDP, while the OECD average is 2.2%. This is unfavorable compared with 3.1% in Germany, 2.8% in France, 2% in the US, and 1.2% in Japan. The Bank of Israel believes that this continued and uncontrolled increase in interest payments on the government debt will reduce the government's ability to maintain infrastructure investments and social needs or freely set budget priorities. These interest payments on the government debt increased to NIS 39.5 billion in 2002, a fifth of the state budget. Economic mismanagement has caused the harshest recession in the country's 55-year history and two years of negative growth. Israel's gross domestic product dropped 1.1 percent in 2002 with unemployment at an average of 10.3 percent. The government ran up a $579 million budget deficit in February, the highest 30-day overdraft on record.

2. *Eliminate Social Zionism.* The kibbutz movement in Israel is symbolic of social Zionism, and it is in crisis. Only limited kibbutzim in Israel, between 35 and 50, are doing well, or in some cases prospering. Though 2 percent of Israel's 6.2 million people live on kibbutzim; they generate 40 percent of the nation's agricultural produce and 10 percent of its industrial output. As Israel's youth flee the kibbutzim, the average age of members have spiraled. Communal financial capabilities for covering retirement and healthcare benefits are on life support as Israelis came to realize the fundamental flaw in social Zionism. As one immigrant stated, "Our basic premise was wrong," "The basic idea was that if we bring up our children in a non-competitive society, they would naturally want to live that way [...] That was a big mistake."

3. *Over Development/Reliance on High Tech.* During the tech boom, Israel over-developed its high tech sector. Investments were made in spite of a general lack of a supporting community of universities and high tech educational facilities and domestic technology demand. Israel counted on being able to leverage preferential access to the US market for military and software products without taking into consideration the high competition with US and other global firms. The dramatic collapse of the Israeli high tech sector also revealed the disproportionate effect over- reliance on a volatile sector can have on a small country as opposed to larger economies in Europe and the United States that have more successfully weathered the storm.

IRMEP's assessment of economic reform in Israel is that it is much too little, much too late, leading to an ACB score of "1 out of 5." Perhaps this can be attributed to ACB's architects. While most are highly capable in securing foreign aid and political support for Israel, none were notable economists. The architects and their network, of course, lay much of the blame for Israel's economic malaise as the effect of Palestinian resistance to occupation.

E. REJUVENATION OF ZIONISM

Zionism, defined as the international movement for the establishment of a Jewish national or religious community in Palestine and later for the support of modern Israel, is enjoying resurgence, though from unexpected quarters:

1. *American Christian Zionist Movement.* Support for Israel by organized Christian groups in the US has undergone explosive growth. Israel has been promoted and accepted as a cause that represents concrete steps toward the fulfillment of scriptural prophecy. One group, the two million-member Christian Coalition, is able to quickly deploy voting guides to over 70 million US households for such causes as the legislative effort to solidify Israel's 1967 borders and occupied territories purely in the name of "protection of religious site access." The return of the Jews to their ancient homeland is seen by Evangelicals as a precondition for the mystical Second Coming of Christ. Therefore, when the Jewish state was created in 1948, evangelicals saw it as a sign. Israel's conquest of Jerusalem and the West Bank in 1967 deepened their excitement, and multiplied their organized support for Israel.

2. *Weakened International Opposition to Zionism.* Twenty-six years ago, the United Nations General Assembly adopted a contentious resolution equating Zionism with racism. Then, as now, Israel mustered the support of the United States (and few other states) to stand by Israel's rejection of the resolution. Although conferences addressing the tie between Zionism and racism are again questioning Israel and the high Palestinian casualties produced by endless conflict, the US has been instrumental in stifling debate through its conspicuous absence at most human rights conferences.

3. *More Effective Deployment of the "Anti-Semitism" Smear Attack.* Critics of Israel in the major broadcast or print media are few in number. In 1919, Morris Jastrow, Jr. wrote the book "Zionism and the Future of Palestine" published by the Macmillan Company. Jastrow correctly predicted that the intertwining of religion and

nationality "political Zionism" would have negative consequences. He posited that whereas non-Jews have only one country and one purported loyalty "Americans are American", the "French are French", etc., Jews are seen as having split loyalties. He believed that they are both citizens of the country in which they live and also supporters of the Jewish state. He worried that Jews living outside of Israel (occupied Palestine) would be seen as being less than totally loyal to the country where they reside. Right or wrong, Jastrow predicted that this political difference adds to the real anti-Semitism that then existed. However, Jastrow failed to predict how effectively smear campaigns would be deployed by Zionist entities such as the Anti Defamation League when small numbers of agents of Israel were actually caught engaging in "activities incompatible with their status as American citizens." The suggestion by Pat Buchanan and other deeply conservative thinkers that "war party" members with undeniably compromising ties to Israel were the primary architects of the US invasion of Iraq have been met with a stifling wall of charges of anti-Semitism and media rebukes. However, though most potential critics of Israel in the mainstream media continue to be effectively muzzled, the charges and evidence are beginning to circulate beyond small groups of intellectuals and patriots.

One religion enjoys no protection. Across the dial of Christian Radio in Bible-Belt America, listeners can hear the shrill condemnations of Islam, and testimony to the ascendancy and righteousness of Christian and Zionist principles, acting in alliance against Islam.

High profile conferences feature sessions by intellectual ideologues such as Daniel Pipes speaking about militant Islam and 15% of Muslims as potential terrorists while Jerry Falwell proclaims that the prophet Mohammed himself was a terrorist. Countless millions of Americans are reading a series of novels called "Left Behind." They are topping bestseller lists all over the country and being made into movies. These books glorify and chronicle apocalyptic times. The setting is the twenty-first century, complete with war planes and TV correspondents. *This Christian fervor for the advance of Israel gives pause to many Jewish leaders.* While these Christians believe that God gave the land of Israel to the Jewish people and that every grain of sand between the Dead Sea, the Jordan River, and the Mediterranean Sea belongs to the Jews, including the West Bank and Gaza, problems exist. The biblical version of the apocalypse either kills off Jews or has them converted to Christianity, making evangelical support a double edge sword that is a poor guide for real geopolitics played out in the Middle East on the ground. In the words of one clever observer it "cuts us out in the fourth act." And what biblical guidance is there for the three million Palestinians who live on the West Bank and Gaza? Some fundamentalists suggest the bulk of them should be cleansed from this God-given real estate and moved to another Arab country. In fact, many evangelicals believe that when Prime Minister Rabin signed the Oslo accords and offered to trade land for peace, it was not only a mistake, it was a sin that he paid for with his own life.

IRMEP assigns a score of "5" to the ACB plan to rejuvenate Zionism. The effectiveness of the machinery in place to promote Zionism is awe inspiring though coming from unexpected, and at times, wholly unwanted, quarters.

III. ACB AMERICAN INTEREST DAMAGE ASSESSMENT

ACB represents a plan for achieving the best possible outcome for Israel. However, the policies that create a favorable outcome for Israel create an equal and opposite negative effect for the United States. In this section, we analyze the extent of the damage and assign it a numerical score.

A. INCREASE US CONGRESSIONAL SUPPORT

A verifiable Israeli influence over the US Congress, indirectly emanating from different quarters of the body of interest groups and lobbying organizations, is tremendously damaging for the United States. As ideologues promoting policies based on Israeli, Zionist or even biblical objectives are effectively enforced by US law and military might, portions of the American ideal begin to wither, die and finally decay.

The first to go is the idea that, as a nation, the United States operates best as a secular entity. The Bill of Rights states, "Congress shall make no law respecting an establishment of religion." By accepting and exporting US power in support of the aims of two religions, Christianity and Judaism, Congress has violated the US Constitution, and itself. Smaller acts, such as distributing communications to US soldiers fighting in Muslim lands exhorting that they "pray for President Bush" are further disturbing signs that the United States separation of church and state has been eroded to the point of collapse.

IRMEP scores the increase in US Congressional Support damage assessment score at the very highest level, "5 out of 5."

B. "PEACE FOR PEACE" PALESTINIAN STRATEGY

The collapse of the Oslo Accords and degradation caused by the Israel Palestinian conflict has left only one party that can effectively enforce solutions to the crisis. The United States. US interests in achieving peace in the region are of high importance. The conflict is seen as the lynchpin of grievances throughout the Arab world. By siding with the interests of Israel, and compromising its role as a neutral broker, the US has compromised its own legitimacy. The chief US interest in the Middle East is promoting a gradual and non-violent political, social, and economic development of the entire region. Favoring only one country makes conflict in vital oil producing regions more likely, motivates militant fundamentalist terrorist networks to act against the US, and strains US relations with the global community.

IRMEP scores US adherence to a "peace for peace" rather than "land for peace" strategy as having a high (score of 4) level of damage to US Middle East Interests.

C. CONTAIN, DESTABILIZE, AND ROLL BACK REGIONAL CHALLENGERS

The Israeli motivated plan to "destabilize" and "redraw the map of the Middle East" may be remembered by future generations as the spark that fell into the tinder box of World War III. While the United States is clearly interested in the reform of governments and institutions across the Middle East, a slower and more gradual approach with lower amounts of bloodshed was clearly the preferable path.

By accelerating conflict and casting aside both international law and alliances in the name of "regime change", the US is increasingly perceived as a rogue state and every bit as much a UN pariah as Israel.

By picking fights with ethnicities and tribes about which it knows or chooses to know comparatively little, the Bush Administration is only beginning to harvest the consequences of ill-advised and ideologically motivated extremism.

IRMEP's US damage assessment score is a solid "5 out of 5."

D. ECONOMIC REFORM

Israel's economic reform is a matter which has little direct affect on US interests. Although Israelis would like to further integrate economies, particularly in the military industrial arena, the US frequently finds that this leads to unintended technology transfers. Israel's attempted sales of radar systems based on US AWACs and the Lavi fighter jet copied from the US F-16 platforms are strategically significant, damaging matters.

The continued dependence of Israel on US aid is a negative factor for the United States. The IRMEP damage score to US interests is material. Ballooning levels of aid to Israel, while insubstantial as a percentage of total US GDP, alienates the global community and Arab states since it is the highest single US disbursement, at extremely favorable terms (equivalent to cash), in the entire US foreign aid budget. This is not good for Israel and in spite of the boon to US arms manufacturers and defense contractor interests written into aid packages, it is negative for the US

IRMEP's US damage assessment score is 2 out of 5.

REJUVENATION OF ZIONISM

Supporting the rejuvenation of Zionism has had a polarizing effect within the United States and damaged the constitutionally protected freedoms of US citizens. As a case study, consider how two ideologically and religiously motivated soldiers departing for different destination countries are now treated by the US government. An ardent and fit Jewish youth with American citizenship can easily travel to Israel and serve in the Israeli Defense Force, or other government branch, for two years, and return to blend back into US society. His or her activities, pledges of allegiance (which nullify US citizenship), and details of military service are of no interest to the US government. He could engage in two years of paramilitary operations against US Arab allies. The soldier could return to the US with an ongoing intelligence liaison to Mossad. None of this will be questioned or investigated in the US.

An ardent and fit Palestinian youth with American citizenship departing for the West Bank faces different treatment. If he is of the minority of ardently religious Muslim Palestinians he faces the wrath of both Israel and the US. He can be detained and imprisoned in Israel if authorities suspect any sympathy or support for Palestinian causes. Pleas to the US counsel in Tel Aviv will lead neither to support nor presence of US representation if the detainment ever reaches a judicial forum, which it may not. If the Palestinian youth joins any group considered to be a militant opposition to Israel (though usually not the United States), he will deeply implicate himself immediately for the crime of association with "terrorist" organizations, subject to detainment as an enemy combatant in Guantanamo Bay, or even execution by US intelligence operatives. Militant opposition to Israel has been completely criminalized in the United States. And Israel itself publicly reserves the right to assassinate American citizens, in the United States, suspected of acting against the interests of Israel.

As a party to the promotion of Zionist over other religiously motivated military activities, the US has subtly codified military and other support of religion in a way that strikes at the very foundations of the reasons for which the nation was formed. By selectively codifying support for Zionism, the US sets itself upon the course of intolerance and wide scale bloodshed. The damage to its reputation as a just, fair, and secular nation has been pre-empted by coalitions of evangelical interest groups and agents of Israel.

IRMEP's US damage assessment score is 4 out of 5. Practically speaking, US policies are becoming indistinguishable from an institutionalized modern crusade against Islam and Arab nations.

IV. CONCLUSIONS

That ACB has realized high levels of implementation is undeniable. However, IRMEP believes that the costs in terms of damage done to US foreign policy objectives and national interests are extremely high.

Though some damage may even be irreparable, IRMEP calls for US policy makers to immediately reconsider of the costs of further ACB implementation. *Following ACB can only generate additional damage to US interests in the future.*

NOTES

1. This is an abridged version from http://www.irmep.org
2. Available at: http://www.israeleconomy.org/strat1.htm